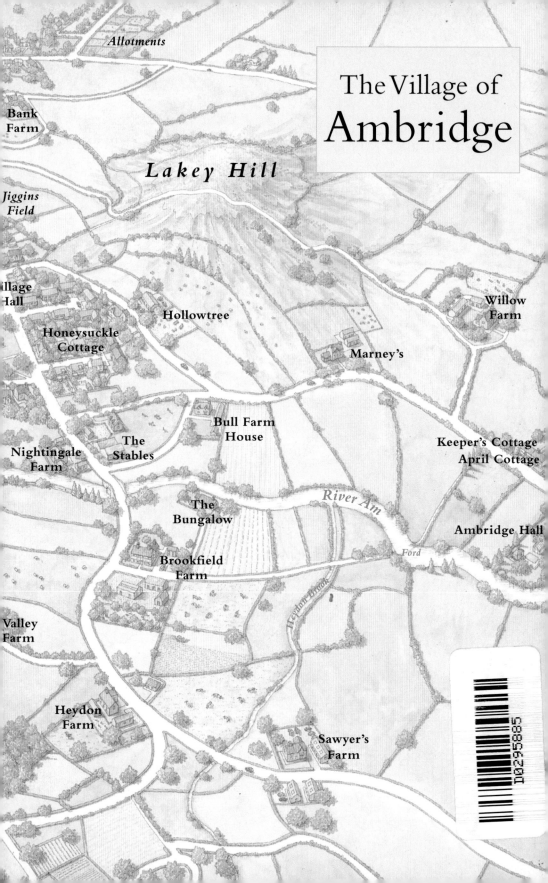

The Archers
ENCYCLOPAEDIA

The Archers
ENCYCLOPAEDIA

This book is published to accompany the BBC Radio 4 serial *The Archers*

The Editor of *The Archers* is Vanessa Whitburn

Published by BBC Worldwide Limited,
Woodlands, 80 Wood Lane, London W12 0TT

First published 2001

ISBN 0563 537183

Commisioning Editor: Emma Shackleton
Project Editor: Helena Caldon
Copy-editor: Trish Burgess
Book Design: Sarah Ponder and Ben Cracknell Studios

Set in Bembo and Frutiger
Printed and bound in Great Britain by Butler & Tanner Limited, Frome and London
Cover printed by Lawrence-Allen Limited, Weston-super-Mare

Special thanks are due to Helen Chetwynd, Researcher, and Camilla Fisher, Programme Archivist, who did most of the hard work in preparing the encyclopaedia. Vanessa Whitburn and Keri Davies did sterling service in reading the various drafts of the text and suggesting pertinent amendments, while Emma Shackleton and Helena Caldon provided much needed editorial support. Above all, the book wouldn't exist without the efforts of the entire cast, writers and production team, past and present, who've made the Archers an enjoyable listen for over fifty years.

J.T. and A.F.

Foreword

As we began the year on 1 January 2001, there was cause for great celebration at *The Archers* as Britain's longest-running drama became fifty years old. But in February we heard of the first outbreak of foot-and-mouth disease, a major, real-life farming issue. There followed weeks of rewriting scripts and rerecording episodes as the disease spread throughout the UK. This incident highlighted one of the key qualities of *The Archers*: while it is a drama set in Ambridge in the county of Borsetshire, after fifty years it continues to respond to real-life rural and farming issues in Britain.

The last half century has seen many changes in our daily lives. In Ambridge today, the horizons of many of the inhabitants and their sons and daughters have changed and grown, too. But the stories continue to strike a chord: during the last year the Grundys sought to re-establish their lives after their eviction from Grange Farm, while Ruth has grappled with, and overcome, breast cancer. Brookfield Farm has finally been handed over to David and Ruth to run. Jill and Phil have moved into Glebe Cottage on their retirement as Dan and Doris did before them. The cycle of life continues. Now the farmers in Ambridge face new challenges for the 21st century: how to cultivate and grow local markets; how to strengthen ties with the consumer; how to grow new markets based on quality and taste. Organics is flourishing, but farmers like Tony and Pat also face challenges – from the supermarkets on pricing and from imported goods, to name but two. And there are challenges for all the inhabitants. The Berrow Estate is aiming to get planning permission to build new houses on some of its land and there are concerns that any development should be controlled and appropriate. Meanwhile, Lower Loxley continues to expand its activities for tourists, and diversification is always on the agenda for some of the bigger farmers in our area. So much to do, then, as we move further into this century.

With over 4.5 million listeners each week, we are delighted that *The Archers* continues to be the most popular non-news programme on BBC Radio 4, and that we are now able to broadcast in Real Audio on the Web for overseas listeners. I don't believe that anyone foresaw the enduring quality of the drama when it was created by Godfrey Baseley. Originally transmitted on the BBC Midlands Home Service on Whit Monday 29 May 1950, it wasn't until 1 January 1951 that it was broadcast to a national audience – at 11.45a.m. on the Light Programme. But by Easter, *The Archers* had proved such a success that it was moved to the prime-time spot of 6.45pm.

Although *The Archers* was introduced as 'An everyday story of country folk', it was created with a remit to educate farmers in modern farming methods after the war. It was part of the armoury of post-war recovery, used literally to help the nation feed itself. This overt educational function was not really dropped until the early 1970s and such script inserts would be quaint today. But I am glad to say that *The Archers* continues to be known for its thorough research and reflection of rural life.

The fiftieth year is the perfect moment to publish an encyclopaedia of the characters and places of *The Archers* – and their archive has been researched and compiled in over 600 entries to provide the most authoritative and comprehensive guide to the people and places of Ambridge and Borchester, from Dan and Doris to Freddie, Lily and Meriel. Browse through it or pick names at random and you will encounter a rich fictional history, for this is a programme which in many ways reflects the changing face of rural middle England in the last half century. It is much more than the sum of its parts, and, although I have edited the programme on a daily basis for ten years, I still stand back from it, from time to time, and marvel at the achievement and enduring nature of what Godfrey Baseley created. Enjoy it all.

Vanessa Whitburn
Editor, *The Archers*

Dorothy **Adamson**

(Heather Barrett)

L ike the eponymous heroine of Joanna Trollope's novel – though without the extra-marital dalliances – Dorothy sometimes chafed against the constraints of being a clergy wife. Soon after her

Birth: 14.01.1945

arrival in Ambridge in 1973, she was heard to complain that she was little more than an 'unpaid curate', though for the most part she cheerfully helped out with bring and buy sales and sponsored fasts. It swiftly became apparent, however, that charity needed to begin closer to home: raising two young children on a vicar's stipend was impossible and Dorothy had to seek paid work. She started off at Carol Tregorran's Pick-Your-Own, before moving up to the 'Gear Change' boutique in Borchester, then the village shop, and, finally, the post of Dr Matthew Thorogood's receptionist. Here, her concern for others led to various indiscretions and Matthew had to re-emphasize the importance of patient confidentiality.

In 1988, the Bishop suggested that Richard think about taking on a parish in the recession-hit North-East. Dorothy took some convincing, but eventually agreed, and the couple were spurred on their way with the presentation by Jill, as church warden, of a cheque and a rosebowl. They repaid the compliment by returning to the village twelve years later for her seventieth birthday party.

Michael **Adamson**

Y ounger child of Richard and Dorothy, Michael was a talented trumpeter. By the time his parents left Ambridge for County Durham in 1988, however, he was no longer living at home, or

Birth: 7.12.1968

he would doubtless have been rapidly recruited into one of the area's famed brass bands.

Rachel **Adamson**

Intelligent and sporty, Rachel attended Borchester Grammar and played in their tennis team right through to the sixth form. Having passed her A-levels in 1985, she took a year off before beginning her English literature course at Lancaster University. The fact that they'd be nearer to their student daughter may well have been a contributory factor in her parents' decision to leave Ambridge for County Durham two years later.

Birth: 19.1.1967

Richard **Adamson**

(Richard Carrington)

Well-meaning, bespectacled Richard was an immediate hit with parishioners when he arrived as Vicar of Ambridge and Rector of Penny Hassett – he later became Rector of Edgeley, too. He flung himself into village life, playing cricket, running the Scout troop and launching appeal funds for church roof repairs and to rehang the bells. With his own finances he was more *laissez-faire*, failing to reclaim his travelling expenses until nudged by the PCC and only reluctantly accepting an old Estate shooting brake to replace his own clapped-out car. Luckily, he had no objection to his wife, Dorothy, working to supplement their income.

Birth: 15.3.1943

Richard faced a dilemma when Christine Johnson and George Barford, a divorcé, wanted to marry in church. The Bishop smartly passed the decision back to Richard and the PCC voted against, but he went ahead with the wedding nonetheless. He later told Phil Archer in confidence that he'd been George's 'Samaritan' when the latter was suicidal, and he felt that George deserved a break.

As they packed up to leave in 1988, the Adamsons may well have remembered their housewarming in the new, modern vicarage when Doris got tiddly on Walter Gabriel's elderflower wine. Happy days, indeed.

Alice **Aldridge**

(Hollie Chapman)

After her first day at school, Alice Aldridge couldn't understand why she was ever expected to go back: 'Why, Mummy? I've been.' It was a shrewd response from a smart child, who is rapidly becoming a street-savvy teenager. Jennifer and Brian Aldridge's youngest, she's into mobile phones, Gucci shoes, and, above all else, horseriding. When her pony, Chandler, was startled by Ed Grundy's reckless driving in summer 2001, Alice took a nasty tumble, but was well enough by the village fête to demonstrate her technical expertise in winning the radio-controlled car race, in partnership with Simon Gerrard.

Birth: 29.9.1988

Brian **Aldridge**

(Charles Collingwood)

Hard though it is to imagine Brian Aldridge in khaki shorts and shirt, he was once a Boy Scout. Perhaps his lifelong readiness to seize business and romantic opportunities whenever they arise stems from that early call to 'be prepared'.

Birth: 20.11.1943

He had few attachments when he came to Ambridge in 1975; his parents had died when he was twenty-eight, and he was only occasionally in contact with his sister, Elizabeth. Seeing his future in large-scale agriculture, he had come to buy Home Farm and an accompanying 1500 acres from Ralph Bellamy. While some of the workers' flats were being reconverted into a farmhouse, he stayed at The Bull and began to make himself known in the area.

Very quickly, he was attracted to Jennifer Travers-Macy. He had always enjoyed being seen with stylish women, and Jennifer not only had style, but the distinction of being a published author as well. He wooed her with golfing lessons and a trip to the Royal Show. Jennifer's disintegrating marriage to Roger acted as a brake on the relationship, but, by February 1976, a divorce had come through. At the end of May, Brian and Jenny, as he called her, were married at the Borchester Register Office. Not only had he acquired a wife to go with his farm, but he had taken on two stepchildren, Adam and Debbie, as well.

Good with stock, he found children much more complex to deal with and was forever seeming to have accidents. Moreover, Adam, unsettled by the way Roger had gone away, could be very badly behaved. Gradually, Brian found a shared language with him through their joint interest in cricket, but it was to be three years before Adam called him 'Dad'. If he sometimes seemed happier spending money, not time, on his new family, he was to be much the same when his own daughters, Kate and Alice, were born.

His marriage has had plenty of awkward moments, largely caused by his lively libido. He became so heavily involved with Caroline Bone in the mid-1980s that he remained jealous whenever he saw her with other men afterwards. Riding instructor Mandy Beesborough, and a member of the Meyruelle twinning delegation, Marie-Claire Beguet, were two others who enjoyed close encounters with him. Even Betty Tucker wasn't safe in her house-cleaning days at Home Farm, when Brian got the hots for her and suggested they went skinny-dipping in the Aldridges' pool. A horrified Betty wasn't interested, and Brian gave up the pursuit when warned off by Jill Archer. He didn't really have the right to complain when Jennifer reciprocated by renewing her relationship with Roger Travers-Macy, but he gave her a hard time about it anyway.

Despite the infidelities, it has been a surprisingly strong marriage, and has needed to be. Kate has tested her father's patience to the limits with her drug use, unsuitable boyfriends and unplanned pregnancies. He took time to adjust to her recent marriage to black South African journalist Lucas Madikane, but suffered his worst moment earlier in 1995, when she had been missing for some months. A young woman of similar colouring, wearing a bracelet with 'Kate' engraved on it, was found at the foot of a cliff, and Brian was asked to identify the body. His relief that it wasn't his daughter gave way to a severe panic attack later.

Alice has, so far, been much less of a handful. Brian struggled not to show his disappointment when she was born in 1988, since he had been hoping for a boy. He didn't spend much time with her as a baby, as he was busy with farm work, and, for a time, campaigning to be elected to the local council. His political ambitions came to an end, when, while canvassing the Grundys in 1989, he sustained a head injury, pushing Joe out of the way of a cow suffering with BSE. Operations to remove a blood clot and cerebral abscess were needed, and the subsequent post-traumatic epilepsy Brian suffered meant that, for a time, he couldn't drive round the farm. Forced to stay at home, he found he was unexpectedly good with Alice, and has lately shown a similar aptitude with his granddaughters, Phoebe and Nolly.

Of all the family, he is probably closest to Debbie. He was quietly pleased when, as a student, she started using Aldridge as her surname. He's also enjoyed seeing her develop into an excellent farmer, despite having had several professional disagreements with her on the way. At times he's been very protective about her boyfriends – with good reason, in the case of Simon Pemberton. But he alienated her by his hostile attitude to Simon Gerrard. Brian couldn't bring himself to attend their wedding, though he was pleased that Debbie wore the necklace he left on her dressing-table the night before.

If there were prizes for being thick-skinned, Brian would win them. In 1997, he risked the wrath of in-laws Pat and Tony Archer by keeping quiet about his involvement in Borchester Land, who were about to become their new landlords. Protests about tailbacks caused by his huge new combine were water off a duck's back, and he was unmoved by complaints about the trial plot of genetically modified oilseed rape grown at Home Farm in 1999, genuinely believing that British farming had to innovate to survive. Only the fact that his nephew, Tom Archer, was acquitted of criminal damage after trashing the crop really bothered him.

In recent years, he's had to face a range of setbacks. Boardroom rival Matt Crawford outsmarted him when Borchester Land evicted the Grundys from Grange Farm, and he has recently lost the contract to farm Estate Land. And at Home Farm, despite having off-farm leisure interests, such as a riding-course and fishing lake, Brian has had to face heavy losses. He is left with some hard decisions to make about the way the farm should be run and the life he and Jennifer want to lead. For a man who likes to be in control, the future looks unsettlingly uncertain.

Jennifer **Aldridge**   née Archer (formerly Travers-Macy)

(Ysanne Churchman, Elaine McNamara, Freda Hooper,
Carol Lynn-Davies, Angela Piper)

When young Jennifer Archer attended Ambridge Village School, wearing a blazer from her previous, private school, the other pupils laughed at her. It was a humiliating experience, since, more than most children, Jennifer always craved approval.

Birth: 7.1.1945

As Jack and Peggy Archer's eldest child, she often had to compete with her sister, Lilian, and brother, Tony, for her parents' attention. With her father's increasing alcoholism causing arguments, she sometimes felt in the way at home. By contrast, her teens were fun, when she found that a touch of make-up and the right clothes could lead to plenty of flattering interest from the boys.

Gary Kenton and Max Bailey were early admirers, but it was to Brookfield farmhand Paddy Redmond that she gave her heart and more. By now a trained teacher, she had already started work at Hollerton Primary School when she became pregnant by him in late 1966. She found breaking the news to her parents extremely difficult, especially since she wasn't willing to name the father. Mrs P and Tony were particularly disapproving, and, although reconciliation was to follow, Jennifer sought temporary respite after the birth of her son, Adam, by moving to take up a teaching post in Bristol.

By May 1968, she was back in Ambridge. A romance with Lilian's former boyfriend Roger Travers-Macy led to a wedding in September of the same year. Together they had a daughter, Debbie, but the marriage wasn't a success. Roger's work in the book trade took him away from home a great deal, and the couple started to grow apart. Within a few years, having achieved some financial independence by working at Grey Gables, Jennifer realized she wanted a separation.

If success as a wife was eluding her, she was having better luck as an author. After having a first novel accepted for publication in 1967, she followed it up with a thriller, *It's Murder*. She went on to write numerous articles for the *Borchester Echo,* and, reflecting her interest in local history, co-authored a study of Ambridge, *An English Village Through the Ages*, with John Tregorran. A shared love of literature was one of the qualities she later found appealing in Debbie's husband, Simon Gerrard.

When her marriage to Roger was in its final stages, Jennifer formed a new relationship with wealthy landowner Brian Aldridge, who had caught her eye at one of Carol Tregorran's dinner parties. Soon he was giving her golfing lessons, and, fairly rapidly, love developed on the links. Once the divorce from Roger had come through, Jennifer and Brian were free to marry in May 1976.

She enjoyed adjusting to the more luxurious lifestyle her new husband made possible, and quickly came to rely on hired help, or her put-upon mother, to take care of all domestic and childcare chores. She felt her energies should be used more creatively, although the Two Jays Craft Studio she opened with Jill Archer soon came to grief.

Two daughters were born to complete the family: Kate in October 1977, and, eleven years later, Alice. Wanting to regain her looks after Kate's birth, Jennifer took up exercising. Concern about her appearance was, in part, a reaction to her husband's wandering eye. Most hurtful was his affair with Caroline Bone. She was furious when she confronted him about it, but, in time, came to accept Brian's protestations that it had just been a meaningless fling.

She was not beyond having extra-marital adventures herself. Village gossip linking her with John Tregorran grew a little overheated, but the same couldn't be said when Roger Travers-Macy returned in 1991. He claimed he wanted to re-establish contact with Debbie, but soon he and Jennifer were meeting on Lakey Hill and reaffirming their old love. Daytime trysts in hotels followed, until Jennifer decided she didn't want the affair to continue. She told Brian everything.

Kate, who always responded badly when her parents were at odds, became an increasing source of worry. Initially, it was only a matter of smoking and minor vandalism, but matters took a more serious turn in 1994, when she simply disappeared from home. There were fears of a tragic outcome, before the wanderer returned, several months later, trailing mud all over the floor.

In 1997, when Jennifer found out that Kate was pregnant, she had a nursery made up at Home Farm, and, after the birth, tried to spend as much time as possible with her new granddaughter, Phoebe. She would have liked to look after her full-time when Kate set off on her travels again, but had to watch while the baby's father, Roy Tucker, took charge.

Jennifer seems to be at her strongest in times of trouble. She ran the farm competently after Brian suffered a serious head injury in 1989, and gave him her full support when Tom Archer trashed his GM trial plot a decade later. She also showed real concern when Debbie was assaulted by Simon Pemberton, and, contrary to Brian's wishes, worked hard to make Simon Gerrard feel wanted in the family.

She is not without faults. She was very ungracious when her mother became engaged to Jack Woolley, leading Lilian to accuse her of being a snob. She's often irritated Tony, by seeming to flaunt her wealth, and, instead of giving the Tuckers credit for their role in bringing up Phoebe, she's more worried about the type of influence they'll have on her granddaughter.

But her heart is usually in the right place. When Kate returned from South Africa, pregnant for a second time, Jennifer's immediate response was honest, maternal relief. She was thrilled by the birth of her second granddaughter, Nolly, and was later surprised and pleased when Kate married the father, Lucas Madikane, in Johannesburg. If she hasn't achieved all she once hoped to in life, she can take consolation from helping hold her family together through many troubled times. Given the volatile mix that makes up the Aldridges, it's a role she will surely have to play again in the future.

Phoebe **Aldridge**

(Laura Poli)

Phoebe Aldridge is the daughter of Kate Madikane and Roy Tucker. A fan of cream cheese, organic yogurt and loud noises, she soon adjusted to Hayley Jordan taking her mother's place when Kate went off to Africa. Subsequently, she was very unsettled when Kate returned wanting to take her to live in Johannesburg. She's a happy child who loves being spoiled by her nana, Betty Tucker, and her grandma, Jennifer Aldridge. If she develops a taste for camping and tie-dyed clothes in the future, she can blame it on being born in a tepee at the Glastonbury Festival.

Birth: 28.6.1998

Alex

Alex was the bosun on Kenton Archer's first Merchant Navy ship, and they kept in touch. In 1988, they set up in business together, selling shares in the intriguingly-named firm Gardenfun to investors as varied as Tom Forrest and Dave Barry. The following year, however, when their company was about to be investigated by FIMBRA, Alex nobly fell on his sword, sacking Kenton to spare him the stigma of possible prosecution.

Allard's Farm

🕭 SEE: *Hollowtree Farm*

Jess **Allard**

(Max Brimmell)

J ess farmed alongside Brookfield and Fred Barratt's farm, making him an obvious choice as third partner when Dan mooted the idea of a dairy cooperative. This became a reality in April 1961, with the formation of Ambridge Dairy Farmers. Sadly, Jess hardly lived long enough to know whether Dan's idea was a good one, as he died the following December.

Death: 1.12.1961

Joe **Allard**

(Ralph Lawton)

J oe was the elder son of Jess Allard, the partner of Dan Archer and Fred Barratt in Ambridge Dairy Farmers. In late 1961, Joe informed them that his father was ill, and, though Jess's dying wish was for his sons (he also had a younger boy, Rex) to carry on after him, Joe and his brother sold out in March 1962. Ambridge Dairy Farmers was reconstituted as Ambridge Farmers Ltd and Phil joined the board.

Rex **Allard**

(Brian Kent)

Son of Jess and younger brother of Joe, there was bad feeling between the brothers when Rex was spotted in Borchester with Joe's fiancée, Ruth. This uncanny echo of the situation between Dan Archer and his brother Ben, who paid too much attention to Dan's fiancée, Doris, did not result in as abrupt a departure for Rex as it had for Ben. Instead, he left Ambridge peaceably when his father's farm was sold in 1962.

Ambridge

Set in Borsetshire's agricultural heartland, Ambridge has the feel of a working village rather than a purely scenic one. Named for its position as a crossing point over the River Am, its roots go back beyond Anglo-Saxon times, when Jiggins Field, then known as Giant's Field, was already under cultivation. Round barrows on Lakey Hill, the impressive landmark to the north of the village, indicate that the area was inhabited in the Bronze Age, while artefacts from a Romano-British settlement, discovered at the north-east corner of the Country Park, and the remains of a medieval settlement, next to Lakey Hill, suggest that occupation has been continuous ever since. (Refer to display boards in St Stephen's Church for further details.) In common with many other rural communities, Ambridge has lost a number of services in recent years, most notably a village school and one of its pubs, the Cat and Fiddle. However, its comfortable commuting distance from Borchester and Birmingham has helped attract a range of incomers to a number of small-scale housing developments within the village. Added to a local population mainly employed in agriculture, equine activities or tourism, the newcomers provide sufficient business to sustain a general store/post office and a thriving pub on the village green, The Bull. The Village Hall, formerly the school building, is at the centre of a range of social activities, including amateur dramatics, meetings of the Over Sixties Club and the local Women's Institute. There are facilities for playing golf, horse-riding or fishing in, or close to, the village, although many residents in search of outdoor entertainment are content simply to sit and gossip by the pond on the village green, or to take their children to play in the Dan Archer Memorial Playground. (See back papers of the book for map.)

Ambridge Farm

Originally one of five farms on the Berrow Estate, Ambridge Farm lies outside the village on the way to Waterley Cross. Ken and Mary Pound were its tenants for thirty years, accumulating such impedimenta as a wuffler, hay knife, butter churn and a 'Farmer's Boy', all of which were disposed of at a farm sale when they left in 1983. The new tenants, dairy farmers Mike and Betty Tucker, started well, Mike building up within two years to sixty-five Ayrshire milkers, thirty-five followers and 165 acres of grassland and arable crops. Betty's farm shop, 'Betty's Barn', was less successful, trading for only two months before closing, and, by late 1985, the Tuckers had serious money troubles. Mike had to declare himself bankrupt, and, in March 1986, the land was absorbed back into the Estate. The new doctor, Matthew Thorogood, rented the farmhouse and converted some of the outbuildings into a surgery, amused to note that under the 1977 Rent Act one of the conditions of tenancy was that he did not use the building for illegal or immoral purposes. On his departure in 1992, the villagers feared they might lose their surgery. They didn't, but it's no longer at Ambridge Farm, which has doubtless been prettified by incomers.

Ambridge Garage

Ambridge Garage, formerly Wainwright's Garage, stood on the site of the old smithy. Paul Johnson bought it in 1967 and dragged it into the late twentieth century by adding a canopy, self-service pump and coffee bar, but he failed to turn a profit and the garage was sold, first to Ralph Bellamy, then to Haydn Evans, who self-importantly renamed it Evans' Garage. Nonetheless, it closed for good in 1981.

Ambridge Hall

Ambridge Hall must surely be the most relaxing and tranquil house in the village, thanks to the powers of Lynda Snell's *feng shui*, which has banished Robert's favourite rug from the hall ('too brown') and resulted in the laying of a new Welsh slate patio. It's chilling to think, however, that had the top copy of Laura Archer's will only been signed, the house would not have been sold to the Snells at all (they bought it for

£160,000 in 1985) but would have gone to Laura's lodger, Freddie Danby, as she had intended.

There have in fact been several owners of this six-bedroomed, yellow-brick edifice, with its gardens that run down to the Am. Built in the 1860s by the Lawson-Hopes for the village doctor, it was occupied a century later by Charles and Carol Grenville. When Carol remarried after her husband's death, she sold the house to Jack Woolley, who sold it on to Laura Archer. The current owner, Lynda, has effected many changes, not least her low-allergen garden with its water feature, and, latterly, under the influence of the Orient, an abundance of wealth corners and wind chimes.

Ambridge Surgery

The bungalow that now serves as the doctor's surgery was originally built in 1974 to be the vicarage. It fell empty when Robin Stokes left the village, and remained so as his replacement, Janet Fisher, lived in Darrington. For a short while, the Church authorities used it as a holiday home for disadvantaged children, before selling it to Dr Richard Locke in 1997, who agreed that one of the rooms should remain available for Janet's use. Apart from this and the doctor's room, it also contains a nurse's clinic, a pharmacy and a waiting-room where the receptionists, including Susan Carter, work. In 1999, some months after Richard had left Ambridge, Dr Tim Hathaway bought it when he took over the practice.

Ambridge Village Hall

Despite the extravagance of Lynda Snell's Christmas productions, there are still those in the village who hanker for the glory days of the old village hall. There, for example, Ned Larkin and Walter Gabriel guested as 'Cliff Pilchard' and 'Elvis Measley', an act that understandably brought the house down. In the late 1970s, Neil and Shula were keen to form a youth club there, but the committee refused. Retribution, however, was theirs when an electrical fault caused a fire in the kitchen extension. Although the main hall wasn't badly damaged, under-insurance meant that repairs would be too costly, so an application went in to convert the former school building, by then standing empty. This was approved, with the decorating done by volunteers.

When the hall needed another refurbishment in 1993, village help was again sought, but it took the intervention of TV troubleshooter Anneka Rice to complete the project. With new yellow and violet gingham curtains, the hall was soon back in business as the home of the playgroup, the WI, the Over Sixties Club and the Christmas show. It has also recently been the venue for Tony and Eddie's joint fiftieth birthday celebrations and Roy and Hayley's wedding reception.

Ambridge Village Shop

As vital to the village as a source of gossip as of groceries, the shop and post office is owned by Jack Woolley. It's undergone many modernizations over the years and collectors of kitsch may still regret the loss of the bead curtain which separated the shop from the stockroom in Martha Woodford's day. Her problems with the electronic till have been echoed more recently in Betty's worries about the computerization of the post office, but perhaps the most controversial innovation was the flashing neon sign which Jack had installed in 1990. A vociferous village campaign led by the doughty Mrs Perkins soon saw to its removal.

The New Age music which Kate introduced during her unsuccessful stint as an assistant may have done something to dispel the bad vibes resulting from two armed raids over the years. The first caused Polly Perks to miscarry and in the second, Jack, Betty, Kate and Debbie were taken hostage. A calmer atmosphere now prevails and the casual customer can call at the shop for everything from tights to fresh pasta. Though supermarket-style baskets are available, Betty and Susan are alway willing to step out from behind the counter to help a young mum with a pushchair or Mr Pullen with picking up his newspaper.

Angus

(Lester Mudditt, Laidlaw Dalling, Andrew Faulds)

Although his dour Scottish family were displeased with his migration to England, Angus and his wife, Jennie, settled well in Ambridge where, as stockman on Fairbrother's farm, he enjoyed a long and happy career. If Angus had been paid on results, he'd have been a wealthy man:

he ran a pedigree herd of Ayrshires, which won many rosettes at local shows, once even beating Dan's Shorthorns.

Anthony

(Adrian Schiller)

Throughout 2000, Phil and Jill Archer kept their accountant, Anthony, crouched over his calculator as they tried to decide how best to divide Brookfield on their retirement. Always against the idea of splitting the farm between the four children, he eventually recommended turning Brookfield into a limited company and issuing different classes of shares.

Edward Antrobus 'Teddy'

Edward Antrobus, or 'Teddy' as his wife, Marjorie, called him, was a man of considerable style. He may have made his career in the army, but he had no intention of roughing it unnecessarily, always taking a beautifully made travelling set, including silver-backed brushes, wherever he went. He dressed impeccably for the mess, using an excellent tailor in Singapore to make up his clothes whenever possible. Apart from soldiering, he greatly enjoyed big game hunting, for which he won quite a reputation in East Africa. Eventually he died in Nairobi, leaving his beloved Marjorie bereft.

Marjorie Antrobus

(Margot Boyd)

Some people are born to be married and Marjorie Antrobus was one of them. She was never happier than when accompanying husband, Teddy, on his army postings. They were together in Burma, Palestine and what was then Rhodesia, but perhaps the happiest memories come from their time together in East Africa. After socializing in the mess or Colonial Club, they would talk on late into the night,

> Birth: 1922

Teddy's stories of the day's big game hunt being swapped for details of how Marjorie found her latest exquisite animal carving. Even without children, they were company enough for each other, so Teddy's death, in Nairobi, left a great gap in Marjorie's life.

On her return to Britain, she settled in Waterley Cross and occupied herself for a time by breeding Afghan hounds. She did this well, with one of her 'girls' even winning second prize at Crufts one year. As something of a Borsetshire celebrity, she was invited to address the Ambridge Over Sixties Club on 'The Colourful World of the Afghan Hound' in the summer of 1984. She was so taken with the village that the following year she bought Nightingale Farm and had it restored to become her new home. Her neighbours realized how serious she was about dogs when she had an outbuilding converted into kennels for her eight Afghans, though Martha Woodford was still taken aback to be asked for sixty pounds of tripe at the shop.

The dogs, especially Portia and Georgina, were good company, but Marjorie wanted a more human element in her life. When a 'Gentleman farmer seeking companionship' placed an advert in the *Borchester Echo*, she replied to the box number, only to be greatly embarrassed when Joe Grundy turned up on her doorstep. There was no question of any romance between them, but they started a low-key friendship, which was of particular value years later, when Marjorie lost confidence after her cataract operations, and Joe found the task of helping her to drive again a welcome distraction from the trauma of eviction from Grange Farm.

Other men occasionally caught her eye. She trampled all over Martha to catch Kathy Perks's wedding bouquet in 1987, when they were both, unavailingly, in competition for Colonel Danby's attentions. Guy Pemberton was another who made her pulse beat a little more quickly. Most unusually, Marjorie harboured some quite uncharitable thoughts when Caroline Bone won Guy's heart instead.

She has always been good at making friends. Despite their intermittent rivalries, she got on well enough with Martha, although the friendship was tested when the latter invited herself for a long stay at Nightingale Farm in 1989. Marjorie's willingness to have a go at bell-ringing, her acting and singing in village concerts, and her invaluable skills as a cricket scorer, have all helped her build a wide social circle over the years. However, she isn't afraid to court unpopularity if she believes it's in a just cause. With Martha's help, she waged a very effective campaign to force the Ambridge Cricket Club to open its annual dinner to women. She also gave great support to the protest against the widening of the Borchester bypass in 1997, and was given a caution by the police for her efforts. Even when the battle was lost, Marjorie wasn't despondent: she collected seeds and acorns from the trees that were felled and planted them in a corner of St Stephen's churchyard, until they were ready to be grown on in the Millennium Wood.

Ever since coming to Ambridge, she has had a close association with St Stephen's. Her organ-playing there has been much appreciated, but the moral support she has given successive incumbents has proved even more valuable. She got on well with Richard Adamson, whom she already knew from Waterley Cross, and was then pleased to recognize his replacement, Jerry Buckle, as someone else who'd lived in Kenya. She was a good friend to Jerry, warning him about the dangers of village gossip when Sharon Richards was given a home at the Vicarage. After Jerry left, it didn't seem that she would get along as well with Robin Stokes, but he was very thoughtful after she lost money to Cameron Fraser, and made sure she was drawn more closely into church affairs. Now she's friendly with Janet Fisher and dismisses concerns about female vicars as irrelevant.

The self-contained flat at Nightingale Farm has brought Marjorie plenty of company as well. Roy and Hayley Tucker, with daughter Phoebe, are only the most recent to have benefited from having her as a landlady, although Hayley occasionally regrets the effect of Marjorie's home-made Dundee cake on her waistline. Previous tenants Nigel Pargetter, Ruth Pritchard and Richard Locke have all been happy to use her as an unofficial agony aunt at times. She certainly knew Ruth was growing close to David Archer in 1988, long before his family did.

Hayley, though, has been a particular favourite. She moved into the flat at a time when Marjorie was having increasing problems with her eyes; trouble with cricket-scoring and totting up the Remembrance Day money progressed to serious difficulty with driving. Hayley was a tower of strength during the months when Marjorie had to wait for her two cataract operations, and was there to share the joy of their successful outcome in 2000. The slight reorganization of rooms at Nightingale Farm needed to let Roy and Phoebe join Hayley in the flat was a small price to pay for having their continued company.

Marjorie might not be as mobile as she once was, but she still loves being with other people, especially younger ones. She was positively the life and soul of Debbie Aldridge's hen party, chatting up the bouncers with the best of them. Most evenings, however, when her lodgers are busy with their own affairs, she has only Nelson Gabriel's old spaniel, Charlie, and her faithful Afghan, Bettina, to sit with her as she busily knits or embroiders. But, as she sometimes tells herself resignedly, no one could ever really have replaced Teddy.

April Cottage

No longer wanting the hassle of renting out April Cottage, the semi-detached property adjoining Keeper's Cottage, Jack Woolley was happy to sell it to Kathy Perks in 2001. The two semis had been built in 1960 by Charles Grenville. Len and Mary Thomas were the first of a string of tenants who were later to include Martha Woodford, who stayed there until her death, and John Archer, who lived there for a time with Hayley Tucker and also used it as a love-nest with Sharon Richards. Compact, with a useful garden, it stands opposite Ambridge Hall.

Anthony **Archer** 'Tony'

(Philip Owen, Colin Skipp)

'The first Archer grandson, eh? Gosh, Peg, aren't we clever, you and me?' whispered an awed Jack Archer when their son was born on 16 February 1951. Anthony William Daniel, as he

Birth: 16.2.1951

was christened, attended private and state schools in Borchester, leaving at sixteen to work for Ralph Bellamy on the Estate and attend day-release classes at the Tech. Following his parents into the pub trade was never an option, and Tony's instinct for farming was borne out when he graduated from the Walford Farm Institute in Shropshire with a distinction.

Taken on as dairy manager by Ralph Bellamy, Tony was the original lad-about-Ambridge, with his free time split between cars, girls and his place in the Ambridge Wanderers football team. After romancing vicar's daughter Tessa Latimer and Christine's groom, Roberta, he nearly came to grief over the bohemian Jane Petrie, who was teaching a summer school at Arkwright Hall. Learning that Tony had ducked work to be with her, Bellamy blamed Tony first for the death of a cow in a thunderstorm, and later, less legitimately, for an outbreak of brucellosis in the herd.

The luckless Lothario was duly sacked and worked briefly at Brookfield before accepting a partnership at Willow Farm with Haydn Evans. Almost immediately, he met farm secretary Mary Weston at a dance and by January 1974 they were engaged. Maybe the fact that they arrived late at The Bull for their own engagement party should have served as an omen: in the summer, Mary wrote from Majorca, where she was holidaying with her parents, to tell Tony the wedding was off. By then, however, he'd already met Pat Lewis, Haydn's niece, who lost no time in proposing to him. They were married in December.

At first, everything seemed to go well for the young marrieds: Tony hoped to increase the size of the herd to sixty cows, and Pat was interested in free-range chickens. Their plan to provide B & B accommodation fell by the wayside, though, when Pat announced she was pregnant, and their first son, John Daniel, was born on 31 December 1975 as the bells rang in the New Year. In 1977, while Pat was away in Wales nursing her mother, something of the old Tony emerged in a flirtation with the milk recorder, Libby Jones, but Pat returned in time to guess what had been going on and to tell Tony she'd be keeping an eye on him in future. Meanwhile, the death of the incumbent tenant, Jim Elliott, had led to a vacancy at Bridge Farm, which both Pat and Tony were keen to take on. Soon the couple were celebrating both the start of their new tenancy and the fact that Pat was again pregnant. Helen was born in April 1979, though a dislocated hip meant that the baby spent three months in a splint. Pat became tired and run down and this initiated a troubled few years for them. Tony contracted tetanus from a rusty nail, then there was a foot-and-mouth scare on the farm, followed by swine vesicular disease. Little wonder, then, that both Pat and Tony were at best ambivalent when she became pregnant again. Thomas (Tom) was born in February 1981, but by this time Tony, in a worrying throwback to his father, had started to drink heavily.

Over the next couple of years, Pat and Tony seemed to drift apart. Pat took up with a women's group, her nascent feminism manifesting itself, to Tony's disgust, in her symbolic cancelling of the *Daily Express* in favour of the *Guardian*. Left in charge of the children once too often while Pat attended a conference in Carmarthen, and needled by a supposed sighting of her in the Goat and Nightgown with her women's studies lecturer, Roger, Tony realized that drastic action was needed. On Pat's return, he disappeared off to a conference of his own and returned pledging to turn Bridge Farm organic. Was Pat with him or not? She was, and since then has stood by him through thick and thin, mud and rain, leek-pulling and carrot-weeding. It was on Pat's initiative that Bridge Farm branched out into yogurt and ice cream production, and, suspicious of their links with organic superstore owner Howard Friend, she was behind Tony all the way when he took a stand against the Borsetshire Environment Trust, who were objecting to the widening of the entrance to the farm shop at Bridge Farm.

Nothing tested Tony's patience more than relations with his elder son, possibly because they were in many ways alike, and there was nothing more poignant than John's furious embarrassment at Tony's dancing when his father acted as roadie for one of his disco gigs. Though Tony took a more relaxed attitude than did Pat towards John's love life, especially his relationship with single mother Sharon Richards, both were delighted when John embarked on a seemingly ongoing relationship with Brummie nanny Hayley Jordan. Sharon returned, however, to break things up, and when, on the morning of Tommy's seventeenth birthday, Tony shouted at John about an unmended fence, he was immediately contrite as he knew John had been more interested in trying to mend things with Hayley. John stormed off, however, on the Ferguson tractor Tony had lovingly restored, only to turn it over in a ditch and die beneath it. Tony found his son's body out in the field, and, while the whole community struggled to come to terms with John's death, Tony had to cope with Pat blaming him for their loss and her sinking into depression a year later. Characteristically, however, they both pulled together when Tom was charged with criminal damage for destroying part of a GM rape crop at Home Farm, and the ensuing rift in the wider family was healed at Pat and Tony's twenty-fifth wedding anniversary meal. With their shop venture in Borchester showing every sign of success, the future for Tony, despite his inherent pessimism, is looking rosier than for some time.

Daniel **Archer** 'Dan'

(Harry Oakes, Monte Crick, Edgar Harrison, Frank Middlemass)

While his younger brothers, Frank and Ben, may have preferred life abroad, Dan Archer belonged in Ambridge and nowhere else. Perhaps his service with the 16th Battalion of the Borchester Regiment during the First World War had given him all the

Birth: 15.10.1896
Death: 23.4.1986

experience he wanted of foreign parts. After his return from the conflict, he promptly put down the roots that were to sustain him for the rest of his life. After his father's early death, he took over the management of Brookfield Farm. With a home and income established, he was free, in 1921, to change the name of his childhood sweetheart, Doris Forrest, to Doris Archer. They were to be married for almost sixty years. A lasting and deep affection helped them face the inevitable troubles their three children were to bring. After spending the Second World War working for the Ministry of Agriculture, Dan hoped the 1950s would see his two sons, Jack and Phil, and his daughter, Christine, settle into the secure kind of life he had made for himself.

His hopes weren't to be realized. Jack's perpetual fascination with alcohol took him away from working on the land to an unsettled life as landlord of The Bull. Christine was to find satisfaction in her work with horses, but the disintegration of her marriage to Paul Johnson caused her parents a great deal of worry. Dan was concerned she was making another mistake when she later married George Barford, though he lived long enough to see that this time she had made a good choice.

Even Phil, who was temperamentally more like his father than the others, gave Dan cause for concern. First there was the tragic outcome of Phil's first marriage to Grace Fairbrother. But there were also regular disagreements between them about the best ways to farm. Dan, a thoroughgoing traditionalist, who only stopped working the land with horses in 1951, wasn't always impressed by his son's enthusiasm for agricultural innovation.

Not surprisingly, Phil often found life easier working for other employers. As a consequence, having managed to buy Brookfield in 1954, when Squire Lawson-Hope's estate was broken up, Dan had to face the possibility that none of his children would want to take it on after him. He was at one time tempted to sell it to Thorpe Wynford, but eventually decided against the idea. Instead, he carried on running the farm astutely and acquiring extra land when appropriate. As a co-founder of Ambridge Dairy Farmers in 1961, he was able to keep Brookfield competitive and had the satisfaction of seeing Phil later become involved once more in running it.

He was unswervingly loyal to family and friends. When his brother-in-law Tom Forrest was accused of killing Bob Larkin, he offered full financial and moral support to help clear his name. Walter Gabriel had frequent cause to be grateful for his friendship as well. When a pack of dogs set about Walter's small flock of sheep, Dan was the first on the scene to chase them off and help assess the terrible damage done. Without Dan's constant willingness to provide good advice, and the loan of a wide range of agricultural implements, Walter would have been forced to leave farming much sooner than he did. In return, Dan greatly enjoyed Walter's company, especially with a pint and pipe to hand.

Throughout all the trials of a farming life – cows falling in slurry pits, lambs lost to lightning, and, above all, an outbreak of foot-and-mouth disease in 1956 that led to the destruction of all the cattle at Brookfield – he always had Doris to buoy him up. Although they took very traditional roles, with Doris responsible for domestic matters while he was very much in charge of the farm, it was undoubtedly a marriage of equals. They were comfortable with each other, his bass-baritone underpinning her lighter voice in their occasional duets. When, in 1967, she became very upset that their unmarried granddaughter Jennifer was pregnant, his calmer, more rational response helped put matters in perspective.

Occasionally, Doris might have wished her husband to be a little less predictable. Sending an identical Valentine's card each year might, at a stretch, be considered romantic but always buying his wife a custard tart when they went out because she had once mentioned that she liked them suggests a certain lack of imagination. But he was capable of the unexpected when he put his mind to it. A Jack Russell puppy, Trigger, made a lively present for Doris one Christmas, and a sun-lounge extension was a welcome birthday gift in 1971. Perhaps the time they needed each other most was when Jack's troubled life came to an end in 1972, the result of all-too-predictable liver failure.

Following Dan's declared intention of retiring, he and Doris moved into Glebe Cottage early in 1970. But he was still working too many hours for her liking. She thought he needed to take better care of himself, and even tried putting him on a new, healthy diet, but couldn't make him give up his favourite meal – beef and mushroom pie.

Ironically, it was Doris who passed away first, in 1980. Although family and friends rallied round, Dan's loss was irreplaceable. The dark purple flowers of the Clematis 'Jackmanii' he planted in her memory provided some consolation for him, but over the next few years his health deteriorated and there were times when he no longer seemed able to concentrate fully on the world around him. His grandchildren were still a great source of joy, however, and it's fitting that his last words were directed to Elizabeth, telling her to be a good girl. He died of a heart attack, over-exerting himself while trying to help a sheep back on its feet.

Almost ninety when he passed away, Dan had played a full part in Ambridge life. He'd served his turn on the Parish Council and been an active member of the NFU. He was to be much missed as a father, grandfather and friend, but people consoled themselves with the hope that death would reunite him with the person who meant most to him – his beloved Doris.

David **Archer**

(Gordon Gardner, Nigel Carrivick, Timothy Bentinck)

Although he may have reflected to his wife, Ruth, that it had been a long time coming, David Archer could not have been more pleased at the start of 2001 when the future of Brookfield was

Birth: 18.9.1959

placed firmly in their hands. Having spent most of his adult life working alongside his father to keep the farm viable, David had assumed that he and his young family would inherit it in due course. But when Phil outlined his inheritance plans, the hostile reaction from David's sister Elizabeth, and, to a lesser degree, his brother Kenton, seemed to threaten a break-up of the whole family business. For a time, David contemplated the unpalatable: leaving Borsetshire and starting life elsewhere. It would have been a huge upheaval, for, perhaps even more than his other sister, Shula, David could not be more firmly rooted in the soil of Ambridge.

As a child, he had quickly shown an aptitude for farming, and his tendency towards practical rather than academic matters became even more pronounced when he went away to boarding school. Having failed his maths A-level twice, he wasn't able to do the course he wanted at university, but seemed quite content to study for two years at the Royal Agricultural College instead. He had a youthful sense of adventure and was happy to go and work on a farm in Holland in the early 1980s, but, by 1983, was ready to return to Ambridge. He didn't always settle easily into working at Brookfield. He considered himself poorly paid, and, in an echo of the arguments that Phil once had with his father, Dan, often felt that he wasn't being given enough say in the running of the farm.

An active social life always helped counterbalance his work. Apart from being a valuable member of the village cricket team, David generally liked to have a romance on the go. An early interest in Michele Brown, a good-looking sheep-shearer from New Zealand, was followed by some entertaining times with fast-living Jackie Woodstock. Then an on-off relationship with design student Sophie Barlow in the mid-1980s appeared to be leading to marriage, until, during preparations for the big day at Felpersham Cathedral, she tearfully told David she couldn't go through with becoming a farmer's wife. His understanding attitude to the news was underpinned by a sense of relief: deep down he realized he needed different qualities in a partner to those Sophie had. Yet, when agricultural student Ruth Pritchard came to Brookfield for a year's work experience, David was slow to get over his initial prejudice about women working on a farm. Gradually, however, Ruth's cheerful, hard-working presence, and her sympathetic ear when David felt newly returned Kenton was getting too much attention, won him over. Love blossomed in the milking parlour and elsewhere, until, by 15 December 1988, he was ready to make Ruth his bride.

Inevitably, a period of adjustment followed; Ruth had to complete her studies at Harper Adams College and then, while a bungalow was built at Brookfield for the young couple, they lived and worked for a time at Home Farm. They returned to Brookfield, and, in February 1993, David became a father for the first time, when daughter Philippa Rose was born. He took on his full share of parenting and became a dab hand at bathing the noisy new baby, although the toll these extra duties took became apparent when he started falling asleep while on duty in the lambing sheds. A son, Joshua Matthew, followed in September 1997, when David showed he took his responsibilities seriously by leaving a cricket match against Edgeley two runs short of a half-century, to be present at the birth. An affectionate father, he quickly came to call his children Pipsqueak and Josh. Family life seemed generally happy, despite the pressures caused by two outbreaks of TB on the farm, until 2000, when Ruth was diagnosed as having breast cancer. Showing sensitivity and strength in equal measure, David tried to support his wife through the ordeal of a mastectomy and subsequent chemotherapy, despite the terrible fear he experienced at the thought of losing her. His obvious love for her eventually swept Ruth's self-consciousness aside, and the marriage emerged from the crisis stronger than ever – a strength symbolized by the eternity ring David bought his wife at Christmas 2000: the words 'Just remember that I love you', a mutual promise made at the time of Ruth's operation, were inscribed inside.

The marriage needed to be strong because this was the time when the future of Brookfield was put at stake by Elizabeth's insistence that she should inherit her share of the business. There was also a realization that, due to the pressures caused by Ruth's illness, the farm wasn't being run as well as it should. An outbreak of mastitis was followed by Phil reluctantly taking Elizabeth's advice and having a consultant draw up survival plans. Feeling betrayed by his father, David was ready to give up the farm and move away. But then his dedication to work, which caused him to suffer an excruciating rib injury during a night-time search for a lost heifer, convinced Phil, like King Solomon before him, that the disputed goods should go to the person who showed most care for them. Almost immediately, David had to contend with the possibility of foot-and-mouth reaching Brookfield. For some weeks, he voluntarily put the farm in quarantine, but thankfully the danger passed.

It's as well for Ambridge that David's staying. He's proved a good friend to many of his neighbours, refusing to testify against the Grundys when Simon Pemberton wanted them evicted, and keeping quiet about his suspicions that Tom Archer was involved in trashing the Home Farm GM trial crop, to give only two instances. Showing an increasing maturity now that he's stepped out from his father's shadow, David is clearly happiest remaining at the heart of a farm that has always seemed at the heart of Ambridge itself.

Doris **Archer**

(Gwen Berryman)

When, in 1958, Doris Archer learned she had been left a lifetime's interest in Glebe Cottage by Letty Lawson-Hope, her thoughts must have gone back forty years. Then in service to the Lawson-Hopes, she can hardly have imagined the independence and relative prosperity she was to enjoy in later life. Her parents, William and Lisa Forrest, had raised Doris and her brothers, Tom and Edward, not to question their lowly place in the social order. Tom was happy to follow his father into gamekeeping for the large local estates, while Doris was only too pleased to be taken on as a kitchen maid, then lady's maid, to Letty Lawson-Hope herself.

Birth: 11.7.1890
Death: 26.10.1980

Even when Doris left service to marry Dan Archer and support him in running his father's farm, she never lost the habits her early working years had ingrained. She was happiest when busy looking after Dan and their three children, Jack, Phil and Christine. She liked nothing better than a long day's baking in the Brookfield kitchen. Pigeon pies were a speciality, but she could turn her hand to all kinds of savouries, cakes, jams and preserves. She was of a generation that believed a woman's place was in the home, and spent a great deal of time ensuring that hers was a home worth living in.

Her concern for the family extended to all its members. She had genuine sympathy for her daughter-in-law Peggy, as she struggled to cope with the difficulties of being married to Jack. When grandchildren arrived in due course, Doris had an especially soft spot for Shula, but Tony, David and the rest could always be sure of some delicious treat if they called on their gran. Of course, some family members were easier to get along with than others, and Doris sometimes found herself biting her tongue when her sister-in-law Laura Archer came to settle in Ambridge. The widow of Dan's brother Frank, Laura wasn't slow to give Dan and Doris the benefit of her opinions on farming and a great deal else. Doris simply couldn't keep quiet when, in 1977, Laura suggested that Doris's winning lemon curd in the Flower and Produce Show was in fact a jar Laura had made and given to Doris a year earlier. Laura was quickly put straight. That jar had been long been disposed of.

Besides Dan and her children, perhaps Doris's greatest concern was for her brother Tom. She was greatly distressed when he was arrested for the manslaughter of Bob Larkin in 1957, and wanted him to move into Brookfield when he was released on bail. She was finally able to relax about her younger brother when he found himself a good wife in Pru Harris.

A chance to chat with friends was never willingly turned down, particularly if Mrs P was the friend in question. While some detail of the church flower rota might start off a conversation, the latest gossip about village life would soon nudge more mundane matters aside. Doris, like Dan, was also a good friend to Walter Gabriel. She did her best to cheer him up when he learned that Mrs P was to marry the second Mr Perkins. When the roof of Walter's cottage was badly damaged in high winds, Doris was happy for him to move in temporarily with her and Dan. Her only condition was that he didn't try to help around the house, especially after his assistance with the washing-up resulted in him ruining two non-stick pans.

Always one to play a full part in village life, Doris helped with fêtes, organized a cottage garden contest for the Festival of Ambridge, and could be relied on to join most fund-raising committees for good causes. She was a loyal member of the Women's Institute, having been a founder member of the Ambridge branch. There was some controversy when Doris, having been nominated as president, was mistakenly thought to be trying to influence the vote by giving away jars of preserves (an affair which would surely, in a later era, have been referred to as 'Chutneygate'). However, Doris's time with the WI was otherwise a happy one. Perhaps her finest moment came in 1965, when she was chosen to represent the institute at a Buckingham Palace Garden Party. She is unlikely to have over-indulged in the complimentary drinks, since she had no head for alcohol. Even a little of Walter's elderflower wine, smuggled into a house-warming party at the Vicarage, left her distinctly squiffy.

Doris liked things simple and certain. Tea was a better drink than champagne, and marriage to Dan was better than anything. Although she left him to make all the big decisions in farming matters, she had her own opinions and would voice them when she considered it necessary. She had a fair understanding of livestock, and kept her own hens until a fox got in among them. Thereafter, she kept only one hen, as a pet.

Staunch Church of England, she valued the traditional ways of doing things and had a strong sense of right and wrong. When a new style of service was used at Family Communion, she would go to Evensong to avoid it. Even her own children weren't exempt from her rigorous views. She disapproved of Christine marrying the divorcé George Barford in St Stephen's, feeling that such a remarriage shouldn't take place in church. Nevertheless, she was relieved that Christine wasn't driven away from Ambridge by the fuss the matter caused.

Her faith was a great comfort in her declining years, when her health started to fail. She suffered a broken wrist when an intruder broke into Brookfield, and then there were painful bouts of arthritis and problems with blood pressure and bad headaches. Finally, after a family tea party at Glebe Cottage, she was found to have passed away peacefully in her chair. At the funeral, her favourite psalm, 'I Will Lift Up Mine Eyes Unto the Hills', was sung, perhaps a reminder of Lakey Hill, which she could see from her Brookfield home, and where, many years previously, a young Dan Archer had wooed and won her for life.

Frank **Archer**

Frank was younger brother to Dan and Ben Archer. After growing up at Brookfield, he wanted to travel, and ended up settling in South Otago, New Zealand, where he married Laura Wilson. Good with livestock, he ran a sheep station until his death.

> **Birth:** 1.6.1900
> **Death:** 30.5.1957

Grace **Archer** née Fairbrother

(Ysanne Churchman)

Grace by name and grace by nature? Well, some of the time. It has to be said that George Fairbrother's only daughter could be spoilt, wilful and manipulative; but she was also warm, impulsive and very, very beautiful. No wonder the young Philip Archer was so captivated by her.

> **Birth:** 2.4.1929
> **Death:** 22.9.1955

Widower George, who'd made his fortune in plastics after the war, bought his farm in Ambridge in 1950 and Grace was quickly absorbed into the village social scene, becoming secretary of the Young Farmers and promoting the Ambridge Tennis Club. She spent New Year's Eve 1950 at Brookfield, where she became dewy-eyed as Dan toasted the new decade. Phil kissed her in the car on the way home and they duly began going out together. They were young, however, and before Grace and Phil could settle down, there were to be many diversions along the way.

The first of these arrived, for Grace, in the form of Alan Carey, the son of the woman her father would eventually marry. Alan had been badly affected by his war experiences in Korea, and Grace thought she could rehabilitate him. Although he proposed, she turned him down, realizing that he was asking more out of a need for security than immutable desire.

Phil was the next one to be tempted, with the arrival at Fairbrother's farm, which he managed, of poultry girl Jane Maxwell. Phil and Grace were already semi-estranged over her father's wish to mine ironstone in the village, and Jane, with her agricultural background, seemed the perfect partner for Phil. When Grace discovered Phil and Jane were together at the bathing pool in the Squire's woods, she rushed there, still pink from her tennis game, to berate him, then tried to pair Jane off with *Echo* reporter Dick Raymond in an attempt to lure Phil back. Jane eventually squared the tricky triangle by leaving the district, and, when Phil saw the Fairbrothers off to the Mediterranean for Christmas 1951, the ironstone scheme having foundered, he realized that he still loved Grace after all.

On Grace's return, she announced that it was about time she became a useful member of the community, and put herself forward to take over Jane's old job. 'The slacks are smashing,' stuttered Phil when she turned up for work looking like a fashion plate, 'and the sweater's just the job. But…' Luckily, Grace had only come for a lesson in poultry-keeping, and, when some day-old chicks in her care died, she soon realized such work was not her forte.

Having successfully schemed to marry her father off to Helen Carey, Grace hated the new regime, which left her without a housekeeping role. She suggested to Christine a partnership in a riding stables at Grey Gables, with Grace providing the money and Chris, the better horsewoman, the expertise. Although Helen supported Grace when George at first opposed the idea, Grace was peeved when it seemed that Helen's apparent bad health might leave her nursing an invalid. She was even more put out when Helen revealed she was pregnant, but was reconciled to the idea by the time of her half-brother, Robin's, birth in 1953.

Phil, meanwhile, ever cautious, had been to see Fairbrother about an engagement between himself and Grace. He was shattered, however, to learn that Grace was a wealthy woman in her own right, which struck at the heart of his intention to be the traditional male provider. He told Grace that he still wished to marry her, but that first he wanted to make £2000 with a pedigree pig-breeding scheme. Unimpressed by this less-than-romantic outcome, Grace took a corner too fast in her car and was knocked unconscious. When she came to, she found herself staring into the eyes of a handsome stranger, Clive Lawson-Hope, who turned out to be the Squire's nephew. He, too, proposed, but the bond with Phil proved too strong, and Grace agreed to wait his stipulated two years. In mid-1953, she took herself off to Ireland for a year's equestrian training, leaving Phil to kick his heels at home. Although when she returned there was evidence of the former, fickle Grace in her flirting with Paul Johnson at her welcome-home party, so Phil finally pinned her down and she accepted his proposal.

To everyone's huge relief, the couple were married on Easter Monday, 11 April 1955, but an immediate disagreement arose over the issue of children. This time it was Grace who wanted to wait, while Phil wanted them straight away. It was only a visit to a friend with a baby with whom Grace was apparently a 'natural' that changed her mind. But Grace was never to be the mother of Phil's children. On 22 September 1955, partly to celebrate Grace's change of heart, Phil arranged dinner at Grey Gables with Carol Grey and John Tregorran. As the foursome sat in the cocktail bar, discussing that day's wedding in Venice of Princess Ira von Furstenburg, Grace realized she'd lost an earring and went outside to search for it. A few moments later, she was back, screaming for help. The stables were on fire.

Phil and John helped her lead the horses out of the inferno, but when Chris's horse, Midnight, for some reason went back in, Grace charged back into the burning building. Seeing the roof cave in, Phil and John rushed in to find her, but she was pinned under a fallen beam. She died in Phil's arms on the way to hospital. Still recognized as one of the most tragic deaths ever in Ambridge, Grace's memory lives to this day in a memorial window in St Stephen's Church, and certainly in Phil's heart. In over forty-five years, despite his happy and enduring marriage to Jill, he has never forgotten the anniversary.

Helen **Archer**

(Frances Graham, Bonnie Engstrom, Louiza Patikas)

Helen's breech birth and dislocated hip, for which she spent three months in a splint, may have affected her early bonding with her mother, but Pat must surely recognize some of her own passionate nature in her feisty daughter. It has to be said that there is, often, nothing wrong with Helen's ideas – it's the way she puts them over that can annoy, as her brother Tom, who's clashed with her more than most, would readily confirm.

Birth: 16.4.1979

Helen's early years were spent much like those of any country child: by the age of eight she was mad about ponies and spent her free time helping her Great Aunt Christine at The Stables. In October 1987, she was delighted when Tony bought her a pony, Comet. Christine lent her a saddle, Kathy bought her a pair of charity shop riding boots and Lynda Snell gave her a hacking jacket that had belonged to one of her stepdaughters. However, it was not Helen's 'second-hand Rose' appearance that caused hoots of derision at the local Pony Club, but rather that of Comet, who was fat, hairy and overweight. Nonetheless, instructor Mandy Beesborough recognized Helen's talent and promoted her within her class. Over the winter, however, tragedy struck. Comet, put in the grain-store overnight to keep warm, was a victim of his own greed. He consumed half of Tony's stored wheat and had to have his stomach pumped, leaving him with laminitis. When he subsequently gorged himself on spring grass, his condition flared up and he had to be put down. Jennifer generously suggested that Helen have her cousin Kate's second pony, Velvet, on a kind of extended loan, and eventually Tony was shamed into buying the animal for his daughter.

Inevitably, as she grew older, the delights of the Pony Club were not enough for the teenage Helen. The Aldridge largesse was extended again, less beneficially this time, when Kate involved Helen in a gang she led and which met in Blossom Hill Cottage, vacated by the girls' grandmother on her remarriage. When Kate left William Grundy locked in the attic, Helen rescued him, but parental feet were firmly put down, the gang's antics stopped, and Helen was banned from seeing Kate.

Helen knuckled down to her schoolwork and passed six GCSEs with good grades. Pat had already made enquiries about dairy courses for her daughter at Reaseheath College, and it was apparent almost immediately that Helen had found her métier. After an initial two years, she signed up for a further three to study for an HND in food technology with management.

When her brother John died tragically in 1998, Helen was a tower of strength to her parents. That summer, however, she rather surprised Pat and Tony, who still needed her support, by telling them that she was not coming back to Ambridge for the holidays but going to work on a dairy farm in Ireland. When Helen did eventually go home, the forthright Hayley lost no time in telling her that she'd shirked her responsibilities. Although Helen backed down at the time, it wasn't long before the two were at loggerheads again.

Hayley and Tom, who'd battled to keep John's organic pig business going, wanted to make sausages and sell them under the name Ambridge Originals. Pat and Tony were wavering when Helen, back from college for Christmas, weighed in. Imbued with marketing theory, she managed to offend all parties when she both opposed the sausage idea and told Pat in no uncertain terms that the Bridge Farm product identity was a mess and the packaging 'folksy'. An alienated Hayley quit the sausage business altogether but the rows contributed to Pat's mounting depression. When Pat took to her bed, Helen had to compromise her placement at a local cheesemaker's to take over in the dairy, but her flow charts and strict hygiene rules caused stress for the staff, who felt that Helen had learned nothing at college about successful people management.

It was sad that Helen felt her family were so occupied with Tom's GM crop trashing in 1999 that she omitted to tell them she'd won the Best Business Student of the Year award at Reaseheath. Fortunately, Pat found out in time, and she and Tony joined Helen for a champagne picnic in the grounds and made a resolution to pull together more in future. Pat and Tony's pride and confidence in their highly competent daughter was evidenced by their asking her, at her twenty-first birthday party, to run the organic shop they were opening in Borchester. Helen accepted eagerly, and, for a time, work seemed fulfilment enough.

In the summer of 2001, however, hints emerged that Helen had formed a romantic liaison, and not an entirely happy one. When her boyfriend was revealed to be gamekeeper Greg Turner, her father, at least, was relieved, having feared an entanglement with a married man. Pat was less sure, and her mother's intuition was proved right when it emerged that Greg was a divorcé and the estranged father of two daughters. But in this, as in everything, Helen has made it absolutely clear that she intends to live her own life.

Jill **Archer** née Patterson

(Patricia Greene)

Those who think Jill Archer's concerns barely extend beyond whether Phil wants one egg or two don't know her very well. Behind the façade of the ultra-traditional farmer's wife is a strong personality, who, just as much as her husband, has been at the heart of Brookfield and the centre of Ambridge life for over forty years.

Birth: 3.10.1930

It's often forgotten that when Phil met Jill she was a free-spirited career woman who wavered over the idea of losing her independence. In fact, she memorably told him on one of their early dates that she could never marry a farmer because she knew nothing about the life and wouldn't be able to support him. Fortunately, she changed her mind, and proved a quick learner.

Phil's first sighting of Jill had been fleeting in the extreme, filming her with his cine-camera at the church fête. This, however, provided him with a good opening gambit when he saw her again, demonstrating the 'House Drudge' in Mitchells of Borchester, and he pursued her relentlessly, persuading her to marry him just four months later, on 16 November 1957.

Jill was an orphan, brought up by an aunt, and she rapidly set about making a comfortable family life for the tragically widowed Phil. Three children – twins Shula and Kenton and then David – were born within two years of marriage, and the youngest, Elizabeth, followed in 1967. She was born with a heart defect, and Jill and Phil needed all their mutual strength during her subsequent operations.

By the mid-1970s, however, with Kenton at sea, Shula at the Tech and the younger two at school, Jill was beginning to suffer from what seemed like 'empty nest' syndrome. She became irritable and run-down, and, in 1976, collapsed on the eve of Shula and Kenton's eighteenth birthday. She was rushed into hospital with acute pylonephritis – a kidney infection arising from the thyroid deficiency myxoedema. By the autumn, she'd regained her strength, branching out into the disastrous Two Jays Craft Studio with Jennifer, and, more successfully, delivering meals on wheels for the WRVS. In more recent years, she established her own on-farm enterprise, bed and breakfast guests, took on Jerry Buckle's bees and was the star – at least in Larry Lovell's adoring eyes – of a couple of Lynda Snell's productions.

Jill has only once looked for paid work outside the home – in 1987, when she thought of being Matthew Thorogood's receptionist. In the end, however, she realized what she'd known all along – that even though her children were notionally off her hands, they still needed her. With their mother always there as a shoulder to cry on, and a plentiful supply of tea and cake, it's no wonder that the Brookfield kitchen has been privy to so many unburdenings.

Jill was thrilled when, after several doomed romances, Shula brought home solicitor Mark Hebden, but in the five years before their eventual marriage, she suffered with Shula all their ups and downs. Once married and trying unsuccessfully for children, Jill was often the focus for Shula's sense of failure, and when Mark was killed in a tragic accident, she was almost as devastated as her daughter. The birth of Daniel, and Shula's remarriage, have been happier times, though Jill was deeply shocked by Shula's affair with Richard Locke and didn't pull her critical punches.

With Elizabeth, too, there have been traumas, notably her abortion in 1992 after her desertion by Cameron Fraser. Jill couldn't accept that, despite offers of support, Elizabeth had killed what would have been her and Phil's first grandchild. For once she could not console her daughter by saying she understood, and the rift within the family took a long time to heal.

If Jill thought her sons might be easier to manage, she was wrong. Kenton's nomadic lifestyle and profligate habits have always been a cause for concern; even his marriage, he had to admit, was initially one of convenience, though not as convenient as the frequent parental handouts. Now that he's a father himself, Jill's only wish is that he'll settle down, but she must recognize this to be the triumph of hope over experience.

Only David, it would seem, hasn't been a huge worry to his mother. Marriage to Ruth seemed a match made in heaven, but Jill learnt a hard lesson when the newlyweds ticked her off for intruding into their life at the bungalow, however welcome her casseroles. But with the birth of Pip, the first Archer grandchild, Ruth was only too glad to turn to her mother-in-law for help, and these days Jill is rarely seen without a couple of grandchildren at her knee. Ruth's recent breast cancer was another severely testing time for Jill as lynchpin of the family.

Bitter wrangling over the inheritance strained even Jill's saintly patience, and, in an outburst at her grandchildren Freddie and Lily's christening, she told her bickering children she'd never been so ashamed of them. As she and Phil finally contemplated their long-awaited move to Glebe Cottage, though, Jill felt understandable pangs about losing her busy Brookfield role, but Phil was quick to reassure her. Since no village or family activity would be complete without Jill's capable presence, great good humour and surprisingly sexy laugh, their retirement is bound to be no more than an extension of Jill's full and satisfying life.

John **Archer** 'Ben'

(Humphrey Morton)

What's in a name? To Dan Archer's younger brother, John Benjamin, quite a lot. Most people knew him as Ben, but Doris Forrest, Dan's post–First World War sweetheart, took to calling him

Birth: 27.5.1898	
Death: 2.8.1972	

41

Johnny. He reciprocated by calling her Dot. When a horrified Dan realized his wife-to-be and his brother were exchanging pet names, honour demanded retribution. These were rugged times. Nothing less than Ben leaving the country would do, and even then, when he reached Canada, he still wasn't sure he'd gone far enough. In 1928, he found a wife of his own, but Simone Delamain was to die only a year later, the shock causing Ben to hit the bottle. He pulled himself round sufficiently to become successful in the oil business, but had little contact with the rest of his family for a long time, until a meeting with Laura Archer in New Zealand led to an invitation to visit Ambridge. Ben duly came in 1969, but too many years had passed for him to pick up the threads easily. Consequently, the Ambridge Archers felt little sense of loss when Ben was unexpectedly recalled to Canada, nor, if truth be told, when word of his death reached the village in 1972.

John **Archer**   'Jack'

(Dennis Folwell)

Jack Archer, Dan and Doris's eldest child, always had good intentions about making something of himself. Unfortunately, his fondness for alcohol all too often undermined his attempts to do so. ATS girl Peggy Perkins certainly had great faith in him. She was impressed by the smart figure he cut in uniform and was happy to marry him in the summer of 1943, when the outcome of the Second World War was still in the balance. Before the war ended, their first child, Jennifer, had been born, to be followed, in 1947, by a second daughter, Lilian.

Birth: 17.12.1922
Death: 12.1.1972

Jack wanted to provide the best for his young family, but the smallholding he worked on in Ambridge didn't seem able to produce the returns he hoped for. Dan and Doris could see what their son couldn't: the gulf between hope and achievement in farming needs to be bridged by sustained hard graft. Sticking at a job wasn't one of Jack's strengths, especially if there appeared to be a quick and easy alternative. When, in 1951, a friend from army days, Barney Lee, offered him a partnership in a Cornish farm, he jumped at the chance. He and Peggy now had three children to provide for, a long-wanted son, Anthony William Daniel, having been born at home earlier that year. But the Cornish venture was a farce. Barney quickly became too fond of Peggy, while Jack, always short of self-confidence, was afraid Peggy was starting to respond. Back the whole family came to Ambridge, where Jack started working with his father at Brookfield. The tensions between him and Peggy increased when Barney followed them to Ambridge. Only a dose of sound common sense administered by brother Phil and sister Chris stopped Jack from walking out on the marriage for good.

When Jack became landlord of The Bull in 1953, following licensee Sam Saunders' retirement, the new challenge should have brought him and Peggy closer together. For a time, he felt capable of anything. As well as his responsibilities at The Bull, he even briefly took on running Walter Gabriel's farm so that Walter could visit his son, Nelson, in Southampton. He enjoyed working on the land again, but Peggy felt he was neglecting the pub. Further problems arose when he started serving after time, and seemed to be developing too great a fondness for the stock. The brewery insisted that Peggy take over the licence. This only compounded Jack's sense of failure and he was to suffer a nervous breakdown that resulted in his being hospitalized for four months. When he returned to Ambridge, he acted as best man for Phil's marriage to Grace Fairbrother. Grace's untimely death seemed to shock him out of his old habits for a time. He started to work hard in his new job as foreman of Carol Grey's Market Garden and took an active interest in his children's education. He was unhappy with Peggy's decision to send Tony to private school, but eventually let her have her way. Anxious that the children should turn out well, Jack could be over-protective, especially of the eldest, Jennifer. He tended to make a fuss about each new boyfriend she had, possibly pushing her into more rebellious attitudes than she might otherwise have adopted. In 1967, he was extremely angry when she announced that she was pregnant but unwilling to name the father. His first instinct was to turn her out of the house. Dan's calmer counsel prevailed, and, by the time baby Adam arrived, Jack was ready to wet the newborn's head with a drop of champagne. While the rest of Ambridge speculated about the father, Jack and Peggy readily made the connection between Adam's bright red hair and that of Brookfield farmhand Paddy Redmond.

While Jack was not always at ease with his parents or siblings, he and Peggy struck up a good relationship with Laura Archer. Aunt Laura gave them considerable financial support over the years. She loaned them much of the money they needed to buy The Bull when it was put on the market in 1959, and later provided cash for it to be modernized and extended. In return, they had a self-contained flat built over the extension and invited her to move in. Laura was at her most generous in 1964, when she made Jack and Peggy a gift of £25,000, which was later increased to £30,000. While some of it was to be held in trust for the children, most was to be used as they saw fit. For once, Jack's expansive instincts coincided with good business sense. He invested some of the money in improving the pub, and lent Ambridge Farmers £3000 towards a new milking parlour and the buying of extra cattle.

If he had been content to concentrate more on business matters, life might still have been good to him. But increasingly he felt the strain of playing second fiddle to Peggy at The Bull. Turning more and more to alcohol for comfort, he added another dangerous habit to his repertoire in 1967, when a cruise holiday he and Peggy took with Fred and Betty Barratt gave him a taste for high-stakes gambling.

Predictably, heavy drinking had a cost. In February 1968, Peggy found Jack unconscious next to an empty whisky bottle. Although he rallied and gave up drinking for a while, it was a battle he wasn't destined to win. Within two years, he was incapable of any kind of work, as his liver started to fail. He was admitted to a clinic in Scotland in July 1971. Too ill ever to leave, he missed daughter Lilian's marriage to Ralph Bellamy that autumn. In January 1972, he passed away. Sadly, Jack's premature death deprived him of the satisfaction of seeing his children reach full maturity and the realization that, by and large, he had passed on more of his good qualities than his bad.

John **Archer**

(Sam Barriscale)

Even the most desultory student of psychology could not but be intrigued by certain events in John Archer's early life and the bearing they might have had on his adult years. It may be nothing more than a coincidence, given his choice of career, that his favourite childhood storybook was *Little Piggly Wriggly*, but it's his fascination with tractors that gives real pause for thought. At the age of two and a half, when being minded by Betty Tucker, he went missing, only to be found playing

Birth: 31.12.1975	
Death: 25.2.1998	

blithely in the cab of Mike's tractor. (Mike had, fortunately, removed the key.) And in 1987, his first experience of tractor-driving, when helping out at Bridge Farm, led to him nearly running over his grandmother.

Despite these portents, it took some time for John to develop a serious interest in farming, his first passion being American football. By the age of fourteen, however, he was demanding a shotgun to shoot rabbits, reading Tony's farming papers and showing a real enthusiasm for things agricultural. The arrival of Sharon Richards and her daughter, Kylie, to live in the caravan at Bridge Farm, however, proved to be a serious distraction. Before long he'd purloined her a television (Tony's own from his private 'den') and was even performing the ultimate sacrifice – helping her to empty her chemical toilet. His parents and grandmother were disturbed by his infatuation, and, when he departed for Brymore School in Somerset (a secondary technical school with a strong agricultural leaning), Pat's tears for her son may have been partly relief at his removal from Sharon's attractions. During holidays from Brymore, however, John was increasingly entrusted with the running of the farm, even though Tony had not been impressed with his school project on Bridge Farm ('The Way Ahead'), which called on his father to keep veg production (Tony's area of responsibility) to a minimum and to expand the dairy side. On leaving Brymore, John airily announced that he'd had enough of education, and, furthermore, that Bridge Farm wasn't the only farm in the world. Then he promptly took himself to Home Farm and asked his Uncle Brian for a year's work experience. At the end of this, however, he did pacify his parents by enrolling for a National Diploma in Agriculture at Borchester College.

Throughout his gap year, John had continued to be besotted with Sharon, and had set up in business raising weaners to Conservation Grade, as well as running a mobile disco. Although his parents felt that he was burning so many candles at both ends that he might self-combust, John was undeterred. Still very much under Sharon's spell, he offered to teach her to drive, but the plan foundered when she crashed his van into Peggy's car. John smoothed things out with his grandmother, but Pat felt that Sharon should have taken the blame and borne the cost of repairs. John retaliated that she could hardly afford to on the pitiful wages Pat paid her at the dairy. The ensuing row led to John storming out to live with Sharon in her house on The Green, but their time together was short-lived and Sharon left for a mother's help job in Leeds. When he finally accepted that she'd gone for good, John told his mother that he thought his heart was broken, but, within a few months, he was taking out an ever-changing succession of girls.

It was Hayley Jordan (now Tucker), whom he'd met at a club in Birmingham, who won his heart. She sought him out at the Lower Loxley Point-to-Point, where he was selling his hot pork rolls, and further proved her devotion by coming to watch him in the Single Wicket Competition. By early 1997, John and Hayley were living together at April Cottage and John was dividing his time between working for his father and raising his pigs, which were now fully organic. But the return of Sharon to the village destroyed this idyll, and she and John began a destructive affair. When Hayley walked in on them, she packed her things and returned to Birmingham, leaving John to send Sharon packing, too, and to plan a miserable Christmas alone.

Realizing that she was the one for him, John was desperate to win Hayley back. When Roy Tucker told him that he'd spent Valentine's night with Hayley but that she'd spent the whole evening talking about John, he was inspired to try a dramatic gesture. At the expensive Mont Blanc restaurant, where he'd booked a table, he produced an engagement ring and asked Hayley to marry him. She said no.

The next day was his brother, Tom's, seventeenth birthday, but John was too miserable to take much notice. When his father nagged him about a fence that he'd failed to mend, John shouted that he'd do it straight away. Tony was in the middle of repairing the farm tractor, so John had to take the cabless vintage Ferguson. When he failed to return for Tom's birthday tea, no one thought the worst until Tony and Tom went out to the fields to look for him. In the mud and rain, Tony found his son lying dead beneath the overturned tractor. The coroner returned a verdict of accidental death.

At his funeral, Hayley paid tribute to John and played 'Wonderwall' by Oasis; Roy Tucker read a poem he'd written; and a tree was planted in the churchyard where Pat, Tony, Hayley and all who loved John go for a moment of quiet thought. His name lives on in the Archer family Bible, where Doris, his great-grandmother, inscribed it when he was born, and his enterprising spirit endures in the pork and sausage business now run by his brother. Sadly, his striking good looks, his sense of fun and his laddish confidence have been lost for ever.

John **Archer (Snr)**

A tenant farmer at Brookfield, John Archer and his wife, Phoebe, had three sons: Dan, Ben and Frank. Perhaps he can be seen as the founding father of an agricultural dynasty. If still alive, he would be Pip and Josh Archer's great-great grandfather.

Joshua **Archer**   'Josh'

He was extremely noisy as a baby, and, although he's calmed down since, Josh Archer can still be quite a handful for his parents, David and Ruth, and older sister, Pip, to deal with. He looked just

Birth: 13.9.1997

like his dad as a baby, but by the time of the millennium village photo, a resemblance to his great grandfather Dan was becoming apparent. Josh loves animals, but loathes having his hair washed.

Kenton **Archer**

(Judy Bennett, Simon Gipps-Kent, Graeme Kirk, Richard Attlee)

Kenton's life is an interesting mixture of cause and effect. Did he run away to sea, as it were, at the age of sixteen because he already felt himself to be a disappointment to his parents? Or was his

Birth: 8.8.1958

seafaring start just the beginning of a long career in dissipation, which has earned him a deserved reputation as the black sheep of the Archer family?

His early years seem blameless enough. The younger of Phil and Jill's twins, Kenton was educated at the village school, then Borchester Grammar, but had no interest in pursuing A-levels, opting instead for a cadetship in the Merchant Navy. He served variously on oil tankers and cruise ships, rising by 1982 to the rank of second officer on an annual salary of £10,000. He was expected at Brookfield on a month's leave in June of the same year, but instead a telegram arrived informing his parents that he'd been promoted and was moving to Hong Kong. Expansively, he invited them to visit, even offering to pay their air fare, but before they could do so, he moved to Bahrain. When he wrote in 1988 to say that he was coming home, however, something in the letter suggested that this would be more than just one of his shore leaves. It implied he was coming home for good.

For nearly fifteen years, Kenton had been a glamorous figure, who swanned back periodically for weddings and funerals, bearing exotic gifts, such as grass skirts from Tahiti. Now, he declared, he wanted to get to know his family again. But would they like what they saw? Phil and Jill certainly seemed won over, Jill throwing a party to welcome Kenton home and Phil buying him an XR3i cabriolet on the business. David was less convinced, fearing that the return of the prodigal would usurp his own position on the farm. Matters were not helped when Kenton began paying attention to Ruth, then a student at Brookfield, but already the object of David's affections. Finally, Kenton admitted the truth. He was taking voluntary redundancy from the Navy and intended working on the farm until he decided what he wanted to do with his life. Phil agreed to pay him a minimal wage, and, to assuage his fears, David was made a partner.

Kenton was not the most reliable of workers. Maybe his body clock was having trouble adjusting to a different time zone, but he missed the morning milking, and, when he offered to 'muck in', did not expect to be taken literally and be given the job of spreading pig slurry. In fact, he rapidly moved away from manual jobs to an area in which he felt his talents would be better exploited – looking into ideas for marketing both his father's pigs and Pat's organic yogurt.

The first half of 1989 was a difficult time for Kenton. Tired and run-down, he underwent blood tests, which disclosed a thyroid deficiency. Then a business that he'd set up with an ex-Merchant seaman chum Alex was investigated by the financial authorities, causing him some sleepless nights. By the summer, however, he had a new project: he was keen to take on the antique shop that Nelson Gabriel was selling. Typically over-optimistic, Kenton bought champagne before the deal had been confirmed, but the sale did go through and Archer's Antiquities opened later that year. Kenton wouldn't have had the wherewithal to buy the shop and business without help from his parents, who gave him an advance on his inheritance, Phil seeing it as a small price to pay for having Kenton at least semi-settled, and, furthermore, no longer a destabilizing threat to the farm. Kenton also needed a cash injection from his sister, Shula, but her husband at the time, the sensible Mark Hebden, insisted on Kenton paying them rent to make up for the interest their money would have earned had they merely left it in the building society. Grudgingly, Kenton agreed, and moved into the flat over the shop.

Archer's Antiquities ran for about two years, during which time Kenton had plenty of disasters. He stripped a bedside table for Jill that subsequently collapsed, and organized a fête auction featuring some wedding presents that had been stolen from Ruth and David. When Mark wanted the shop premises to set up his own legal practice, Kenton knew his books would come under scrutiny, and showed Nelson a sheaf of unentered 'business' receipts, including some for whisky and a television. In the end, he was lucky that Mark bought him out for the same amount as Kenton's original investment. He briefly partnered Nelson Gabriel in another antiques business in the Old Market Square, but the call of the wide blue yonder was too much for him. After attending a family wedding in Australia, Kenton met up with old friends and decided to stay, involving himself in running charter yachts.

His reappearances in Ambridge since then have tended to spell trouble. Resurfacing for Phil and Jill's ruby wedding anniversary in 1997, it emerged that Kenton had not just huge tax debts but a wife, Mel, whom he'd married to gain Australian citizenship. And when he popped up again for his mother's seventieth birthday in October 2000, he initiated a discussion about the Brookfield inheritance, which, with some justice, resulted in Kenton being cut out altogether, though Phil later changed his mind. With the birth of his and Mel's baby, Meriel, in May 2001, it remains to be seen whether fatherhood might finally make Kenton grow up.

Laura **Archer**   née Wilson

(Brenda Dunrich, Gwenda Wilson, Berry McDowall)

Laura Archer, Dan's sister-in-law, was not a woman to let the grass grow under her feet. Most areas of village life, including the WI, the WRVS, several committees for community action

| Birth: 29.8.1911 |
| Death: 14.2.1985 |

and the Parish Council, all felt the benefit of her zealous involvement at some point during her twenty-eight years in Ambridge. Indeed, some of the older residents still twitch nervously when they remember her relentless campaign to smarten up the streets and gardens of Ambridge for 1974's Best Kept Village award (sadly, to no avail that year).

She had come to England in 1957, after the death of husband, Frank, prompted her to relocate from their farm in South Otago, New Zealand.

After a brief stop in Stourhampton, where she outstayed her welcome with her friend Nellie McDonald, Laura settled in Ambridge. A woman of considerable financial means, Laura's generous nature coincided with her wish to play an active role in the business affairs of the village. Although Dan turned down the offer of an interest-free loan in 1958, the following year Jack and Peggy were pleased to accept help in buying The Bull. Further funds to pay for its modernization were forthcoming, and Laura even lived for a short time in a flat over the pub.

She was to become very close to Jack and Peggy's children. When Lilian was looking for somewhere to set up a riding school in 1967, Laura let her use some of the land on Barratt's Farm, which she had purchased a couple of years previously. She also showed a practical, as well as good-hearted, approach to the problems caused by Jennifer's unexpected pregnancy. Tony wasn't forgotten either, although Laura's hopes of buying Paunton Farm for him fell through.

The hundred acres of farmland that Laura had bought with Barratt's Farm were rented to Ambridge Farmers Ltd in 1965. She made another significant purchase in 1973, when Jack Woolley sold her a large Victorian house beautifully situated by the Am. It cost more than Laura could comfortably afford, and a complicated deal involving a fictitious finance company had to be arranged before the sale went through. Once it was in her ownership, Laura renamed the house Ambridge Hall.

As Robert and Lynda Snell were to find out some years later, Ambridge Hall was an expensive house to run. To help with the cost of maintaining it, Laura took in a retired colonel, Freddie Danby, as a bed and breakfast guest in 1976. Since the two of them seemed to get on well, Laura was hurt to discover that Freddie was looking for alternative accommodation the following year. A shrewd word from Jill Archer helped resolve the situation. Freddie liked Laura's company, but wanted evening meals as well as breakfast prepared for him. Sure enough, he was content to stay once Laura agreed to take on the extra work, although it was a while before they could work out a realistic rent for him to pay.

Over the next few years, they became close friends and even holidayed together in Malta. In tune with the times, and hoping to save money, they experimented with making Ambridge Hall self-sufficient. Damsons and herbs from the garden were made good use of; less successful were their attempts to create coffee from barley and other grains. Their tendency to treat livestock as friends rather than food didn't help the cause either. They showed appropriate resolve in buying a piglet from Tony, but, once it had been named Edric, its chances of turning up on a plate became diminishingly small.

During a visit to a smallholding, undertaken in the interests of researching self-sufficiency, Freddie realized how strongly Laura disapproved of unmarried couples cohabiting. Anxious to protect her reputation, he said he ought to marry her, or, alternatively, leave Ambridge Hall. But Laura wasn't worried that others might misinterpret the nature of their friendship. She turned him down and things carried on just as comfortably as before.

It was as well that Laura could be thick-skinned about gossip. In 1981, whispers spread that she was having an affair with Joe Grundy. It's certainly true that she was making regular visits to Grange Farm at that time, but only to do some cleaning. Joe Grundy had seen her accidentally kill a deer on Jack Woolley's land during the course of a driving lesson from Jill. Help with the Grundy housework was the terrible price he exacted in return for his silence. This wasn't her first brush with the Grundys. In 1973, she campaigned vigorously to save the village pump from being knocked down for road widening. Her campaign, and the pump, came to an abrupt end, when the Grundys' heavy lorry crashed into it.

In February 1985, when picking snowdrops for Freddie in Leader's Wood, Laura broke her ankle, slipped into a ditch and became thoroughly chilled. She was taken to Borchester General suffering from pneumonia, but was discharged, apparently recovered, after a week. Six days later, she died of heart failure. She had intended Freddie to inherit Ambridge Hall, but the only copy of her will that could be found was unsigned. As Laura's executor, Phil Archer placed adverts in the New Zealand press, trying to trace any next of kin. Judy Wilson, the granddaughter of Laura's younger brother, came forward to claim her inheritance. Ambridge Hall was sold and Freddie had to leave. Although Laura hadn't managed to leave him anything financially, it's unlikely Freddie would have swapped the memories of his feisty, life-enhancing landlady and friend for any money.

Mel **Archer** née Hardiment

It fell to the former Mel Hardiment to tell her in-laws, Phil and Jill, in a long-distance phone call that she and Kenton were married: he had

Birth: 12.2.1972

unaccountably failed to mention it. You'd think he'd have been proud to have bagged blonde, twenty-something Mel, but it emerged that the marriage had been one of convenience so that he could stay in Australia. Kenton assured his parents, however, that his feelings for Mel had turned to love, and, in May 2001, Mel gave birth to a daughter, Meriel.

Meriel **Archer**

In a sense, proud grandmother Jill learnt about her sixth grandchild and third granddaughter before she had even been born. Thanks to the time difference between England and Australia, Jill was phoned by Kenton on Thursday 10 May, to be told that Meriel had arrived Down Under at 6.20a.m. – on 11 May. Two weeks overdue, she weighed 8lb 6oz when she emerged after a long labour for her mother, Mel.

Birth: 16.5.01

Pat **Archer** née Lewis

(Patricia Gallimore)

It's tempting to wonder whether, given the speed of their courtship, Pat and Tony ever had time for that 'getting to know you' phase, which might just have given Tony some clues about the woman he was to marry. Was the Conservative young farmer so reassured by the fact that Pat drank gin and tonic that he failed to check on her politics (Labour)? Did she ever tell him that she'd played county netball, or, even more significantly, been county champion at javelin? The sporty side of Pat is little in evidence these days, and, though she did captain the ladies' football team during her early years in Ambridge, that was probably as much a sign of her feminism as her athletic prowess. If nothing else, however, Tony should have been alerted to the nature of the fiery Celt he'd fallen for when Pat, the niece of his farming partner, Haydn Evans, proposed to him in 1974. Two months later they were married.

Birth: 10.1.1952

From the start, Pat, who at home had tended a pedigree herd of Welsh Blacks, resolved to be a hands-on farmer's wife, and this determination didn't waver through the move from Willow Farm to Bridge Farm in

1978 and the birth of three children. By the early 1980s, however, the combination of two school-age children and a toddler, the hard daily graft on the farm, and, it has to be said, living with the lugubrious Tony, had all taken their toll. More for stimulation than consolation, Pat began to look for activities off the farm, attending CND meetings and enrolling in a women's studies class. When, in early 1984, she announced her intention of taking the children with her on a CND march, Tony was outraged, and even the vicar had to reprimand her when her contributions to the bookstall at the fête were deemed to be too political. When Pat attended a conference entitled 'Women as Economic Units', Tony finally snapped, seeing perhaps that the writing on the wall wasn't just 'Weapons Out'. (Rumours abounded that Pat had been seen with her women's studies tutor, Roger, in a dark corner of a student pub.) Pat duly gave up her course and joined Tony wholeheartedly in their new venture, which was to turn Bridge Farm organic.

Since then, Pat has reverted to her former enthusiastic involvement on the farm, pioneering deals for her organic yogurt and ice cream, first with a delicatessen in London, then with the upmarket Underwoods Food Hall. At the same time, she has maintained her interest in the wider world, searching her conscience when Peggy offered to pay John's boarding fees for Brymore, which, although a state boarding school, smacked to Pat of private education, and taking a stand on the recent threatened closure of Loxley Barrett School. On women's issues, too, she has remained active, though in a rather more personal, practical way. It was Pat who offered Sharon Richards a job in the dairy and a home in the Bridge Farm caravan for herself and her baby daughter. She has twice sheltered Kathy Perks when Kathy's marriage was in trouble, leading Tony to accuse her of running a hostel for the homeless. Pat's championing of Sharon was especially poignant as her subsequent relationship with John caused Pat much heart-searching over what she had thought were her liberal principles. Was she unhappy about John and Sharon, she had to ask herself, because Sharon wasn't good enough for her son? In the end, though, her instinct was right, whatever its origins: Sharon's reappearance in John's life was a factor in his split with Hayley and thus, indirectly, in his death in February 1998.

As Christmas 1998 approached, Pat had to admit that the usual seasonal circus was leaving her cold. Getting through John's birthday on New Year's Eve and the anniversary of his death on Tom's seventeenth birthday took a heavy emotional toll, and, by Easter, Pat was at breaking point.

Taking to her bed, she was diagnosed with depression and prescribed tablets, but her recovery was probably helped just as much by a thaw in her relationship with Hayley and a talk with Mike Tucker, who'd been through similar despair. Emerging tentatively back into normal life, Pat was immediately caught up in Tom's prosecution for trashing a crop of GM rape. Although she was terrified that Tom would go to prison, Tony knew his wife's old fight had returned when she vowed to support her son in his determination to plead not guilty. Pat's total recovery was marked by her idea to open an organic food shop in Borchester – to be run by her daughter, Helen.

Pat's character these days is more warm than abrasive, though she's still capable of clashing with her headstrong daughter, most recently over her worries about Helen's relationship with Greg Turner. Unlike Tony, who will never be resigned to his lot as the poor relation to his well-off sisters, Pat knows that if she and Tony are still tenant farmers, it's not because they haven't had the chance to buy their farm. She has the rare gift of being able to compare herself with those worse off than herself – her dairy worker Clarrie, for example – and, given the growing appetite for all things organic, she realizes, in the rare moments of calm between hoeing cabbages and potting yoghurt, that she and Tony should really be counting their blessings.

Philip **Archer** 'Phil'

(Norman Painting)

Born on St George's Day – Shakespeare's birthday – Phil Archer is, like his stellar twins, the archetypal Englishman. A practical farmer with an abiding love of the countryside, his outwardly unemotional reserve conceals a sensitive side, which revels in music and song. But, above all, it's his courage in the face of life's adversities, his integrity and kindness that mark him out as quietly heroic.

Birth: 23.4.1928

As Dan and Doris's younger son, Phil, like Christine, profited from his place in the family. During the slump of the 1920s, money was tight, and elder brother Jack didn't have the advantages that, with better times, came Phil's way. He was educated at the village school and then the grammar school, and progressed to the Farming Institute. From 1951 to

1962 he worked as a farm manager, first for George Fairbrother, then for Charles Grenville, until leaving to join the recently formed Ambridge Farmers, working in partnership with his father.

If the young Philip Archer's career path was assured – he was always going to be a farmer – his relationships with women in the early days were rather more arbitrary. Although attracted to Fairbrother's daughter, Grace, Phil hesitated about a commitment, and, while she turned down two proposals from other men, he dallied with the girl who looked after the poultry, Jane Maxwell. In the end, though, true love won the day, and Phil and Grace were married on Easter Monday 1955. Less than six months later, however, she died in a horrific fire at the Grey Gables stables, and Phil was alone again, though not for long.

In July 1957, he noticed a pert blonde in a yellow dress at the church fête, filmed her on his cine camera – and the rest is history. Jill and Phil married later the same year, and their enduring marriage has become totemic in Ambridge and beyond as everything a union should be. In 1970, when Dan finally retired, Phil and his wife, Jill, moved into the Brookfield farmhouse, where they continued to raise their four children. They seem to have had only three rows in nearly forty-five years – one over the twins' education, one when Jill sided with some squatters at Rickyard Cottage and one when a crying baby belonging to Jill's B & B guests kept Phil awake at night. Otherwise it's been a partnership of mutual support, with Jill agreeing to run the farm when Phil won a round-the-world trip as an essay prize in 1968, and, in later years, encouraging him with his exercises after a hip replacement operation.

It's not that their marriage hasn't been tested. Tension between their elder son, Kenton, and David led to Jill persuading Phil to make David a partner in the farm. Daughter Shula tried Phil's patience with her disastrous boyfriends, never more so than when Nigel Pargetter, supposedly sleeping on the sofa, tried to get into bed with him in the middle of the night.

One of the most trying times, however, was Elizabeth's abortion in 1992. Confronting Cameron Fraser, the father, Phil told him he was the most amoral human being it had ever been his misfortune to meet, and no one was in any doubt that he meant it. There was a fearful reminder of the tragic loss of Grace when Shula's husband, Mark, was killed in a car accident in 1994; and, again, six years later, when Ruth was diagnosed with breast cancer, Phil went through similar emotional turmoil with David.

Phil's sense of justice made him an excellent JP during his time on the Borchester Bench, and a respected chairman of the local NFU. He plays the organ in church and the piano for the Christmas show, and has always had a soft spot for pigs, keeping a succession of Large Whites in the Brookfield orchard. He was close to tears when Brookfield's TB-infected cattle twice had to be sent for slaughter in the 1990s, but even at the end of his working life was still coming up with ideas, such as the extended grazing regime, which, prophetically, harked back to the more extensive way of farming Phil had been brought up with.

In his dealings – and frequent clashes – with his son, David, who farmed alongside him from the early 1980s, Phil had the percipience to see shadows of his relationship with his own father, never clearer than in David's wish for Phil to retire so that he and his wife, Ruth, could run the farm. Like Dan, though, Phil hung on. It was only when Jill injured her knee, precipitating an enforced house swap between the inhabitants of Brookfield and the bungalow, that Phil realized that the time had perhaps come to vacate the farmhouse for good. He couldn't have foreseen the ensuing strife in the family, however, as David and his sister Elizabeth, in particular, became locked in battle over the inheritance. On New Year's Eve 2000, Elizabeth let slip that her father had secretly been seeing a consultant about the possibility of rationalizing the farm. David, who'd been promoting a suckler beef idea, was devastated and it was only after he had, almost literally, laid down his life to save a fallen heifer, that Phil realized once and for all that he should have followed his first instinct, which had been to leave the farm to his son. With Phil and Jill now enjoying retirement at Glebe Cottage, and the Herefords installed at Brookfield, it's up to Ruth and David to respond to whatever changes may be in store for farming in the wake of the nationwide foot-and-mouth outbreak of 2001.

If he had one wish, he told the family at New Year 2001, it was to see Brookfield carry on as it always had, as a mixed family farm. Nothing can ever be certain in agriculture, but Phil's stewardship of Brookfield did everything to keep it that way. He's passed on to David and Ruth the trust that had passed from his own father, which he took so seriously and fulfilled so well.

Philippa **Archer** 'Pip'

(Elina Gill, Helen Inglis-Palmer)

Named after her granddad Phil, and Aunt Rose on the Pritchard side of the family, Philippa Rose was Ruth and David Archer's first child.

Birth: 17.2.1993

Usually called Pip, or even Pipsqueak by her father, she is a girl of strong likes and dislikes. She loves living on a farm and says she wants to be a farmer when she grows up. She's keen on strawberries, too, and sometimes even seems quite fond of her younger brother, Josh, although she was anything but welcoming when he first appeared. Unhappy at having to share her parents' affections, Pip threw tantrums, until being allowed to show Josh to her admiring classmates at school suggested he might have some good points. She seems a good-hearted girl and took great care in making up a shoebox full of gifts in response to an appeal for Kosovo. Tact isn't her strongest point, however. After Ruth's mastectomy and chemotherapy, Pip commented that her cropped hair made her look like a loo-brush. But she soon got the knack of the special way she had to hug her mum so as not to hurt her, and clearly adores both parents.

Ruth **Archer** née Pritchard

(Felicity Finch)

For quite a time after she arrived at Brookfield in July 1987, in search of work experience before starting at college, Ruth Pritchard felt an outsider.

Birth: 16.6.1968

Although she had grown up in Prudhoe, Northumberland, it wasn't living in a new part of the country that bothered her – it was the negative attitude David Archer showed towards having an, as yet, unskilled woman working on the farm that caused problems. Being Martha Woodford's lodger wasn't much fun either; an irredeemably nosy landlady was the last thing Ruth needed after a hard day's work.

Things started to improve after she accepted Mrs Antrobus's offer of the flat at Nightingale Farm as alternative accommodation. Mrs A's friendly but non-interfering approach was rewarded when she became the first to learn of Ruth and David's growing love, which was to result in marriage by the end of 1988. Jeans and a T-shirt have normally been Ruth's favourite style, but for the wedding she wore a 1930s-style ivory silk dress with a long ivory veil. She didn't concede too much to tradition, however; the ceremony, conducted by the Reverend Carol Deedes, contained no promise to obey.

Despite the demands marriage made upon her time, Ruth turned down David's suggestion that she give up her agricultural course at Harper Adams College. She also resented what she saw as Jill Archer's attempts to domesticate her. Ruth's lack of enthusiasm for cooking and housework were to become a long-running source of tension between her and her mother-in-law, particularly on those occasions when circumstances dictated that Ruth and David share the Brookfield farmhouse with Phil and Jill.

In order to have a breathing space while a bungalow was built for them at Brookfield, Ruth talked David into becoming Steve Manson's replacement at Home Farm, on the understanding she could do her year's practical placement there as well. It wasn't an altogether successful move; David quickly went back to working at Brookfield, and Ruth didn't get on well with the new foreman, Bill Knowles. He treated her with a singular lack of respect, but Ruth had the last word when she was able to show Brian Aldridge that Bill had been fiddling the Home Farm feed bills.

When there was a delay in the completion of the bungalow, Ruth and David moved briefly into the Nightingale Farm flat again, only to have their still-unopened wedding presents stolen. Fortunately, some of them were later recovered at an auction Kenton organized for the village fête. When the bungalow was finally ready to move into, Ruth became so fed up with Jill constantly popping in to help around the house that she even had the locks changed. The rapprochement between the two was a long process, arising partly out of their shared sympathies for Shula at the time of her ectopic pregnancy, Ruth's elation at passing her final exams, the support she gave Jill at the time of Elizabeth's abortion, and the birth of Ruth and David's first child, Philippa Rose, or Pip, in February 1993.

Despite difficulties in breastfeeding Pip, Ruth took to motherhood very quickly, but was determined that it shouldn't stop her playing an active part on the farm. She'd already shown initiative in organizing a feed co-op among the Ambridge farms, and, in 1997, while pregnant with a second child, tried to convince Phil and David to expand the dairy herd. Although Phil respected her opinions, and showed as much by offering her a full partnership in the business that year, there was no immediate expansion. It wasn't until some months after the premature birth of Joshua Matthew, or Josh, in September 1997, that new stock was brought in, despite Phil's opposition. When an outbreak of TB followed, introduced by one of the new heifers, Ruth blamed herself for the inevitable slaughter of the infected cattle.

She was asked to address the Royal Agricultural Society 'Young Perspectives' conference in 1998. She told her audience farmers could survive the difficult economic climate by concentrating on food quality rather than on the scale of production. It was a philosophy she and David were later to put into practice when they bought some Herefords and set about establishing themselves as suppliers of traditional beef. However, before she could return to concentrating on agricultural matters, Ruth had the trauma of breast cancer to negotiate. When the lump she found in May 2000 proved to be malignant, she underwent a mastectomy, and, subsequently, a gruelling course of chemotherapy. Unusually young to contract such a cancer, Ruth's greatest fear prior to the operation was the thought of leaving her children motherless, while afterwards she took a long time to feel physically comfortable again with David. Her closest friend of recent years, Usha Gupta, was a great help in allowing Ruth to talk openly, while her parents, Heather and Solly Pritchard, were a great source of strength as well.

The experience gave her a new perspective on what was most important in life. When the arguments over who would eventually inherit Brookfield blew up, courtesy of sister-in-law Elizabeth, Ruth told David time was too precious to spend in argument, and suggested that they should move to live elsewhere. Eventually Jill dissuaded her from thinking along those lines. Like her mother-in-law, Ruth had grown to love life in Ambridge and was hugely relieved when Phil finally decided that the farm would eventually go to her and David. Although her treatment has so far been successful, Ruth is a realist and knows that there is no guarantee she will remain free of cancer. However, she looks to the future with some optimism. The running of the farm is very much in her and David's hands; their two children are growing up healthy and happy, there is a third on the way, and a concerned reaction to her illness showed how much she is valued in the village. Now, as she brings the herd in for afternoon milking, or attends to another of the Brookfield chores, she knows the days of being an outsider in Ambridge are long since past.

Simone **Archer** née Delamain

French-Canadian Simone Delamain found Ben Archer's Borsetshire accent irresistible when they met up in the 1920s. Attraction turned to love, and then marriage. Tragically, Simone was to die a year after the wedding. For a time, her grief-stricken husband turned to alcohol for consolation. Even when he gave it up, he never found another woman worthy to replace Simone as his wife, so had to be content to die a widower.

Birth: 1900
Death: 1929

Thomas **Archer** 'Tom'

(Tom Graham)

Pat and Tony's third child had a quick and easy birth, arriving early, possibly for the only time in his life. Childhood enthusiasms for *Thunderbirds* and his mountain bike, on which, with a trailer, he once did deliveries for the village shop, were soon replaced by more appropriate adolescent passions, such as cricket. In this, as in everything else, Tommy (as he was known till his late teens) had to perform in the shadow of his brother, John, and when, in 1997, team captain Sean Myerson told him he'd be playing twelfth man or nothing, Tommy was bitterly disappointed. But Tommy didn't always lose out to his brother. He didn't do spectacularly well in his GCSEs, but celebrated nonetheless with a party in the Village Hall, which he'd persuaded John to book as if for a Young Farmers' function. In the fuddled light of the next day's hangover, and in view of the damage that Tommy's rowdy friends had caused to the hall, it didn't seem like quite such a good idea, and Pat had to reprimand both her sons for their thoughtlessness.

Birth: 25.2.1981

Tom's life changed dramatically on his seventeenth birthday with the death of his elder brother. At first annoyed that John was cutting into his party time by not returning home for tea, Tom had the devastating experience of being with his father when Tony found John's body. Afterwards, Tom was withdrawn. Together with John's girlfriend, Hayley, though, he was quietly determined to keep John's pig business going, missing college to do so. He finally persuaded his parents that he should give up his A-levels, instead combining a part-time course at Borsetshire Agricultural College with work at Bridge Farm and with the pigs.

Tom's somewhat naive approach to the business, however, led to ructions early in 1999 when he and Hayley had the idea of marketing pork and leek sausages under the label Ambridge Originals. True, they'd worked out the cost of a vacuum packer and labels, but Hayley's place in the business had never been clearly defined, and Tony insisted that she could be no more than an employee. Tom was already battling with his sister, Helen, who insisted that the sausages, if made at all, should be sold under the Bridge Farm label. Eventually, Tom had to give way on both counts, but as a protest made his parents cancel the party they'd planned for his eighteenth birthday in the function room at The Bull.

The inhabitants of Bridge Farm had always been among the most concerned in the district about the trial plot of genetically modified rape which was being grown on Home Farm land by a biotech company, feeling that it was a genuine threat to their organic status and thus their livelihood, though Brian pooh-poohed the idea. The identity of the group who trashed a third of the crop in May remained a mystery until the day after the Single Wicket Competition, which Tom had finally won. It was then that he was arrested on suspicion of criminal damage after his name was linked to a van at the scene. A balaclava found in his room hardly helped his case.

Tom was, in fact, proud to admit his involvement, and was convinced that he should plead not guilty so that, when the case came to court, the full issues would receive a wider airing. There was a drawback, of course: if found guilty he would have a much greater chance of going to prison.

By the time the case came to trial in October 1999, Usha, acting for Tom, had lined up a barrage of expert witnesses to support his defence that he had 'lawful excuse' for trashing the crop, while the prosecution aimed to prove that he was no more than a common criminal. When, after much deliberation, the jury returned a 'not guilty' verdict, there was much jubilation in the Archer camp, though Brian was understandably furious. Tom soon enjoyed getting back to normal life, though the bail conditions that had prevented him from seeing his girlfriend, Kirsty, still applied, as she was herself on bail for another crop trashing in Northamptonshire.

With Kirsty's case taking a long time to come to court, Tom's attentions wandered elsewhere, and soon he was going out with Lauren, a long-legged blonde. When Kirsty walked back into his life almost a year after they'd been forced to part, the timing could not have been worse. The old attraction was still there, and Tom, with the foolishness of youth, began seeing both girls. When he found himself recruited for Lynda Snell's *Mikado*, closely followed by both his girlfriends, neither of whom knew about the other, he found himself in a situation which itself encapsulated a perfect light operatic plot. Inevitably, however, the truth came out and Tom was chastened – at least temporarily.

The highlight of 2001 for him was acting as best man at Roy Tucker's wedding to Hayley Jordan in May. Although initially dismayed when he found out about the formal attire he was expected to wear, Tom took his duties very seriously, perusing several books on wedding etiquette and perfecting jokes for his speech. He stoutly maintains, however, that it'll be a while before he gets himself tied down. As Kirsty is an independent sort of girl, this probably suits her just fine. Bless him, he's got some growing up to do yet.

Arkwright Hall

Recently restored by the Landmark Trust to provide holiday accommodation, Arkwright Hall stands proudly next to its own lake in the Grey Gables Country Park. A Victorian building with seventeenth-century origins, the Hall was bought in 1959 by Charles Grenville. John Tregorran supervised the renovations necessary to make it a community centre for the village before Harvey Grenville moved in to act as warden. For a time, the building was well patronized, especially when a youth-orientated Cellar Club was opened in September 1963. Jack Woolley became the new owner in 1965, installing Sid Perks to run it as a leisure centre. However, this wasn't a successful venture, and, within a couple of years, the Hall was closed. Robin Freeman was appointed warden when it reopened as a field study centre in 1970, with Gordon Armstrong later being given responsibility for managing the lake as a wildfowl sanctuary. After Robin left Ambridge, Arkwright Hall was unoccupied and fell into disrepair until 1999, when Jack, with time on his hands after retiring, offered the building to the Trust. With Lewis as supervising architect, they restored it to its former glory.

Gordon **Armstrong**

(Gordon Gardner, Tom Coyne)

Newcastle-born Gordon Armstrong, whose powerful physique had been honed by hours of judo practice, swept into Ambridge in 1971 like a tower of testosterone. He had been taken on as assistant keeper to Tom Forrest on a year's trial basis and soon showed himself equal to the work. However, it was his recreational activities that had the most obvious impact on village life.

He started by falling in love with Michèle Gravençin, but soon turned his attentions to a series of other eligible young women. He became friendly with Angela Cooper, Jennifer Travers-Macy, Jane Dexter and Susan Harvey, among others. His most serious relationship was with Trina Muir, but this gradually became unstuck as Gordon made it clear he had no intention of marrying.

He put a lot of effort into increasing the number of wildfowl in the Country Park before taking over as head keeper when Tom Forrest retired. He also worked hard to arrange birdwatching trips for disabled children at the Arkwright Hall lake, and wrote about some of his experiences in a series of articles for the *Borchester Echo*. But by 1978, Trina had left Ambridge and Gordon was feeling restless himself. Handing in his resignation to Jack Woolley, he set off to become head keeper for Lord Netherbourne's estate, where he doubtless took good care of the wildlife and set many other hearts fluttering.

Ted **Arnold**

Ted Arnold took over as manager of Charles Grenville's Market Garden after Arthur Howell, the previous manager, left Ambridge. While his disabled sister, Dorothy, looked after their home, Ted made such a good impression at work that Jack Woolley soon poached him to take charge of the gardens and greenhouses at Grey Gables. Unfortunately, the only thing Ted really wanted to grow was his bank account. He stole money from Mr Woolley and Laura Archer before being caught and put on probation. Prudently deciding to leave the past behind him, he then moved permanently to Borchester.

Arthur 'Art'

Always known as 'the YTS lad', Arthur arrived at Bridge Farm on a Youth Training Scheme in 1986. Tony was not overly impressed with his work, even less so when poor Art passed out in the winter cold owing to inadequate clothing. Pat interceded on Art's behalf, but, just as she'd persuaded Tony to keep him on, Art announced he'd fixed himself up with a job near Waterley Cross.

Atkins' Farm

Amos Atkins gave up the tenancy of Coombe Farm to buy Wagstaff's Farm in 1954. Renamed Atkins' Farm, it was never much of an advert for Borsetshire methods of agriculture, since Amos was neither a good farmer, nor a pleasant neighbour. After his death, early in 1955, the land was bought by Dan Archer and subsumed into Brookfield. The farmhouse was then let to Len and Mary Thomas.

Amos **Atkins**

(Wortley Allen)

Originally a tenant farmer on Coombe Farm, Amos Atkins bought a farm of his own in 1954. He took little care of his cattle, and wasn't much bothered when they strayed on to Dan

Death: January 1955

Archer's land. He was more concerned that Phil and Jack Archer shouldn't pay court to his niece Audrey, who came to housekeep for him. He hit a new low when he started setting gin traps in open fields. When Simon Cooper, Tom Forrest and Jack Archer went to complain, they found him dead at the bottom of his stairs – a sad end to an unhappy life.

Audrey **Atkins**

(Pauline Seville)

Timid Audrey Atkins came to Ambridge to keep house for her Uncle Amos. She wasn't good in company, even fleeing polite conversation from Jack and Phil Archer. Overworked and unpaid by Amos, she tried running away, but only got as far as hiding in Walter Gabriel's house. Her crush on John Tregorran led to some tensions with Carol Grey. These culminated in Carol accusing of her of being careless with Amos's effects when £300 was unaccounted for after his death. Fortunately, Len Thomas discovered the missing money behind a loose brick in the kitchen, clearing Audrey of all suspicion.

Piggy **Atkins**

For the pigsticking enthusiast, Joe Grundy's great friend Piggy Atkins was the man to know. A butcher in Penny Hassett, Piggy inherited his pigsticking skills from his father, who harried many a wild boar in the 1930s. Piggy's wife, Rosie, may have had other interests. She featured strongly in a photograph album of Percy Jordan's, bequeathed to Walter Gabriel in 1985. Whether she spent all her time with Percy discussing the thrill of the chase is uncertain.

Jean-Paul **Aubert**

(Yves Aubert)

Jean-Paul is the gastronomic genius of Grey Gables, whose culinary expertise has been delighting diners there since 1983. At the same time, his intolerance of any interference from above has been a source of constant frustration for Jack Woolley, and, latterly, Caroline Pemberton. He's often found reasons to resign, whether through disgust at catering for murder mystery weekends, or simply through irritation at changes to the running of the restaurant and health club. For a short time he even defected to Nelson's Wine Bar, where his refusal to freeze leftover food cut right into Nelson's profits. He has little respect for other people's cooking, reserving particular contempt for vegetarians and 'those damp mattresses that you English call quiche'. Lately, he's taken a dislike to Simnel cake, after judging a seasonal cake-making competition at The Bull. For all the unpredictability of his temperament, Jean-Paul's cooking leaves his customers in ecstasies, a fact Roy Tucker tried to make use of before proposing to Hayley Jordan at New Year 2001. Jean-Paul has often said he's happy working at Grey Gables until he has saved enough money for his own restaurant. His many admirers hope that day is still a long way off.

Avril

It's no wonder that Ambridge villagers shun the metropolitan life if every time they have dealings with Londoners they turn out to be as stroppy as Avril. The delicatessen she managed was one of the first outlets for Bridge Farm's yogurt in 1988, but Avril made Pat's life a misery, constantly varying the order and trying to drive down prices. When she eventually stopped taking their produce, Pat and Tony breathed a heavy sigh – of relief.

Baggy

Garage mechanic Baggy's relationship with the Grundys has often blown hot and cold. He lent his friend Eddie money to make a demo record in 1981. When the money wasn't repaid on time, he ill-advisedly threatened Joe about it, only to find himself being chased away by a kettle-wielding Clarrie. Later, he and his partner, Sylvia, together with their half dozen children, ended up staying at Grange Farm in a bus and tepee, while Baggy was supposedly going to mend the farm track. When the work didn't materialize, they were sent on their way.

In company with Eddie, he stage-managed a corn circle hoax in 1991. Elizabeth Archer, investigating the phenomenon for the *Borchester Echo*, quickly realized that aliens intelligent enough to travel interstellar distances would be unlikely to do so simply to imprint the shape of Eddie's horned hat in a cereal field. Perhaps Baggy's finest recent moment in Ambridge was his performance in the 1998 production of *Jack and the Beanstalk*. In the words of his good friend Snatch Foster, who acted with him, Baggy could have been born to play the rear end of a cow.

Harold **Bagley**

A jug of wine, a loaf of bread and Harold Bagley: the recipe for the perfect picnic, as long as you forget to bring Harold. He was a grumpy fellow, who tried to convince George Fairbrother that public opinion was against the Makemerry Fair in 1955. He also made a point of marching through Dan Archer's newly planted fields to assert the public right of way. No wonder Walter Gabriel and Tom Forrest didn't want to see such an argumentative chap elected to the Parish Council.

Mabel **Bagshawe**

It was preserving pans at dawn in 1983 when Mabel fell out with Mrs P in a complicated saga involving two pots of plum jam and the alleged poisoning of Mabel's budgie. A huffy Mrs P refused to sit next to her arch-enemy on the coach for the Over Sixties' outing to Weston-super-Mare, but felt guiltily responsible when Mabel got left behind and no one noticed. A blithe Mabel, however, simply made her way home on the train.

Max **Bailey**

(Alaric Cotter)

A handsome-looking engineering student, eighteen-year-old Max Bailey would have melted the heart of many an ice maiden in 1961, the year he met Jennifer Archer on a skiing holiday in Switzerland. He lived in Wolverhampton with his father, his mother having died some years previously. Jennifer was so keen to impress that she pretended to be older than sixteen. They holidayed together in France in 1962, and were still close enough for Jennifer to spend Christmas with him and his father in 1966. But by then she was pregnant with Adam, so Max was gently eased out of the picture.

Christine **Barford** 'Chris' née Archer, formerly Johnson

(Pamela Mant, Joyce Gibbs, Lesley Saweard)

After two boys, Doris Archer was delighted when her daughter was born. Christine's early years were trouble-free, winning a scholarship to grammar school and then walking into a job, first as an outside milk sampler at the Ministry of Agriculture, then a lab job at Borchester Dairies. Here, however, Doris's worries began, for Christine embarked on a doomed affair with her married boss that seemed to set the tone for her love life. Her first proper boyfriend, Dick Raymond, was a reporter with the *Borchester Echo*, but he was destined for higher things and was soon dispatched to be a junior correspondent in South-East Asia. He and Christine corresponded, and she still considered herself in love until she heard from a passing caravanner that Dick had become engaged to a wealthy tea-planter's daughter – yet another heartbreak for her.

> **Birth:** 21.12.1931

Luckily, Chris had rediscovered another passion. She was by now running a riding stables with Grace Fairbrother, and local horse-fancier Reggie Trentham was training her, with some success, to ride in meets and point-to-points. The Squire's nephew, Clive Lawson-Hope, proposed, but she was confident enough to turn him down, and, within six months she'd met Paul Johnson, the man she would eventually marry. Their engagement was sudden – Chris simply turned up at home wearing the ring – and not without its problems. Paul's pretentious mother, Hilda, thought Christine wasn't good enough, and kept everyone in suspense as to whether she'd attend the wedding, which took place on 15 December 1956. Chris wore white lace with paper taffeta petticoats, with bridesmaids in turquoise. Her brother Phil, sadly widowed, filmed the occasion on his cine-camera.

Chris continued her equestrian pursuits, buying a new horse, Red Link, which she entered in the Horse of the Year Show, but, after a year of marriage, she was troubled enough by her failure to conceive to visit a specialist. She was told to relax and give it time. Paul, meanwhile, was working in the business he'd inherited from his father, but, by 1960, had to sell out to Charles Grenville, who kept him on as manager. Restless, however, Paul talked of leaving Ambridge. Chris dutifully said she'd go wherever he wanted, but even her loyalty was tested when he began a flirtation with an old flame, Marianne Peters. He subsequently resigned from his job, trained as helicopter pilot (financed by Chris) and moved them to Newmarket, where he intended going into aerial crop-spraying. The venture was not a success, and, on their return to Ambridge the following year, Chris was determined to put down roots for good. Paul resumed work for Grenville, and the marriage seemed to go through a period of consolidation when they adopted a baby, Peter, in 1965. For some years, Chris was centred on a wholly domestic world, running the village playgroup and becoming president of the WI, but all too soon Paul came up with a new proposition – selling horseboxes in Europe. This was another abortive scheme, but, ever the charmer, he wangled himself an engineering job in the oil industry, first in Germany, then off the Welsh coast, and, finally, a desk job in London. Throughout all this, Chris was adamant that she would not leave Ambridge again, partly for the sake of Peter's schooling and partly because she had by default made a career at the riding stables, which she was now running for Lilian. Later, when Paul's affair with his boss's PA came to light, she might have wished she'd endured the upheaval. Contrite, Paul returned to Ambridge, though another worry line was etched on Chris's forehead.

Although she always defended him publicly, Chris knew her husband was a dreamer, but, in 1977, even she was aghast when he set up a fish farm in the old trout hatchery at Grey Gables. Disaster struck in October when leaves clogged the pump and all the fish died; uninsured, Paul had no option but to file for bankruptcy. Phil and Dan moved swiftly, safeguarding Christine's future by buying The Stables for her. Paul, however, felt patronized by the Archers, and Chris returned home one day to find a note saying he'd gone for good. After days of frantic worry, he was eventually traced to Hamburg. Chris flew out to plead with him, but he refused to return and she had to come home in the knowledge that her marriage was effectively over. Her one concern was to make a secure life and home for herself and Peter. She decided to move to the farmhouse at The Stables; ironically, the Maori name given to it by its former owner, Laura Archer, had been 'Onemomona' – home, sweet home.

Paul, however, was still dragging her down. He missed one bankruptcy hearing and was summonsed to attend again, when he was suddenly killed in a motorway accident. A distraught Christine had him buried in Germany, sensing perhaps that there was no point in bringing him back to Ambridge, which he'd only ever wanted to get away from. Since her move to The Stables, Phil and Doris had noted George Barford's frequent visits, but, when Phil raised the matter, he was told firmly that Chris and George were just good friends. When George proposed in late 1978, however, Christine accepted. The couple persuaded Richard Adamson to take a controversial decision to marry them in church on 1 March 1979, Christine radiant this time in a dress of cream and old gold satin.

She was forty-seven, and, after the initial family prejudice against George had subsided, Doris must have breathed a sigh of relief. 'Our Chris' was settled at last and has remained so ever since. In this time, she built up The Stables and had a share in a racehorse with Brian. She was also the inspiration behind the Dan Archer Memorial Playground, built in the village in 1996 to mark her father's centenary. Her retirement in 2001 means that, bad back permitting, Chris can at last make more of her leisure time, enjoying the tranquil life in Ambridge which eluded her for so many years.

Ellen **Barford**

(Penelope Shaw)

Formerly married to George Barford, Ellen bore him two children, Terry and Karen, but they parted in 1970, partly as a result of his drink problem. Ellen was not best pleased to have been cast aside, and confided to Nora McAuley that she had no intention of divorcing George as she was Roman Catholic. Anyway, she contended, he found the situation convenient.

The antics of their teenage son meant the couple were forced to remain in contact, and, though Ellen was sometimes keen to involve George in sorting out Terry's misdeeds, she was equally likely to turn round and blame him for all Terry's problems.

In 1978, she conveniently forgot her religious convictions and changed her mind about a divorce when she wanted to remarry. Her Damascene conversion came just in time for George, who was able to propose to Christine Johnson. But if Terry had suffered while his mother was struggling to bring him up on her own, it was Karen who felt slighted by the remarriage. Terry told his father that Ellen was concentrating so much on her new husband that Karen felt left out.

George **Barford**

(Graham Roberts)

<table><tr><td>Birth: 24.10.1928</td></tr></table>

Although he came highly recommended by Lord Netherbourne, when Yorkshireman George Barford arrived in 1973 as Jack Woolley's gamekeeper, some in the village found him reclusive and rather blunt. Bull barmaid Nora McAuley sensed what the problem was, and it was to her that George confessed that he was an alcoholic, and had been for six years. This had contributed to his walking out on his marriage to Ellen, by whom he had two teenage children, Terry and Karen. In April the following year, Tom and Pru found George unconscious after a suicide attempt. George might have continued his erratic existence, but the forthright Nora announced that she was moving in to take care of him, and – daringly for Ambridge at the time – they began living together. The relationship was not without its problems: a jealous Ellen made trouble, Nora miscarried and Terry seemed to be turning into both a delinquent and a drunk. George sought consolation in music, joining the bell-ringing team, singing a solo from *Ruddigore* in a Gilbert and Sullivan evening, and taking up once again a youthful interest in the cornet. But Nora's support for George started to wane when she quit The Bull for a job at the canning factory. The ex-policeman in him shrewdly saw through her feeble excuses of 'overtime', and he told Tom he knew she had someone else. In parallel, however, George had himself been striking up a new friendship – with Christine Johnson. Her husband, Paul, had left her and she'd moved to the farmhouse at The Stables. George and Nora were her nearest neighbours, and George was quick to offer his services chopping logs and helping her son with his homework. When Nora admitted her affair and told him she was leaving, George confessed to Christine that his main emotion was one of relief, and promised to take young Peter fishing.

After the turbulence of life with Paul Johnson, the now steady influence of George must have been a relief for Christine, too. He sought her advice about buying a dress for Karen's birthday, and took her to a rehearsal of Hollerton Silver Band, which he hoped to join. What moved things on, however, was Ellen's timely request for a divorce. Suddenly George was free to marry. He lost no time in proposing to Christine, now a widow, and must have thought Christmas had come early, when, in late 1978, she agreed, just as he was offered a promotion to the job of sporting manager at Grey Gables. There was an element of snobbery in the Archers' attitude to George at first, but he won them round, just as his dogged desire to have his wedding to Christine in church swayed vicar Richard Adamson into marrying them in St Stephen's on 1 March 1979. Tom Forrest, George's long-time colleague, was best man.

Although his personal life was more fulfilling than for years, baggage from George's former life, in the shape of his son, Terry, refused to stay safely in Left Luggage. George had been thrilled, when, after a troubled adolescence, Terry had joined the Prince of Wales's Own Regiment, but in 1984, he sustained head and neck injuries when his army jeep was in collision with a civilian car. George flew out to Berlin to be at his son's bedside, and when, a few years later, Terry decided to leave the army, George was again on hand to urge him into a future in gamekeeping. The only grouse Terry was interested in, however, was on the label of a whisky bottle. George took the blame for his son's lack of direction in life, almost turning to drink himself in his frustration. Fortunately, his wife, his work at Grey Gables and his commitment to the greater good were stronger than the attraction of alcohol, and George threw himself into his new role as chairman of the Parish Council, which was involved in a scheme to build low-cost housing in the village.

If George could be accused of anything, it is over-zealousness. In 1993, his determination to rid the shoot of vermin led him to use a banned poison, endrin, with which he baited some eggs. Unfortunately, they were eaten by vicar Robin Stokes's dog, Patch, who died, and George suffered many long dark nights of the soul before confessing everything to Christine, and then to Robin. In the summer of 1997, he spent night after night in the Country Park looking for poachers, only to receive a bad beating for which Eddie Grundy was wrongfully arrested. George remained jumpy until the real culprit, Clive Horrobin, was behind bars, and, although he returned to work, much of his old vim and vigour had gone. In November 1998, he told Jack Woolley he wanted to retire, and, though he grumbled about the time it was taking, was secretly flattered when Jack found him impossible to replace. George therefore stayed on part-time, working with Greg Turner and young William Grundy, whose interest in wildlife he'd done so much to foster. George's long career was crowned with the presentation at the Game Fair of a long service medal, and at his retirement party with the gift of a pair of silver pheasants, which

Christine has never once complained about polishing. In retirement, too, George has plenty to occupy him, not least the overgrown garden at the Police House. In his role as Ambridge's tree warden, a job he inherited from Tom Forrest, he was instrumental in setting up the Millennium Wood, and his performance as Pish-Tush in *The Mikado* threw him once more into the musical limelight.

Both George and Christine had endured rocky relationships before, but for the past twenty-odd years their marriage has brought the couple nothing but happiness. Despite his frequent disagreements with Jack Woolley, and his contempt for the chocolate drops to which Jack treated his dog, Captain, George was moved, when he retired, to admit that it had been a privilege to work for him. There can't be many people, in Ambridge or anywhere, who can claim to be as fulfilled on both counts.

Karen **Barford**

The younger child of George Barford and his first wife, Ellen, Karen was only eight when her father left the family home in 1970 – her brother Terry was ten. In 1978, George enlisted the help of Christine Johnson in choosing a dress for Karen's birthday, but in 1980, with Chris and George an item and her mother remarried, Karen complained that she felt left out. One can only hope that she's a happier adult than she was a child.

Birth: 4.6.1962

Terry **Barford**

(Paul Draper, Jonathan Owen)

Terry's social workers over the years may well have put him down as the so-called typical product of a broken home. Indeed, Terry himself was never slow to blame George's desertion of the family for his problems, but in truth, of course, he was the architect of much of his own doom.

At fifteen, Terry was found breaking and entering a furniture store and put on probation. When he left school the following year, he made his

Birth: 18.6.1960

way to Ambridge, doing casual work at Brookfield before becoming an apprentice on Jack Woolley's estate. But it wasn't until, to George's delight, Terry joined the Prince of Wales's Own Regiment of Yorkshire that he found some stability in his life. By 1984, he was enjoying life as a lance corporal, had developed a talent for boxing and acquired a girlfriend called Anita. He left the army five years later, and, building on previous skills, was taken on as a trainee gamekeeper by Brian Aldridge. Finding it hard to fit into civilian life, however, he turned to his old comforter, drink, quit his job and packed his bags. He was last heard of working in a bar in Berlin – a case of 'Auf wiedersehen, Ambridge'.

Mr **Barlow**

(Gordon Walters)

In 1960, Mrs Turvey was so appalled by the heaps of scrap that Walter Gabriel kept in Parson's Field, which adjoined her garden, that she bought the lot off him. It proved so worthless that she was unable to sell it on, whereupon she called in a friend to help out. Mr Barlow went to Walter, pretending to be interested in any scrap metal he might have for sale. Sure enough, Walter couldn't resist the thought of a quick profit, and promptly bought all his junk back from Mrs Turvey.

Sophie **Barlow**

(Moir Leslie)

Far from disapproving of David's choice of girlfriend, Phil Archer was so taken with red-haired fashion student Sophie Barlow that he grew a beard again on the strength of her saying she liked

Birth: 1962

it. The daughter of an architect, Sophie met David at a Young Farmers' dance in 1983, and had an on/off relationship with him over the next four years. She briefly went out with Mark Hebden, but became committed to David when she accepted his proposal in 1986, made while watching the wedding of Prince Andrew and Sarah Ferguson on television. They tried to buy a house at auction, but were outbid, which proved to be a blessing in disguise. Sophie, who had impressed a top fashion house with one of her shows at Grey Gables, accepted the offer of a job in London. When she came back to discuss arrangements for the wedding, she broke down in Felpersham Cathedral, telling David she wanted to focus on her work rather than marry. If the truth were known, he hadn't really missed her while she'd been away, so was relieved at her decision. They remained good enough friends for her to accompany him to Jethro Larkin's funeral soon after, but David hasn't heard anything of her, or her sister, Chloe, in a long while.

Hugo **Barnaby**

(Michael McClain)

Hugo Barnaby, cousin to John Tregorran, came to Ambridge in 1968 from the USA, where he had made a name for himself in the world of antiques and fine art. Once living in Glebe Cottage, he wrote, and had published, his 'spiritual memoirs'. He was fleetingly attracted to Fiona Watson, but developed a deeper affection for John's wife, Carol. At times, the strength of Hugo's feelings threatened to unbalance the warm friendship he had with the Tregorrans, never more so than when he misinterpreted the suggestion that he take over one of John's lecture tours as a sign that he was no longer welcome in the village. He certainly made his mark on it, turning Nightingale Farm into a rural arts centre, after buying it from Lady Isabel Lander in 1970, and being the driving force behind a tree survey in the area. In 1971, he returned to the States, was made vice-president of the American Fine Arts Society and became engaged to a delightful woman called Stephanie. The engagement didn't work out, and he came back to Ambridge for a while, hoping to pay court to Carol once more. Getting nowhere, he went back to America for good in 1976.

Irene **Barraclough**

Irene Barraclough, a resident of Manorfield Close, had lived for ten years in Ambridge and had hardly ever needed to visit the doctor's surgery

Death: 9.7.1996

before she was diagnosed as having cancer in 1996. Richard Locke spent a great deal of time treating her, and made such a favourable impression that Irene changed her will to leave one-eighth of her estate to him. She actually passed away while he was with her, a circumstance that added to her son, Ken's, unjust suspicions that Dr Locke might not have given her the best possible care.

Ken **Barraclough**

(Richard Hague)

K en Barraclough didn't often make the journey from Dorset to Ambridge to see his mother, Irene, while she was alive, but made himself known around the village after her death, when he accused Richard Locke of negligence and abusing his position as a doctor to influence Mrs Barraclough's will. An independent review followed Ken's complaint to the Health Authority in 1996. After the General Medical Council decided that the case should not be referred to the Professional Conduct Committee, Ken accused Richard of murdering his mother, only to be told a few home truths by the understandably angry doctor.

Badger **Barratt**

W hen the bucolically-named Badger ('Brock', presumably, to his nearest and dearest) was pensioned off as huntsman by the Squire, Christine Archer was pleased to exploit his equine expertise by taking him on to help out at the riding stables. His hacking jacket was hung up for good, though, on his death in 1960.

Death: 1960

Betty **Barratt**

(Brenda Dunrich)

W hen Betty Barratt's husband, Fred, left her for another woman in 1968, Betty soon took up smoking. Some might have said she was exchanging one noxious weed for another. The years since Fred's retirement from farming had been difficult for her. She was aware of some of his womanizing and was embarrassed by his slanderous tongue. There had been good times earlier: shared holidays with Dan and Doris Archer, and a cruise undertaken with Jack and Peggy Archer. But Betty always regretted that she and Fred lost their only child, a little girl, within months of her birth. Not naturally gregarious, Betty took some persuading to join in village life, but enjoyed being involved with the WI once Doris had coaxed her into going. A short spell working in the office for Ambridge Farmers Ltd was less successful, since Betty had no talent for organization.

She hoped Fred's retirement would mean a move to the sea, but they only got as far as Hillside Cottage in the middle of Ambridge, and the marriage soon went into terminal decline. After the break-up, she had the satisfaction of refusing to return some property Fred had bought in her name. It's unlikely that she spent any of the income from it in his new Borchester greengrocery.

Fred **Barratt**

(Tommy Duggan)

In 1960, while chair of the local NFU, Fred Barratt spoke to Dan Archer about the problems facing small-scale farmers like themselves. As a result, they agreed to try to amalgamate their dairy operations, and, with Jess Allard, formally started operating as Ambridge Dairy Farmers Ltd in April 1961. The company was expanded and renamed Ambridge Farmers Ltd the following year, when Jess had died and been replaced by Phil Archer.

Fred, and his wife, Betty, became good friends with Dan and Doris, and holidayed with them in Ireland and Guernsey. Then things started to go wrong. Gout and rheumatism forced Fred into early retirement. With his property disposed of in 1965, he spent his time drinking, womanizing and spreading malicious rumours. Jack Woolley threatened to disclose one of his romantic misdemeanours to Betty unless he stopped making unsubstantiated claims about Nelson Gabriel and the mail van robbery. Without warning, in 1968 he left both Betty and Ambridge. Dan discovered him running a greengrocery in Borchester. Now involved with another woman, Fred was bitter about some property he had bought in Betty's name, which she was refusing to return to him. He felt that Jack Woolley was in some way to blame. While nothing more is known of his greengrocery ventures, it is believed that, by this time, Fred stocked a fine selection of sour grapes.

Barratt's Farm

Not many of Shula Hebden Lloyd's clients being put through their paces at The Stables realize they are riding on what was formerly Barratt's Farm. Originally, it was known as Sixpenny Farm before Fred Barratt bought it. On his retirement in 1965, he sold it to Laura Archer, who leased most of the farmland to Ambridge Farmers Ltd, keeping the farmhouse and a couple of acres for herself. She named the house 'Onemomona', a Maori word meaning 'home, sweet home', in honour of her New Zealand connections. When Lilian Archer was hoping to establish her own riding school in 1967, Laura let her set it up on her property, and later sold both house and land to her. Lilian renamed it 'The Stables' and kept it on until she left Ambridge with husband Ralph Bellamy in 1975. Christine Johnson then took it over, and continued living and working there after her marriage to George Barford in 1979. By 1998, she was pleased to be able to share the responsibilities of running the riding school by going into partnership with Shula, who in 2001, took sole charge of The Stables on Christine's retirement.

Major Barrington

(Self)

Thanks to his work at a Cotswolds game farm, Major L. Barrington had a reputation as something of an expert on the care of game birds. He came to Ambridge to discuss the shoot on the Bellamy Estate early in 1966 and his opinions were highly valued by Ralph Bellamy, Jack Woolley and Tom Forrest, among others. It is not known if he was connected to the Borsetshire Barringtons.

Dave **Barry**

(David Vann)

Dave Barry's attitude to policing was something between Claude Rains in *Casablanca* and Arnold Schwarzenegger in *Robocop*, and the luckless Eddie Grundy spent much of the early 1980s

Birth: 1945

having his collar felt by the dapper detective. Dave got off on the wrong foot with the inhabitants of Ambridge when he arrested Nelson Gabriel, the villagers' very own Arthur Negus/Arthur Daley, on suspicion of handling stolen goods. Unable to prove the case, he told Lynda Snell in pique that a table she'd bought from Nelson for £2000 was a fake, and subsequently transferred his energies to more manageable crimes such as missing bicycles.

In 1984, Dave moved his zebra-print cushions and smoked-glass coffee tables into the former Ambridge police house, and, before long, teacher Kathy Holland was poring over his paint charts. They were together for two years, but she spurned him to marry Sid Perks, only to be tempted back into Dave's arms for a brief affair. When she ended it, he became morose and misogynistic, attempting to blackmail Kathy and swigging Scotch in the street. But his mother must still love him: in 1990 he moved to St Albans to be near her.

Mr and Mrs **Barton**

The Bartons moved to Ambridge in 1989, where they took up residence in Glebelands, shortly after Mr Barton's retirement as a solicitor. His wife quickly became a stalwart of the Ambridge WI, but has been a little less regular in her attendance recently. Mike Tucker derives a great deal of innocent pleasure when delivering the milk by asking whatever happened to their son Dick.

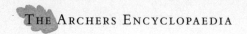

Albert **Bates**

(Ralph Lawton)

In the spring of 1964, PC Bates arrived in Ambridge, bringing with him his Worcester-born wife, who gave birth to their first child in October of that year. His parents, who were keen to see the village that their son spoke so much about, came to visit for the summer, staying at Rickyard Cottage when they did so. By 1967, their quietly conscientious son earned himself promotion, and left to take up his new job in Borchester.

Anne **Baxter**

Anne runs a thriving cheese-making enterprise near Ambridge, where Helen Archer did her college placement. Anne is obviously well placed in the Borsetshire good food and healthy eating mafia: it was through her intervention that Howard Friend agreed to meet Helen and her brother, Tom, and subsequently to sell Bridge Farm sausages in his superstore.

Mrs **Beard**

When James Bellamy was born in March 1973, his proud father employed Mrs Beard as his nanny. However, she proved to be no Mary Poppins, insisting on a strict routine for the baby, wishing to be referred to as Nanny Bellamy and emphasizing that 'Nanny knows best'. When she committed the further offence of falling out with Mrs Blossom, the housekeeper, Ralph Bellamy sacked her in July.

Dr **Beck**

(Janet Dale)

A cardiologist who's been working for some time at Felpersham Hospital, Dr Beck dealt with Elizabeth Pargetter's referral in March 2000. She was very encouraging about Elizabeth's cardiac problems, which she didn't consider life-threatening at that stage, but recommended an operation to replace the leaky valve before the end of the year, stressing that it had a success rate of 96 per cent. At the time, Elizabeth wasn't very reassured, and later used pressure of work as an excuse to postpone the procedure, with the result that she suffered cardiac arrest in January 2001. Dr Beck performed the operation on a resuscitated Elizabeth a few days later.

Ronnie **Beddoes**

(Harry Littlewood)

Thirty-six-year-old Ronnie Beddoes was intended to be only a temporary manager at The Bull, covering while Jack and Peggy were on holiday in 1966. He was so good at his job, however, that he was persuaded to stay on. Jack became jealous, not simply of the competent way Ronnie worked, but of the attention he was paying Peggy. It was probably for the best, then, that Ronnie left The Bull in April 1969 to go and work at Grey Gables, where he also made a good impression, before quietly leaving for another post.

Tim **Beecham**

(David Parfitt, Tim Brierley)

It was only natural that when Nigel Pargetter was thrown into the Lower Loxley lily pond during his fortieth birthday bash in 1999, foremost among those giving him a soaking was his good friend Tim Beecham.

Birth: 1968

Not particularly gifted in passing his accountancy exams, Tim was nevertheless a natural at romancing women, and used his stint as chairman of the Young Conservatives for social rather than political purposes. He enjoyed going out with Rachel Adamson in the mid-1980s, but that didn't preclude him developing an unrequited passion for Peaches, the barmaid at the Cat and Fiddle. Perhaps not quite gallant enough to be considered a true gentleman, in 1986 he found himself in court for spray-painting a speculative message about Elizabeth Archer's underwear on a wall opposite the Borchester Magistrates' Court. Later he won a bet with Nelson Gabriel about the likely duration of a vow of chastity Elizabeth had made. Nigel floored Tim when he heard about the bet, but then, when marrying Elizabeth, was still prepared to consider him as best man, until Debbie Aldridge, as chief bridesmaid, ruled Tim out as unsuitable. Middle age may since have toned him down a little, but if you ever need someone prepared to drop their shorts in a really high-class establishment, Tim is still undoubtedly the man.

Mandy **Beesborough**

Thinking of flame-haired temptress Mandy Beesborough can still bring a smile to Brian Aldridge's face, as well as a tremble to his knees. Mandy was running the Pony Club in 1987, when Kate Aldridge was a member. She introduced herself to Kate's parents when she wanted to discuss Home Farm as a possible venue for the club's Christmas rally. Brian was much impressed, and found opportunities for further meetings. However, he went too far in inviting her to join his party at the races at the very time his daughter Alice was being born. An irate Jennifer wasn't having any of it and, in consequence, neither was Brian.

Birth: 1953

He was interested enough to want to send flowers when Mandy had a riding accident in 1992, and was pleased that she still had the Aldridges on her Christmas card list a couple of years later. Reports that she was sighted at a recent Darrington Easter Service may yet spark a religious revival in one small, Home Farm-based corner of Ambridge.

Marie-Claire **Beguet**

(Juliette Mole)

A butcher's wife with intense brown eyes, Marie-Claire stayed at Home Farm in 1993, as part of a town-twinning delegation from Meyruelle. Her understanding of cricket, which she'd played on the beach as a child, appealed to Brian Aldridge. There may have been other elements to the attraction, since bystanders watching them go round the Arts and

Crafts Centre in Borchester together felt they generated enough sexual chemistry to run a small pharmaceutical plant. Brian's wife, Jennifer, wasn't sorry to see Marie-Claire go home.

Admiral **Bellamy**

(Fred Yule)

Although his estate bordered Lakey Hill, Admiral Bellamy didn't feature large on the Ambridge landscape, though he did once condescend to open the church fête. Mrs P, in fortune-telling mode, analysed his handwriting, somehow correctly surmising the salt tang of the sea. When, in 1955, Bellamy retired – to a seaside resort, inevitably – his son, Ralph, took over running the land, and Squire Lawson-Hope, who'd just sold his own estate, bought the Admiral's house.

James **Bellamy**

While Ralph Bellamy was arguing with a nurse who insisted he scrub up and put on a gown before entering the delivery suite, his wife, Lilian, was giving birth. James Rodney Dominic arrived

> **Birth:** 30.3.1973

on 30 March 1973, a much hoped-for son and heir for the man who was effectively squire of Ambridge. Even before the baby's birth, Ralph had put his name down for his old school (so convinced was he that the baby would be a boy) and had engaged a nanny, Mrs Beard. She, however, was not a success, and her services were dispensed with in July.

In the meantime, on 13 May, the baby had been christened, with John and Carol Tregorran and Ralph's protégé, Tony Archer, as godparents. James was only a toddler when his parents left for Guernsey, from where he was sent to boarding school and played in the cricket and basketball teams. In 1986, he was reputedly tall and good-looking, at least in Walter Gabriel's eyes, though Walter reckoned this was the legacy of the Archer side of the family. By the early 1990s, he was working in London and Lilian, now a widow, bought him. He was, nonetheless, too busy to have his mother to stay after her cosmetic surgery in October 2001. One imagines this supremely selfish young man living life in the fast lane, with sharp suits, a snazzy car and a succession of well-connected girlfriends.

Lilian **Bellamy**   née Archer

(Margaret Lane, Elizabeth Marlowe, Sunny Ormonde)

Erupting back on to the Ambridge scene at Nelson's funeral, with the characteristic demand: 'What do I have to do to get a drink around here?' Lilian has already caused much hand-wringing in the Archer family in the months since her return. A heavy smoker and drinker, Lilian's outspoken views seem designed to puncture what she sees as the insularity and smugness of village life.

Birth: 8.7.1947

She hasn't always been such a trial to her relations. Jack and Peggy Archer's middle child, she was excited at the age of fourteen to receive a pony, Pensioner, for Christmas. The next year, she enterprisingly started a Hay and Fodder Club to provide food for the animal over the winter, aiming to save five shillings a week in the summer months by doing odd jobs. While her sister, Jennifer, was enjoying wild parties at college and getting pregnant by Phil's cowhand, Paddy Redmond, Lilian was going out with Roger Patillo (Travers-Macy) and studying hard at Felpersham Riding Academy, with a view to setting up her own stables. This she did in 1967, with help from her Aunt Laura.

In 1968, she was swept off her feet by Lester Nicholson, a handsome pilot officer in the Canadian Air Force. She married 'Nick' a year later, but he died suddenly in March 1970, having gone back home to receive treatment for an ear complaint. A subdued Lilian returned to Ambridge and took up the threads at The Stables, and before long the eye of self-styled squire Ralph Bellamy had alighted on the young widow. She hostessed a couple of his dinner parties before he cunningly bought his way into her affections by acquiring a horse, Red Knight, which he entreated her to ride at a local point-to-point. She won her race and Ralph won his bride. They were married on 3 September 1971. After their honeymoon in Venice, she moved into the considerable splendour of the Dower House – a far cry from the rooms above a pub where she'd been brought up – and in time bore him the son and heir he wanted. As ever, there was a price to be paid for her luxurious lifestyle. Ralph was both authoritarian and chauvinist, forbidding Lilian from riding whilst pregnant, and trying to interfere in Trina Muir's consequent appointment at the riding school. When, as a result of his ill health, the Bellamys decided in 1975 that they must leave Ambridge to give Ralph complete rest, Lilian went with very mixed feelings. They spent a peripatetic year visiting Canada and cruising the Mediterranean before settling on Guernsey as a suitable place (and tax haven) to see out the rest of their well-heeled days. They lived on a friend's yacht while the house they'd found was remodelled to their specifications, but within a year Lilian was restless. Wearied by the endless round of bridge parties and gossip, Ralph noticed she was drinking to excess, and, as her phone calls home became more and more discontented, both Peggy and Doris were worried. When Jennifer visited in 1978, she returned unable to give much comfort. Lilian, she reported, was bored out of her mind.

Jennifer was soon back on a plane again, when, in September 1979, Ralph had a heart attack. Although he wasn't on the danger list, Lilian felt responsible, was depressed and turned to drink again. Her conscience didn't prick her for long, however, because after Ralph had a second attack and died in January 1980, Lilian told her sister that her overwhelming feeling was one of relief. She was free! She could wash that man right out of her hair and shake off the Guernsey blues by packing up and leaving. Curiously, however, this is just what she didn't do.

She came to stay in Ambridge for a while, and was anything but the grieving widow. Peggy was tight-lipped when her daughter went out drinking every night: The Bull would have been one thing, but this was at The Cat and Fiddle with the Grundys. Since Lilian had inherited the Estate on Ralph's death, it was no wonder Eddie began to brag that he'd got a 'special understanding' with his landlady, though Lilian always had the hauteur to slap him down if he got too familiar. In truth, Lilian didn't really know where her life was going, as she confided to Chris, on whose behalf Ambridge Farmers had acquired The Stables from Lilian in 1978. She offered Chris monetary help to start up riding holidays, but had the sense not to support Nelson financially in his sauna and massage parlour venture. Instead, he asked her for a £5000 loan for the antique shop. Lilian again refused, but offered him a partnership. A year later, Nelson was urging her to take over complete financial responsibility for the business and live in Ambridge, but she declined and got her money out.

In December 1989, having come to Ambridge in the past fourteen years only for weddings (Chris's) and funerals (Dan's and Doris's), Lilian arrived on what was ostensibly a Christmas visit. She told Jennifer and Peggy she had a boyfriend called John with a yacht, but she was still drinking heavily and became dewy-eyed when the trio reminisced about happier times. At the Estate office, she went through the files, then asked for the key to the Dower House. Having evaded questions, not least from her brother, Tony, who was one of her tenants, she finally announced she wanted to sell the Estate. In 1994, she effectively severed the last of her ties in Ambridge by selling Blossom Hill Cottage to buy her son, James, by then twenty-one, a flat in London.

Lilian's recent appearance in Ambridge was closely followed by that of her youthful lover, Scott – an actor/model more likely to be seen striking a pose in a catalogue than appearing in a production of *The Caucasian Chalk Circle*. Unceremoniously and publicly dumped by him for the physically firmer charms of Brenda Tucker, Lilian leant heavily on a sympathetic Jennifer and an increasingly exasperated Brian, who watched a year's supply of gin disappear before his eyes. After vain attempts to reshape herself at the gym, Lilian opted for cosmetic surgery to enhance her failing looks. When the scars, literal and metaphorical, have faded, there can be no doubt that she'll be all too ready to relaunch herself into the world and the Ambridge scene. But will the world – let alone Ambridge – ever be enough?

Ralph **Bellamy**

(Jack Holloway)

Although he'd taken over the running of his father's estate when the Admiral retired in 1955, Ralph Bellamy's presence wasn't felt in Ambridge until 1963, when he swept into the village determined to make the land work a little harder for him. He had a fiancée in Cambridgeshire, but he called off the wedding when his father fell ill, and, on his death in 1964, inherited everything. He promptly disposed of his father's assets, buying the Grenville estate with Jack Woolley when it was sold off in 1965. Ralph, however, was the countryman, the agriculturalist and the driving force in the arrangement, and it was on his say-so that the pair disposed of the poultry unit and the market garden.

Birth: 26.2.1925
Death: 18.1.1980

Ralph was the bluff, hail-fellow-well-met type. Rugged, confident and above all wealthy, he had no trouble in attracting women, though he nearly came unstuck when the estranged husband of one of his girlfriends, Clare Madison, threatened an alienation of affections charge against him. Ralph retaliated like a shot, setting a private detective on the husband, and within two months he'd collected enough evidence both to stop the action and to prevent Madison from divorcing his wife as a result. Ralph rebounded from this excitement into an affair with Valerie Woolley, the wife of his business partner, but it fizzled out in the face of the overriding importance of commercial interests. Bellamy and Woolley were trying to push through a development scheme in Ambridge, and Ralph needed his eye on the ball. He was less downhearted than Jack when the plan was turned down, but the setback made him more determined than ever to farm on a larger scale. Already an exponent of the 'big is beautiful' idea, he was to prove himself absolutely ruthless in getting what he wanted, as the widowed Lilian Nicholson would shortly find out.

But his marriage to her was still some years off. In the meantime, Ralph continued his private expansion scheme in Ambridge, snapping up anything that came on the market like a man in a game of bucolic Monopoly. In three years, he bought some shooting rights from Woolley, two garages (Paul Johnson's and one in Penny Hassett), Blossom Hill Cottage and the Dower House, where he installed Lilian after their wedding in 1971. His courtship of her had all the hallmarks of a Bellamy campaign: he bought a horse, Red Knight, which he demanded she ride, commissioned a portrait of her astride it and presented her with a knuckleduster diamond. Who could resist? His treatment of her brother, though, caused some friction in their early married life, which was otherwise harmonious. Ralph had first taken on Tony Archer as long ago as 1966, offering him some practical experience before he went to college. When he qualified, Ralph employed him again as dairy manager, but, while Tony was mooning around over one of his girlfriends, a heifer was killed when a thunderstorm brought down a tree. Tony was again the whipping boy when brucellosis was discovered in the herd, and Ralph fired him.

After the birth of James in March 1973, Lilian found that Ralph had very strong ideas about his son's upbringing. He rejected Jennifer and Roger Travers-Macy as godparents in favour of the Tregorrans. He then sacked James's nanny, Mrs Beard, for imposing too strict a routine on the baby – pretty rich for someone as didactic as Ralph, though this may just have been a ploy to get Lilian to spend more time with her son and less at The Stables. Whether it was business burn-out or the demands of a young child at the age of nearly fifty is unclear, but, in June 1974, Ralph visited a Harley Street specialist, who told him he needed complete rest. In November, Ralph and Lilian told Peggy that, as a result, they were leaving Ambridge, though she could stay on at Blossom Hill Cottage, and that they'd retain the Dower House for James to inherit.

By 1976, after a year's travelling, they were installed in Guernsey. The following year, Tony visited to ask to be considered for the tenancy of Bridge Farm. Ralph was as peremptory as ever, pointing out how much it would cost to build up a dairy herd and telling him that Brian was willing to pay nearly £30 an acre just for the land. Tony went home seething with Brian, but his anger later changed direction when he learnt that Ralph had rung Brian inviting him to make an offer only after Tony had expressed an interest. However, Ralph thought better of it, or Lilian intervened, because a week later she arrived in Ambridge with a letter offering Tony the tenancy.

The Bellamys had gone to Guernsey for peace and quiet, and that was what they got. Even Ralph found life there a bit tedious, but it irked the lively Lilian more. He was agitated by seeing how much she was drinking, and when, in late 1979, he had a heart attack, Lilian felt it was her fault. Ralph was discharged from hospital and told to keep to a strict regime, but in January 1980, he suffered a second attack and died. His funeral was held in Guernsey on 21 January, and there was a memorial service in Ambridge ten days later. At St Stephen's, where a munificent Ralph had once paid for the bells to be rehung and the roof repairs to be completed, friends, family and tenants past and present remembered a man whose large heart had finally given out, leaving a son who was only seven and Lilian a widow for the second time at the age of thirty-two.

Bellamy Estate

❧ SEE: *Berrow Estate*

Jim **Benfield**

When TB was suspected in the Brookfield herd in 1994, it fell to ministry vet Jim Benfield to check over the cows. Phil was already reeling from the death of his son-in-law, Mark, in a car crash, and news that Jim had found eleven reactors was another body-blow. Jim could give little comfort: he told Phil they might have to think in terms of slaughtering the whole herd.

Jim **Benson**

(Ronald Baddiley, Monty Crick)

Jim was an agricultural worker on Fairbrother's farm. Something of a gruff individual, he hated being thanked for anything and was once sacked for insulting Helen Fairbrother. She'd innocently taken an interest in a tractor he was trying to start and her questions irked him. Eventually he was reinstated and told Phil that on the whole he thought Fairbrother was a good boss, albeit one who sometimes called a funny tune.

There was trouble at home when Jim's half-brother, Stan, turned up, having deserted and stolen money and cigarettes from the NAAFI. Fearful of facing the music, he was holed up in Copley's Spinney and reliant on Jim and his wife, Mary, for food. To add insult to injury, Stan, who'd once gone out with Mary, was making up to her and causing bad feeling. Phil judiciously advised Jim to go and see Stan's CO on the quiet, even giving him £2 towards the rail fare. Stan eventually gave himself up.

When Charles Grenville took over the Estate in 1959, he offered the Bensons a brand new cottage, but they preferred to stay put, and Jim was given charge of the dairy stock.

Mary **Benson**

(June Spencer)

Wife of farm worker Jim, Mary was brave to settle in Ambridge at all. When the couple surprisingly refused Charles Grenville's offer of a brand new cottage in 1960, it emerged that Mary was terrified of insects and wildlife, and couldn't contemplate a move to the cottage as it was in the woods.

Before marrying Jim, Mary had gone out with his half-brother, Stan, something of a ne'er-do-well, who rolled up in Ambridge in 1951, having gone AWOL from the army. He was sleeping rough but depended on Jim and Mary for food, and took the opportunity to see if Mary still had feelings for him by flirting with her. Jim, luckily, shrugged it off, saying Mary was too good-hearted and Stan was making a fool of her.

In 1955, Mary was instrumental in clipping Jim's wings. He wanted to set up on his own, so had applied for the tenancy of Amos Atkins's farm. Jim wanted Dan Archer, who was interested in buying the land, to withdraw his application, but Mary, believing Jim couldn't afford the tenancy anyway, told Dan to do no such thing. Dan was happy to accede to her request, and the land was duly added to the expanding Brookfield empire.

Sue **Bent**

(Linda Polan)

In name alone, Sue Bent may not have sounded especially glamorous, but perhaps to make up for her monosyllabic moniker, she wowed the menfolk of Ambridge with her beehive hairdo (this was 1965) and her pungent Californian Poppy scent. Arriving at The Bull to replace Polly Mead, who'd moved on to the Regency Hotel in Borchester, in 1966 they swapped jobs, Polly returning to the beer pumps at The Bull.

Jonathan **Bentley-Jones**

In 1992, Jason the builder discovered an unusual shard of pottery during building work at St Stephen's, and vicar Robin Stokes called in the county archaeologist, Jonathan Bentley-Jones. He and his colleagues identified the pottery as Saxon, and were further interested in some ancient timbers below the floor of the bell tower. They decided against a full excavation, however, and the timbers were re-covered to rest in peace.

Berrow Estate

It was all so simple in the old days, when Squire Lawson-Hope owned the Estate. Since he sold up in 1954, the land has repeatedly changed hands, sold first to Fairbrother, then to Grenville, then to Ralph Bellamy and Jack Woolley. It was Ralph and Lilian Bellamy, though, who really changed the face of Ambridge.

When he left the village in 1975, Ralph broke the Estate into three, retaining 1000 acres as an investment, selling a further 1000 to a Mr Barnet and 1500 to Brian Aldridge. Then, in 1990, his widow, Lilian, sold off her 1000 acres, letting in the crass arriviste Cameron Fraser. After he'd gone bankrupt, a return to the old order seemed possible with the arrival of patrician Guy Pemberton, but his ill health and subsequent death left the land in the hands of his ultra-suave son, Simon. Simon can be credited with setting up the business units at Sawyer's Farm, but, morally discredited in the village, he was forced to put the Estate up for sale again in 1997. There was much secrecy before Brian Aldridge finally admitted that he was a member of the consortium that had bought it, but this sharp practice has proved a poisoned chalice for him. His co-director Matt Crawford enjoys playing boardroom games, and, with two development schemes already proposed, who knows what Borchester Land might next have in store for the village?

Beryl

(Marian Kemmer)

A long-time casual worker on the Bridge Farm vegetable crops, Beryl has a cool line in saucy banter which has often embarrassed a blushing Neil Carter. When she tried the same tactics on Tom Archer in 1998, however, he got his own back by inviting her to meet a hunky admirer called Eric. She jumped at the chance but was, for once, dumbstruck when she found out that Eric was Tom's Duroc boar.

Beverley

Beverley was brought in to cover as manager of the conference operation at Lower Loxley in 1999, when Elizabeth Pargetter was expecting the twins. As the range of activities available there expanded, she was given a permanent position, and proceeded to carry out her duties with quiet authority until she was made to feel uncomfortable in the summer of 2001. By then Elizabeth, wanting to resume full-time work herself, had started subjecting her manager to constant criticism. Beverley wasn't prepared to suffer in silence, so she left, having found work elsewhere, allowing Elizabeth to resume in sole charge of conference business.

Susan and Mrs **Blake**

(Carol Lynn-Davies, Margery Field)

Wanting to provide her sick mother with a special Christmas dinner in 1959, fourteen-year-old Susan Blake tried to steal a hen. Hearing from Ned Larkin and Jack Archer that the young girl had been running the household single-handed during her mother's illness, Doris Archer got people in the village to put a hamper together. When Mrs Blake subsequently went into hospital, Susan stayed with Tom and Pru Forrest, and afterwards Charles Grenville paid for her and her mother to have a month's holiday by the sea.

Rose **Blossom**

(Anne Offord)

Originally an Essex girl, Mrs Blossom was housekeeper to Brigadier Winstanley. On his death, she moved to Manorfield Close, where she had special permission to keep the Brigadier's golden retriever, Amber. In 1971, she agreed to act as live-out housekeeper for the Bellamys, and continued in that role for their tenant when they moved to Guernsey. On her death in 1986, Freddie Danby

Death: 15.4.1986

acquired the tenancy of her bungalow, though presumably not her Ford Escort and white stilettos.

Blossom Hill Cottage

Blossom Hill Cottage stands on a side road off the Borchester Road, not far past Grey Gables. With a thatched roof, beech hedge and climbing roses round the porch, it looks the epitome of the rural idyll. Its current owner, Usha Gupta, loves living there now, but seriously considered leaving in 1995, when racist graffiti appeared on its walls during a hate campaign against her. The cottage had also seen plenty of drama during the occupancy of its previous tenant, Peggy Archer: first there was a burglary, then shortly afterwards a fire. When Peggy left to marry Jack Woolley, her granddaughter Kate Aldridge used it illicitly as a base for her gang of teenage friends. It was Kate's discovery of a letter in the attic that led, indirectly, to Peggy's wartime sweetheart, Conn Kortchmar, appearing in Ambridge. Before Peggy moved in, the cottage belonged to Ralph and Lilian Bellamy, who had bought it for £6500 in 1971. Roger Travers-Macy had been renting it from John Tregorran before this, and John had previously been renting it from Mike Daly. The history of the cottage before 1952, when Mike bought it from Squire Lawson-Hope, is a mystery Usha would love to look into one day, when she's got time.

Joe **Blower**

(Leslie Bowmar)

Joe was an old friend of Dan's and a fellow tenant farmer on the Squire's Estate. Like Dan, he was horrified about George Fairbrother's proposed ironstone mine, and, when offered compensation, felt that it would be small recompense for the loss of his farm. Joe was something of a Dr Doolittle with animals: his hound pups frequently won prizes at the fête, and he bred Siamese kittens. When he sold one to Walter for Mrs P, it came with its own diet sheet.

In the early days, Joe was seemingly a jolly fellow, who liked a bet, but it all started to turn sour for him with a downturn in the pig business and a bad harvest. He announced he was done with farming and was looking for another job. Having bought his farm from the Squire, its subsequent sale left him in the money. He acquired a car, began dressing like a fop, and, to Walter's disgust, started paying court to Mrs P. This culminated one Christmas in his giving her a handsome clock and taking her to the pantomime (Hiss, boo). Shortly afterwards, to Walter's undisguised relief ('He's behind you!'), his money ran out and he left Ambridge for good. (Hurrah!)

Craig, Colin and Lee **Bonnetti**

The Bonnetti brothers are the sort of workmen who give cowboy builders a good name. Engaged to refit the Bridge Farm kitchen at the end of 1988, they ripped out the old one only to disappear for days. A frantic Pat and Tony, facing the prospect of a kitchen-less Christmas, learnt that Craig had gone off in the van with all the tools and none of the family knew where he was.

An apparent glimmer of hope when Colin and Lee delivered the new units was swiftly extinguished when they confessed they had no idea how to fit them. Exasperated, Tony called in the helpful Mr O'Hara, only to have Craig arrive, disgruntled that the kitchen fitting had now gone to someone else. Craig confessed that he'd fancied a weeks' pampering with his girlfriend on a health farm, but, fearing Lee's wrath, had simply taken the van and been too frightened to come home. When Pat and Tony refused to pay the balance on the kitchen for the trauma they'd been through, the Bonnettis threatened legal action. No wonder that these days everyone uses the chirpy Brummie, Jason.

Harry **Booker**

(Alex Johnston, Gareth Armstrong)

When he left the army in 1973, Harry Booker and his wife, Marilyn, needed somewhere to live, so they stayed with her parents, Ken and Mary Pound, at Ambridge Farm, until they bought a house in Penny Hassett. Harry didn't really get on with his in-laws; he didn't want to do farm work and turned down a job Ken had arranged for him at Ralph Bellamy's garage.

Determined to make his own way financially, he was taken on as a mini-bus driver for a short-lived Ambridge to Borchester service before having spells driving the school bus and being a taxi-driver. He seemed to have found his niche when he started training as a postman in 1974, and certainly showed initiative in swinging the post bus across a field to avoid an attempted robbery the following year. To supplement his income, he briefly provided a home-delivery service for groceries, and dabbled in the second-hand car trade, although almost got his fingers badly burnt when he bought a Jaguar cunningly constructed from two separate cars.

A keen sportsman, he captained the cricket and football teams and was a key darts player for The Bull. When the post bus was withdrawn from service in 1983, he stopped coming to Ambridge, preferring to spend his time in Penny Hassett. Some people do.

Marilyn **Booker** née Pound

Marilyn was relieved when she and husband Harry were able to buy a house in Penny Hassett in 1974 and move there with their children, Lisa and Robert. She hadn't enjoyed staying with her parents, Ken and Mary Pound, prior to this because Harry didn't really get on well with them.

Birth: 1951

During her years as an army wife, she'd developed a taste for a good standard of living. Harry was always aware of the need to earn extra cash to support this, and Marilyn helped out by joining her parents in running the farm shop they set up in 1976. In contrast to her husband, she was all in favour of Borchester Grammar becoming an independent school, only to be disappointed when she realized it was then too expensive to send their children there.

Not a great extrovert, Marilyn was happy to lend a hand with the administrative side of the local talking newspaper, but generally kept more in the background than her husband. Consequently, her absence was perhaps less marked than his, when she and Harry gradually stopped coming over to Ambridge in the early 1980s.

Mr **Booth**

Enthusiastic campanologist Mr Booth suffered for his art a year after joining the St Stephen's bell-ringing team in 1998: his car was stolen while he was at a practice, and later found miles away, completely burnt out. Eyebrows were raised when Jolene Rogers' car was seen parked all night outside his house, though purveyors of unlikely gossip were disappointed when it transpired that Jolene had actually been with Sid at the time, but hadn't wanted to leave her car on show at The Bull.

Borchester

It's a pity that the coachloads of American and Japanese tourists en route for Oxford or Stratford-upon-Avon rarely have time to stop, for Borchester has much to recommend it. Six miles from Ambridge, Borchester, originally a Roman settlement, has been a commercial centre since the Middle Ages, as evidenced by the Old Wool Market (now luxury flats). The modern-day equivalent, the part-pedestrianized shopping centre, offers the usual multiples, and Pat and Tony Archer's Ambridge Organics is to be found in nearby Harcourt Road. Public buildings include the hospital, schools, colleges and the Magistrates' Courts, though, sadly the assembly rooms have been replaced by a multistorey car park. For entertainment, there is a leisure centre and the riverside park with its bandstand, where Mark and Shula Hebden once sheltered as Mark sang 'Isn't It a Lovely Day to Be Caught in the Rain'. A fellow film fan was Mark's father-in-law, Phil: in 1951, he took Grace Fairbrother to see *All About Eve* at the Astoria. Today's Romeos head for the back row of the small multiplex near Radio Borsetshire, and patronize Borchester's many pubs and restaurants. The Goat and Nightgown near the Tech was the favourite haunt in the early 1980s of both Pat and her women's studies lecturer, Roger, and of Jennifer and John Tregorran.

Ricky **Boyd**

(Leslie Dunn)

Ricky Boyd was a regular bad hat and no mistake. In 1960, after being stood up by Tina Paget at the Borchester Palais, and he acted threateningly towards her in John Tregorran's shop, until clunked over the head with a paperweight. Walter Gabriel and Sally Johnson were to find him trying to set fire to one of Charles Grenville's barns some time later. Ricky knocked Walter out and waved a knife at Sally. He was taken to trial in Borchester in 1961, and, shortly afterwards, Boyd was doing bird.

Bridge Farm

Covering 140 acres to the south of Ten Elms Rise and bordered by Heydon Berrow, Bridge Farm has been organic since 1984 and Pat and Tony gained the coveted Soil Association symbol for their produce a year later. With the help of Clarrie Grundy and Colin Kennedy, Pat runs the dairy, producing delicious yogurt and ice cream, while Tony is in charge of cropping and the dairy herd. He has had to extend his range of vegetables to supply their shop, Ambridge Organics, on a year-round basis. The shop in Borchester is particularly important to the couple, as a previous venture, a farm shop, failed.

Although the house is an unremarkable Victorian red-brick edifice, Pat and Tony are happy there: it's been the only home their children Helen and Tom have ever known. Even the tragic death of their elder son, John, in a tractor accident in one of the farm's fields served only to bind them more strongly to the place.

Spanner **Bridges**

(David Perks)

When Roy Tucker finally made a statement to the police following the racist attacks on solicitor Usha Gupta, he named Spanner as one of the main movers in the neo-fascist biker gang he'd become mixed up with. Spanner – presumably named after his weapon of choice – was arrested and charged not only with the attacks on Usha – a street mugging and a more serious ammonia-throwing incident – but with the trashing of Mike Tucker's market garden in a revenge attack on Roy. Released on bail, placed under a curfew and warned by the police not to interfere with witnesses, the none-too-bright Spanner promptly phoned Roy and threatened more violence unless Roy withdrew his statement. Roy went straight to the police, earning himself a savage beating from self-styled 'friends of Spanner'. In September 1995, Spanner and two others appeared in the Crown Court. Spanner pleaded guilty on the first charge of robbery and mugging, and Roy, now recovered from his injuries, gave evidence against him. The jury found Spanner guilty by a majority verdict of ten to two, and he was sentenced to ten years, three of these for the racial motive to the crimes. In a final act of poetic justice, the judge ordered his bike to be sold and the money to go to Usha.

Colonel **Bridgewater**

Retiring chairman of Borsetshire County Cricket Club, Colonel Bridgewater was persuaded by Shula to make a speech at the Ambridge Cricket Club dinner in 1999. What Shula hadn't appreciated was the Colonel's penchant for telling off-colour stories. Neil Carter and Sid Perks enjoyed the entertainment, though wondering what their respective spouses would have thought had they been present. Peggy Woolley considered the speech downright sexist, and Jack agreed with her, though not without a hint of merriment in his eye.

Ann, Peter and Stephen **Briggs**

In 1976, Ann and her salesman husband, Peter, were living in two damp rooms on the Penny Hassett road with their son, Stephen. Sid Perks came to the rescue by renting them Rose Cottage, but the Briggses were a bad lot: Stephen was caught stealing in the shop at the tender age of four, and the family fell behind with the rent. Eventually, they did a moonlight flit.

Enoch and Bri **Broddy**

(Kenneth Shanley, John Baddeley)

Natives of Walsall, Enoch and his son, Bri, made their living in dubious ways. In 1980, they convinced Mrs P to part with an 'Act of Parliament' clock made by Richard Harper for £100, when, as John Tregorran told her when he found out, it could have been worth £1000. After Peggy learned what her mother had done, she informed PC Coverdale, but there was little he could do, as no law had been broken. However, the Broddys had an all-round reputation for sharp practice, so Coverdale started taking a keen interest in them, with the result that they decided it would be better to leave Borsetshire. John Tregorran later found the clock on sale for £550 in a rather dubious antique shop in Felpersham. He arranged for Peggy to buy it and then resell it for £1100 to a reputable dealer.

Brookfield Bungalow

After Ruth and David Archer were married in 1988, the question of where they were to live didn't present an immediate problem because Ruth still had her agricultural course to finish. But Phil and Jill Archer wanted their son and new daughter-in-law to stay at Brookfield, so they set about choosing the right spot for a new home to be built. By January 1990, the foundations of a bungalow were being dug out in Little Field, and, after a temporary setback when the first building company involved went bankrupt, David and Ruth were ready to move in on 12 September. The bungalow enjoys river views and has a garden, which tends to be neglected unless Bert Fry has a chance to help out with it. With their children, Pip and Josh, starting to grow older, by 1999 David and Ruth were starting to find the bungalow too constricting for the needs of their family. A temporary move into the main farmhouse, while Jill recovered from a leg injury and found living in the bungalow easier, whetted their appetite for a permanent move. By the autumn of 2001, their hope had become a reality, as Phil and Jill moved to Glebe Cottage, leaving the bungalow to be developed as a future source of revenue as a holiday home.

Brookfield Farm

Having decided to back David's idea for a Hereford herd against a possible rationalization plan, Phil must have thought by early 2001 that he could finally relax. Like every other farmer in the country, however, he was shaken by the scale of the nationwide foot-and-mouth epidemic and willingly supported David's wish to quarantine the family on the farm. For Phil, of course, it was a dreadful reminder of when Brookfield had itself been struck by the disease in 1956 – and when it was twice struck by TB in the 1990s.

Every year that they lived at Brookfield, Phil would take Jill on a stroll round the farm in the spring. No doubt he'd reflect on the hard work which had taken it from the original 100 acres first rented, then bought, from the Squire by his father to the 400-plus acres it is today. Brookfield has indeed seen many changes over the years. The pigs may have gone, but the sheep flock – some destined for Hassett Hills lamb – still grazes Lakey Hill and the expanded dairy herd is thriving on its extended grazing regime. Holiday lets and the farmhouse's additional bathroom, once so useful for Jill's B & B guests, and now to Ruth and David's still-growing family, only go to show that diversification can have benefits all round.

Betty **Brown**

Daughter of the Penny Hassett garage owner, Jim Brown, seventeen-year-old Betty was considered rather forward in her manner for 1955, at least by Dan Archer. For one thing, Betty was known to cadge lifts home from men after skittles matches. She did once convince Dan to take her all the way to Penny Hassett, but not before he insisted Jack accompany them, in case the teenager's fevered imagination got carried away en route.

Charles **Brown**

(Geoffrey Lewis)

A somewhat incompetent criminal, Brown was a professional gambler who, in 1967, had to go into hiding with his brother from a gang of thugs demanding protection money. Arriving in Ambridge, he passed himself off as a pig farmer at Paunton Farm while planning the Borchester mail van heist, but was charged with involvement in it when the van was discovered under a stack of bales at the farm.

Fay **Brown**

(Linda Polan)

Fay was Charles Brown's girlfriend, but posed as his wife at Paunton Farm while he hatched plans to carry out the Borchester mail van robbery with Nelson Gabriel. When Nelson arrived, she left for London, from where she was supposed to contact Sid Perks, then working as Brown's farm labourer. Fay fell ill, so Nelson's girlfriend, Gloria, made the call, but the line was being tapped by the police and both women were arrested.

Michele **Brown**

(Ann Portus)

Michele grew up on a sheep station in Milton, New Zealand, so shearing the Home Farm and Brookfield sheep in 1976 came as second nature. She arrived in Ambridge, redolent of travel and adventure: Laura Archer was reminded of home, while Shula, feeling restless at the confines of village life, was pleased to share a European holiday with her. Michele unsettled some of the men as well. Neil Carter had to accept that she was joining him in the Nightingale Farm flat on a platonic basis only; Kenton Archer went out with her a few times, but it was David Archer, whom she was willing to help with his A-level maths, who was most smitten by her, even missing a day's harvesting to picnic with her.

She spent some time in London, before the allure of Ambridge drew her back to take up a waitressing job at Grey Gables. She annoyed Jack Woolley by pressing for union representation among the restaurant staff, but he was impressed enough by her work to help her fight the expiry of her visa, only to see her head off for the United States at the beginning of 1978.

Geoff **Bryden**

(John Dexter, Geoffrey Lewis)

Villagers wondering who was going to take over from Constable George Randall in 1955 were pleased to find that his replacement, PC Bryden, was genuinely interested in getting to know the people on his new patch. By the time of Bob Larkin's shooting in 1957, he knew enough of the area to carry out all the inquiries needed in a thoroughgoing way. He wasn't flashy or obtrusive in his approach to policing, but, by 1964, had made a good enough impression on his superiors to be promoted to a position in Borchester.

Eve **Buckland**

In 1955, Eve came to Ambridge with her brother when he swapped places for a while with its vicar, John Ridley. She liked the village, and John Tregorran thought she might like the vicar, too, so he arranged for her to stay on after Ridley's return. But conscious, perhaps, of the disastrous fallout of the actions of her Biblical namesake, the vicar wasn't tempted and Eve returned to London.

Norris **Buckland**

(Harold Reese)

Along with his attractive twin sister, Eve, Norris came to Ambridge on an exchange with the incumbent vicar, who took on Norris's parish in London. Known for his outspoken sermons and his cack-handedness at cricket (he once shied a ball through Ben White's window), he was disturbed to discover acts of vandalism at St Stephen's that couldn't be blamed on a misjudged outswing. All in all, the exchange wasn't a wild success, and the Bucklands returned to London.

Jeremy **Buckle** 'Jerry'

(Michael Deacon)

In the two years from January 1989 to December 1990 that the Reverend Buckle spent as Vicar of Ambridge (he was also Rector of Edgeley and Penny Hassett and agricultural adviser to the diocese), Jerry made many friends (and some enemies) with his green-leaning sympathies and highly practical strain of Christianity. His eminent father had worked in government in Nairobi, and Jerry met his wife, Frances, there when he was a lieutenant in the Grenadier Guards. He left the army after developing pacifist beliefs, and he and his wife farmed in Derbyshire, Jerry entering the Church after she died of breast cancer in 1976. Jerry was never afraid to involve himself in controversial issues, even introducing the proposed Borchester bypass, rural unemployment and lack of housing into his sermons. Turning words into deeds, he offered Sharon Richards and Clive Horrobin a home before their baby, Kylie, was born, and worried about Sharon's lack of maternal instinct and her smoking. After the birth and Clive's desertion, Mrs Antrobus warned him about the wisdom of his living with an unmarried mother, but Jerry was still sorry to see Sharon move out. After a missionary-type trip to Mozambique, Jerry wrote to the church wardens telling them he intended to stay in Africa. His belongings were sold and Sharon was given £100 from the proceeds.

Birth: 10.01.1938

Bull Farm

If you've ever wondered where Jean Harvey laid her head after a tough Parish Council meeting or a disappointing demonstration at the WI, you now have your answer. She and her accountant husband, Charles, bought the house in 1975, after the farm's previous owner, a Mr Martin, emigrated and the farm was broken up. At the auction, which took place at The Drum and Monkey in Borchester, Phil Archer snapped up the thirty-five acres of land that bordered Brookfield, but Mr Hopkins from Hollerton was a disappointed man. He bought 10 acres with an eye to getting planning permission, but was refused. Luckily, Tony stepped in to rent it from him at a cost of £100 a year. The Harveys, whose daughter,

Susan, has long grown and gone, gained some new neighbours in 2001 in the shape of Shula Hebden Lloyd, Alistair and young Daniel.

The Bull

When Kathy Perks asked Graham Ryder to value The Bull as part of her divorce settlement, he estimated a sum of £300,000 – a huge rise from the £5,300 Jack and Peggy Archer had paid in 1959. When Sid and Kathy themselves had had to raise a purchase price of £250,000 some seven years before, they'd achieved this by taking out a loan and getting Guy Pemberton to invest. Sid therefore blenched at parting with £60,000 to Kathy, but his new live-in lover, Jolene Rogers, looks sure to put cash in the till with her money-spinning ideas, such as 'The Bull Upstairs'. She has also revived interest in quiz nights and darts.

Dating back as it does to the fifteenth century, and with its very own ghost (a Civil War drummer boy), Jolene's are far from the first innovations The Bull has seen. It's had the Playbar (a coffee bar), a steak bar, a Civil War-themed restaurant serving olde Englishe grubbe, and now the Family Room. Where there was once a bowling green, there is now a boules piste and extensive gardens, with resident peacock. Sid serves stirrup cup when the Hunt meets outside The Bull, and can be relied on for refreshments at the village bonfire and grand Christmas lights switch-on on the green. Cheers!

Joan **Burton**   née Hood

(Nona Blair, Esma Wilson)

The youngest of Percy and Betty Hood's daughters, Joan proved herself a bright spark by doing well in her GCEs in 1956. The spark soon became a star when she took the leading part in the Ambridge Ciné Club's first film.

Her mother wanted her to go out with Dusty Rhodes, but Joan's preference for Jimmy Grange proved to be a wise one when Dusty revealed himself to be a petty thief who made off with the Youth Club money. Desperately upset when her family decided to head north in April 1959, Joan gave a rather less heartbroken Jimmy a bird book as a token of her undying love. Within a couple of months, she'd run away from her parents to come back to Ambridge. Although her Uncle Doughy sent her home, she soon returned with permission, and started work for Carol Grey.

In 1962, after studying at Studley College, she met Nigel Burton while she was working for the Grenville estate. She married him in 1964 and had a daughter, Juliet, the following year. Thereafter she worked part-time in the Brookfield office before leaving quietly to concentrate on her family.

Nigel **Burton**

(Bryan Kendrick)

Nigel Burton came to Brookfield in 1961, taking charge of the dairy in place of Jimmy Grange. Anxious to have some privacy, he upset Doris Archer by asking for a key to his own room in the farmhouse and told her he would do his own cleaning and tidying up as well.

For a time he went out with Janet Sheldon, but grew cool about the relationship when she repeatedly cancelled dates at short notice. He found himself more suited to Joan Hood, whom he married in 1964. An opportunity to take over one of the estate farms, Thornton, arose and Nigel decided it was time for him and his wife to move on. They had not been running the farm long before, in 1965, they had their first child, a daughter called Juliet.

Mike **Butcher**

Mike Butcher lent Eddie Grundy a sizeable amount of money in the summer of 1999. Clarrie didn't know about the arrangement, until she took a call on the day the first repayment was due. Eddie tried to pretend that Mike was a friend of friend, but Clarrie soon worked out that he was an unofficial moneylender. Desperate to stave off bankruptcy, the Grundys went back to him in January 2000, but this time Mike considered them too much of a bad risk. Being turned down by a loan shark brought home to them just how desperate their situation was.

Amy **Butler**

(Patricia Gibson)

Amy spent nine years from 1960 to 1969 as barmaid at The Bull, though during the last couple of years was often off sick, thus failing to pull her weight. The highlight of her time in Ambridge seems to have been cooking for Dan and Nigel Burton when Doris was visiting Christine in Newmarket. Although others gossiped freely about the arrangement, Amy left the village without ever revealing whether Dan preferred her lemon meringue to his wife's.

Marjorie **Butler**

(Kathleen Canty)

After Phil's entanglement with the sultry poultry girl Jane Maxwell, Dan and Doris were relieved when, in 1955, he appointed Marjorie Butler to succeed her. Reliable and self-motivated, she was also no oil painting. There must have been something in the air, or perhaps the pig swill, however, on Fairbrother's farm because in no time Marjorie announced that she was soon to be a changed woman who took more part in village life. The next thing Phil knew, she'd permed her hair and asked if Chris would go with her to buy a suit.

From then on it was all downhill. She persuaded Phil to give work to her new boyfriend, Ginger Green, but when he abruptly disappeared, it transpired that he was married. A defiant Marjorie told Phil that she intended to go on seeing Ginger, and before Phil could object, handed in her notice. Seeking her at Ginger's lodgings, Phil learnt that Marjorie had indeed been there looking for him – after he'd departed with his wife. The humiliation was too much for Marjorie, who left the area. It would never have happened if she'd stuck to pigs and poultry.

Alan **Carey**

(Dudley Rolph)

Post-traumatic stress wasn't recognized in the 1950s, but it's clear that this is what Alan Carey was suffering from when he arrived in Ambridge with his mother, Helen, as guests of the Squire. Fighting in the tank corps in the Korean War with his twin, Rex, Alan had been badly shot up and had seen his brother burn to death. As a result, he was moody and anti-social. Simple country pursuits, such as rabbit-shooting, were an unwelcome reminder of being under fire, and he took to disappearing off by himself until Grace Fairbrother took up his neuroses as a cause, hoping to rehabilitate him. Charmed by her concern, Alan proposed, but, after thinking it over, she decided that he was more in need of a nursemaid than a wife. He took her refusal badly, and, given his mental state, even the brittle Grace must have had some misgivings when he announced that he was going climbing in the Lake District to get over her. In nearby Yorkshire, however, a short while later, he met Ann Fraser, whom he married at Whitsun 1952.

Christopher **Carter**

After a straightforward labour, Susan Carter was distressed when her son, Christopher, was born with a cleft palate and hare lip. It was three months before he could be operated on, by which time Susan was overcoming her initial coldness towards him. Fortunately, the operation was a complete success. When he was five, he was greatly disturbed at his mother going into prison; he refused to talk to her while she was there, and then wouldn't let her out of his sight when she was released. Always quite a lively lad, he made the mistake of using eggs when imitating his father, Neil's, juggling tricks, but successfully managed to train his hamster to go round its wheel to music for the pets' karaoke at the 1997 village fête. He shows some promise as a cricketer, having managed to bowl Eddie Grundy at the Single-Wicket Competition, albeit with a no-ball.

He could do with developing a little more common sense, however. In October 1999, he and Ed Grundy let off a number of fireworks near the turkey shed at Grange Farm, causing the death of half the Grundys'

Birth: 22.6.1988

turkeys and leading his father to hope he won't turn out like his uncle Clive Horrobin.

Emma **Carter**

(Jane Collingwood, Felicity Jones)

Blue-eyed Emma spent quite some time in a premature baby unit after being born a month early and then contracting jaundice. She later resented being overshadowed by the attention given to younger brother, Chris, after he'd been operated on to correct a cleft palate, and was deeply upset by the teasing she received at school when her uncle Clive Horrobin was involved in the raid on the village post office. Even worse was facing up to her mother going to prison at the end of 1993.

Birth: 7.8.1984

She went on to be bullied by a fellow pupil, Karen Irving, but eventually got on to better terms with her, as well as developing friendships with Brenda Tucker and Ed Grundy. Her GCSE results were disappointing, but rather than retake them, she went to work in the Lower Loxley café in 2000.

Her friendship with Ed Grundy caused the greatest trauma of Emma's life in the autumn of 2001, when, as a passenger in a car he was driving illegally, she was caught up in a terrible crash. For a time her parents, Neil and Susan, were afraid they had lost her and are only now coming to terms with the severity of the injuries their daughter suffered.

Neil **Carter**

(Brian Hewlett)

As Neil gives iron injections to a new litter of piglets, or uses a tractor to turn the compost mountain at Willow Farm, he appears to be a farming man born and bred. But he was very much a town boy, when, on the recommendation of an Agricultural Training Committee, he first came to Ambridge in 1973. He quickly established

Birth: 22.5.1957

himself in the village football team, but acquiring the agricultural skills he was now going to need took considerably longer.

Lodging with the Woodfords, he worked alongside Joby at Brookfield. Initially, he seemed careless, failing his proficiency test on a tractor because he left the fore-end loader up, and forgetting to close the gate between pens at Hollowtree, with the result that two pigs died after a fight. Gradually, though, he showed ability in his work and decided he wanted to specialize in livestock after completing his apprenticeship. Phil Archer recognized that the young man had promise, although occasionally he needed a sharp reminder to pull his socks up.

It certainly took him time to make progress on the romantic front. An early involvement with Sandy Miller, who planted marijuana on him during a police raid on a party, led to Neil getting a criminal conviction and having to paint Walter Gabriel's porch as part of his Community Service Order. As he moved into his twenties, he tried to develop other relationships: Maggie Price became a good friend, Vikki Schofield liked Neil, but not his game-shooting habits, while Julie, the barmaid at The Bull, was engaged to him for a while before deciding they weren't really suited. The great, unrequited, love of his life was Shula Archer, who would occasionally go out with him if there was no one else around, but could only think of him as a friend.

It wasn't until Susan Horrobin won a pig at the Ambridge fête in 1983, and Neil offered to build a pen for it, that his love-life found a more permanent direction. When he took Susan for a short break to London at the end of the year, and she insisted on separate rooms, he found it was very much a case of stable-doors being locked after the horse had gone. Susan was pregnant. They married, set up home in Neil's flat at Nightingale Farm, and, by August 1984, had been joined by a daughter, Emma Louise.

Shortly afterwards, their landlord, Hugo Barnaby, wanted to sell Nightingale Farm, and, despite Neil's misgivings about living so close to the Horrobins, the Carters moved to No. 1, The Green. To supplement Neil's income from Brookfield, he had an egg-round, with the hens kept in Bill Insley's barn at Willow Farm. Salmonella was later to disrupt this enterprise, but by then Neil had been left the barns and 8 acres following Bill's death. He had a passion for pigs, and now used some of the land to set up his own small breeding unit. Whatever troubles were later to hit the Carter family, he always managed to keep this venture going, and was even able to provide Bridge Farm with organic weaners when John, then Tom Archer, decided to go into the pork business.

A second child, Christopher John, was born in 1988. Neil was worried when Susan had difficulty bonding with her son, who was born with a cleft palate, but her maternal instincts soon revived. Having two children to provide for added greater weight to Susan's argument that her husband should aim for a more lucrative career than farm labouring. Eventually, her persuasion paid off when he took a position as a feed sales representative with Borchester Mills. If Susan felt the new job improved the Carters' social standing, her brother Clive's raid on the village shop in 1993 brought nothing but shame and trouble on the family. Neil had to look after the children alone, as Susan was sentenced to six months' imprisonment for attempting to pervert the course of public justice. He found some consolation in talking over his troubles with family friend Maureen Travis. Unfortunately, Mo, as she preferred to be called, was interested in more than talking. Neil resisted the temptation and concentrated on helping Susan readjust when she came out of prison.

Although he stayed six years with Borchester Mills, he was never comfortable with the job; he was not a natural salesman and didn't enjoy wearing a shirt and tie, but the final straw came when he had to chase the Grundys for payment at the time of their greatest economic hardship. For some days he pretended he was still going to work before admitting to Susan that he'd walked out on his job. As the 1990s came to a close, he struggled to find more than casual employment, and, at one stage, was even reduced to walking Mrs Antrobus's dogs for money. This made it all the more galling, early in 2000, when Phil and David Archer decided it was no longer economic to stay in pigs, and had to retract an offer they'd made asking Neil to take charge of Hollowtree once more.

Far worse was to come when daughter Emma was seriously injured in a car crash, late in 2001. Neil was one of the first on the scene, cradling her while her life was in the balance, as they awaited the arrival of the ambulance. Now it will take all of Neil's patience and dedication to help Emma back to anything like a normal life. But the outlook isn't all bad for him: his skills are often in demand on the Ambridge farms; he gets a fair price from Tom Archer for his organic weaners, and he's recently started joint ventures with Eddie Grundy and Betty Tucker, dealing with compost and free-range eggs respectively. He might never become a high-flier, but, whether as a stalwart of the cricket team, a bell-ringer, conscientious worker or simply as a loving father and husband, Neil Carter will always be a much-valued character in Ambridge.

Susan **Carter**

(Charlotte Martin)

The strong loyalty Susan Carter shows towards those she loves is matched only by the frustration she feels that they rarely share her aspirations to get on in life. As the eldest child of Ivy and Bert Horrobin, she often had to help look after her four brothers and her sister, Tracy, while they were growing up in their council house on The Green. Unlike the others, she was never afraid of hard work, and, when the chance came in her first job, at The Bull, to convert from part-time to full-time hours, she readily accepted it.

Birth: 10.10.1963

Winning Pinky the pig at the village fête the following year, 1983, allowed her to get close to the man she was most interested in. Neil Carter helped her look after Pinky; she assisted him with his hens when he sprained his ankle, and, almost inevitably, romance followed. In January 1984, Susan was pregnant; by the end of February, she and Neil were married. Daughter Emma Louise was born a month early and had to be kept in the premature baby unit for some days. Not unnaturally, Susan was depressed by this, but her spirits were soon lifted when Emma proved to be hale and healthy. A further boost came when Hugo Barnaby offered the Carters £4000 to leave the flat in Nightingale Farm so that he could sell it. With a baby to look after, they were given priority on the council housing list and soon moved into No. 1, The Green, five doors away from the rest of Susan's family.

Marriage suited her, although she was briefly jealous when she thought Neil was spending too much time with the new Brookfield farmhand, Ruth Pritchard. A more serious problem arose following the birth of a second child, Christopher John, in June 1988. Blaming herself for the cleft palate he was born with, Susan found it difficult to bond with him, until a surge of maternal feelings overwhelmed her when she thought he was at risk from some livestock. Once he had been operated on, Susan was so proud of Chris that she unintentionally neglected Emma for a time.

The difficulties she experienced in having her own children made her sympathetic when her brother Clive's girlfriend, Sharon Richards, became pregnant, so she and Neil let the young couple stay with them for a while. In 1993, Clive was to make much greater demands when he went on the run after raiding the village post office. Unable to turn her back on her brother, Susan provided him with food and shelter, only to be arrested and charged with harbouring a criminal once he'd been caught. Mark Hebden did his best to defend her in the Crown Court, just before Christmas, but couldn't save Susan from being sentenced to six months' imprisonment.

It was the worst period of her life. She desperately missed the children and couldn't let Neil kiss or touch her when he visited. The right to a weekend at home was lost when she briefly absconded to attend Mark's funeral. On leaving prison, she tried to slough off the experience by leaving her clothes behind and buying a whole new wardrobe. The process of feeling comfortable with her husband again wasn't helped by Mike Tucker passing on erroneous gossip about Neil and Mo Travis. After some full and frank discussions, during which plates were smashed when Susan pushed Mo against a dresser, she realized Neil hadn't been unfaithful, and grew close to him again.

Her time in prison disrupted Susan's efforts to make her family upwardly mobile. She'd proved herself highly competent when offered a secretarial job in the Berrow Estate office, had been the driving force behind the Carters buying their council house, and had even coaxed Neil into taking white-collar work with Borchester Mills. She didn't enjoy Simon Pemberton assuming responsibility for the Estate on Guy's death, but was even more unhappy when Borchester Land took over in 1997. Insulted that Brian Aldridge wanted to keep her on as a glorified cleaner rather than secretary, she handed in her notice and was soon working as a receptionist at the surgery. She got on well with Richard Locke, so was perhaps more upset than most when the doctor decided to leave Ambridge in the wake of his affair with Shula. Susan gave an Extraordinary General Meeting of the cricket club the benefit of her opinion on the matter, resulting in Shula making an embarrassed, hasty exit from the Village Hall.

She's never been slow to say what she thinks. Neil got the full force of her temper when he gave up his job as a feed rep. She slighted Ruth Archer publicly after Brookfield withdrew their offer of a job to Neil, although had the grace to try and make amends when she realized that Ruth, diagnosed with breast cancer, had more pressing concerns. Trying to remedy the financial insecurity caused by Neil's departure from Borchester Mills, she took on part-time hours at the shop, as well as continuing at the surgery. Briefly she acted as an amanuensis to Julia Pargetter when that august lady was trying to write a romantic novel.

With Clarrie Grundy, Susan invented its most successful passage, to fill in a gap where Julia's dictation had accidentally been wiped off tape.

Seeing her own hopes of a materially better life stalled by her husband's lack of ambition, Susan may have hoped for better from her children, only to be disappointed when Emma's poor GCSE results in 2000 were followed by a decision to work in the café at Lower Loxley rather than train for a more demanding career.

The disappointment this caused was put into perspective by Emma's dreadful accident, in September 2001, in a car driven by Ed Grundy. Now Susan's ambitions for her daughter only extend to hoping that, one day, she'll make a full recovery.

Elizabeth **Cartwright** née Aldridge

Sister to Brian Aldridge, Elizabeth Cartwright lives near Strathclyde, where her husband used to lecture. Her two children, Clare and Robert, have now left home. Liz, as she prefers to be called, made a bad impression on her last visit to Home Farm, when her forcefully stated opinions about the way it was run managed to make Jennifer feel very inadequately briefed. Liz and Brian rarely get together these days, with Brian considering his sister to be overbearing and insensitive. Definitely an Aldridge, then.

Martin **Carver**

Overbooking at Grey Gables meant that agricultural valuer Martin Carver was left without a room during a visit in 1992. Foolishly, he accepted the offer of hospitality at Grange Farm, only to find himself being grilled by Joe Grundy about the value of their herd. Martin said the cows were worth £500 a head, not the £250 Joe had told the taxman. He agreed to write to the Revenue free of charge, but passed up the offer of an overnight stay. Finding the sensory experience that is Joe's bedroom too overpowering, he headed off to Brookfield instead.

Cat and Fiddle

For many years the Cat and Fiddle co-existed happily with The Bull, each pub having its own distinctive clientele. With Dick Pearson as landlord, the Cat had something of a spit and sawdust image, which suited regular customers, such as the Grundys, Baggy and Snatch Foster, exceedingly well. When Peaches was employed as a barmaid in the mid-1980s, its appeal broadened, and Tim Beecham, to cite only one example, couldn't call in often enough. Ray and Maureen Notley took the pub over in 1989, hoping to position it further upmarket, with the result that Joe and Eddie Grundy were thrown out at the grand re-opening for not being dressed smartly enough. The change in image didn't last long, and, by the middle of the 1990s, the Cat, which was known to be lax about underage drinking, had become the haunt of the village's younger element. New landlords Sean Myerson and his partner, Peter, showed a more competitive approach to winning business, and introduced wide-screen TV and a happy hour to increase custom. They also succeeded in winning staff from The Bull, most notably Owen the chef. But with the rural market constantly under pressure, the brewery took the opportunity of Sean and Peter's move from Ambridge in July 2000 to close the pub for good.

Elsie **Catcher**

(Thelma Rogers, Mary Wimbush)

'Elsie Catcher, Milk Snatcher' would have made a satisfyingly euphonic playground chant at the Ambridge Village School, but for the fact that free milk was still being served at the time of Elsie's retirement as headmistress in July 1967, after she had completed forty years in office. Despite referring to her as 'Old Mousetrap' behind her back, the great majority of her pupils respected and liked her. Outside the demands of her job, she was a keen ornithologist and also served a turn as secretary to the Parish Council.

Robin **Catchpole**

(Edward McCarthy)

Roving reporter Robin spent only a year in Ambridge, but managed to ruffle plenty of feathers. Meeting Shula, then engaged to Mark Hebden, at the Landscape Survey Exhibition in 1981, he laid siege to her and declared undying love. Shula rebuffed him, but his avowal made her question her feelings for Mark, and Robin was a definite factor in the cancellation of their wedding later that year.

Arrogant and confident, with a degree in history and a taste for Scotch, Robin thought he was a cut above his lowly job on the *Borchester Echo*, and, like Simon Parker before him, believed he was destined for greater things. He was certainly not suited to the realities of life in the farming fraternity: he deplored Neil Carter's battery hens, and his critique of the Wildlife and Countryside Bill did not go down well locally. Robin, however, felt he'd found his niche and started freelancing on the side. He was delighted when an article he'd written on conservation was accepted, he told Shula, by an 'important' magazine. In March 1982, he was sacked from the *Echo* over yet another contentious piece, and left to work on a fringe magazine in London.

Susan **Cattermole**

(Penelope Shaw)

Martha Woodford had no reason to be fond of Susan Cattermole. In 1973, there were a number of thefts from the village shop and Stan Cooper, father of shop manager Angela, began to wonder if the new assistant, Martha, was being light-fingered. Martha was put in the clear only when Jack Woolley caught Susan Cattermole stealing. Susan and her husband had seven children and a liking for evenings spent at the Cat and Fiddle to support. Letting his heart overrule his head, Jack didn't even report her to the police.

David **Cavendish**

(Geoffrey Lewis)

Many factors have contributed to Tony and Pat Archer's enthusiasm for organics, but a generally unacknowledged one, perhaps lodged deep in Tony's psyche, is the influence Dr Cavendish had on him as a child. The doctor, who got on well with all Jack and Peggy's children, was a great believer in the medical benefits of fresh produce. In the mid–1950s he set up a treatment centre at the Manor House, based on healthy living, asked Carol Grey to provide him with fruit and vegetables grown without artificial fertilizers, and approached Ben White to make bread according to a favoured recipe.

He was attracted to Carol, but formed a closer relationship with Eileen Rawlings, whose parents invested in the health centre. When Eileen's brother, Peter, stole Mrs P's handbag, the doctor kept him out of trouble by assuring PC Bryden he would take full responsibility for Peter's future behaviour. His own actions weren't above reproach, however. He was a misery about John Tregorran's Makemerry Fair coming too close to the Manor, but, worse still, in the summer of 1956, his business failed and he left Ambridge without repaying the money John had lent him to put towards a new surgery.

Stephen **Chalkman**

Stephen Chalkman, who served on the Borsetshire District Council Planning Committee in 2001, was often seen in the company of Andrew Eagleton, a member of the Borchester Land board. When Borchester Land were interested in building a controversially high number of executive homes in Ambridge, and, at the same time, Chalkman acquired a Jaguar from Eagleton's London dealership, Brenda Tucker became suspicious. It was subsequently discovered that Chalkman's wife, Mererid, was serving on the board of Borchester Land's parent company under her maiden name. Although Matt Crawford assured Brian Aldridge he had no idea corrupt practices were taking place, Borchester Land rapidly did a rethink on its planning proposals, while Mererid was obliged to relinquish her position.

Paul **Chubb**

Paul, a 6ft 2in pilot in the Fleet Air Arm, wooed Caroline Bone in 1984 with his descriptions of reverse thrust engines, but she had to confess that they were wasted on her – she didn't even understand how her hairdryer worked. He waltzed her off to Walberswick for a romantic weekend nonetheless, but soon afterwards dropped her to marry someone called Philippa.

Al **Clancy**

(Ed Bishop)

Retired college professor Al Clancy and his wife spent some of the autumn of 1996 at Ambridge Hall as part of a house swap they had arranged with the Snells. Al wanted to research the Borsetshire roots of a number of families who had ended up in his home state of Kansas. He was especially pleased to find a poem hidden under the binding of an old book at St Stephen's; it had been written by Josiah Goodall, an agricultural radical, before his deportation. The discovery nicely rounded off what had been an enjoyable visit for the professor.

Mary Jo **Clancy**

(Maxine Howe)

Wife of Al Clancy for thirty years, Mary Jo always got value for money when she stepped on the weighing scales. At home in Kansas, she had a refrigerator with double doors, and while on a house swap at Ambridge Hall, quickly developed an appreciation for cream teas at Grey Gables and Pat Archer's ice cream. A generous woman, she untethered Lynda Snell's goats because she thought they looked depressed. Unfortunately, this led to a Quentin Tarantino-style slaughter of garden plants. On leaving Ambridge, Mary Jo left Lynda the ideal present – a pink padded lavatory seat.

Bill **Clifford**

(John Baldwin)

When Terry Barford first got into trouble in 1976, Bill was the probation officer assigned to the case. It helped that they had football in common, though Bill followed Derby County while Terry supported Leeds. When Nora and George confided in Bill about Terry's drinking, he was keen to help, but Terry pre-empted his concern by stealing a car and being sent to a detention centre.

Harry **Cobb**

(Charles Leno)

Handyman Harry was one of Walter's great rivals for Mrs P's affections. He helped with the cellar work and behind the bar at The Bull, but it was when he found time to mend Mrs P's leaky tap that their friendship flourished. (He even confided in her his greatest secret: his luxuriant locks were dyed.) Though he gave her a mynah bird for her birthday, she preferred Walter's gift of a budgie, and in 1971, when his bronchitis got the better of him, Harry retired down south.

Graham **Collard**

Graham was herdsman at Brookfield from 1977 to 1991, and gave faithful service, not even taking time off when a cow trod on his foot. No wonder Jill Archer was astounded to learn when he was made redundant to make way for Ruth that his pay-off would be a mere £2000. The blow was softened for Graham and his wife, Val, however, by his new job at Hollerton, and they left Rickyard Cottage, freeing it for holiday lets.

Damien **Colleymore**   'Droopy Drawers'

Damien Colleymore stands as an inspiration to ugly ducklings everywhere. Considered a wimp at Borchester Green School, where he was a classmate of John Archer and Roy Tucker, he acquired the nickname 'Droopy Drawers' when he almost lost his shorts at the top of some wall bars in the gym. Yet by the summer of 1997, Damien had developed such devastating good looks that when Lynda Snell wanted to cast him in *A Midsummer Night's Dream*, jealous John, afraid Hayley Jordan might fall for him, steered Damien away by claiming that Lynda's productions were so awful, no serious actor would be seen near them.

Clarice **Conway**

(Gwen Muspratt)

Clarice Conway fell for Doughy Hood during his days as a ship's baker. For a while they wrote to each other, but when Clarice's musings turned to matrimony, Doughy ended the correspondence. Not one to give up easily, in 1958 Clarice tracked her loved one to Ambridge and produced a letter which, she claimed, showed Doughy meant to marry her. Rita Flynn, Doughy's latest girlfriend, was less than impressed. She snatched the letter, and a fight followed, in which Clarice came off worse. Deciding that Doughy wasn't the only baguette in the bakehouse, on 30 April 1958 she promptly left Ambridge for good.

Coombe Farm

Coombe Farm has played an important part in Phil Archer's life. Bought by George Fairbrother in 1953 when Amos Atkins gave up his tenancy, the land was used first for Fairbrother's Herefords and then for Phil's pedigree pig-breeding scheme. When Phil and Grace married, Fairbrother agreed to let them have the house for £1 a week, and it was in the Coombe Farm dining-room that Grace told Phil she'd changed her mind about having children. After her death, Fairbrother took the practical decision to divide the house in two. Phil remained in one half, and the other half was occupied by the new herdsman and his wife, Mr and Mrs Rodgers. When Phil met Jill, his head was in such a whirl that he invited her out on the second anniversary of Grace's death without noticing the date. Realizing halfway through dinner, he explained his predicament and they picked flowers from the Coombe Farm garden to lay on her grave. Phil and Jill spent their early married life at Coombe Farm, and Shula, Kenton and David were born there, but in 1962 they vacated it for Allard's Farm, which they renamed Hollowtree.

Roger **Coombes**

In 1984, sensitive, intellectual Roger, Pat Archer's women's studies lecturer seemed to her the antithesis of her boring, boorish husband. Despite the feminist slant of his lectures, he brought out the coquette in Pat, who cut her hair and began wearing eye make-up. Though there is no evidence that theirs was anything more than a friendship, gossip elevated it to a quasi-affair. Pat finally saw sense, quit Roger's course and turned, with Tony, to organics. They have never looked back.

Bess **Cooper**

(Peggy Hughes, Gertrude Salisbury, Peggy Hughes)

Wife of Brookfield farmhand Simon Cooper, Bess was fond of simple pleasures. She enjoyed a glass of stout at The Bull and loved receiving flowers on her birthday. The money she earned working on Dan Archer's smallholding was put straight into saving for that acme of 1950s domestic luxury, a television. She hoped that she and Simon might one day buy the smallholding themselves, but, when her husband became unwell and died in 1957, she left the village to live with one of her sisters.

Simon **Cooper**

(Eddie Robinson)

One of nature's gentleman, Simon Cooper always wore a hat, even when mucking out the pigs at Brookfield. He gave Dan Archer twenty years' loyal service as a farmhand, although Simon's wife, Bess, might have preferred him to strike out more on his own.

A keen country sportsman in his spare time, Simon was awarded a Hunt button for meritorious service, but perhaps his greatest enthusiasm was reserved for shooting. When Tom Forrest found him with a pheasant in one hand and gun in the other, he naturally thought Simon had been poaching. Simon had actually confiscated the bird and gun from Jimmy Wharburton, but kept quiet about it rather than get the young man into trouble.

Seeing his co-worker Len Thomas being given extra responsibilities made Simon worry that he was going to be replaced. Increasingly unhappy, he resigned when an accountant was brought in to review his work on the Brookfield smallholding. Only when he realized that he wasn't being accused of fraud did Simon withdraw his resignation. He wasn't to stay much longer on the farm, however, with ill health forcing him to retire in 1956. He took up gardening work for a short time thereafter, and could sometimes be seen in Ambridge, bending over the petunias, with his hat still firmly in place.

Stanley **Cooper** 'Stan'

(Geoffrey Lewis)

Respiratory problems forced Stan Cooper to give up work as an engine driver after forty years' service with Great Western Railways. Asked to manage the village shop in 1972 by Jack Woolley, widower Stan took the job on. He hoped that, with his daughter, Angela's, help, he could operate it as a newsagent's and post office, while even offering customers haircuts as well. In addition, he agreed to drive the engine on the Ambridge Park Railway, but was badly scalded by the steam cock during the official inauguration.

When business at the shop proved slack, he left Angela in charge and started to work at Ralph Bellamy's petrol station. But the arrangement didn't last long: Angela, aggrieved when her father told her to stop seeing Gwyn Evans, ran off to marry him and settle in Canada. Stan was so distraught at this, he told Martha Woodford that Angela hadn't been his daughter at all. He started drinking heavily, and, unable to fall in with Mr Woolley's plans for the shop, decided to leave the village altogether in 1973. Haydn Evans gave him a lift to Hollerton Junction, where, fittingly, he left the district on a train.

Dick **Corbey**

(Geoffrey Lewis)

After Jack Archer's death in 1972, Peggy arranged for Dick Corbey to manage The Bull on a temporary basis. He was so efficient that she offered a three-month extension to his contract, despite several customers, her son Tony in particular, not warming to him. Tony's reserve was justified. First, Dick's surname came into question, when it was discovered that he'd been known as Watkins and Delahay in the past; then he helped himself to some stock and disappeared. The police caught up with him in Manchester, where he eventually pleaded guilty to theft.

Eva **Coverdale** née Lenz

(Hedli Niklaus)

Home Farm may not have seemed the most obvious place for German au pair Eva Lenz to come to in 1978, given that she suffered from hay fever and found the dawn chorus disturbing. Neil

Birth: 10.3.1959

Carter fancied his chances with her, but once Nick Wearing had offered to take her badger-watching, she was putty in his hands, despite already having a boyfriend, Mark, back in Germany. Nick didn't reciprocate Eva's feelings, and, with Mark's parents, Mr and Mrs Freidal, applying pressure on her, Eva went back home for a while, before returning with a diamond ring on her finger.

The engagement quickly fizzled out, but soon stern words from DI Coverdale, when he found Eva riding a bicycle without lights, stirred something deep and primeval within her. At first the good constable resisted her advances, until, having rescued her from Eddie Grundy's unwelcome offers of help when Eva had a puncture, Coverdale could resist no more. They started going out together, and the strength of their relationship became clear when even the prospect of having Kate Aldridge as a bridesmaid didn't stop them tying the knot. Marriage was followed by a move to Plymouth, where the dawn chorus may have proved less troubling.

Detective Inspector James **Coverdale**

(Leon Tanner)

Constable Coverdale's clumsy handling of minor infractions of the law quickly made him unpopular when he was assigned to Ambridge in 1979. Whether it was Jennifer's parking, or Sid's

Birth: 1948

turning-out time at The Bull, if there was an undiplomatic way of making a point, Coverdale would find it. The only unqualified fan he had in the village was the German au pair, Eva Lenz. They didn't have the most romantic start to their relationship; it began when he called to give her an unofficial warning for not having lights on her bicycle. At the time, he had a fiancée, Sandra, but once she'd decided country life wasn't for her, the courtship between Coverdale and Eva moved on apace. They married in 1980, and, the following year, moved to Plymouth, where Coverdale had requested a transfer.

Sixteen years later, and now a detective inspector, he came back temporarily to help run the investigation into the assault on George Barford. He seemed determined to nail Eddie Grundy for it – perhaps, some said, because Eddie had once been a rival for Eva's hand. He was also briefly seen at Nelson Gabriel's funeral in 2001, but is not thought to have any plans for a permanent return.

Craven

(Martin Julier)

An associate of the menacing Spanner and a fellow neo-fascist biker, Craven was mixed up in the racist attacks on Usha Gupta that so shocked Ambridge in 1995. After Roy Tucker went to the police and admitted he knew something about the thuggery, Spanner and Craven were arrested and charged with GBH against Usha, and criminal damage following a 'warning' attack on Mike Tucker's market garden. Both were released on bail but were placed under a curfew and warned not to interfere with witnesses. Unlike Spanner, Craven did at least observe these conditions. Following a brief appearance in the Magistrates' Court in August, Spanner, Craven and another gang member, Pete, were committed for trial at the Crown Court in September. Although Craven's decision to plead guilty to the first charge counted in his favour, he was still sentenced to seven years in jail. Assuming good behaviour, he must already be a free man and roaming a shopping centre near you…

Matt **Crawford**

(Kim Durham)

Peckham-born Matt doesn't think much of the peace and quiet of the countryside. Still, if he continues persuading the board of Borchester Land to increase its housing and leisure developments, soon there may not be much peace left for him to worry about. He came to prominence in 1997 by selling the woodland that was cleared to widen the Borchester bypass. Not slow to scent a profit, he was also in on the ground floor of Borchester Land when it was set up in the same year to buy Guy Pemberton's estate land.

Since then, he's been a constant thorn in Brian Aldridge's side, always trying to maximize the consortium's profits, whatever the cost might be in local goodwill. He tried to push through a housing development on Sawyer's Farm, which only failed when Lynda Snell found the protected plant *Gentianella anglica* on the site; he was the driving force behind the Grundys' eviction from Grange Farm, and was taking the lead in promoting a new housing scheme in 2001, until his plans got into a legal tangle. Lilian Bellamy seemed to find him fascinating, but Debbie Gerrard, whom he tried to chat up, thinks him odious. Hers is probably the majority opinion in Ambridge.

Tommy **Croker**

If it's the big band sound with toe-tapping dance rhythms you want, Tommy Croker's the man to get in touch with — at least that's Jack and Peggy Woolley's opinion. They've booked Tommy and his band for several big events at Grey Gables, including Guy and Caroline Pemberton's wedding party and Jack's own celebration for his eightieth birthday. Younger members of the village, however, aren't generally so keen on him, while it's rumoured that Tommy Croker Junior (alto sax, occasional maracas) has got his eye on his father's place in the spotlight.

Baroness **Czorva**

(Brenda Dunrich)

Vying with Madame Garonne for the title of most enigmatic character in Ambridge, Baroness Czorva arrived in 1954 and stayed innocuously enough at The Bull, claiming to be there for the sale of the Squire's effects at the Manor. Her real function, however, was to make contact with thriller writer and former secret agent Mike Daly, telling him that a certain third party was expecting to see him. He promptly left the village.

Mike **Daly**

(John Franklyn, Michael Collins)

'The name's Daly, Mike Daly.' Well, almost. Mike swaggered into Ambridge in 1952 and rented Blossom Hill Cottage, ostensibly to write thrillers. Before long, though, Reggie Trentham was on to him as a fraud, and gatecrashed a tea party with Mike's so-called fiancée, Valerie, in tow. The full story, when it emerged, was far better than thriller material.

Mike was, in fact, a sort of secret agent who'd been dropped into occupied France but had ended up in Dachau. Certified dead by a pro-British German officer, he was smuggled out and given a new identity as Major John Smith of the Pay Corps. Major John was then cashiered to attract the interest of, and thus flush out, enemy agents. Phew!

Luckily for the smitten Reggie, Valerie, herself an agent, was only posing as Mike's fiancée, and he married her while Mike abruptly left the village. Two years later, Mike returned to ask Valerie to work with him on a special mission, but her life had by then taken a different turn. Instead, a Baroness Czorva contacted Mike, told him a 'certain party' was waiting and he disappeared, presumably back into the bowels of MI6.

Frederick **Danby** 'Freddie'

(Norman Shelley, Ballard Berkeley)

A chivalrous bachelor, who had seen his fiancée of six months killed in a hunting accident when he was a young man, Freddie Danby perhaps found the greatest contentment of his life in the company of Laura Archer, with whom he started to lodge in 1976, after his retirement from the army.

Birth: 1.11.1912

For the next nine years they shared a life of, sometimes, shabby gentility. Freddie lost a position working for a charity soon after coming to Ambridge and went on to work part-time as a garage forecourt attendant and then golf club steward, but never seemed to amass much money. When circumstances were especially straitened, he and Laura would attempt self-sufficiency by growing their own vegetables and keeping livestock. They grew increasingly comfortable with each other until, afraid that village gossip might misinterpret their relationship, Freddie felt obliged to propose marriage. To his relief, Laura refused; they both knew they were better off simply as companions.

When an incorrectly completed will meant that he had to leave Ambridge Hall after Laura's death, instead of inheriting it as she'd wished, Freddie went to stay at Mrs Blossom's cottage in Manorfield Close. Then, in 1988, deciding an old friend who had fallen ill needed his company, he said his final farewells in the village and left to live in Bristol.

Bob **Dancer**

(Patrick Connor)

In the days of mods, rockers and moody motorbikers, Bob Dancer was a rebel with a firework. In 1962, he lit it and placed it under Pensioner, one of Lilian Archer's horses, inevitably causing the animal deep distress. Retribution came on Bonfire Night, when his motorbike was set ablaze by a firework let off next to it. By common consent, Lilian was the number one suspect.

Scott **Daniels**

(Peter Meakin)

With his waxed chest, the better to show off his glistening 'six-pack', actor/model Scott arrived in Ambridge in May 2001 as Lilian Bellamy's toyboy lover, and left under a cloud, having dallied with Brenda Tucker and broken her heart. He and Lilian had scandalized the village with their antics on his Harley-Davidson and their 'dirty dancing' at Jolene's line-dancing class, but Scott got his come-uppance when Brenda's protective brother, Roy, defended her honour with a well-aimed punch which left him worrying about his immaculate bridgework.

Darren

At the height of her involvement with the WRVS in the early 1980s, Jill Archer organized country holidays for deprived children. Eleven year-old Darren was sent from Liverpool's Strawberry Fields to Brookfield, where he confessed that his brother was doing time and his dad was a convicted housebreaker. The person who befriended him in Ambridge was Joe Grundy but whether Joe passed on any of Alf's tips – or vice versa – is not recorded.

PC **Davies**

(Rob Swinton)

Industrious PC Davies has been kept busy in various capacities by the inhabitants of Ambridge. In 1994, he investigated Kate Aldridge's disappearance, and, five years later, interviewed David Archer after he and Ruth had witnessed the trashing of the Home Farm rape crop. After Dave Barry, he's probably Sid Perks's least favourite policeman: a good spin bowler who plays for Borchester Police, he once got Sid out for a duck.

Revd Carol **Deedes**

(Angela Thorne)

Carol Deedes was the female deacon who married Ruth and David Archer in December 1988. She prepared them for the ceremony by seeing them for a premarital chat, and then holding a rehearsal nine days before the real thing. Those who attended the wedding couldn't help noticing that she was rather glamorous. It's not thought the same was ever said about the Reverend Jerry Buckle.

Jane **Dexter**

(Eileen Barry)

Jack Woolley soon warmed to the good-looking, London-based PR lady, Jane Dexter, who organized a sales conference at Grey Gables in 1977. At her suggestion, he went to London to interview a young Italian candidate as a potential manager for Grey Gables, but was really more interested in getting to know Jane better. Higgs, Jack's chauffeur, showed his more scampish side by misinforming people that Jack had taken Jane to Paris.

Having agreed to act as an agent for the conference side of Grey Gables, Jane started spending more time in Ambridge. Gordon Armstrong grew very keen on her, while Jack took any chance to see her, even though she'd made it clear to him that theirs was a business relationship only.

Eventually he got the message that his attentions weren't wanted, and, afraid he'd made himself look foolish, backed off. Even so, Jane, probably wisely, thought she'd be better off focusing on her activities in London, and off she went.

The Dower House

Ralph Bellamy acquired this elegant property, with its slate roof and large garden, in 1970. He and Lilian lived there until they left Ambridge in 1975, after which it was rented to Arnold Lucas and other unnamed tenants. It must have been standing empty, though, in 1990, when Lilian Bellamy obtained the keys from the Estate office and had a final look round before selling it, along with the rest of the Berrow Estate, to the slimy Cameron Fraser. When Guy Pemberton bought the Estate in 1992, he had to spend a lot of time and money ripping out the worst excrescences of Cameron's flashy taste, and the house today is much as he left it after his heart attack. There is a study with computer and fax, a polished floor with rugs in the hall and a splendid painting of a beef shorthorn in the sitting-room. When the Grundys were evicted in 1999, Caroline, Guy's widow, took pity on her godson, William, and offered him the self-contained flat within the house. He accepted with alacrity, and now the only challenge is keeping an eye on his light-fingered brother, Ed, when he pays a friendly call.

Barbara **Drury**

(Ysanne Churchman)

Barbara, wife of Constable Colin Drury, didn't really enjoy life in the country. Aware that her husband's job might one day lead to a clash of loyalties, she avoided making close friendships until, upset at Colin turning down a sergeant's job in Felpersham in 1976, she confessed to Nora McAuley that she was lonely. Even after this admission, she was very particular about what she got involved with: she helped out with the disabled children's lessons at The Stables, but refused to make costumes for the revue. She was delighted when Colin's promotion in 1979 meant that they would be going back to town life.

Colin **Drury**

(John Baddeley)

Colin Drury was Ambridge's bobby for twelve years, against the wishes of his wife, Barbara, who longed for a return to the bright lights. Jovial Colin, however, thrived on rural life, and even when his area was increased to cover Penny Hassett and across to Hollerton, he could be seen zipping enthusiastically around in his panda car. In 1967, Colin had been in the job only a few months when he proved his worth by spotting that the Borchester mail van hadn't passed him at its usual time. Investigating, he found it in a ditch and his dogged inquiries led to the arrest of Charles Brown. Nelson Gabriel has gone to his grave, however, without ever revealing whether the £500 that Drury found down the side of an old armchair in Walter's shed was really, as Nelson claimed, a gift for his father, or whether it was part of the robbers' ill-gotten gains.

When not policing, Colin threw himself into Ambridge life, once taking part in the sack race at the fête and winning a dozen eggs. His sense of justice, however, led him to confess that he'd won only by tripping up Gordon Amstrong. Barbara eventually got her way when Drury was promoted to sergeant, which meant a town posting, and they departed in 1979.

Gerald Grosvenor, **Duke of Westminster**

(Self)

Ambridge folk were dumbfounded when Caroline Bone, as she then was, revealed that Gerald Grosvenor, Duke of Westminster, had used to tie her up at parties – until she added that she'd been about six at the time. As chairman of the NSPCC's Centenary Appeal in 1984, the Duke was in Ambridge to attend a fashion show at Grey Gables. Jack Woolley was thunderstruck when he brought with him his even more illustrious relative... Yes, HRH The Princess Margaret.

Alice **Dyer**

Alice was the daughter of Bess Cooper's brother, Edward. Blind since the age of three, she loved having piano lessons, but there was no money for her to have an instrument of her own, until her father and her Uncle Simon saved up secretly to buy one. On Christmas Day in 1951, Alice was brought into the living-room and seated in front of it. As she reached out, touched the keys and started to play, she cried with happiness.

Percy **Edwards**

(Self)

In a community so dependent on its livestock and with such a rich variety of bird life, who better to be the celebrity guest at the Village Hall Christmas concert in 1963 than the famous bird and animal impersonator Percy Edwards? His appearance was a wild success, though whether the entertainer would have survived the direction of Lynda Snell, in recent years Ambridge's self-appointed Christmas entertainment supremo, is another matter entirely.

Britt **Eckland**

(Self)

Clarrie Grundy was right to be suspicious in 1992 when her husband Eddie encouraged sons William and Edward to enter a colouring competition to win tickets for *Aladdin*. The prize included meeting the star of the show – the beautiful film actress Britt Eckland. When, with help, his children came up trumps, Eddie was too overwhelmed to speak to Britt at first, though he became more loquacious after a drop of champagne.

Clarrie subsequently forced him to take down a signed photograph in the bedroom by threatening to withhold his conjugal rights. Unknown to her, Eddie simply relocated the picture to his workshop.

Jim and Meg **Elliott**

Meg and Jim were tenants at Bridge Farm immediately before Pat and Tony Archer. On Jim's death in 1977, Meg thoughtfully put money behind the bar at The Bull for friends to have a drink in his memory. She then decided to live with her son, a doctor. The house contents were sold and Meg, equally considerately, moved out early so that the house could be redecorated for Pat, Tony and baby John.

Dave **Escott**

(Charles Collingwood)

A sales rep for a paint company, Dave Escott was all gloss and no undercoat. Arriving at The Bull in 1974, he lost no time in chatting up Nora McAuley and Polly Perks, until he discovered Peggy Archer was the owner, whereupon he turned his charms on her. He said he was leaving his company to set up Escott Design Services, and persuaded her to let him redecorate the Ploughman's Bar at no cost, hoping that it would act as an advertisement for his talents. Peggy was won over enough by him to agree, but drew the line at becoming his business partner.

Although Peggy said she didn't want any commission for putting work his way, Dave was irrepressible and sent her a cheque when she helped him get the chance of some design consultancy at Grey Gables. Jack Woolley, jealous to see Peggy's attention focused elsewhere, looked into Dave's background and discovered that he was an undischarged bankrupt, who had no right to be setting up new businesses. His dark secret uncovered, decorating Dave dashed off, leaving only a bouncing cheque to pay for his stay at The Bull.

Angela **Evans**   née Cooper

(Elizabeth Revill)

There can't be many people who had such an eventful time in Ambridge as did Black Country girl Angela Cooper, as she then was, when she arrived in 1972 with her father, Stan, to run the village shop.

A qualified ladies' hairdresser, she acted as village postmistress and was soon to be seen whizzing about delivering newspapers on her scooter, but no sooner had she witnessed the plane crash on Heydon Berrow in September than her father had an accident at the inauguration of Jack Woolley's railway in the Country Park. While he was in hospital, she was assaulted by a stranger, who was eventually arrested, but not before a traumatized Angela had crashed her scooter and had herself been hospitalized.

Things looked up when she fell in love with Gwyn Evans, but her father was against the match, believing he came from the same mould as his no-good brother, Dylan. The tragic pair were forced to run away together, and, in April 1973, Stan heard by letter that they'd been married by special licence and were emigrating to Canada. They settled in Vancouver, where Gwyn found work in a shoe shop, ushering in a temporarily more tranquil existence.

Evans Farm

SEE: *Willow Farm*

Dylan **Evans**

(Donald Houston)

Son of Haydn and brother of Gwyn, Dylan was a wastrel. Having courted Shula Archer with a wood carving and been entrusted with the sale of a grandfather clock from Brookfield, rumours about his rascally nature began to leak out. He had no qualms about letting himself be baled out by Angela Cooper, who would later marry his brother, Gwyn, but, by the time he left Ambridge in November 1972, he had still run up a raft of debts.

Gwyn **Evans**

(John Ogwen)

Son of Haydn Evans, and thus Pat Archer's cousin, Gwyn was the lucky recipient of the 100-acre Willow Farm, which his father bought for him in 1972. Dogged by the reputation of his feckless brother, Dylan, Gwyn's love for Angela Cooper was opposed by both families, so the couple eloped and emigrated to Canada. The marriage foundered, but Gwyn never returned to the land of his fathers, opting instead for Canadian citizenship.

Haydn **Evans**

(Charles Williams)

Pat Archer's Uncle Haydn was not only the means by which she was introduced to Tony but was for several years a feature of the Ambridge agricultural scene in his own right. Haydn originally bought Willow Farm for his son, Gwyn, but, when Gwyn emigrated to Canada, Haydn and Tony became partners, with Tony taking over the house and Haydn moving to Martha Woodford's old cottage in Penny Hassett. After Tony and Pat's marriage, Haydn tactfully decided to leave them to run the farm, and bought the garage from Ralph Bellamy. When Tony and Pat moved to Bridge Farm in 1978, Haydn got on less well with his new partner, Mike Tucker, and was dismayed when Mike announced he intended taking on contract milking work as he couldn't afford to buy enough cows to make a profit from dairying alone. Pat and Dan intervened to smooth out the quarrel, but Mike alienated Haydn even further by uprooting the farm's eponymous willow trees and selling the wood to Joe Grundy.

By 1981, Haydn was looking longingly towards the greener grass of home, and he eventually sold the farm and the garage and retired to Wales.

'Evans the Muck'

Back in 1985, when Pat and Tony Archer were converting their land to an organic system, they were keen to take advice from anyone with experience. One such person was 'Evans the Muck', a Welsh farmer who knew more about organic manures than anyone else in the business. He must have advised them well, since Pat and Tony's organic enterprises have flourished.

George **Fairbrother**

(Leslie Bowmar)

A bluff businessman who'd made a fortune in plastics after the war, George was not just an ignorant 'townie'. A keen fisherman, he had a strong feeling for stock, and was quick to spot the young Philip Archer's potential. Employing him as his farm manager virtually straight from college, he gave Phil a free rein with the day-to-day running of the farm, though he liked to be involved in the decision-making. Over the years, Fairbrother's agricultural interests included Ayrshires, Herefords and a large commercial poultry flock, as well as compost, and, with Carol Grey, fruit.

Like many incomers to the village, he often found the parochial nature of Ambridge frustrating. He couldn't understand why there was no local enthusiasm for an ironstone mine, which would have provided jobs and trade, though he could see that he was the one who'd transgressed the boundaries when he was fined both for setting fire to bracken without a licence and for not treating his cattle against warble fly.

Having married the former Helen Carey, who gave him a son, all was going well for Fairbrother until his daughter, Grace, was tragically killed. He never properly recovered, and he and Helen left the village in 1959.

Helen **Fairbrother** née Carey

(Joy Davies)

A charming, cultured widow aged forty-two, Helen Carey was an old friend of the Squire, but, when she and her son, Alan, came to stay with him in 1951, she probably never imagined that she'd find in Ambridge the man she was to marry, nor that she'd become a mother again after twenty-five years.

It was Grace who initially did the matchmaking between her father and Mrs Carey, though the transparency of her schemes made George and Helen smile. After the ironstone débâcle, the Careys and the Fairbrothers spent Christmas on the Riviera, and early the following year, George had a revelation whilst fly-fishing: he had genuinely fallen for Helen. He didn't propose, however, until Helen heard that Alan was getting married, after which things moved quickly, and they beat the youngsters to the altar by getting married at Easter 1952.

Relations with Grace, whose nose was firmly out of joint, were tricky, even more so when Helen gave birth to a son, Robin, in 1953. Things improved once Grace and Phil were married, and Helen supported a broken George after Grace's death. She was sad to leave the village in 1959 and returned later the same year to finalize details of the church window that George had commissioned in his daughter's memory.

Robin **Fairbrother**

When twenty-year-old Elizabeth Archer disclosed in 1987 that she had a new boyfriend, Rob, Jill was both pleased and curious – until, that is, he turned out to be Robin Fairbrother, half-brother of Phil's first wife, Grace. All Jill's old insecurities about Grace's place in Phil's life resurfaced and she refused to let Robin near Brookfield, still less invite him to the family meal usual on these occasions. The romance continued, however, helped on Elizabeth's side no doubt by the fact that the handsome wine importer was a sophisticated thirty-four years old and owned a BMW and a house in the Dordogne. Jill was counselled by wise Walter Gabriel, and was about to relent and invite Robin to lunch when Elizabeth was the one who received a shock: it transpired that Robin, though separated, was still married. Worse still, when Elizabeth phoned him in London, his wife answered the phone and told her that Robin didn't want to speak to her. When Robin reiterated this in Nelson's Wine Bar, saying he was trying to repair his marriage, a furious Elizabeth tested his wine-tasting skills by throwing a glass of house red in his face.

Birth: 6.2.1953

Helen **Fairlie**

After Roger Travers-Macy stopped working as Laura Archer's chauffeur, he was replaced by Helen Fairlie, who took on housekeeping duties, too. She got on well with her employer, and also found a useful role for herself in the village when she took on delivering groceries to one or two people. However, by 1974, Laura was feeling the financial pinch, and, unable to continue running a car, had to let Helen go.

Felpersham

Thank heavens for Felpersham! When the bright lights of Borchester pall, this cathedral city is only seventeen miles from Ambridge, whose residents have not been slow to partake of its delights. With its regular market, and late-night shopping on Thursdays, no retail stone is left unturned. Gourmets can feast at the well-regarded French Horn, or, for rather more downmarket tastes, the canal-side pub that Pip Archer likes because she can feed the ducks, or the American Diner, where Caroline treated the Grundys on the fateful day they returned home to find they'd been made bankrupt. Felpersham's excellent hospital, where Freddie and Lily Pargetter were born, has a specialist Breast Unit, where Ruth Archer was diagnosed with breast cancer. In happier times, Ruth attended the salsa club in Felpersham with her friend Usha Gupta, while Roy Tucker studied at the same university where Simon Gerrard teaches. And Felpersham hasn't lost touch with its past: there's an annual procession known as the 'Riding of St George'. In 1984, David Archer helped with the Young Farmers' float, which was entitled 'England's Bounty', while, the following year, Mr Gill from the building society gave a passable impersonation of England's patron saint.

Sheila **Ferguson**

(Linda Polan)

A woman ahead of her time, at least for Borsetshire, the outgoing Sheila was a fellow student in Jill's French class at the Tech in 1977. Phil was positively bedazzled when she roared up the Brookfield track on her son's motorbike and revealed that her husband encouraged her taste in eye-popping outfits. It was with culture, not couture in mind, however, that she and Jill booked a short break in Paris. Phil approved of the three-day jaunt, but was less keen when Sheila considered extending it by a week. In the end, three days were more than enough for Jill, who failed to keep up with the cracking pace set by her new-found friend. Even at the airport on the way home, Sheila kept up the pressure, smuggling through more than her duty-free allowance, including a bottle of Cointreau for the law-abiding Phil. When she delivered this gift to Brookfield, she further divulged that she and Jill had enjoyed some male company whilst abroad. Although Phil might have excused this had they been practising their French vocabulary, he was less than amused to find out that the men in question were Henry and Clive – from Scarborough.

Colin **Finch**

(Sean Baker)

The appropriately named Dr Finch was one of five expert witnesses called for the defence in the trial of Tom Archer for trashing a crop of GM rape in 1999. Cool under cross-questioning, he denied he was being alarmist in stating that, as a result of genetic modification, cross-pollination and horizontal gene transfer were real possibilities. There was a place for research, he said, but he felt it should be in a controlled and protected environment.

Janet **Fisher**

(Moir Leslie)

There were ructions in the village in 1995 when Janet, a former nurse who was already Vicar of Darrington, was put forward to take on St Stephen's under a reorganization which would also combine Ambridge with Penny Hassett and Edgeley. Peggy Woolley was outraged at the prospect of a woman vicar, and worships at All Saints, Borchester to this day. Bert and Freda Fry and Susan Carter were also reluctant converts to the idea, though Janet has proved an excellent priest. She initiated the millennium bells appeal, has introduced new hymn books, and, with Usha Gupta, went on the Jubilee 2000 Third World debt march to Cologne.

The most testing time of Janet's entire ministry, though, came early in 2001, when she found herself attracted to the local doctor, Tim Hathaway, with whom she'd worked on a tasteful nude male calendar in aid of the Borsetshire Rural Stress Line. Although she didn't quite fall, she stumbled, and it was only a reprimand from her bishop that made her tell Tim there could definitely be nothing between them. As she works to repair her position in the community and he to repair his marriage, it remains to be seen whether they can put the mutual attraction behind them.

Louis **Fisher**

Nelson was thrilled when he persuaded the *Borchester Echo*'s very own Egon Ronay, the estimable Louis Fisher, to sample the wine bar's cuisine during a brief spell in 1990 when Jean-Paul had been lured away from Grey Gables to work there. Louis came, saw – and wrote nothing, for no review ever appeared. Did the proof of the pudding repose on a sub-editor's spike? Nelson accused Jack, the *Echo*'s proprietor, of sabotage, but Jack denied it.

Derek and Pat **Fletcher**

Perhaps mellower now than when he first came to Ambridge, Derek Fletcher has even been known to laugh occasionally, usually when Jolene is behind the bar at The Bull. Derek and his wife, Pat, certainly didn't seem given to merriment when they originally moved into Glebelands in 1983. They found country life most off-putting, especially when Susan Carter's pig, Pinky, got loose and wrecked their back garden. As if that wasn't enough, the Housing Department responded to the Fletchers' complaint by confirming Susan was entitled to keep a farm animal on council property. No wonder Derek's moustache bristled with indignation.

Complications with a fish pond ordered from Nigel Pargetter and having their garden vandalized were to follow, but gradually Pat and Derek became more attuned to village life. Derek went to Meyruelle in 1994 as part of the town-twinning process, and also became a member of the Parish Council, only to offer his resignation when Janet Fisher became the Vicar of St Stephen's. In recent years, Pat has had to put up with her husband constantly complaining about backache. When it all becomes too much for her, she takes solace in contemplating the fish pond, which is attractively fringed with ornamental gnomes.

Rita **Flynn**

(June Spencer)

In the 1950s Rita came from Ireland to work for Doughy Hood and struck up a friendship with the bachelor Phil. Grace understandably took umbrage when Phil borrowed her car to run Rita to the station and returned it damaged, but that was the least of Phil's worries. On the journey he'd discovered that Rita was not just married, but married to a violent ex-con who'd just come out of prison in Aberdeen. Not quite, then, a desirable future wife for the Brookfield son and heir.

Rita lived in a caravan on Doughy's land, and he became inordinately fond of her, even making a will in her favour. She stayed in and around the village for ten years, loyal to her job at the bakery, despite a flirtation with the idea of being a kennel-maid for Bill Sawyer. In 1961, however, she fell for a fellow countryman Michael O'Leary, the foreman of a road-mending gang, and returned to the Emerald Isle with him.

Wayne **Foley**

(Ian Brooker)

King of the jingle, soundbite supremo Wayne is Brenda Tucker's mentor at Radio Borsetshire and a favourite with all her family. Mike has him to thank for superb publicity for the pick-your-own strawberries he used to run with Neil Carter, while Wayne made Betty Tucker's day by inviting her on to his show on her fiftieth birthday, a gesture he repeated, at Clarrie's request, for Joe Grundy's eightieth. The recent success of 'Joe's Jottings' has been but one more sign that Wayne truly has his finger on the listeners' pulse.

Pru **Forrest**   née Harris

(Mary Dalley, Judi Dench)

After suffering a stroke in 1991, Pru Forrest kept asking for her wedding ring, since a loss of sensation on her left side meant she could no longer feel its reassuring presence on her hand. It was typical that, at a time of great anxiety, Pru needed to be sure that her bond with Tom Forrest still held good.

Birth: 27.7.1921	
Death: 11.11.1998	

Of course, in the days when she was still Pru Harris and lived in Firs Cottage with her mother, there had been admirers other than Tom. Joe Grundy, for one, had liked seeing her serve behind the bar of The Bull. Indeed, so affected was Joe by the occasional innocent kiss and cuddle he had with Pru that, forty years later, he was to send flowers to the nursing home she had moved into, and, after her death, was discovered by Mrs Antrobus, standing in mourning at Pru's grave. Another young buck in search of Pru's hand was Bob Larkin. She turned him down when he proposed to her in 1957, though she may have hoped his suit would spur Tom Forrest into more decisive courting. She and Tom had become friendly after the death of Pru's mother and were eventually to marry in September 1958, after the trauma of Tom's trial for the manslaughter of Bob Larkin had reached a satisfactory resolution.

A month after their quiet wedding, a mobile X-ray unit found a patch on Pru's lung. She had to go into a sanatorium until June the following year, when a delighted Tom was able to bring her home again.

When young Susan Blake's mother had to go into hospital in 1960, Pru and Tom looked after Susan for a while. Pru became fond of her, and, when Susan left, wondered if she and Tom might foster a little girl. Pru's medical record and Tom's court case threatened to be obstacles to fostering, but the child welfare officer was impressed by the Forrests and gave them the go-ahead. Instead of a girl, though, Pru became a foster mother to Johnny Martin and Peter Stevens. Like Tom, she had her work cut out as a parent, but was proud to see her young charges blossom in the loving home provided at Keeper's Cottage.

She kept on working as a barmaid until Sid and Polly Perks took over management of The Bull in 1972 and found they couldn't afford to keep her on. As a protest, Pru told Tom he had to stop drinking there in future. For a time, the poor man was reduced to sitting in a field by the pub and having his friends bring out pints of beer for him. But Pru's anger softened when she found another income for herself by taking on the housekeeping at Brookfield. At first, it was a short-term arrangement, while Jill Archer was away for a while, but she proved so invaluable that she was asked to help with the cleaning on a permanent basis. She was soon back on good terms with the Perkses and even offered to help out on any occasions they found themselves short-staffed.

In 1976, Tom was invited to manage Jack Woolley's new garden centre, with Pru as his assistant. Within a couple of years, disappointing profits persuaded Jack to bring in an expert, Jim Bolton, to take charge. While Tom moved on to manage Jack's fishery, Pru continued to work at the garden centre.

She was kept busy at home as well. There were all Tom's clothes to buy, sloe gin to be made, and any number of entries to be prepared for the Flower and Produce Show each year. In 1985, she became positively obsessive, hoping to achieve a record fifteen first prizes. Unfortunately, her determination to win meant there was nothing in the house Tom could actually eat.

Although in many ways a quiet person, Pru plucked up the courage to give the welcoming speech when Terry Wogan arrived at the Grey Gables golf course for a celebrity match in 1989.

She sometimes suffered from migraines, but was clearly abnormally unwell in the run-up to the 1991 Flower and Produce Show. When she suffered a stroke, all the other villagers pulled out of the categories Pru had entered. Tom was greatly moved by the number of prize certificates she was awarded. Although he hoped to look after her at home without professional help, a second, more serious stroke led to Pru moving into The Laurels nursing home. Occasionally, she managed to come out, spending her thirty-seventh wedding anniversary at home in 1995, and enjoying Christmas dinner at Brookfield in the same year. For the last months of her life, she was reunited with her beloved Tom, as he joined her at The Laurels. She died six days after he did, seemingly having lost the will to live once he had gone. Johnny and Peter both managed to attend the funeral, where Jill read John Clare's poem, 'Love Lies Beyond the Tomb'. When she reached the lines which spoke of 'the fond, the faithful and the true', many in the congregation considered them a very apt description of Pru and Tom.

Thomas **Forrest** 'Tom'

(George Hart, Bob Arnold)

Birth: 20.10.1910
Death: 5.11.1998

The two bells hung most recently in the St Stephen's bell tower are dedicated: 'In Memory of Tom Forrest – Bell-ringer and Tower Captain – and his devoted wife, Pru'. It seems natural that Ambridge should remember Tom and Pru jointly, for, despite marrying relatively late in life, they grew to be very close in the thirty-seven years they shared together. No one was surprised when they died within a week of each other, in November 1998.

Tom, younger brother to Doris Archer, had not always seemed as keen on companionship. Although he had enjoyed being part of the Ambridge soccer team as a youngster, was a conscientious bell-ringer and church warden, and took a lifelong pleasure in singing, whether at church or at The Bull, he was most at home working alone in the woods, taking good care of his game birds. As soon as he was old enough, he had followed his father, William, into gamekeeping. For over sixty years he worked on shoots for, among others, the Lawson-Hopes, Charles Grenville, and, finally, for Jack Woolley, for whom he worked as sporting manager. He understood what made for a healthy woodland as well as he knew how to tickle a trout clean out of the water.

Doris often worried that Tom didn't have a wife to look after him. She and Dan made sure he regarded Brookfield as an open house, and Tom was often glad of the good meal he could always expect there. But, by the time he was in his mid-forties, no one really expected him to change his bachelor ways. That is, until they saw how well he was getting on with the barmaid at The Bull.

Initially, Tom's reason for spending time with Pru Harris was to act as executor of her mother's will. However, it soon became clear to everyone, except Tom himself, that he and Pru would make a very good match. Perhaps the strength of his feelings only became clear to Tom when a rival appeared on the scene. In 1957, Ned Larkin's ne'er-do-well brother, Bob, appeared in Ambridge and had the temerity to propose to Pru. Tom was heard to say he would 'bash Bob Larkin's face for him' if he kept making a nuisance of himself. It was a phrase that was to rebound on Tom, for, shortly after, he was to catch Bob poaching in the middle of the night. In the struggle between them, Bob was killed when his gun accidentally went off. Tom was arrested and charged with manslaughter.

The reports of previous bad blood between the two of them could have had a major impact on the verdict, but the jury at the trial quickly realized that Tom was innocent and acquitted him. To his astonishment, a great reception was prepared for his return home. Twelve men towed his car into Ambridge, while the Hollerton Silver Band thundered out 'For He's a Jolly Good Fellow'.

Tom finally proposed to Pru in February 1958, but, not allowing romance to compromise his professionalism, delayed the wedding until September, when his pheasants had been put out to cover. Then, in 1960, Charles Grenville had Keeper's Cottage built for the couple because Tom's old home was going to be too close to a new bypass. Also in 1960, unable to have children of their own, Tom and Pru investigated the possibilities of fostering. A little boy called Johnny Martin came to stay for the occasional weekend and got on well with Tom, as they went fishing together. When Johnny absconded from his children's home with a friend called Peter Stevens, Tom and Pru decided to foster both boys. Over the next few years, the two youngsters caused them plenty of problems. In 1967, Tom offered his resignation to Jack Woolley because Peter had been painting offensive graffiti on Jack's wall. Fortunately, the offer was refused and, influenced by Tom's example, Johnny and Peter eventually grew into responsible and industrious young men.

Tom retired as sporting manager in 1976, but was subsequently persuaded to manage Jack Woolley's garden centre and then fishery, as well as continuing to assist with the shoot from time to time.

He was not without flaws. One was his weakness for biscuits, particularly custard creams and ginger snaps. During a sponsored slim, he even resorted to snaffling the odd piece of shortbread from Jack Woolley's office, for which Jack's dog, Captain, got the blame. Tom might also be considered unenlightened on the question of women's rights. He resigned as an umpire in 1990 after a disagreement with Clarrie Grundy about women playing cricket, and was even less happy when Janet Fisher became Vicar of St Stephen's in 1995. He could also be rather too keen in his rivalry with Bert Fry over their entries to the annual Flower and Produce Show. Even on the one occasion when they ceased hostilities and won a prize for a joint entry, Tom would only let Bert have a copy of the winning certificate.

In truth, if Tom seemed a little more irritable in his last years, it was largely because Pru was no longer living with him. After suffering two strokes in 1991, she had to move into The Laurels nursing home. Although Tom visited her whenever he could, he was never completely happy again until, with his own health failing, a double room became available at The Laurels and he joined her there in 1997.

When, a year later, Tom and Pru passed away, Christine Barford had the idea of arranging a horse-drawn hearse for their funeral. It is a touch Tom would have appreciated, for, in an increasingly mechanized age, he always kept faith with the old ways when he could. Although his distinctive voice is now no longer heard passing on the country wisdom he acquired from a lifetime's work, he is not forgotten. Whenever the bells of St Stephen's ring out, something of Tom Forrest still resonates in Ambridge.

Andy **Foster**

(Peter Meakin)

Andy Foster was the assistant official receiver who, together with valuer Charles Waring, came to Grange Farm in February 2000 as a consequence of the Grundys' bankruptcy. They valued all the livestock and machinery on the farm in preparation for a farm sale that was to follow. Eddie Grundy wasn't impressed by the visit, but grudgingly accepted Andy's suggestion that, in return for a fee, he should continue to milk the Grange Farm herd until the sale.

Bruno **Foster**

Bruno is the son of Snatch Foster and the godson of Eddie Grundy. In spite of this, he behaved impeccably at his christening, in stark contrast to bawling Alice Aldridge, with whom he was christened. To clear up a long-standing controversy in the village: he wasn't named in honour of Giordano Bruno, the sixteenth-century Italian philosopher, or St Bruno of Cologne, the twelfth-century German churchman, but after Frank Bruno, the British heavyweight boxer and pantomime star.

Birth: 1989

Snatch **Foster**

Snatch once refused to dress up for a gangster and moll night at the Cat and Fiddle, but, by common consent, looked just the part of a petty criminal anyway. One of Eddie Grundy's closest friends, he has a similarly pragmatic approach to right and wrong: if you're not caught, it can't be wrong. Together they poached the Home Farm fishing lakes early in 2000, only one of many dubious ventures they've undertaken together.

His enthusiasm for boxing was reflected in the choice of name for his son, Bruno. He also briefly showed an interest in acting, when he played half of a pantomine cow in the 1998 Ambridge production of *Jack and the Beanstalk*, with the other half being played by his great drinking companion, Baggy. Although generally quite a cheerful character, Snatch has known heartache in his life, never more so than when the Cat and Fiddle closed. Still, never one to shirk a challenge, he's trying to adjust to drinking in The Bull instead and may one day succeed, if perseverance counts for anything.

Frances 'Fran'

Over the summer of 1988, just before he got things together with Ruth, David Archer went out with a nurse who had worked at Felpersham Hospital. Fran, as she liked to be called, was a thirty-three-year-old divorcée with two children, Rosie and Sarah. Caroline Bone was an old friend of hers and had actually attended Fran's wedding.

Phil and Jill weren't happy about their son going out with a divorced woman, but didn't need to worry for long: not wanting to lose her sense of independence, Fran soon told David that the relationship was over.

Jean **François**

The tall, slightly balding figure of Jean François appeared in Ambridge for the town-twinning ceremony of 1994. He took advantage of his stay to pick up the rudiments of cricket from Neil Carter. Returning the favour, he insisted that Neil should learn something about boules during a corresponding visit to Meyruelle the following year. Neil's efforts during the eventual tournament between the two villages ensured only a narrow defeat for Ambridge.

Basil **Franklin**

(Donald Scott)

When Nelson Gabriel went to his father for £3000 on leaving the RAF in 1961, it was to set up in a light engineering business in Borchester with Basil, also a former airman. The hapless Walter willingly invested the remains of his football pools winnings and the business at first prospered, but Basil and Nelson soon parted company, and Nelson had to find another partner.

Alan **Fraser**

(Crawford Logan, Peter Wickham)

Ambridge folk realized that Alan Fraser was no ordinary bloke when Tom Forrest, paying a neighbourly visit to the man renting The Lodge in 1981, was mistaken for a burglar and nearly strangled by him. Sid Perks concluded he was ex-SAS but it was only when Fraser started courting Caroline Bone that the full story of his mysterious past came out.

He'd left school at eighteen, he told her, and joined the Army, serving in the Parachute Regiment and helping to defend NATO's Southern Flank in Greece. He'd also, he added casually, worked as a courier – but of what? – and a bodyguard. As if further proof of a dodgy past were needed, Nelson Gabriel and Fraser finally settled a 'financial' matter, dating from the time they'd both been in Venezuela together.

Caroline was understandably keen on the blue-eyed fitness fanatic and spent many nights at The Lodge despite his sparse possessions – a sleeping bag, trunk and a handful of books. His frequent unexplained absences failed to put her off, but, early in 1982, Fraser disappeared again, this time for good. Caroline wasn't forgotten. He left her a red rose in an empty vodka bottle.

Ann **Fraser**

(Noreen Baddiley)

When Grace Fairbrother turned down his proposal, Alan Carey moped off to visit friends in Yorkshire. There he met Ann Fraser, with whom he had rather more success, for she speedily agreed to marry him. News of their engagement, early in 1952, prompted George Fairbrother to propose to Alan's mother, Helen, but it was not a double wedding: George and Helen married in Ambridge at Easter, and Ann and Alan in Yorkshire at Whitsun.

Cameron **Fraser**

(Delaval Astley)

There were mixed opinions in Ambridge when Scottish businessman Cameron Fraser decided to buy the Berrow Estate, the rump of what had been the Bellamy Estate, in 1990. Elizabeth Archer

Birth: 31.10.1954

was quickly won over by his self-confident manner, Jennifer Aldridge found him charming, while even Pat Archer was impressed by the interest he took in the land he was going to buy. Brian Aldridge didn't take to him, however. An initial coolness arose when Cameron accidentally caused one of the Home Farm deer to abort, but the dislike was intensified by jealousy when Cameron starting going out with Brian's former lover, Caroline Bone. Surprisingly, it was Jean-Paul at Grey Gables who gave the most accurate early assessment of the newcomer. That man, said Jean-Paul, looked 'suspicious'.

Cameron claimed he had not had the happiest of childhoods. As his parents lived abroad, he was farmed out to family friends during holidays from his Edinburgh boarding school. The sense of being unwanted was made worse when he started work in the City and fell in love with an undergraduate. He asked her to marry him, but she laughed the proposal off. As Cameron was later to explain to Elizabeth during a trip to the south coast, he became very cautious about his feelings thereafter.

How well he was able to hide his emotions wasn't at first clear in Ambridge. His romance with Caroline seemed to be going well and he appeared to have a positive approach to developing the Estate. However, his response to Shula Hebden's ectopic pregnancy, when his only concern was to get someone into the Estate office to cover for her, was an early sign that he could be heartless. Failing to attend Jack Woolley and Peggy Archer's wedding was, in Caroline's opinion, equally inconsiderate.

The relationship with Caroline struggled on into 1991. In a rare moment of candour, Cameron admitted having previously spent six months in prison as a result of insider dealing. He was worried that the case Mike Tucker was bringing against the Estate, following the loss of an eye, could result in a further term of imprisonment. In the event, farm manager Geoff Williams was held responsible, but any relief Cameron felt was soon tempered by Caroline telling him that their relationship was over. He told her she could not be serious, but she was.

This was the opportunity the still impressionably young Elizabeth Archer had been waiting for. She found Cameron's man-of-the-world stance irresistible, and even took up riding again so that she could go cubbing with him. He had made his home in the Dower House, and now it became an occasional love-nest for the two of them. Nigel Pargetter, unswerving in his devotion to Elizabeth, was appalled. Cameron warned him to keep away from her, and was petty enough to block an application Nigel had made to the Borsetshire Architectural Trust.

Cameron could be small-minded in other matters, too. Frequent disagreements with Shula over the use of Estate cottages and the timing of contract work led to him complaining to Rodway & Watson over her head. No sooner had Shula threatened to stop handling the Estate account than Cameron got into a tangle and pleaded with her to take it on again. An attempt to sell Red House Farm in 1992 didn't go well either. Phil Archer became annoyed when Cameron's solicitors insisted the deal had to be completed within six weeks. Despite the heavy-handedness of this approach, the sale looked as though it would go through, until other factors got in the way.

First, there was Elizabeth's realization that she was pregnant. She imagined that Cameron would be delighted when she gave him the news, but his only response was to offer to pay for an abortion. Deeply hurt, Elizabeth said she wasn't going to see him again. Nevertheless, she tried to believe that, underneath the apparent indifference, he really cared for her. By now, however, Cameron's second tranche of troubles was taking up a great deal of his attention.

A series of phone calls to the Estate office in March 1992 showed that he had got himself into real financial difficulties. When Elizabeth relented and agreed to meet him, he admitted that he had mishandled funds he had been investing for other people. He blamed some supposed friends, who, he said, had given him bad advice.

Elizabeth believed his version of events, and, after he had reaffirmed his love for her, she was willing to go off secretly on holiday with him. As they drove down the M40 in his Jaguar, she spoke happily of their love for each other and of what having the baby would mean to them, oblivious to how uncomfortable he seemed with this type of talk. That he didn't share her vision only became clear to Elizabeth when they had turned off the motorway for some food. After waiting fifteen minutes for him to return from the toilet, she was shocked when a waiter told her that Cameron had already driven off.

Not only had he abandoned his lover, he had left a lot of other people in the lurch as well. Caroline and Mrs Antrobus, among others, had trusted him with money that they were never to see again. When the Fraud Squad contacted Rodway & Watson in May, the full extent of his wrongdoing became clear. He had been taking money that investors wanted placed in low-risk government stock and using it for high-risk stock market deals, the whole operation coming unstuck when these didn't work out. As a result, his assets, including the Berrow Estate, had to be sold to pay off his creditors. He had taken advantage of too many trusting people in Ambridge to be missed. Elizabeth, in particular, was long to remember the hollow promise of his final words to her. When he said, 'I'll be back in a minute,' she really thought he meant it.

Robin **Freeman**

(Peter Kenvyn)

A botanist appointed as warden of the Arkwright Hall Field Centre in 1970, Robin Freeman had led a troubled life. During the Second World War, he had been held in a Japanese prisoner-of-war camp, and later, he and his wife, Zoe, were to suffer the death of their only child. Matters didn't improve when they came to Ambridge: Zoe was in a disturbed frame of mind and needed psychiatric treatment when she started smashing equipment at the Field Centre. When she made advances to Phil Archer, Robin felt obliged to tell him that Zoe was a nymphomaniac.

After Zoe left him for good in 1973, Robin had to fight to keep his job, since the Field Studies Council wanted a married man in the post. With support from Dan Archer and Jack Woolley, he contested the decision and was allowed to stay on, with a housekeeper coming in to take charge of domestic matters.

Excited to discover that Jiggins Field had once been Giant's Field and had Anglo-Saxon connections, he started an archaeological dig there. But he had no emotional ties in the area once Peggy Archer had made clear that she wasn't interested in him romantically. As a result, he was content to leave for a new academic job in October 1974.

Zoe **Freeman**

(Margot Young)

Prone to severe bouts of depression ever since her only child died as a toddler, Zoe Freeman was never really at peace during her stay in the village. She'd come with her husband, Robin, when he started work at Arkwright Hall, but the surroundings didn't suit her. After a bout of breaking laboratory equipment in the Field Centre, she accepted the need for psychiatric treatment, but didn't respond particularly positively to it. She seemed to crave more affection that her husband could provide and was drawn to Alan Nicholas, a musician who was staying in the district temporarily. Phil Archer proved attractive to her as well; she made excuses to call on him and even managed once to get him into a passionate embrace, only to be interrupted when Shula walked in.

In early 1973, she was keeping company with another man. Peggy, who was aware of the problems in the Freemans' marriage, gave instructions that she wasn't to be served at The Bull, but, in the long run, it didn't do any good. By July of that year, Zoe had decided she could never be happy with Robin or country life, and walked out on both.

Howard **Friend**

(Geoffrey Whitehead)

'No friend of mine', as Tony Archer is fond of saying, Howard tried to use his influence with the Borsetshire Environment Trust to block Bridge Farm's plans to open a farm shop in 1993. The real reason, however, was Howard's own 'organic superstore' which was due to open. Relations improved when Bridge Farm agreed to supply him, provided they could keep their own label, and Helen later persuaded Howard to stock Tom's sausages, too.

Bert **Fry**

(Roger Hume, Eric Allan)

In the opinion of erstwhile employer Phil Archer, Bert Fry never does a job the short way if a long way is possible. As he's shown in ploughing matches against, among others, David Archer and Brian Aldridge, speed is of little consequence to Bert; it's how straight you plough your furrow that matters.

Birth: 1936

He came to Brookfield in 1988, after losing his position as foreman on one of the Berrow Estate farms. Originally, he was acting as cover for Ruth Archer, while she completed her studies, but, in the event, it was Graham Collard who was asked to leave on her return. Bert had already established himself as being skilled in handling the arable cultivations, and, while lacking Neil Carter's expertise with pigs or Ruth's gift for working with cattle, he has shown himself capable of working with all types of livestock. His steady, if unspectacular, approach to his work has generally outweighed the impact of his occasional errors, although he definitely wasn't popular when his use of the wrong locking pins on the cattle-feed mixer wagon resulted in a feed bucket wrecking the mixer paddle.

Aside from his work, he has many other interests. His flair for creating poems and pithy sayings was soon noted by Elizabeth Archer, who wrote about him in the *Borchester Echo*. A short period of local celebrity followed, with Bert even appearing on television. More recently, he used his talent for word play by producing a series of fiendishly cryptic quiz sheets, sold in aid of the Church Bells Fund. For a time he was considered something of a pub quiz maestro as well, until it was discovered he had simply found Sid's source material and was memorizing the answers beforehand.

He has appeared in a number of village shows and has also been a bastion of local sporting life in his capacity as a cricket umpire. When a few errors started creeping in to his handling of matches in 1997, he took a lot of persuading to attend a refresher course on the rules. Subsequently, he infuriated the Ambridge team by repeatedly referring to the rule book on the most trivial of occasions.

In 1990, Jill Archer persuaded him to become a deputy warden at St Stephen's, and he has taken his duties there seriously ever since, although there was some question about his continuing when Janet Fisher arrived. A traditionalist in most things, he was so strongly opposed to having a woman vicar that he was even in two minds about attending Martha Woodford's funeral. A phone call from Janet, and the realization that Martha would have wanted him there, finally persuaded him to go. Since then, he has become used to having Janet in post, and continues to play a full part in parish life. He winds the church clock on a weekly basis and also enjoys any chance to buttonhole visitors and tell them something of the history of St Stephen's.

One of his main interests is gardening. He takes great pride in keeping the flowerbeds at Woodbine Cottage in immaculate order, but his greatest efforts are reserved for his vegetables, the finest of which are always destined to appear in the Flower and Produce Show. He considered Tom Forrest a great rival, never more so than when Mrs Antrobus wanted some strawberries for Open Day teas. Ultimately, Bert had the grace to admit that Tom's strawberries tasted vastly superior to his own, and he even asked for some spare runners. However, there is still a certain uneasiness between Bert and another keen grower, George Barford, following the great onion unpleasantness at the 2000 show. George was horrified to see some of his prize specimens seemingly spirited to Woodbine Cottage overnight. Bert dismissed the charge that he'd been cheating as ludicrous, as well he might. Ed Grundy and Fallon Rogers had been responsible for the big vegetable switch as a way of entertaining themselves during the long, slow Ambridge evenings.

He is even more jealous and protective of his wife, Freda, than he is of his vegetables. He was unsure about her taking up work at The Bull, until he realized she would be working only in the kitchens, away from the unwelcome attentions of the customers. Unfortunately, in 1995, he became convinced that Owen, the chef, was making advances of his own. Changing his customary seat at the bar, Bert was able to peer into the kitchen and see that nothing was amiss. He and Freda have a strong marriage, run, unsurprisingly, on very traditional lines, with Bert happy never to be allowed into the kitchen. They have one adult son, Trevor, and a granddaughter, Amy, whom Bert dotes on. For such a strongly built, work-hardened man, he has a genuinely deft touch with youngsters, and was often able to entertain or pacify Pip Archer as a baby when others failed.

Woodbine Cottage has been the Frys' home since Bert started working at Brookfield. Although finding it quite chilly before central heating was installed, they seemed perfectly settled there, until a lorry smashed through the garden and into the front wall in 1999. Having been temporarily re-housed in the Brookfield bungalow, there was some doubt as to whether they would want to move back. But both Bert and Freda were delighted by the way the Archers had the cottage upgraded and were pleased to return, in March 2000.

Bert worries that his working future is now less secure than his home. Although the average age of agricultural workers is high, he has often worried that his increasing years leave him vulnerable to being laid off. The recent restructuring of the farm, involving the loss of the pig enterprise, but including the development of a new beef herd, seems to ensure employment for a while longer at least. He's certainly fit enough to keep working – perhaps not quite at the peak he reached when he won the Fittest Person in Ambridge competition in 1991, but still undaunted by the challenges of a hard outdoor life. Never a sprinter, Bert is happy to keep ploughing a long straight furrow for as long as anyone wants him to.

Freda **Fry**

In her quiet, unassuming way, Freda Fry has made a place for herself in village life since coming to live at Woodbine Cottage with husband Bert in 1988. Apart from working part-time as a cleaner at Brookfield, she's also a mainstay of the kitchen at The Bull, where her calorie and cholesterol-rich dishes melt in the mouth of any customer with a relaxed attitude to clogged arteries and sudden cardiac arrest. She always got on well with Kathy Perks, but had some difficulty adjusting to the livelier, more youth-friendly culture Jolene introduced to the pub.

At home, Freda is queen in her own kitchen, and devotes considerable time to preparing jams, pickles and other comestibles for the annual Flower and Produce Show, where she generally does well. She surprised a number of people by taking on the role of the fairy in the 1998 pantomime, *Jack and the Beanstalk*, but is generally happier letting Bert be the extrovert in the marriage. She was thrilled at the recent improvements made to Woodbine Cottage, and would be happy to see out her days there, as long as son Trevor and granddaughter Amy remember to visit from time to time.

Nelson **Gabriel**

(Jack May)

'He was the sweetest man I knew,' said Elizabeth Pargetter in her eulogy at Nelson's funeral, unconsciously echoing the words Nelson had used about his father. 'Sweet' might not have been the

| Birth: 1933 |
| Death: 2001 |

first word that sprang to mind for many in the congregation (D.I. Jim Coverdale, for one) but it's certainly true that to know Nelson was to be seduced by his charismatic personality, whether in his wine bar or the CID interrogation room.

It's typical of Nelson that he managed to get through his National Service in the RAF without ever flying a plane; he nonetheless signed on for a regular engagement, and was promoted to sergeant. After serving abroad, he left the RAF in 1961 and persuaded Walter to invest £3000 in a light engineering business in Borchester. It was the first of many times that the gentle old man would subsidize 'his' Nelson with a substantial payout. The early 1960s were golden years for the debonair Nelson. Having sold out his business to Carol Grenville and Paul Johnson, he partnered Tony Stobeman in a casino and chain of betting shops, and revelled in a life of luxury. He went out briefly with Jennifer Archer and some of the village girls, but had other things on his mind than marriage. He was too busy masterminding the Borchester mail van robbery.

In late 1966, Walter returned alone from a cruise, while Nelson stayed abroad. The following year, a packet of money and a letter in Nelson's writing arrived for Walter from the pilot of the charter plane that had been bringing Nelson home. The plane had crashed and Nelson, his father learnt, was dead. In fact, he was just down the road at Paunton Farm, the villains' hideout, where he was respectfully addressed as 'Boss'. After the heist, he vanished and was not tracked down by Interpol until 1968. He was brought home to be tried at the Assizes, where, despite his fingerprints having been found on a whisky bottle at the farm, he was acquitted.

Nelson wisely lay low for over ten years, dabbling in property and taking his father on the occasional flash holiday. In 1980, though, he was back in Borchester, purchasing an old warehouse in West Street, which he converted into a wine bar. When the shop next door became vacant, he tried to persuade Clarrie Larkin to work at his putative sauna and massage parlour, but, when local folk, not least her boyfriend, Eddie Grundy, took the idea badly, decided to open an antique shop instead. It was through antiques that Nelson came to the attention of the police once more. He was accused of being part of a ring, but yet again they couldn't make the case against him stick, and Nelson was able to toast his freedom with a glass of robust red.

'Of all the gin joints in all the world...' Nelson might well have muttered *sotto voce*, as was his style, when tall, auburn-haired Rosemary Tarrant swept into the wine bar in 1986 to announce that she was his daughter. It was left to Walter to explain that if Nelson had gone a little pale when she'd disclosed that she was to train as a police cadet at Hendon, it was only because he'd been 'picked on' by the police in his youth.

Nelson might have tapped his father for cash over the years, but there was no doubting his genuine, if often wryly-expressed, affection for him. When Walter fell ill, Nelson moved to Honeysuckle Cottage to look after him, and he admitted after his death in 1988 that the old man had been a guiding influence in his life. Shortly afterwards, the wine bar lease came up for renewal and Nelson sold the antique shop to Kenton to pay for it. He became something of a mentor to the young entrepreneur, though Kenton never exhibited Nelson's skill in any department. Nelson finally had to take him in hand and go back in with him in a lock-up shop in the Old Market Square. Here Nelson briefly employed Debbie Aldridge, offering her a partnership, and was disappointed when she opted for a career in farming.

Nelson's love life, which had been discreet, not to say quiet, for years, enjoyed a revival when he became active as escort not just to Julia

Pargetter but to her sister, Ellen. On New Year's Eve 1996, following the relaunch of the wine bar as a café-bar, Nelson and Julia kissed in the ballroom at Lower Loxley. Never quite comfortable with his final attempt to move with the times in business – he had trouble with the new cappuccino machine and couldn't settle on the right music for the ambiance he wanted to create, trying everything from Pulp to Vivaldi – he decided to spend Christmas 1997 in Spain with the rival sisters. This was the last the village saw of him. Nigel was charged with shipping out his possessions from Honeysuckle Cottage, and, a few weeks later, a letter posted in Madrid announced that Nelson was winding up his business interests and pulling out altogether. Nelson's solicitors were saying nothing, but a repossession order on the cottage suggested that times had been hard. In April 1998, Nelson rang Elizabeth to wish her a happy birthday, and, or so she later said, she had a funny feeling it would be the last time she spoke to him. When news of his death came, it was from Argentina, but no one knows what he was doing there, or the exact circumstances in which he died. The death certificate, when translated from the Spanish, merely stated elliptically: 'heart failure'.

Nelson's funeral, held at St Stephen's on 6 April 2001, finally brought him home to be buried alongside his parents. For years, he'd been a shoulder to cry on for the bright young things of Ambridge – Mark and Shula, Caroline, Elizabeth and Nigel. For Julia, he'd been a suave and witty companion, and a comfort in the dark days of her drinking. For all Ambridge, though, he'd been an enigma, and he died that way. As for the proceeds of the mail van robbery...we'll almost certainly never know.

Walter **Gabriel**

(Robert Mawdesley, Chris Gittins)

'All the beasts of the forest are mine; and so are the cattle upon a thousand hills.' When Walter Gabriel chose these lines for his epitaph, they were certainly appropriate. Walter was a great animal lover, and, though a woefully inept farmer, a considerate stockman. But at the same time those words illuminate only one facet of his kaleidoscopic personality.

Birth: 25.8.1896
Death: 3.11.1988

Walter was one of several brothers from a large family. His grandmother, whose sayings he frequently quoted, and whose remedies cured many an Ambridge ill, had sixteen children and forty-eight grandchildre, and the Gabriels had by tradition been the Ambridge blacksmiths. In 1951, however, Walter was a tenant of the Squire and Brookfield's neighbour, but he drove Dan Archer to distraction with his delapidated fences, broken-down buildings and constant cadging. Walter also liked a drink, and, on one occasion, Phil and Dan had to stick his head under the village pump. He was always, however, a faithful friend, and the life and soul of any party with his famous euphonium. Sadly, his singing voice was not up to much, sounding, according to Dan, like a rusty nail being shoved through the bottom of a cocoa tin.

Walter eventually bought his farm, in 1954, but sold it to Thorpe Wynford three years later. He then acquired Honeysuckle Cottage with three-quarters of an acre and set himself up as village carrier. Almost immediately, his usual luck prevailed: his bus was stolen and the seats slashed. Phil, Walter's godson, had them repaired as a surprise.

Walter's own 'surprises' over the years did not work out so well: he once rotovated Mrs P's garden only to find that she had just planted out her spring seedlings. And when he stayed with Dan and Doris during repairs to his cottage, he helpfully scoured two of Doris's non-stick saucepans, and fitted new door handles – the wrong way round. But it was impossible to be angry with Walter for long, and Doris duly baked him a cake for his efforts.

Walter seemed to inspire affection – even the redoubtable Mrs P fell under his spell. Walter was wildly jealous of her other suitors, but their friendship survived her remarriage, and, when she returned to the village, they took up where they'd left off. The formality with which they addressed each other ('Mrs P, ma'am' and 'Mr Gabriel') belied a deep, if often exasperated, affection, though, when he did finally propose, Mrs P turned him down.

The loss of Walter's wife, Annie, at a young age had left him free to idolize his only son, and much of Walter's energy (and funds) went into keeping Nelson on the straight and narrow. One of the most heart-rending times for Walter was when Nelson staged his own death in a plane crash to avoid detection for the Borchester mail van robbery. When Interpol tracked him down, no one but Walter was convinced that Nelson was 'h'innocent', and, when his son was acquitted, the gleeful pair went off on a cruise, one of many lavish foreign holidays they took together.

Back in Ambridge, Walter was an organic part of the village scene. With Ned, then with Jethro Larkin, and with Tom Forrest, he played dominoes in the pub, though his annual rivalry with Tom over the Flower and Produce Show was well documented. In 1982, Walter 'fed' his marrow with sugar and water, so determined was he to win, but the scheme backfired all round when it exploded – in Tom's hands. At village fêtes, too, over the years, he made his mark, most notably when he bought an elephant, Rosie, who, with her baby, Tiny Tim, appeared at the summer festival in 1965. But the village knew better than to be surprised: already that year Walter had bought a balloon called Pegasus and a stuffed gorilla, George, that pointed the way to his Ambridge junk yard.

For if Nelson was, to put it politely, an entrepreneur, he got it from his enterprising father. Over the years, Walter had interests in a pet shop, two junk shops and a caravan site, and was all set to establish a craft studio when he realized it would mean upping his rates. But he was always a craftsman who liked working with his hands. His woodcarving business had such success that he had ended up buying in rocking chairs to satisfy his eager clientele, and he restored both a steam engine and an unusual form of glockenspiel called an autoglockenpolypon. His attempts to build Mrs P a TV set back in 1952 foundered, however, when he failed to understand the technical terms in the book he was following. Walter was always more of an instinctive worker.

After Nelson settled, relatively speaking, in Borchester, Walter took huge pride in the antique shop and wine bar, subsidizing its many renovations to keep up with popular taste. After one such make-over in 1985, Walter installed himself at the bar with his budgie, Joey, advising the customers to try Nelson's 'jerkins' (gherkins) before ticking them off for smoking and being too rowdy.

But The Bull was Walter's natural home. In 1988, his ninety-second birthday party was held there, with food supplied by Mrs P. Walter, who'd once tried to claim he was 'Lord of the Manor' of Ambridge, was instead declared a freeman of The Bull – a title rather more worth having. Sid Perks declared that in future, all his specials (his diabetic ales) would be on the house and Walter chuckled that Sid would regret it because he intended 'going on for ever'. That was in August. By November he was dead, carried off by pneumonia, and found by his son.

The funeral was held on 8 November and was marred only by the escape of Joe Grundy's sheep, which held up the service. If he'd been present, Walter would no doubt have let out a furious tirade, followed by a wickedly funny revenge. But he was gone. His inimitable greeting – 'Hello, me old pal, me old beauty' – had been heard for the last time.

Bert and Annie **Garland**

(Reg Johnston, Joy Davies)

The truth about Bert Garland was less pretty than his name. In 1961, he perpetrated a fiddle over a tractor deal that led to Paul Johnson resigning from Charles Grenville's employ when the accounts failed to tally. Bert's usually cowed wife, Annie, insisted he confess or she'd go to the police. Bert sent Johnson and Grenville £100 each, and, later, thoughtfully, £10 to Lilian for her pony – but the damage was done.

Madame Denise **Garonne**

(Irene Prador)

Madame Garonne, Charles Grenville's housekeeper for some years, enjoyed passing on gossip. On one occasion, she told people she'd seen Carol Grey make a late-night departure from Blossom Hill Cottage, without bothering to find out that Carol had simply been seeing a drunken John Tregorran safely home. Still, being indiscreet is one thing, being an international diamond smuggler quite another, yet that's what the *Borchester Echo*, in December 1959, revealed to be her true trade. Who'd have thought it?

Lucy **Gemmell** née Perks

(Tracy-Jane White)

Sid and Polly's only child, Lucy, weighed in at 6lb 12oz at 2.30 in the morning. She had a busy childhood, with ballet, riding and piano lessons, though she was denied her greatest wish – a puppy

Birth: 12.12.1971

– and had to make up an imaginary one, Crackers, instead. In 1982, her mother was killed in a car crash, but Lucy passed her eleven-plus exam nevertheless and went on to Borchester Grammar. There, fatefully, her form teacher was Kathy Holland, who was soon advising Sid on problems with his pre-teen daughter, such as her need for her first bra. Having dealt with the loss of her mother, once again the bottom dropped out of Lucy's world: Sid and Kathy fell in love and Lucy was jealous. After at first refusing to attend their wedding, she did go, but not before she'd placed a bouquet on Polly's grave with a card saying 'Goodbye Mum'. With the marriage a reality, Lucy had to find other outlets for her resentment, such as the environment and religion. She studied ecological science at Nottingham University, but failed to get her degree, having been distracted in her final year by a Kiwi, Duncan Gemmell. She married him in October 1994 and they settled in New Zealand.

Deborah **Gerrard**   'Debbie'   née Aldridge

(Tamsin Greig)

Debbie Gerrard is as comfortable swinging a huge combine round the Home Farm wheat fields as drawing up marketing plans for the Hassett Hills consortium of lamb producers, which she

Birth: 24.12.1970

chairs. In her enthusiasm for the practicalities of farming, she seems much more like her stepfather than she is to anyone else in her family.

Only five when her parents, Roger and Jennifer Travers-Macy, divorced, Debbie adjusted to her mother marrying Brian Aldridge shortly after much more calmly than her half-brother, Adam, did. The gift of a skewbald pony called Moonbeam no doubt helped Brian win her approval.

A keen student, who hated missing days from primary school, she seemed equally happy when she moved on to Cheltenham Ladies' College. A teenage fascination with the pop group Wham! didn't distract her from her studies, and she did well enough at A-level to be accepted to read French and English at Exeter University.

Although Jennifer had some concerns about the effect student life was having on her, it wasn't until Debbie suddenly announced she was taking a sabbatical that it became obvious something was badly wrong.

As Debbie finally told Brian, an unhappy love affair with a lecturer, Simon Gerrard, was the root of the problem. When Simon came to Ambridge, hoping to put things right, Brian's heavy-handed response made Debbie think about accompanying her lover to Canada, before deciding they didn't have a future together. While she was helping start up a riding enterprise at Home Farm, life produced another surprise. Her father, Roger, reappeared when she was celebrating her twenty-first birthday at Grey Gables. He said he wanted to get to know her again, but his main interest was in Jennifer, with whom he started an affair. Debbie rapidly found herself caught in the emotional crossfire between her mother, father and stepfather that ricocheted over the dining-table and echoed in fraught conversations in the lambing shed. She showed considerable maturity in telling Roger to leave Jennifer alone before any more damage was done.

Brian wanted her to complete her degree, but she'd lost interest in it. Passionate about horses, she persuaded him to let her take over the management of the riding course. Then Julia Pargetter came up with another offer: Debbie could become Nigel's assistant at Lower Loxley. It was a shameless piece of matchmaking, intended to push Elizabeth Archer out of the picture, but Nigel knew what his mother was up to, and had a good laugh about it with Debbie.

She also had the opportunity to work in the antiques business in 1994, when Nelson Gabriel offered her a partnership. Unsure about working in such a cut-throat environment, she opted to put her energies into Home Farm instead. She built up the riding course and helped with the fishing lake, but gradually found herself drawn more into crop and stock management. Persuading Brian to trust her judgement on agricultural matters was a long haul, and she was at one point tempted to leave for a friend's PR company. But, over time, Brian has come to acknowledge her competence, and she's had the satisfaction of seeing him change some of his farming practices in accordance with her views.

Her good looks, intelligence and lively sense of humour have always attracted men, but her self-confidence has sometimes frightened them off. She got on well with Civil War enthusiast Richard Locke, and took part in a re-enactment of the Battle of Hassett Bridge with him. However, despite Martha Woodford's chatter, they were never really more than friends. Things were more serious with farm worker Steve Oakley, but he was edgy about their different backgrounds, and finally accused her of only wanting a bit of rough. In 1997, Simon Pemberton used more than words when Debbie told him their relationship was over – he beat her up. To add insult to injury, his remorseful act in court resulted in his getting only a very light sentence.

Debbie has been no stranger to traumatic events. When Clive Horrobin and Bruno Wills raided the village shop in 1993, Debbie was one of the hostages and was to be disturbed by the experience for some time after. Nor will she ever forget Mark Hebden's tragic swerve, which saved Caroline Bone's life, and, perhaps, even her own. Her relationship with half-sister Kate has sometimes been strained, but she was a great support during Kate's first pregnancy, and was subsequently touched when asked to become Phoebe's guardian in a New Age naming ceremony. She gets on well with Kate's new husband, Lucas, and adores baby Nolly. Although there's a considerable age gap, Debbie has always got on well with her other half-sister, Alice, and has stayed in touch with Adam during his time abroad.

When Simon Gerrard contacted her in the summer of 1999, Debbie wasn't sure if she wanted to become involved again. Having agreed to a meeting, she quickly found his wit and ebullience as irresistible as ever. While Brian was horrified to see her move in with a man who was so much older, Debbie appreciated being with someone who wasn't intimidated by her strength of character. Simon's suspension from Felpersham University on a charge of sexual harassment dredged up some old ghosts, but, once the allegations had been dropped, she had no hesitation in marrying him.

Debbie had always got on well with Elizabeth, having provided a lot of support after her break-up with Cameron Fraser, so Elizabeth was a natural choice to be a witness at the wedding. The hen night was a hoot and the honeymoon in Canada was great fun, too, though Debbie clearly sees her future in Ambridge, where she would eventually love to try running her own enterprise – with Simon's support of course.

For a long time Debbie remained a Travers-Macy, then Macy, to please her father; as a student, she chose to become an Aldridge, in recognition of Brian's role in bringing her up; then, in the face of some opposition, she became a Gerrard. Being happy would be so much easier if she didn't always have to divide her loyalties.

Simon **Gerrard**

(Garrick Hagon)

'Excuse me…I seem to have got myself completely lost,' said the good-looking Canadian wandering round Ambridge in the summer of 1991. He was trying to find Home Farm, but, not for the first or last time, Simon Gerrard had taken a wrong turning somewhere.

A widower, he had come to teach French Canadian literature for a year at Exeter University. He started a relationship with one of his students, Debbie Aldridge, and they got on so well that she was thinking of going back to Canada with him. Then she discovered he was seeing another woman as well, and, heartbroken, retreated to her parents' farm. Finally, he caught up with her, and, using every last ounce of his charm, persuaded her to at least talk to him.

They spent some time together in Ambridge, with Simon vowing he wouldn't leave without her. Brian Aldridge was appalled to see Debbie linked to a man almost twice her age. When he discovered Simon apparently treating her roughly, he threw him out of the house. Debbie, furious at her father's intervention, immediately walked out as well. In the end, however, she decided she had too much to lose, and Simon went back to Canada alone.

Over the next few years, he moved from one college to the next, never really settling down. He found a new lover, Katherine, but wrecked that relationship by getting drunk at a party and going off with another woman. No one really matched up to Debbie for him, so, when the offer of a lectureship at Felpersham University came up in 1999, he had a dual purpose in recrossing the Atlantic.

At first Debbie was quite cool about meeting up again, but Simon was persistent in asking. Soon she was helping him choose a flat in Borchester and the love affair was back on. Jennifer Aldridge quickly spotted the new spring in her daughter's step, and, although she had reservations when she realized Simon was the cause, she soon succumbed to the charm offensive he waged over dinner at Home Farm. Simon tried to put Brian at ease as well by asking informed questions about agriculture. As far as Brian was concerned, this was like a burglar politely asking the whereabouts of the family silver. Heatedly, he warned Debbie that Simon was only interested in her because she would one day inherit the farm. This hostility merely pushed Debbie closer to Simon, who was delighted when she changed an earlier decision and agreed to move in with him.

Happier than he had been in years, Simon got on increasingly well with Jennifer, who liked having someone to talk books with. He even won over Kate Aldridge with his attentions to her baby daughter, Phoebe, and seemed generally well liked elsewhere. Tony Archer didn't think much of him, considering his ingratiating manner to be smarmy, but that was very much a minority opinion.

Work was going well, too, but what Simon enjoyed most was becoming involved in traditional village life. Following the hunt was fun; playing the Sheriff of Nottingham to Debbie's Robin Hood in the pantomime even more so. It was a shame Debbie had to spend so many nights in the lambing sheds, but even that had its compensations. He dined out on the story of delivering a lamb himself.

It was all going too well to last. In February 2000, Debbie found him at home one afternoon when he should have been lecturing. Hugely embarrassed, he told her he had been suspended while an accusation of sexual harassment was investigated. Debbie wanted to believe him when he said the girl involved was a fantasist, but couldn't help seeing parallels with the way he had treated her as a student. Once again, Simon had to be very persuasive before she fully accepted he was telling the truth. Brian wasn't such an easy proposition. When he heard the news, he felt he had been right to be suspicious all along and couldn't resist saying so. Simon then had the pleasure of telling him that the accusation had been withdrawn, and that the girl who made it was leaving the university.

Over a celebratory meal, Debbie, feeling guilty that she had ever doubted him, accepted Simon's proposal of marriage. Their wedding was on 12 May, with an old friend of Simon's, Bondi Blanchard, acting as best man. The highlight of the day was provided by Pat and Tony Archer, who took the newlyweds to their reception on a decorated tractor and trailer. If Simon was offended that his new father-in-law had felt unable to attend, he made every effort not to show it.

The honeymoon was in Canada, where Simon introduced his bride to glamorous cousin Lindsay and her anthropologist husband, as well as to a favourite uncle, whose sprightliness belied his seventy years of age. Debbie was left with an overall impression of marrying into very academic stock.

The next step, back in Britain, was deciding where to spend their married life. Taking over Grange Farm after the Grundys' eviction had briefly seemed an option, but Matt Crawford hadn't really been serious about letting Borchester Land sell it to the Gerrards.

For the time being, the Borchester flat is still home, but it's unlikely to stay that way for ever. Simon loves the idea of living in the countryside, in a strong settled marriage, with a patch of land to look after, and, who knows, maybe even children running through the fields to complete the picture. He's enjoying the rural idyll and has convinced himself that his old womanizing habits will never undermine the little piece of paradise he's finally found for himself.

Albert **Gibbs** 'Bert'

(Graham Rigby)

Bert, who farmed at Meadow Farm from the late 1950s until his retirement in 1979, was a bit of a misery, who seemed to think the world was against him: some blamed the death of his only son. He tried to sue the *Borchester Echo* after a misprint suggested he'd been fined for effluent disposal, and got into an altercation with the vicar, Richard Adamson, no less, who was electrocuted by a wire fence across a footpath. When, shortly afterwards, one of Bert's heifers strayed and died on Lakey Hill after eating a plastic bag, Bert concluded it had got out over the pulled-down fence and claimed Richard was to blame. To make matters worse, the heifer was not insured as Bert was between policies, but the magistrates found in the vicar's favour, fining Bert £5 for obstructing a right of way. Bert had already tried to enlist the help of the NFU via Phil, but they could do nothing to help him. Nonetheless, having characteristically shot one of Jack Woolley's deer that had ventured on to his farm, Bert presented Phil with a haunch of venison as thanks for his advice and support. When Bert sold up, Phil bought 30 acres of his land.

Jolyon **Gibson**

(William Tapley)

To Jennifer and Brian Aldridge, public school-educated Gibson seemed a much better boyfriend for their daughter Kate than Roy

Tucker. They were wrong to think so. His idea of a suitable Christmas present for Kate in 1995 was a bottle of pills on which she almost overdosed. John Archer warned the drug-dealing Gibson he wasn't welcome in Ambridge, but it was Roy who fought with him and sent him packing after Gibson boasted he'd slept with Kate. When last heard of, he was on remand for drugs offences.

Glebe Cottage

No wonder Shula found leaving Glebe Cottage a wrench. Set prettily beneath its thatched roof and within a walled garden, the only drawback to the place is its size: Dan and Doris Archer added a so-called conservatory but the property has only two bedrooms.

Glebe Cottage is only in the Archer family at all because it was left to Doris, initially for her lifetime, by her grateful employer, Letty Lawson-Hope. While she was still living at Brookfield, Doris rented it out, first to Ned and Mabel Larkin, and then to Hugo Barnaby, and she and Dan moved there on his retirement on 1970. A few years later, they managed to buy the freehold, and, on her death, Doris left the cottage to Shula, on the understanding that Dan could see out the rest of his years there. Shula subseqently lived there with her first husband, Mark Hebden, and together they contemplated the knotty problem of rethatching the roof, an operation that was delayed over the summer of 1986 so as not to disturb a colony of roosting bats. On Mark's death, Jill helped Shula plant a buddleia in the garden. As part of Phil's retirement plan to hand over the running of Brookfield to David and Ruth, he and Jill moved into Glebe Cottage in September 2001.

Glebelands

Glebelands is a small development of houses built in 1978/9 on a plot of land belonging to Jack Woolley, which lies between the village green and the River Am. Originally there was strong opposition from the Parish Council to the idea of new housing being located in such a scenic spot, and, even when the go-ahead was finally given, Colonel Danby and Laura Archer politely made clear to Jack that they would be ensuring the builders stuck rigidly to the agreed plans. Derek and Pat Fletcher were among the first to move in, as were Mr and Mrs Patterson, who took up residence at No. 11. Very quickly, the Pattersons were applying for planning permission to extend: they wanted to add a utility room and a second bathroom. Possibly Mr Patterson – Barry to his friends – had used up too much of the original space in storing his football memorabilia, since, according to Mike Tucker, who delivers to No. 11 on his milk round, Barry is fanatical about football, and was willing to pay a very high price for World Cup tickets in 1998.

Debbie **Glover**

(Esma Wilson)

Debbie Glover was awkward: she gave Jack Archer a mouthful when, as foreman of the Market Garden, he sacked her in 1957, and later created trouble for Jack's brother, Phil, by spreading untrue stories about him and Rita Flynn. Perhaps feeling more settled once she was working for Toby Stobeman, she tipped off PC Bryden about the imminent theft of a bus. Grateful to Walter Gabriel for the hamper he tactfully gave her one Christmas when she and her mother were penniless, she returned the favour by giving him Butch the bulldog when he was in search of a pet.

Lady Mercedes **Goodman**

The Spanish wife of Sir Sidney Goodman, Lady Mercedes is ever willing to spend the profits from her husband's canning factories, and especially enjoys shooting and going to health clubs. Although she's one of Julia Pargetter's closest friends, she didn't feel able to lend Julia all the money required to pay off the latter's gambling debts early in 1999. Perhaps she needed the cash to invest in moisturizers, since, despite the health-giving effects of her various dietary regimes, some people consider her sun-soaked skin a little leathery.

Sir Sidney **Goodman**

(Roger Hume)

Knighted for services to industry, Sir Sidney owns canning factories both in Spain, the home country of his wife, Mercedes, and in Borchester. For a time in the 1980s, he served as a county councillor in Borsetshire. An indication of his lifelong political leanings can be gleaned from the knowledge that as a young man he volunteered to fight in the Spanish Civil War – on Franco's side.

He certainly couldn't be accused of wishy-washy liberalism in his business dealings. Usha Gupta appeared to have won a significant victory for the workers at the Borchester canning factory in 1992, when she manoeuvred management into agreeing to enter pay negotiations with the union, once she'd discovered men and women there weren't being paid equally. But Sir Sidney didn't take defeat lightly, and retaliated by ensuring that Usha, and her legal partner, Mark Hebden, then lost a contract to deal with the building of a new shopping centre – the developer coincidentally being a close friend of Sir Sidney's.

Friends such as Julia Pargetter note that these days he is showing his age, and, with one serious heart attack already behind him, sadly speculate that he may not have long left for further wheeling and dealing.

Gerry **Goodway**

Surprisingly little is known about Gerry, considering that he's been part of the Ambridge scene for years, acting as Tony's best man and godfather to John Archer. An agricultural contractor, he can often be seen around the lanes and fields during silage, hay-making and harvest. In his spare time, he's a member of Borchester Round Table, where he may well be the life and soul of the party. At work in Ambridge, however, he's the strong and silent type.

Jimmy **Grange**

(Alan Rothwell)

Originally young farm worker Jimmy Grange was apprenticed to Dan Archer for only two years, but in the end stayed on at Brookfield for a good while past his finishing date of October 1959. Combining skiffle-playing with agriculture, hot-blooded Jimmy was an attractive figure to Ambridge's teenage girls, with Joan Hood being his most devoted admirer. He was slightly less enthusiastic about her, so was quite relieved when she left the village with her family, only to be less delighted when she later returned alone.

He developed his own crush on Carol Grey, whose encouragement of his folk-singing he had interpreted as meaning something more. He was mortified when she made his mistake clear, and resolved never to go back to her cottage. Hazel White, whom he met at Borchester Tech, was more responsive, and, although Jimmy got into a fight about her with Gary Kenton, they got on well enough to spend a weekend in London together. Jimmy left Ambridge in 1960, shortly after a scuffle he had with Ricky Boyd resulted in Mr Grenville closing the Youth Club. It's not known if he ever made anything of his musical ambitions.

Grange Farm

After the Grundys' long tenancy ended in eviction in April 2000, Grange Farm found a new occupant when retired farmer Oliver Sterling bought the farmhouse and an accompanying 50 acres from Borchester Land. Although he needed builders to do some serious renovation before moving in, Oliver knew that any property comprising six bedrooms, two bathrooms, a parlour, kitchen, scullery and large cellars has plenty of potential for development. Certainly the Grundys loved living there. Clarrie was particularly proud of the improvements she wrought after joining the household in November 1981. She was responsible for two new bathrooms being put in, and was especially pleased with having the second one, a competition prize, put en suite in the master bedroom – although Eddie did take some convincing that it needed walls around it. Eddie drew more satisfaction from the new milking parlour he fought to have built, after a fire in 1996 destroyed the original one. Eddie's father, Joe, would simply have been happy to see the tenancy pass on to his grandsons, William and Edward, in due course, but it wasn't to be. Still bitter at losing the farm, Joe cheers up when given any opportunity to reminisce about the pop concert and car boot sales that were held there in his time, or, most memorable of all, the remains of a German plane that was discovered on their land in 1995.

Michèle **Gravençin**

(Lorna Phillippe)

Michèle arrived from northern France in 1970 as au pair to the Brookfield brood. Her uncle was a farmer, so she was no stranger to country life, and soon no stranger to Tony Archer's sports car either, as he romanced her for a time. But her real sweetheart was Gordon Armstrong, Jack Woolley's underkeeper. They were unofficially engaged when Michèle had to rush home as her mother was seriously ill. Maman subsequently died and Michèle never returned.

Ginger **Green**

When a woman called Helga turned up at Fairbrother's farm in 1956 asking after her husband, Phil Archer knew something was amiss with the young man, Ginger, he'd recently employed, believing him to be the boyfriend of poultry girl Marjorie Butler. When questioned, Ginger promptly disappeared – as did Grace's engagement ring. This was later retrieved, but the hapless Marjorie was still smitten and Phil found himself tracking Ginger to his digs on her behalf. Unaccountably, both he and Helga had vanished.

Ivan **Greenwood**

Hardyesque Ivan was a long-serving cowman at Sawyer's Farm, working under several Estate owners, but his great misfortune was to end his working life in 1991 – the time of Cameron Fraser. Cameron at first agreed to Shula's suggestion that on his retirement Ivan should be offered Ivy Cottage at a reduced rent, then reneged on the deal. Ivan is now presumably in a council flat – if not a cardboard box – in Borchester.

No. 1, The Green

One of twelve compact houses on The Green, No. 1 was council property until 1991, when Susan Carter persuaded husband Neil that they should buy it. It was in a poor state of repair, but they thoroughly decorated and modernized it, at the expense of some acid comments from Lynda Snell, who thinks their neo-Georgian front door was an error of judgement. With the Carter children, Chris and Emma, growing up, conditions have become increasingly cramped, but on their current income there is little prospect of the Carters being able to move elsewhere.

Ann **Grenville** née Prescott

(Heather Canning)

Ann Prescott was the junior partner in a London gown shop, who, on becoming re-acquainted with Harvey Grenville after an interval of seventeen years, decided to move to Borsetshire to be closer to him. Setting up shop a few doors away from John Tregorran's antique business, she enjoyed living in the area – so much so that plans for her and Harvey to marry were temporarily jeopardized when he wanted to resume work for the Foreign Office, which would have meant moving from Ambridge. Eventually they did marry, and, after Harvey was made redundant from the Estate in 1965, quietly moved away after all.

Harvey **Grenville**

(Ronald Baddiley)

Rather short on self-confidence, bearded Harvey Grenville stayed with his distant cousin Charles when he first came to Ambridge in 1961, before moving into a flat at Arkwright Hall after taking up the wardenship there. Perhaps being best man when Charles married Carol Grey put ideas in his head because he soon found himself falling in love with Ann Prescott. He gave up the idea of resuming work for the Foreign Office when it seemed this would stop Ann marrying him, and continued with his new job, as a supervisor for the Estate, until Charles died in 1965.

Oliver **Grenville** 'Charles Grenville'

(Michael Shaw)

A shrewd businessman, Charles Grenville was also good at winning the respect of those who worked for him. Phil Archer didn't get on with him straight away when Grenville purchased the

Death: 21.1.1965

Fairbrother Estate in 1959, but gradually came to realize that his new employer had the type of vision necessary to cope with changing agricultural times. Carol Grey developed more than a liking for him: she fell in love and married him. In December 1962, a little over a year after their marriage, a son, Richard Charles, was born. The following year, in a traumatic car crash, Grenville lost a leg, while his passenger, Janet Tregorran, was killed. Injury didn't stop him pursuing his wide-ranging business interests in companies that dealt with agricultural machinery, animal foodstuffs and farm contracting. Appropriately, given the reach of his investments, one business was called the Octopus Trust Ltd. Restless for new challenges, in 1965 he decided he wanted to settle in the United States, despite Carol's disapproval. While in New York, he suffered a major haemorrhage, probably caused by a bug he'd picked up many years earlier when working in Africa, or travelling in the Far East. On his death, his possessions were divided between Carol and Richard.

Richard **Grenville**

(John Offord)

Having lost his father, Charles Grenville, when he was just over two years old, Richard soon had to get used to having a stepfather around, after

Birth: 13.12.1962

THE ARCHERS ENCYCLOPAEDIA

his mother, Carol, married John Tregorran. He wasn't too enthusiastic about the arrival of his half-sister, Anna Louise, in 1969, but seemed happy to settle into boarding-school life, along with fellow villager David Archer. Insecurity caused by John Tregorran's repeated absences on lecture tours briefly triggered off some behavioural problems, such as petty theft, but by the time he'd taken his A-levels, Richard was becoming considerably more mature.

Grey Gables Country Club

Built in a mock Gothic style during the Victorian era, Grey Gables is one of the best country house hotels in the whole of Borsetshire. It has twenty-four rooms in the main house, with a further thirty-six in the annex, each with en suite bathroom and impressive views of the surrounding 15 acres of garden. The Royal Garden Suite is generally agreed to be the most favoured set of rooms. Beyond the gardens lie a golf course and the Ambridge Country Park. If guests require other forms of exercise or relaxation, a health club, with swimming pool, gym, sauna and tanning facilities, is also available. A first-class restaurant, under the supervision of Jean-Paul Aubert, offers well-regarded French and English cuisine, while there is also a bar and lounge for guests to relax in. The ballroom, with its delicately fashioned chandelier, is consistently popular as a venue for wedding receptions and other celebrations, while function rooms can be booked for conferences. (If live music is required for any event, the Tommy Croker band are often available at short notice.) In 1962, ownership of the hotel passed from Reggie Trentham to Jack Woolley. On his retirement, Jack passed the running of the hotel on to Caroline Pemberton, who employs a wide range of staff to keep it running smoothly, including Roy Tucker as a trainee assistant manager, and Lynda Snell, who works on reception.

Grey Gables Lodge

Uncomfortable with living at Grey Gables, newlywed Peggy Woolley was glad to act on Caroline Bone's suggestion that the hotel's lodge might make a better home. Formerly used by employees of Grey Gables, the black and white timbered building was in a bad state of repair, but Jack and Peggy had extensive repairs made before moving in on 11 June 1991. The kitchen, finished in antique oak, and the conservatory are much admired features; the electronic cat-flap is now worked by Bill and Ben, since the much-lamented Sammy is no longer around to shed hairs on the all-pervasive beige carpet.

Elaine **Griffiths**

For once Tony had cause to thank Lynda Snell when in 1989 she extolled the virtues of Bridge Farm's organic milk to Elaine, a dairy representative from mid-Wales. Tony had already cunningly given Elaine, who was desperately seeking suppliers, the impression that he might possibly be able to spare her some of his surplus when, in fact, he was anxious to sell to her. Lynda's paean of praise clinched the deal.

Basil and Valerie **Grove**

(Michael Ford, Pat Driscoll)

If Doris was pleased when her daughter found herself a job at Borchester Dairies, she was less so when rumours reached her ears of Christine's affair with her married boss. Snooker-playing Basil, thirty-three and saddled with wife Valerie, who 'didn't understand him', asked Chris to go away with him at Whitsun 1951 as Valerie was herself away. But when she returned unexpectedly, the trip was off the agenda, as was any further hanky-panky.

Alfred **Grundy**

(Terry Molloy)

The elder son of Joe and Susan, Alf Grundy has brought little credit to his family during a lifetime largely spent paddling in the shallows of non-violent crime. He started early, stealing chocolate from Woolworth's, before graduating to receiving stolen copper

Birth: 13.11.1944

wire in 1980, when he was supposedly a legitimate dealer in scrap metal. At this point, Joe said he was disowning him, and contact between Alf and the rest of his family became extremely intermittent thereafter. After spending some time in prison for breaking and entering offences, he showed up briefly at Grange Farm in the summer of 1986. He stayed long enough to empty William's money box and steal Eddie's car stereo, before heading off to resume his criminal ways elsewhere. In the run-up to Eddie's fiftieth birthday, early in 2001, Clarrie contacted him to see if he could contribute any memories of the brothers' years growing up together. He could, but, sadly, nothing suitable for repetition in mixed company. Later in the year, he met up with Joe for his father's 80th birthday. Apparently untroubled by any desire to revisit Ambridge, Alf continues to weave his own path through life. Those he comes into contact with would still be well advised to count the spoons after he has gone.

Clarrie **Grundy**   née Larkin

(Heather Bell, Fiona Mathieson, Rosalind Adams)

As the Grundys prepared for a dispersal sale, in a prelude to leaving Grange Farm in 2000, Eddie wondered why his wife, Clarrie, hadn't left him years previously. Quite simply, she answered, it was

Birth: 12.5.1954

because she loved him. Indeed, only someone with her exceptionally loyal and loving nature could have withstood all the buffeting that life as a Grundy has brought her.

Clarrie's parents, Jethro and Lizzie Larkin, originally had great hopes for her, and were disappointed when, after she lost her job at a travel agent's in 1976, she seemed content to take on housework around the village. In truth, Clarrie has always seen work as a way of supporting her family rather than an end in itself. She's worked part-time in The Bull for many years, fitting the hours in around her duties at the Bridge Farm dairy. At times of increased financial stress, she's taken on extra employment, such as cooking for a dogs' weekend at Grey Gables, and stuffing envelopes for a mail-order underwear company, who never got round to paying her.

Right from the start of her relationship with Eddie Grundy, she needed to have some income of her own. She was attracted to him when he came to make improvements to the kitchen at Woodbine Cottage in 1980. Aware of Eddie's interest in becoming a country singer, she offered to pay for a demo tape he was making, and even ended up buying her own engagement ring when Eddie finally proposed. Jethro was dead set against the marriage, but Clarrie showed an independent spirit in walking out until he relented and agreed to give her away.

Clarrie made up a bridal suite in her new home at Grange Farm, hanging blue curtains and finding a bedspread to match. By the time she and Eddie returned from their honeymoon in Torremolinos, in November 1981, the room was being used to store unwanted furniture, as, not for the last time, Joe Grundy unwittingly put a spoke in Clarrie's plans. The arrival of children soon complicated family life further.

William was born in February 1983. It was a difficult birth, and Clarrie said she never wanted another child, but was soon pregnant again, giving birth to a second son, Ed, while staying with her sister, Rosie, in Great Yarmouth, in September 1984. Heartache was added to the trials of looking after young children when Clarrie lost her father to an accident at Brookfield three years later.

While she would very much have liked to have had a daughter as well, perhaps as an ally in the otherwise all-male household, Clarrie proved an extremely caring and conscientious mother to her sons. William has proved to be a source of pride, but Ed has become an increasing cause for concern – never more so than when his joyriding habits led to Emma Carter being seriously injured in a car crash. Although raising a family, trying to keep Joe and Eddie out of mischief, and holding down various part-time jobs have never left Clarrie with much time to herself, she has always maintained other interests. An avid reader of romances, she also enjoys cooking traditional food, and has a real talent for cake-baking – a useful skill for someone who has served her turn as secretary of the local WI. Perhaps her greatest passion is reserved for travel. She loves going to France, and for a time hoped the family would move to a French farm. She was one of the prime movers in Ambridge being twinned with Meyruelle, and was delighted when one of her French friends sent tickets for the Japan v. Jamaica match in the 1998 World Cup. She thoroughly enjoyed taking William and Ed over to see it, although she had to retrieve the tickets from Dr Locke first – Joe and Eddie hadn't been able to resist the opportunity of trying to make a few bob from them. She also has fond memories of a coach trip to Jersey, when the driver, Austin, was captivated by her, and continued sending postcards and valentines long after the trip was over. Clarrie didn't think much of Eddie's jealous response: getting a tattoo of a heart with 'Eddie and Clarrie' underneath, as proof of his affection.

Since life hasn't always been quick to provide what Clarrie wants for herself and her family, she's often tried to nudge it along by entering competitions. She won a fridge shortly before her wedding, and, in 1993, was delighted to win a fully fitted luxury bathroom. She was less happy about being accidentally locked in it, along with Lynda Snell, after Joe botched a demonstration of how to work the sliding doors. More recently, a modest scratch card win enabled her to buy Ed a longed-for electric guitar as some recompense for all the upheavals the family experienced in 2000.

That was the year when Clarrie most needed good fortune, but found it wasn't forthcoming. Despite all her efforts to take on extra work, the mounting pile of bills at Grange Farm led inexorably to bankruptcy and eviction. She tried to keep up a brave face for her family's sake, but couldn't restrain tears when the family dog, Tess, came running back from her temporary home at Brookfield at the very moment the Grundys were leaving the farm for the last time.

Clarrie found the months cooped up in the cramped, noisy conditions of Borchester's Meadow Rise flats thoroughly dispiriting, but never lost her determination to hold her family together as they fought through the crisis. Finally, she received her due reward, when Eddie brought her unsuspectingly to Keeper's Cottage and revealed that they were to be the new tenants. The bottle of champagne Joe had cooling in the mop bucket was a nice touch, but most important of all for Clarrie was the sense that, finally, she and her family were home again in Ambridge.

Edward **Grundy**   'Eddie'

(Trevor Harrison)

A great country and western enthusiast in his spare time, Eddie Grundy has experienced enough twists of fate to fill a rhinestone-studded songbook. His dreams of handing on Grange Farm to his sons, William and Ed, ultimately proved no more substantial than those he once had of being a successful singer and recording artist. But

Birth: 15.3.1951

where a lesser man might have crumbled under the weight of troubles he's seen, particularly in recent years, Eddie continues to duck and dive, mixing hard work and hard scheming in equal measure to make a living for his family at the financially challenged end of Ambridge.

He hadn't planned to follow his father, Joe, into farming, preferring instead to try his hand at scrap-metal dealing in Gloucester before working for a plant hire firm in Hollerton. However, when half the Grange Farm herd became infected with brucellosis in 1978, and Joe's main response was to start drinking, Eddie felt his place was at his father's side, trying to get the farm back on its feet. Over the next few years, he combined a variety of jobs with helping out on the farm, before the realization that he couldn't inherit the tenancy unless he worked with his father for at least five years out of seven, led him to take up farming full-time. He certainly had the capacity for hard physical labour, although his failure to master the niceties of good agricultural and financial practice constantly undermined his efforts to make Grange Farm pay.

More money would certainly have been handy in his courting days. For a time, Eddie was intent on marrying divorcée Dolly Treadgold, but ultimately found her too flirtatious for comfort. Jethro Larkin's daughter Clarrie was a much better match, although it took Eddie quite a time to realize it. As he and Clarrie were gradually growing close, country singer Jolene Rogers was tempting him to put more time into his music. He and Jolene made a record together, but, when the recording company became bankrupt, a chastened Eddie was finally ready to commit himself to Clarrie. They married on 21 November 1981, with Eddie's brother, Alf, as best man. Eddie's eye has occasionally wandered since; circus performer Maxine the Mohican fascinated him briefly in 1990, and there is still a certain electricity between him and Jolene. But for the most part, Eddie realizes that Clarrie is the only woman who could have put up with him for so long, and he's loath to do anything that might put their marriage at risk.

Their two sons, William and Ed, have been a source of pride and consternation in equal measure. Having devoted considerable time to teaching William the best ways to poach all manner of wildlife, Eddie was naturally taken aback when his law-abiding elder son opted to become a gamekeeper. They had a serious clash when Eddie took trout from Brian Aldridge's fishing lakes, an action that William feared might cost him his job. Younger son, Ed, who has a much more elastic notion of right and wrong, seems closer in temperament to his father, though Eddie was distressed when Ed's joyriding caused Emma Carter serious injury in September 2001.

With no great talent for making agriculture pay, Eddie has fallen back on a wide range of money-making schemes to try and support his family. Cider-making, holly-selling and raising turkeys for the Christmas market have all been Grundy ventures. At one time selling personalized number plates looked as though it might be a money-spinner, and selling the accidental daubings of one of the Grange Farm cows, Poppy, promised to take Eddie into the high income bracket, until the poor beast passed away and Eddie's attempts to forge her style were unmasked. Other scams have brought him too close to the wrong side of the law for Clarrie's liking, never more so than when selling stolen venison indirectly led to his being arrested for an assault on George Barford. Fortunately, the real culprit, Clive Horrobin, was found before Eddie was taken to court.

The arrest was only one of a series of disasters that befell him in the late 1990s. The destruction of the milking parlour in a fire was followed by a Notice to Quit order from the Grundys' then landlord, Simon Pemberton. The eviction was successfully contested, and Eddie heroically tried to build up the family's finances by investing in a herd of Jersey cows. But as farming hit a nationwide crisis of ever-falling prices, Eddie wasn't really equipped to keep the farm afloat. A series of diseases affected the herd, causing the loss of milk income, while feed bills and rent arrears rapidly amassed. In desperation, Eddie turned to loan shark Mike Butcher, but could stave off the crisis only temporarily. Despite helpful cash advances from members of the Archer family, notification of bankruptcy came on 27 January 2000, and, by April, Eddie and family had been evicted from Grange Farm by Borchester Land.

The next few months were bleak. Rehoused in a rundown block of flats in Borchester, Eddie watched as his father became increasingly depressed and Clarrie wore herself out trying to hold the fragmenting family together. After a phase of listless self-pity, when he tried dead-end jobs on a building site and as a delivery man for Hurry That Curry, Eddie was spurred into more positive action by his father's two-day disappearance during a confused attempt to walk back to Grange Farm. As a first step back to normality, Eddie got hold of a large caravan and parked it illegally near the pheasant pens on the Estate shoot. The Grundys moved in temporarily, while Eddie plotted to find them proper accommodation. Freed of the expense of running a farm, he raised enough money from contract work to persuade Jack Woolley to let the family take on the tenancy of Keeper's Cottage. Clarrie's delight on being shown her new home made all Eddie's efforts seem worthwhile.

The loss of Grange Farm was caused partly by the flaws in Eddie's character; the fact that he managed to bring his family back to Ambridge is a testament to his good qualities – above all, his tenacity and determination. Maybe when he's got time, between running a compost business, laying patios and doing anything else he can find to make money, he'll even get round to writing a song about it all.

Edward **Grundy** 'Ed'

(Barry Farrimond)

Most people assume that Ed Grundy was named after his father, Eddie, but his mother, Clarrie, claims Prince Edward was the inspiration. The other name she fancied was Barry, after her favourite singer, Barry Manilow. Edward it was, however, and Ed he's since become to family and friends alike – except for Clarrie, who still uses his full name, especially if she's having words with him.

Birth: 28.9.1984

He was a placid baby, happy to sit quietly for hours, until a much grumpier side was displayed when he had to start going to school, and tried to get out of it by throwing his lunch-box out of the window. From early on he showed musical talent, not so much when bashing away at the piano with elder brother William, but more when he had to sing. He made a good impression at the Christingle service in 1994, and sang a solo at the carol concert the following year, despite almost losing his voice shouting at an Aston Villa match his father had taken him to shortly before.

When he entered the talent contest in 1996, Clarrie was convinced he was going to show the Grundys up by performing something hideously raucous, but instead he and Eddie duetted with the Boyzone ballad 'Father and Son'. As a result, Ed won second prize in his age group. Tellingly, William had already offered to be his manager, on the understanding that he took 85 per cent of the prize money.

The two boys had a typical brotherly relationship: at times they were rivals for their parents' attention and financial resources; on other occasions they formed a team, as in 1998, when they ran a scam selling badly embroidered cushion covers Ed had stolen from school, and which they purported had been made by Clarrie. For some time, it seemed as though Ed would turn out to be the more responsible of the two. He was good at saving money, whereas William always spent his. When Clarrie took them to see the Japan v. Jamaica match in the 1998 World Cup, Ed was even in a position to lend his brother £25 spending money. However, while William showed increasing maturity as he trained to become a gamekeeper, Ed appeared to go the other way.

He marked his fifteenth birthday by getting drunk on home-made apple brandy. A couple of months later, he and Chris Carter were responsible for killing half the Grundys' turkey flock by letting off fireworks too close to their shed. About this time, he was also discovering girls. Hoping to impress Emma Carter with his nerve, he climbed up on the roof of St Stephen's, got horribly stuck and needed Janet Fisher to talk him through a descent. But what really seemed to push him into full teenage rebellion was his family's eviction from Grange Farm.

While William had his own flat at the Dower House to go to, Ed had no choice but to accompany the rest of the Grundys to their dismal new accommodation in Meadow Rise. After growing up in a spacious farmhouse, he loathed being squeezed into a flat, particularly when he realized he was meant to share a room with his grandfather, Joe. Soon he was either arguing furiously with his parents about his right to play music full blast, or staying out to all hours with anyone who could put up with his company. He landed himself on William as often as he could, caused the Carters some concern by spending more time with Emma than was good for her exam revision, but mostly seemed to enjoy the company of a new friend he'd made in Borchester – Jazzer – of whom Clarrie strongly disapproved. On his frequent trips back to Ambridge, Ed had nothing better to do than make a nuisance of himself outside The Bull.

Life got more stressful at Meadow Rise when his father tore down the makeshift tent Ed had made in the middle of the flat, in his continued determination not to share a room with Joe. Even when Eddie bought a caravan for the family in Ambridge, Ed preferred spending his time at Jazzer's, or hanging round the now generally empty flat with his new mates. He and Fallon Rogers organized a party there for Emma Carter's sixteenth birthday, which all went wrong when friends of friends gate-crashed and started to cause havoc.

Ed's soft spot for Emma had already led him into trouble when he wanted to go with her on the village millennium trip to Blackpool, but didn't have the money. During a visit to the Dower House, he stole £50 from Caroline Pemberton's purse. Although he seemed full of remorse when William made him confess what he'd done, he was actually very pleased with himself when he was allowed to work the debt off – he felt he'd got one over on Caroline.

Some of his youthful energies were channelled into being part of a band called Dross, which he formed with Jazzer and Jazzer's brother; he also developed a taste for lawbreaking, and, egged on by Jazzer, took to breaking into cars in order to joyride. After going to an open-air concert in September 2001, he persuaded Emma to come back to Ambridge with him in a car he had 'borrowed' from William. When a deer ran out in front of them, Ed couldn't avoid crashing. He showed considerable courage in pulling Emma away from the burning wreck, but knows that he is ultimately responsible for the major injuries she sustained. It is not yet clear whether the accident, and subsequent court appearance which led to a fine and community service, will make him take a more sober approach to life in future, or whether he'll simply go from bad to worse.

Joe **Grundy**

(Reg Johnston, Haydn Jones, Edward Kelsey)

Determined to prevent bailiffs taking action over the bankruptcy of Grange Farm in January 2000, Joe Grundy, armed with a shotgun, took up sentinel duty in the yard. It was a short-lived

Birth: 18.9.1921

gesture, stemming from a deep sense of shame that the tenancy of the farm had been lost in his lifetime. When the loss of the business was followed by eviction from the farmhouse, with the Grundys having to accept council accommodation in Borchester, Joe suffered a major breakdown. He killed the family's ferrets with a lump hammer, believing this was the best response to a council edict that they couldn't have pets. Shortly after, in a highly disturbed state, he left a note saying 'Sorry' to his family, then set off, trying to get back to Ambridge. It was a journey that almost cost him his life. Caught in the open, he would have died of hypothermia, had he not been found in a ditch by his grandson William.

Joe had been set on returning to the village for many reasons, but, above all, because he couldn't bear to be too far from the grave of his wife, Susan. They'd married in 1941 and stayed together for the next twenty-eight years, until her death. Thereafter, Joe always remembered it as a happy marriage, and, for the most part, it had been. For a short while he was so taken by Pru Harris, at the time of Tom Forrest's trial for manslaughter, that he would have contemplated leaving Susan for her if Tom had been convicted. But, this interlude apart, he generally accepted what he considered his responsibilities as a husband, as well as those as a father to two growing lads, Alf and Eddie.

They weren't easy to deal with after losing Susan, and Joe often felt the lack of female companionship. He was a rival to Bill Insley in courting Martha Woodford, until he started finding it too much like hard work. Adverts in a lonely hearts column brought a brief friendship with Sandra Haimes, and also a rather awkward meeting with Marjorie Antrobus. There was also a dalliance with one of Robert Snell's business contacts, Patience Tait, but the woman who has played the biggest part in Joe's life in recent years has been his daughter-in-law, Clarrie, who joined the Grundy household on marrying younger son Eddie in 1981.

Grange Farm was in a fairly chaotic state at the time. Joe, never the most punctilious of farmers, had let it go into decline after Susan's death, and seemed to lose all interest in it when brucellosis was diagnosed in half his dairy herd. Elder son Alf was more interested in pursuing a criminal rather than agricultural career, but Eddie opted to help his father out, with a view to one day taking over the tenancy. They started up a turkey enterprise and managed to render the farm finances temporarily stable. When Clarrie joined them, Joe grudgingly had to adjust his notions of what constituted acceptable décor and hygiene for a farmhouse, but grew to be very fond of her, especially when she gave birth to the grandsons, William and Ed, who would ensure the continuation of the Grundy line.

Joe constantly looked for ways to supplement farm income by other means. Poaching often filled the family pot, especially on Bonfire Night, when there were plenty of other explosions to put the likes of Tom Forrest or George Barford off the scent. The land at Grange Farm was rented out for activities as diverse as pop concerts and auto-cross, while the craze for mineral water led Joe to explore the potential of bottling a spring he and Eddie discovered when burying a calf in 1991. Like most of his other schemes, this came to nothing when neither Jack Woolley nor

Cameron Fraser were willing to invest in it.

Not for the first time, Joe considered himself let down by the great and good of Ambridge. Successive landlords found him and his family difficult to deal with. Simon Pemberton tried to evict them after the milking parlour burned down in 1996. Brian Aldridge was generally more sympathetic when Borchester Land took over the Estate, but even he couldn't prevent their loss of the tenancy, for which Joe still holds something of a grudge against the Aldridges. He has mixed feelings about the Archers, too, blaming Phil and David for conspiring against him when he was convicted of not dipping his sheep properly. He disparaged the creation of the Dan Archer Memorial Playground as another landmark to the greater glory of the Archer family, until his campaign to have Susan commemorated as well led to a small garden dedicated to her memory being incorporated within it. Never afraid of going against the grain, he left the congregation of St Stephen's to become a Methodist, although never quite embracing the ideal of temperance.

As visitors to The Bull have sometimes found to their cost, he is usually willing to dispense rural wisdom for the price of a drink. He knows the full eighty-one verses of 'The Hobhound of Ambridge', and can chill the marrow of an audience with his rendition of the Borsetshire ghost story 'John Briar and the Squire'. For a time he was even a celebrity on Radio Borsetshire, telling country tales in 'Joe's Jottings', until it was realized most of his stories were pilfered from other sources.

Thanks to Eddie's unwavering resolve to bring the Grundys home, Joe is now once more securely established in Ambridge. His perennial complaint of farmer's lung, which in the past frequently stopped him doing heavy work whenever anyone else was available to do it, seems to be in abeyance. Inspired by the example of his grandfather, who lived to be ninety-five, he can reasonably look forward to some good years ahead, with plenty of time to be spent in the convivial company of Jolene at The Bull, rather than in trying to scratch out a living from the unforgiving land at Grange Farm.

Susan **Grundy**

Whenever Joe Grundy wants to make a point about the qualities desirable in a woman, he invokes the memory of 'my Susan'. She married him in 1941, incurring the wrath of her parents to

Birth: 6.3.1923
Death: 1969

do so. Her mother, a deeply religious woman, felt Joe was such an unsuitable choice of husband that she could never bring herself to speak to him after the wedding.

Having grown up on a farm, Susan was quite capable of helping Joe run Grange Farm reasonably successfully. She was a good wife, not only skilled at producing marmalade but also happy to cook her husband his favourite meal of steak and kidney pie every Saturday for the twenty-eight years of their marriage. She was an equally devoted mother, and what little sense of ethics her sons, Alf and Eddie, possess they inherited from her, not their father. Her sudden death in 1969 was keenly felt by all of them. Joe, who found her collapsed on the scullery floor, misses her still, but draws comfort from regularly visiting her grave in St Stephen's churchyard. On his initiative, a small garden area within the Dan Archer Memorial Playground is dedicated to Susan's memory.

William **Grundy**

(Philip Molloy)

Whether setting traps for rats, strengthening the pheasant-rearing pens against predators, or seeing off crows and magpies, William Grundy takes his duties as underkeeper on the Estate shoot

Birth: 9.2.1983

extremely seriously. He's also proving to be a likeable, if untidy, tenant at the Dower House, where he lodges with his godmother, Caroline Pemberton. Clarrie Grundy takes considerable pride in watching the way her elder son is developing into a hard-working and responsible member of the Ambridge community; she's only too aware that, given the other male Grundys' propensity for flouting the law, and some of William's own behaviour in the past, he might very well have turned out differently.

He didn't make the best of starts, being born two weeks overdue and then proving to be a fractious baby. He wasn't any easier as a toddler, when he greeted younger brother Ed's arrival by some attention-seeking tantrums and long spells hiding under the table. Loxley Barratt Primary School didn't look as though it was going to bring out the best in him either, though Clarrie's fears that he wouldn't settle there proved to be unfounded. At home he could be a handful, not least when, at six years old, he decided to play with Joe's shotgun, blissfully unaware of the danger he was creating, until the gun went off – fortunately harming no one.

Soon the Grundy flair for trying to profit in unorthodox ways started to show. He had a go at selling the number plates from one of Eddie's cars, and not only admired Bert Fry's prize apples at the Flower and Produce Show, but decided to pinch some as well. By the time he was twelve, he was being initiated into the art of poaching trout from the Home Farm fishing lake, and being taught the mysteries of ferreting for rabbits by his father. Although he said he didn't want to become a farmer, he was clearly good at handling cattle and other livestock around Grange Farm. A dormant interest in wildlife started to burgeon again as he looked after a variety of injured or orphaned animals, including Lucky the duck and the unimaginatively named Stripy the badger. It was when he wanted to know more about the best way to look after a baby jackdaw that William had one of his first encounters with Jack Woolley's gamekeeper, George Barford.

George was to have a considerable influence as William, going through secondary school without any clear idea of where his future lay, became interested in the possibility of gamekeeping. It wasn't an instant conversion to being an upright citizen, however. He was caught poaching again at Home Farm by Debbie Aldridge and Steve Oakley in 1995, and was later discovered smoking behind the Village Hall when he should have been at school.

A cigarette may inadvertently have played a large part in changing William's behaviour. He was upset when he thought the fire in the Grange Farm milking parlour and outbuildings, in which the family's farm dog, Gyp, died, may have been caused by one of his carelessly discarded stubs. Faulty wiring proved to be the real cause, but the experience served to shake him up. When Jill Archer gave the Grundys a replacement dog, Tess, William took charge of training and caring for it. He also showed an increasing interest in the Estate shoot. George, impressed enough by his attitude to tell Jack Woolley he might one day make a good keeper, started using him as casual labour.

Much more enthusiastic about practical than academic work, William kept making excuses to take time off school. Apart from helping Debbie Aldridge at lambing time, he had his own pedigree Jersey cow, Posh Spice, to look after. Godmother Caroline had provided the money for Posh, to replace an earlier cow of William's – Ginger Spice – who had been the first calf born to the herd re-established after the fire. William took great pride in preparing Posh for the Felpersham Show, where she won fourth prize in 1998. She had a calf in turn – Baby Spice – before being sold to help alleviate the Grundys' mounting debts.

William repaid a more personal debt to George Barford by successfully searching for him after an assault by deer poachers left him wounded in the Country Park. With encouragement from George, and a promise from Jack Woolley that he would be taken on as an underkeeper if he did well in his exams, William finally got down to working on his GCSEs and performed creditably well. When Brian Aldridge masterminded the absorption of the Grey Gables shoot into the larger Estate enterprise, he agreed that William should be kept on, now answerable to head keeper Greg Turner. They worked well together and seem to develop a mutual professional respect.

Where William's working life began to unfold well, his domestic arrangements were badly hit by his family's eviction from Grange Farm. It was during the turmoil this caused that Caroline offered him his own rooms at the Dower House, thus sparing him the misery of life in Meadow Rise flats. When grandfather Joe could no longer stand living in Borchester, and went missing while trying to return to Ambridge, it was William, with the help of his working dog, Meg, who found him. Angry with his father for not facing up to the problems that led to the loss of Grange Farm earlier, William became furious when he subsequently realized that Eddie was taking revenge by poaching the Home Farm fishing lakes again. His response clearly showed he was maturing into an independent and strong-minded young man.

With a job and accommodation in place, some villagers wonder when he's going to get himself a serious romantic attachment. He used to get on well with Brenda Tucker when they were children, and had something of a crush on Debbie Aldridge when he helped her with lambing. For the time being, however, his priorities appear to lie elsewhere. While he's learning how to run a large-scale shoot, any Borsetshire Lady Chatterleys looking for a spare gamekeeper must learn to be patient.

Basil **Guinness** 'Lofty'

(Rikki Fulton)

Escaping on holiday to Edinburgh in 1951 from the clutches of one Basil (Grove, her married boss at Borchester Dairies), Christine Archer immediately fell for another, this time a likeable Scots lad known as Lofty. The attraction was mutual, and, since he wanted to be a farmer, it could have been a match made in heaven. Chris wanted him to visit Ambridge, but, although he sent her a Christmas card, he never ventured south of the border.

Shiv **Gupta**

(Shiv Grewal)

Usha's Coventry-based older brother, Shiv, is a rock in times of trouble. In 1995, he offered moral support by coming to stay with Usha during the trial of the thugs who had subjected her to racist attacks. Something of a gourmet himself, he wasn't impressed when Usha's boyfriend, Richard Locke, offered him a lunch of peanut butter sandwiches with half a tomato, although a mutual passion for cricket later helped some kind of friendship develop between them. Shiv had been a good enough cricketer to have a trial for the county, and enjoyed arguing with Richard and David Archer about who had been the greatest all-rounder in the world.

He used his own experience of moving from a smaller firm to a larger one to encourage Usha to go ahead with the merger of Hebden & Gupta with Jefferson Crabtree in 1996. A couple of years later, it was support of a different kind he offered, when Richard's affair with Shula Hebden came to light. Shiv was pleased his sister showed such a positive attitude to the end of the relationship, and later heartily approved of her picking up the threads of her love life with Adrian Manderson.

Usha **Gupta**

(Sudha Bhuchar, Souad Faress)

Usha Gupta's earliest memories are of Kampala in Uganda, where her father worked as a doctor. She wasn't there for long because when Idi Amin decided to expel the Asian community, the

Birth: 1962

Guptas moved to join family members in Coventry, where Usha completed her schooling. Having trained in London to become a solicitor, she moved back to Coventry, where she started going out with a junior hospital doctor, Rajiv. Within a short while she began to feel restless, so, in 1991, when Mark Hebden decided his Borchester practice needed another partner, she put her relationship on hold, and moved to Borsetshire.

Shula Hebden was unsettled by how well Usha and Mark got on, but theirs was strictly a business relationship. The new partner was clearly hard-headed: she rejected Mark's original offer of a 70–30 split in the business, insisting on full equality in the partnership. It took her a while to get used to the politics of market-town life. She successfully supported Susan Carter's fight for equal pay in Sir Sidney Goodman's canning factory, only to be surprised when a close friend of Sir Sidney's subsequently withdrew the contract for a shopping centre from Hebden & Gupta. She was soon up to speed, however, and, by the time of Mark's fatal accident in 1993, was able to take full responsibility for running the practice, with the help of an old university friend, Nick, as locum.

For her first couple of years in the area, she lived in the flat over the office, but was gradually attracted by the idea of living in Ambridge. She liked the friendliness of the villagers; Jill Archer invited her to supper, Bert Fry and Neil Carter initiated her into the mysteries of socialising at The Bull, while Marjorie Antrobus, mistakenly believing Usha to be an expert cook, positively insisted she address the WI on 'A Taste of India'. When Blossom Hill Cottage came up for sale, she decided it was time to experience the joys of rural life, and, despite an unhelpful attitude from Peggy Woolley, who was handling the sale for her daughter Lilian, bought it in September 1993.

At first she encountered only minor problems, such as Bert mistaking her intentions for the garden and digging most of it up. But when she became subject to a series of racist attacks in 1995, her faith in country living was tested almost to destruction. The ordeal began when she was mugged after an evening out with Dr Richard Locke. Next, a rock was thrown through a window at Blossom Hill Cottage, then a swastika and racist slogans were painted on the walls. The hate campaign culminated in ammonia being thrown at Usha's face by helmeted thugs outside The Bull. Although her arms blocked most of the ammonia, she suffered some corneal abrasion, and, for a time, was worried about losing her sight.

This last assault made her decide to sell up and return to city life. She put the cottage up for sale and was in negotiations to sell the business as well, when Richard intervened to stop her going. He and Usha had grown close during the course of her troubles. She'd let him move into her spare room, as a business arrangement in the first place, but they quickly became more to each other. Richard was prepared to buy the cottage himself, but wanted Usha to stay with him – he loved her. With his support, she coped with the prosecution of her attackers, 'Spanner' Bridges and Craven, although it was a long time before she felt comfortable in the company of Roy Tucker, who had been a friend to her assailants.

Operating as a stand-alone solicitor was becoming increasingly difficult, so, in 1996 she joined forces with the Felpersham-based firm of Jefferson Crabtree. She was constantly kept busy, defending Eddie Grundy against an unfounded charge of assault on George Barford, among other cases. Acting on a suggestion from one of her new colleagues, she also decided to work for her Higher Court Advocacy exams, at the expense of taking any holidays.

Richard was also being kept busy, particularly by the complications that arose from the death of Mrs Barraclough. Inevitably, the relationship suffered, and, by April 1998, Usha was confiding in Shula that things weren't going well. All the more humiliating, then, for her to discover that Shula was actually having an affair with Richard at the time. She suffered real pain as he moved out of Blossom Hill Cottage and then left Ambridge altogether, but at least she had the consolation of telling Shula exactly what she thought of her.

She didn't let it stop her passing her advocacy exams, nor from continuing to take an active part in village life. She helped Janet Fisher train for the Jubilee 2000 march in aid of cancelling Third World debt and walked the Birmingham to London leg with her. Her friendship with Ruth Archer, which had been close enough for her to act as an honorary supporter at Pip's christening, when her Hindu faith ruled her out from being a godmother, deepened further as she helped Ruth come to terms with the effects of her breast cancer. Her legal skills were much in demand as well. Kathy Perks and Roy Tucker both had occasion to use her services, but perhaps the client with most to thank her for was Tom Archer, who, largely thanks to Usha's efforts, was found not guilty in his landmark GMO trial.

She sees her parents, or Ma and Pa, as she calls them, from time to time, and meets up with her brother, Shiv, whenever she can. Her Auntie Satya can be an overbearing presence whenever she comes to Ambridge, but Usha is always grateful for her concern and loves her cooking. But there's another reason for the sparkle lately in Usha's eye: after a brief flirtation with Shiv's friend Ashok, a more serious relationship seemed to have started with barrister Adrian Manderson. Will it go anywhere? Don't expect Usha to tell you. Like the expert solicitor she is, she always knows when to keep her own counsel.

Sandra **Haimes**

(Gillian Goodman)

Delighted to get a response to his lonely hearts advert in the *Echo* in 1987, Joe Grundy smartened himself up for his dates with Sandra Haimes. She was impressed enough to visit Grange Farm with her son, Jason. It wasn't Clarrie going to kill a chicken that put her off, or Eddie leaving Tex the ferret under the sofa; she even took the news that Joe was only a tenant farmer in her stride, and almost coped with Eddie asking for a loan to pay the rent: it was William and Edward locking Jason in the coal cellar that finally convinced her Joe wasn't suitable husband material.

Mr and Mrs **Hall**

(Philip Garston-Jones)

The Halls and their son, Leslie, who were spending a camping holiday at Brookfield in 1956, happened to choose a week when Doris was away. Mrs Hall assumed Dan was a widower and insisted on cooking him faggots and peas for his tea. After the Halls' tent caught on fire and there was no room at The Bull, Dan put them up in the house until they were able to improvise a new shelter with some canvas normally used on the hayricks.

Mr **Hannan**

(Martyn Read)

Mr Hannan was the prosecutor at the Magistrates' Court hearing when Tom Archer appeared there in 1999 accused of trashing a crop of GM rape at Home Farm.

Mr **Hapgood-Harman**

Mr Hapgood-Harman, whose formal title suggests that he might have been one of the old school, was editor of the *Borchester Echo* until his retirement in 1976 cleared the way for the young pretender, Simon Parker. He had to step in again the following year, however, when Simon fell out with the *Echo*'s proprietor, Jack Woolley, and again in 1978, when a restless Simon left for Kathmandu.

Gilbert **Harding**

(Self)

A major media star of the 1950s, Gilbert Harding was to experience national fame as a panel member of the TV quiz show *What's My Line*. He also appeared in a Cliff Richard film and conducted an interview with Mae West, but it's debatable whether his finest moment wasn't opening the 1952 Ambridge village fête. Mrs P got in a real lather in case he spoke to her. Given Mr Harding's reputation for acid comments, perhaps it's as well he didn't.

Ronald **Hardwicke**

Whisper the name Ronald Hardwicke among certain members of the British expatriate population in Spain and you will see grown men quiver. Ill-advisedly, Julia Pargetter borrowed £30,000 from him in 1998 to cover some gambling debts. Unable to repay him, she returned to Lower Loxley. When well-spoken Hardwicke found he wasn't getting the response he wanted from e-mails and phone calls to her, he sent round a couple of his highly muscular business associates, who had a word with Nigel. Subsequently, Julia sold some jewellery, begged money from her children and finally managed to pay off the debt.

General Sir Borthwick **Hare**   'Bunny'

(Bernard Brown)

Freddie Danby couldn't have been more surprised to see who was escorting Marjorie Antrobus to the Ambridge barn dance in October 1987 – his old commanding officer, Bunny Hare. Bunny was no stranger to the battlefield, nor, as it proved, to the dance floor, where he took over calling from Nigel Pargetter and made the evening go with such a zing that Marjorie called a truce with Martha Woodford over their rivalry for Freddie Danby's attentions.

George **Harper**

When Ambridge's cricket team was looking for an umpire in 1996, Phil suggested George Harper, who is retired and lives at Waterley Cross. Sid wasn't keen, saying that George was too old and that his sight was failing. It took some time before Sid himself noticed that Bert had taken to wearing a white coat and was practising flailing arm movements in the pub. Bert eventually got the job.

Birth: 1.7.1920

Charles **Harvey**

(Victor Lucas)

Charles came to Ambridge with his wife, Jean, and daughter, Susan, in 1975, when he bought Bull Farm. An accountant by profession, he spent little time at home, although did set about growing his own vegetables soon after arriving. When pigeons started damaging the crops, he followed Carol Tregorran's advice and asked a Borchester shooting club to come and deal with them. Unfortunately, the directions given were a little hazy and the club members went to Ambridge Hall instead, where Laura Archer was startled to see what looked like a small invasion force enter her garden. Charles smoothed over the incident by sending her a dozen bottles of wine.

He showed his generosity again, some time after, by arranging to pay for the floodlights so that Ambridge Wanderers could replay Jephcott at the Borchester United ground. Ever busy with his work, he hasn't been as involved in village life as his wife, but is always willing to stop and chat, especially if it gives him the chance to mention how well Susan is doing, now that she's working in the south of England.

Jean **Harvey**

(Patricia Gibson)

One of life's great organizers, Jean Harvey has been active in many aspects of village life since coming to live at Bull Farm with her family over a quarter of a century ago. With previous experience as a WI president, she lost no time in bucking up the Church Fund Appeal and taking on the organization of the village fête. Finding a like-minded spirit in Laura Archer, they soon became firm friends.

In 1979, Jean was elected on to the Parish Council and, for many years, was a mainstay of its activities, apart from a brief period in 1986, when she and her husband, Charles, went to Singapore for six months. She was also active in delivering meals-on-wheels and was involved in the town-twinning project with Meyruelle in 1994. She takes great pride in her appearance, never settling for less than the best, according to Peggy Woolley. After more than twenty years of active service on the Parish Council, she finally retired in June 2000. Her many well-wishers hope that the extra time she's gained thereby can be put to good use in pursuing her twin passions of gardening and golf.

Susan **Harvey**

🙢 SEE: *Jean Harvey, Charles Harvey*

Siobhan **Hathaway**

(Caroline Lennon)

As soon as Siobhan saw Honeysuckle Cottage in March 1999, she fell in love with it. She was moving to Ambridge from London with her husband, Tim, and the picturesque dwelling

Birth: 13.6.1965

perfectly fitted her image of what country life should be. Having precisely planned her life in terms of travel, marriage and her career as a translator up to that point, she felt a village was the best place to start a family. She quickly discovered a downside to the rural idyll: no sooner had her pregnancy ended in miscarriage than all of Ambridge seemed to know about it, thanks to Jason the builder, who had put two and two together when he realized the Hathaways had dropped their plans to have a nursery.

She worked through a profound sense of loss and even managed to maintain her friendship with Elizabeth Archer, who was about to become a mother herself. A new job, working for a publishing company, provided satisfying challenges, but meant she was abroad a lot of the time. When village gossip revealed that Tim had been getting too close to Janet Fisher during her absences, she accepted his assurances that nothing serious had happened, but could be forgiven if she was left with some doubts about the strength of the marriage.

Tim **Hathaway**

(Jay Villiers)

Tim trained to be a doctor in the army, had a practice in Islington, but quickly seemed at home with country living when he took over Richard Locke's practice in 1999. George

Birth: 4.2.1960

Barford soon decided that the new doctor was the sort of 'incomer' Ambridge could do with, while Susan Carter, who continued as a practice receptionist, summed him up as being trustworthy. He tried hard to support his wife, Siobhan, through the aftermath of her miscarriage, although initially found it difficult to talk about his own sense of loss. In an attempt to get her out of the house and active again, he went horse-riding with her for an afternoon, without admitting that he had almost no experience himself, till his lack of control on Marcellus made it obvious he was a novice.

When Siobhan started spending time away from home for work reasons, Tim found himself drawn to Janet Fisher. He followed a kiss under the mistletoe by giving her a scarf, which he'd originally bought for Siobhan. Janet backed off before anything more could happen, but tongues had already started wagging, somewhat damaging Tim's trustworthy image. Whether he had done long-term harm to his marriage remained to be seen.

Audrey **Hebden** 'Bunty'

(Sheila Allen)

Elizabeth was unkind about Bunty's 'rent-a-tent' outfit at Mark and Shula's wedding, but Shula made strenuous efforts to get on with her rather bossy mother-in-law. When Bunty gave her some

Birth: 20.2.1922

curtains patterned with swans, however, Shula was quick to pass them on to Clarrie Grundy, saying the birds looked more like vultures. Devastated by Mark's death, and initially suspicious of Daniel's adoption, Bunty's relations with Shula are these days pretty harmonious.

Joanna **Hebden**

With her flaming red hair and brown eyes, Mark's younger sister, Joanna, could have been a luminous beauty in the pre-Raphaelite style. Sadly, she was anything but fragile at the time of Mark and Shula's planned wedding in 1981. She was desperate to be a bridesmaid, but was two stones overweight, so her mother put her on a diet. The wedding was cancelled, and, when Mark proposed again, Joanna's ambition was, thankfully, not resurrected.

Mark **Hebden**

(Richard Derrington)

Birth: 20.2.1955
Death: 17.2.1994

Shula was annoyed when her father invited Mark to help with the haymaking: after just a few weeks, she was already finding her new boyfriend a touch boring. But the blue-eyed, black-haired solicitor hadn't always been such a goody-goody: he joined the school choir at the age of ten but got the sack a year later for smoking. He learnt a lesson, however, and promptly gave up.

Mark, in fact, was made of strong stuff: maybe the martial arts he'd studied (he was Borchester Under-14 Judo Champion) gave him the focus he needed. Although he'd once been afraid of heights, he joined the Borchester Buzzards Hang-Gliding Club, and, later, the Borchester Skydivers, and on matters of principle, especially in court, nothing would get in his way. Defending a couple of hunt saboteurs in 1980, he spoke out against the 'socially acceptable amateurs' on the bench – one of whom was Phil Archer. The ensuing bad atmosphere didn't stop him, however, from proposing to Shula at New Year.

She accepted and the wedding date was set, but, over the summer, she had doubts, and they only eventually married in September 1985. In the meantime, during their split, Mark had dallied with Shula's arch-enemy, Jackie Woodstock, who moved in with him at Penny Hassett. He then became engaged to blonde, bubbly Sarah Locke, with her Klosters perma-tan, but yet again was unlucky in love when his wedding to her was first postponed, then cancelled. Shula, who'd by now realized that Mark was the man for her, was relieved, and saw him off at the airport to Hong Kong, where he'd accepted a timely job offer, and where he might mend his broken heart. A year later she flew out to see him, but their time together was strained. The following month, to confound her, Mark returned and proposed on Lakey Hill, thereafter their special place.

If anyone thought the pair could breathe a sigh of relief and sink into the blissful comfort of the marriage bed, however, they'd have been wrong. Mark became a busy local councillor for the SDP, and as a member of the Planning Committee had to tell his father-in-law that he'd be voting against his barn conversion plans. Then, no sooner had Mark and Shula decided they were ready to start a family than Mark took on a job in Birmingham. The commuting, and Shula's failure to conceive, put strains on them both, and, in March 1989, after a big row, Mark took off to stay with his friends Marian and Johnny in Moseley. They soon made up, however, and Shula saw a gynaecologist, who told them to 'keep trying'. Mark was thrilled when Shula became pregnant in October 1990, and did his best to sustain her when the pregnancy was found to be ectopic. It was another low in their relationship, and Mark was wounded when he found Shula had been to Matthew Thorogood and had asked to be put on the pill. By early 1991, however, he was cracking open the champagne as a result of Shula's admission that she couldn't imagine life without children.

Realizing that he, too, had to put something into the equation, Mark resigned from his Birmingham firm and set up a practice in Borchester, taking on Usha Gupta as a partner. The only person not pleased was Kenton, who feared that part of Mark's thinking was to keep an eye on the investment he and Shula had made in the antique shop he was running in the same premises. But yet again, when the signs of domestic harmony were better than for some time, life intervened. Shula was distraught when her sister, Elizabeth, told her she'd aborted her baby, though judicious Mark believed that only Elizabeth had the right to decide. Nine months later, after the birth of Ruth's baby, he supported Shula when she concluded that she wanted a child at any cost, including IVF, and he went along with the often undignified procedure with great good humour, even giving Shula her hormone injections. Their first attempt in June 1993 was, sadly, unsuccessful, and, though they could have made another attempt in the autumn, Mark was by then defending Susan Carter for hiding her fugitive brother, and life was just too busy. By February 1994, however, the time seemed right.

On 17 February, Mark warned Shula he might be a little late home as he had a tricky injunction case to handle. She wasn't best pleased, as she was hosting Caroline Bone's hen party and Mark had promised to wait at table. In the event, Mark called her from the car to say he wouldn't be late after all – but in fact he never made it home. Overtaken by a reckless driver on a blind bend, and swerving to avoid Caroline, who'd been thrown from her horse as a result, Mark crashed his car into a tree. He died instantly.

His funeral was held at St Stephen's, where he and Shula had been married. Mark never knew that Shula was pregnant, and that she would bear him the child they'd both longed for. Just over a year after his death, on what would have been Mark's fortieth birthday, Shula and Caroline climbed to the top of Lakey Hill. 'I'm on top of the world,' Shula revealed, had been Mark's rather lame joke about the place. And she also told her friend how, when they'd lost their first baby, she and Mark had clambered all the way up and had yelled out their pain into the wind.

After everything they'd been through together, it's no wonder it took Shula a very long time to work through her grief. But Mark is certainly not forgotten. His carefully tended grave in the churchyard, and the Cricket Club's Mark Hebden Memorial Trophy, awarded each year to the winner of the Single Wicket Competition, keep his memory alive. The inscription on the trophy perhaps best sums him up: 'In memory of a Talented Player and a Valued Friend'.

Reginald **Hebden**

Father of Mark and Joanna, and married to the overpowering Bunty, mild-mannered Reg was a solicitor until his retirement. The Hebdens were concerned when Shula's new husband, Alistair Lloyd, wanted to adopt Daniel, fearing for their grandparents' rights, but, after Jill and Phil's tactful intervention, Reg was reassured and talked his wife round. He and Bunty now enjoy helping out with Daniel during the school holidays.

Daniel **Hebden Lloyd**

(Dominic Davies)

Shula's miracle baby, Daniel, was conceived by IVF and born, weighing 7lb 12oz, after his father, Mark's, death. Although he was a placid baby, Shula has nonetheless had many worrying times with him. When he was eight months old, she feared he'd contracted meningitis, though thankfully it was another, unnamed, virus. When Daniel fell ill in 1998, though, a diagnosis was not so speedy, and it was almost with relief that Shula learnt he had systemic juvenile rheumatoid arthritis, a treatable condition.

> **Birth:** 14.11.1994

Shula was already seeing Alistair Lloyd, whom she married in 1999 with Daniel as ring-bearer. His stepfather has encouraged Daniel's interest in wildlife, allowing him to keep a hamster and stick insects and taking him on vole and hedgehog hunts. When Daniel drew a picture of Alistair entitled 'My Dad', it confirmed Alistair's decision to adopt him, though there was a nervous moment when Daniel made a point of showing the adoption social worker his biological father's grave, conveniently next to a nest of stag beetles in which he was interested. After the adoption hearing, he enjoyed a noisy fast-food lunch and has much else to look forward to: with the move to The Stables, there is at last room in his bedroom to lay out Mark's old train set.

Shula **Hebden Lloyd** née Archer

(Judy Bennett)

These days a respectably married mother of one, owner of the Ambridge riding stables, church warden and valued member of the community, it's hard to remember Shula as the wild child she once was. But her father Phil's reputed favourite had a troubled adolescence, then took off overland to Bangkok, and, as she hit forty, embarked on a scandalous affair with the village doctor. Maybe showjumper Ann Moore was right when, assessing Shula's chances as a competition rider, she concluded that Shula had the potential, but was rather headstrong.

> **Birth:** 8.8.1958

Kenton's twin, Shula was judged 'a bit backward' at the village school but gained five O-levels at the grammar. Her future career posed a problem, though: her parents wanted her to train as a vet, but Shula's real passion was horse-riding. To pacify them, she did one year of her A-level course before dropping out in favour of a secretarial and business studies course at the Tech, which prudent Phil had insisted on as a fall-back. In parallel, however, Shula was spending all the time she could at her Aunt Lilian's riding stables, schooling her favourite horse, Mr Jones. On Lilian's advice, she signed up on a horse management course, but at the end of it there was no job for her, and she had to brush up her shorthand and typing and settle for the job of office junior at Rodway & Watson's estate agents.

Shula found the work dull, but there were other distractions, such as good-looking Nick Wearing, who was doing a year's placement at Brookfield. Together they embarked on a round-the-world trip, but he abandoned her in the Far East and she came home dejected, having had her passport and money stolen. Nick, in Phil's eyes at least, was the latest in a long line of undesirable boyfriends, probably the worst of whom had been journalist Simon Parker, who took Shula's virginity in a Netherbourne cornfield in June 1977. With Shula's reinstatement at Rodway's, however, Phil didn't have long to wait before an apparently more suitable candidate appeared in the shape of solicitor Mark Hebden. Patrick Lichfield's photos show Shula radiant in a white, high-necked dress when she and Mark married in September 1985. Their courtship hadn't been all straightforward. She'd been swayed by Robin Catchpole and had been out with Nigel Pargetter and Martin Lambert, but Mark was, she now knew, the man for her.

The prototype yuppy couple, they set up in a flat in the Old Wool Market in Borchester before moving to Glebe Cottage, which Doris had left to Shula on Dan's death. Shula took on a new role as agent to the Berrow Estate, while Mark climbed the corporate ladder. When Shula got a craving for peanut butter in February 1987, neither was thrilled to think she might be pregnant, as a baby wasn't yet part of their plans. But she wasn't, and all was well. In 1988, however, they decided they did want to start a family, and Mark suggested they move closer to Birmingham when he got a job with a bigger firm there. But he soon realized that it would be impossible to prise Shula away from her close and loving family.

A year on, and still no sign of a baby; Shula had a 'well woman' check and then saw a gynaecologist. This revealed she'd had endometriosis, but she was told there was no reason why she shouldn't conceive. When she did, though, in October 1990, the pregnancy was ectopic. Shula lost a fallopian tube, and she almost lost Mark as well when she became withdrawn. The rift was repaired, but there was to be no escape from baby traumas. In April 1992, discovering that her sister, Elizabeth, was unhappily pregnant, Shula wanted to adopt the baby. When Elizabeth had an abortion, followed swiftly by Ruth's successful pregnancy, Shula was devastated, but it crystallized her determination to have a child, and she and Mark sought IVF treatment. Their second attempt was successful and Daniel was born in November 1994. By then, however, Mark was dead, and Shula had to cope with life as a widow and single mother.

She returned to work in May 1995, and was thrown together with Simon Pemberton, who was running the Estate for his father. Although he was arrogant, Shula felt for his isolation in the village, and they began seeing each other, but he betrayed her with another woman. When she finished with him, his response was to hit her. In 1997, Shula quit her job as Agent to the Estate in protest against Simon's heartless attempts to evict the Grundys, and, learning later that he'd also hit Debbie Aldridge, Shula persuaded her to go to the police and offered to give evidence herself. At the subsequent court hearing, however, Simon got off with a fine.

In late 1997, she met vet Alistair Lloyd, who took an instant shine to her. Shula's response was more measured, and, when Daniel was hospitalized in April 1998, she found herself attracted to the local doctor, Richard Locke, who'd been such a support. Richard felt the same, and left his partner, Usha Gupta, for her, but Shula was out of her depth. She tried to tell Alistair of her deception, but, reluctant to hurt him, fudged telling him the truth. Inevitably, the full story came out, and Shula felt – correctly – that she'd badly mishandled the whole thing.

In the end, Alistair forgave her and they were married on 24 December 1999. Although Daniel at first refused to speak to his mother when she returned from honeymoon, he accepted the new arrangement well, and, in a curious legality, both Shula and Alistair formally adopted him.

Shula wanted no part in the long drawn-out Brookfield inheritance dispute and was delighted when it was resolved in David's favour. The chain of house moves which took Shula, Alistair and Daniel to the stables makes perfect sense, as Shula had bought the riding school from her aunt in the summer of 2001. She has her work, her family, her friends, the man and the child she loves. It seems unlikely that even Shula could want for more.

Robert **Heriot**

(Robin Bailey)

Robert Heriot was an artist whose services John Tregorran called on, in 1966, when he wanted a valuation on some canvases Ralph Bellamy was selling. When he came to Ambridge, Robert also took the opportunity to paint portraits of Richard Grenville and Hazel Trentham, while at the same time becoming very friendly with John's business partner, Dawn Kingsley. Some people assumed that he and Dawn would get married, but, although she went away with him for a while, nothing more permanent materialized.

Heydon Berrow

Heydon Berrow, which has Heydon Rise as its high point and then slopes down to Heydon Wood, is a large area of common land to the south of Ambridge. In the summer of 1998, the wooded area was filled with birdwatchers hoping for a glimpse of a black woodpecker, never before seen in Britain. George Barford worried about the effect on his game birds of having so many people tramping around, while other villagers found difficulty coping with the sudden influx of traffic. All in all, then, it was quite a relief when the woodpecker decided to move on.

John **Higgs**

Apart from a spell working as a handyman in the garden centre, John Higgs has spent most of his time with Jack Woolley, acting as a chauffeur. He was noted for having a permanent grin when he first came to Grey Gables in 1966, possibly connected to the fact that some women considered him irresistible. There's no doubt he found the smart cars he drove for Mr Woolley gave him a certain cachet when courting a lady friend in Hollerton.

Over the years another passion has developed: a love of gardening. He became so skilled at it that Mr Woolley, employing a horticultural form of *droit de seigneur*, once entered some of Higgs's chrysanthemums and dahlias in a flower show under his own name.

A lifelong smoker, and occasionally given to drinking too much, Higgs has always enjoyed a game of cards with Bert Horrobin, but doesn't like spending time with Grey Gables chef, Jean-Paul. The whole village wondered what type of Widow Twankey he would make in the 1998 pantomime, only to be denied the chance to find out when he lost his voice at the last moment. Generally happy with his lot, let no one whisper the word 'retirement' in his presence.

Hilda

Distantly related to the Grundys, Aunt Hilda was said to be on her last legs in 1992. Eddie headed up to see her in Aberdeen, making sure he was armed with photos of William and Edward looking at their best. He was delighted to return with the news that Hilda was sure to leave them something in her will. She also sent a message to Joe, saying that he was forgiven, though it's not clear what for. Sadly, however, Hilda is no longer with us, and her hints of leaving a substantial inheritance came to nothing.

Corinne **Holford**

(Barbara Flynn)

In October 1999, Corinne was the barrister prosecuting Tom Archer for his part in the destruction of the trial GM crop at Home Farm. Suggesting that he hadn't acted with 'lawful excuse', but had been prompted by sheer hotheadedness, she seemed on top of the case with her astute questioning of the toxicologist Professor Armstrong. She also subjected an expert called by the defence, Colin Finch, to some intelligently probing questions about horizontal gene transfer. However, in spite of her best efforts, the jury wasn't persuaded and chose to acquit Tom.

Steve **Holland**

(Colin Starkey)

It's fortunate that Kathy Perks was seeing policeman Dave Barry when her ex-husband, Steve, turned·up in Ambridge in 1985, wanting her back. Fearing Steve's temper, Kathy was scared to see him, but Dave brooked no nonsense when he explained to the errant Steve that, far from wanting a reconciliation, Kathy intended filing for divorce. Steve duly returned to Chesterfield, where, it was rumoured, he would waste no time in consoling himself.

Hollerton

There have been many brief and not-so-brief encounters at Hollerton Junction, Ambridge's nearest railway station since Beeching's axe fell at Borchester. Caroline Bone was touched when Robin Stokes turned up to collect her there one rainy night, advancing their romance a notch, and there a choked Sid saw off his daughter, Lucy, to Nottingham University. The rail link has made Hollerton, once a small market town, a target for developers in recent years, and alarm bells rang in Ambridge when plans were mooted to merge Loxley Barrett School with Hollerton's primary. Both schools have been saved – for now. Hollerton has something to offer both the musical and sporting resident. Its Silver Band welcomed Tom Forrest home after his acquittal on a manslaughter charge in 1957, and George Barford was later a keen band member, playing the cornet. The Hollerton Point-to-Point was a fixture of the Ambridge calendar in the 1950s. Mike Daly rode the Squire's horse to victory there in 1952, and, the following year, Christine Archer, riding Midnight, was pipped at the post by Reggie Trentham on a grey. She did, however, have the satisfaction of beating Clive Lawson-Hope.

Hollowtree Farm

Formerly known as Allard's Farm, it was bought by Phil Archer in August 1962 and the land incorporated into Ambridge Farmers Ltd. Phil, Jill and their three children (Elizabeth was not yet born) moved from

Coombe Farm into the farmhouse and renamed it Hollowtree. When Phil and Jill moved to Brookfield in 1970 on Dan's retirement, the house was sold to Nelson Gabriel, who converted it into flats and even lived there himself for a while. It was later bought back by Brookfield and became their pig unit. In one of Hollowtree's most memorable moments, Phil Archer was discovered there playing a piano that Joe and Eddie had abandoned in a shower of rain. Jethro Larkin, who had previously accidentally dropped a bale of hay on Phil's head, became convinced that his employer was temporarily disturbed, but the pigs munching nearby recorded no complaint. Indeed, productivity at Hollowtree may even have gone up. Latterly, Hollowtree has stood empty and silent, its contentedly grunting inhabitants disposed of when Brookfield went out of pigs. But with David's new beef scheme, the buildings have once again been pressed into use.

Holly

While Holly was going out with John Archer, in 1993, Pat hoped that this diligent young woman would set him a good example. But Holly's desire to do well in her exams and read history at university could never compete with the rather more earthy charms of Sharon Richards, whom John was managing to see at the same time. He got Holly a good luck card for her exams, but then took Sharon for a drink. That says it all, really.

Home Farm Estate

As befits the largest privately-owned farming operation in Ambridge, Home Farm has the largest farmhouse. It was built in the eighteenth century, converted into flats just after the Second World War, then reconverted into a single home when Brian Aldridge bought it from Ralph Bellamy in 1975. The solar-heated swimming pool he had installed in the garden three years later attests to the lifestyle enjoyed by Brian, his wife, Jennifer, and their family. The kitchen is sumptuously appointed and the dining-room, bedrooms and even the office are all fitted and decorated to expensively high standards. Walking round the farm, the visitor soon notices the Rookeries, three farm workers' cottages now rented out as holiday homes, as well as the large fishing lake and the riding course that Brian instituted when he decided to diversify his sources of income. A wide range of arable crops is grown, including linseed and rape, although the only livestock to be seen are sheep and deer. The large size of the fields and field entrances are often commented on; both Brian and his stepdaughter, Debbie, believe in the economies of scale, though Debbie is more environmentally conscious and has encouraged several initiatives, including beetle banks, to give wildlife a foothold on the farm.

Honeysuckle Cottage

One of the most picturesque cottages in Ambridge, with its central position overlooking the duck pond and village green, half-timbered Honeysuckle Cottage has recently been refurbished and extended by its new owners, Tim and Siobhan Hathaway. They were intrigued to find a 1950s photograph of a couple taken in the garden, who were identified as Walter Gabriel and Mrs P. Siobhan has had it framed and it hangs in the house in their honour.

Walter had bought the cottage in 1957 from Tim Wainwright, attracted by its three-quarters of an acre and good outbuildings. From it he ran his carrier's business, but, as with his farm, maintenance was never Walter's strong point, and, by 1977, the thatch was wearing thin and death-watch beetle discovered. Both were duly repaired. After Walter's death, Nelson himself lived in the cottage, continuing despite himself to do the garden and tend the productive plum trees. This could be why, after Nelson's funeral, the Hathaways were disturbed by the sound of digging – not the ghost of Nelson, but, it was rumoured, some of his former 'associates' looking for the loot from the fabled mail van robbery of 1967.

Hood's Farm

❧ SEE: *Kenton's Farm*

Arthur **Hood**   'Doughy'

(Arnold Ridley)

Baker 'Doughy' Hood learned his trade as an apprentice to Ben White, so it was only natural that, after many years working at sea, he should take the chance to buy Ben's bakery when it came up for sale in 1956. He didn't have the most auspicious of starts: in May of that year, he fell down a well, leaving all the bread to get burnt. With Rita Flynn as his assistant, he struggled to stay independent at a time when small bakeries were being bought up by big firms. He refused to sell the business to Hollerton Bakeries in 1960 because they wouldn't promise Rita a job as manageress.

He'd become very fond of her. Despite her protestations, he decided to leave her all his property in his will, so was naturally upset when she became engaged to Michael O'Leary and subsequently left Ambridge. For a while Laura Archer was a partner in the bakery, but, once she withdrew, Doughy saw no reason to refuse an offer from Juniper Bakeries. Thereafter, he had a series of odd jobs before leaving to join his nephew, Percy Hood, and his wife, Betty, in the North. At one stage he considered returning, but ultimately opted not to.

Betty **Hood**

(Dorothy Smith)

Betty was Percy Hood's wife, and mother to four children, Diana, Margaret, Joan and Roger, of whom Joan was the most troublesome. Not wanting to see this awkward teenager going out with skiffle-playing Jimmy Grange, Betty tried to steer her in the direction of Dusty Rhodes, only to be horrified when she learned of Dusty's criminal tendencies. After moving back north with the family in 1959, she was upset that Joan ran back to Ambridge, but later gave pemission for her difficult daughter to stay in the village, working for Carol Grey.

Cyril **Hood**

(Peter Howell)

It was typical of Bishop Cyril Hood that in the midst of the unkind gossip about Janet Fisher's relationship with Dr Hathaway he should make a point of being seen with her at one of her Easter services in 2001. He is a man of simple pleasures, who, on his first visit to Ambridge in 1987, derived more pleasure from a lunch of cheese and water than from the lavish feast Jack Woolley intended him to eat at Grey Gables. Of course, it's possible he'd simply lost his appetite, as he had been trying some Grange Farm scrumpy earlier in the day, when dropping in on villagers.

As a friend of the groom's, he was pleased to officiate at Jack Woolley's wedding to Peggy Archer, and showed good sense, as well as an open mind, when counselling Caroline Bone and Robin Stokes before the marriage that never was. When, in 1996, there was controversy about Janet's appointment to St Stephen's and the merging of the Ambridge parish with Edgeley, Penny Hassett and Darrington, he didn't duck the issues involved, but came to a meeting at the Village Hall to hear people's concerns. He is generally well liked and respected.

Percy **Hood**

(Ronald Baddiley)

When Percy Hood came to Ambridge with his wife and four children in 1956, he was making a return journey. Before the Second World War, he'd lived and worked on a smallholding in the village, until the agricultural depression drove him to leave the area and find work as a bailiff. On coming back, he set up in dairy farming at Court Farm, with the help of Dan Archer, who lent him some milking equipment. He should have felt at home, especially with his Uncle Doughy running the local bakery, but he never seemed completely at ease. Several of his cows were lost to yew poisoning, and he didn't get on well with Estate owner George Fairbrother. Without saying what he was up to, he went off for a short while in 1959, before coming back to announce he

Death: 1970

was going to take work as a bailiff again, this time on the Scottish border. Sure enough, he sold up and took his family with him. Little was heard of him thereafter, till news of his death filtered through in 1970.

Bert **Horrobin**

(William Eedle)

It's anyone's guess whether Bert will reach retirement from his work in road maintenance before a lifetime's heavy drinking and smoking takes its toll. Never the most cheerful of characters, he was inclined to disown his daughter Susan when he found out she was pregnant, but relented in time to be present for her marriage to Neil Carter. He's seen two of his sons, Clive and Keith, serve time in prison, while his other children, Stewart, Gary and Tracy, haven't given him much to smile about either. A night spent playing cards with John Higgs is about the best life has to offer Bert these days.

Clive **Horrobin**

(Alex Jones)

Clive Horrobin was only eleven when Tom Forrest caught him trespassing in the Country Park. Breaking rules was nothing new to Clive; while his sisters, Susan and Tracy, were generally well behaved, he was more like his brothers, Gary, Keith and Stewart, none of whom had much respect for authority. Where, to another youngster, the telling off from Tom Forrest might have been a turning point that set him back on the right track, it simply turned out to be a minor milestone on Clive's journey into troublemaking and criminal behaviour. By the time he was seventeen he had made his girlfriend, Sharon Richards, pregnant. When her parents threw them out, they lived with Clive's mum and dad, Bert and Ivy, for a short while. Then they took up an offer to use the spare room in his sister Susan's house, but made themselves unpopular by not doing their share of the household duties. The Reverend Jerry Buckle tried to help out by letting the young couple move into the Vicarage, but

Birth: 9.11.1972

Clive wasn't interested in becoming a responsible parent. He walked out on Sharon before the baby was born, helping himself to her ghetto-blaster on the way.

He drifted for a time, using his talent for fixing cars to pick up odd jobs. By April 1991, he was apparently keen to move back in with Sharon and their baby daughter, Kylie, but they were quite happy without him. Following this rebuff, Clive told Susan that he was a reformed character. This claim seemed less credible, when, having given up a job in a garage, he became hugely drunk at The Bull and made an obnoxious nuisance of himself at the Carters, when he went there looking for Sharon. Susan tried to make allowances for her brother, but Neil didn't believe he'd changed for the better.

By April 1993, Clive's behaviour was definitely on a downward spiral. With a thuggish young friend, Bruno Wills, he led an armed raid on the Ambridge post office. Kate and Debbie Aldridge got caught up as innocent bystanders, but it was Jack Woolley who suffered most. The shock of the raid caused him to collapse, and, when Betty Tucker tried to phone for an ambulance, Clive's response was to rip the phone off the wall before he and Bruno managed to get away. When they were caught later, Clive showed there was little honour among thieves by giving the police statements against his accomplice and their getaway driver.

Anxious not to go to prison, Clive escaped from remand and looked to Susan for help. She made the mistake of letting him stay for a night. Thereafter he extorted money, clothes and food from her by threatening to tell the police she had already helped him. The escape didn't work out: he was recaptured, found guilty and sentenced to six years in prison. He gave little sign of feeling remorse when Susan was subsequently given a six-month prison sentence for harbouring him while on the run.

Unsurprisingly, Betty was deeply upset by the raid, and, more than anyone, seemed concerned as Clive's release date approached in June 1997. The terms of the release dictated that he should live in London, but that didn't stop him turning up at Susan and Neil's house in July. He claimed that he wasn't going to stay, as a friend was setting him up with mini-cab work in the big city. However, he then used a fall his mother had as an excuse to stay on in Ambridge, saying that he needed to look after her. Not many people were happy to see him around, although Lynda Snell trusted him enough to let him help collect props for her production of *A Midsummer Night's Dream*. What she didn't realize was that he was using the opportunities this afforded to research the layout and contents of the houses he visited. After someone tipped off the police that he was breaking the conditions of his parole, Clive had to be careful not to be too visible in Ambridge. He wasn't best pleased when he worked out that George Barford must have been the source of the information against him.

A series of burglaries then occurred in the village, including one at George and Christine's home. Worse was to come when George, keeping an eye on the Country Park at a time when there'd been an outbreak of deer poaching, was attacked by an unidentified assailant and left with a broken arm, broken ribs and his face a mass of bruises. Eddie Grundy, who had been selling venison of dubious provenance, was suspected of being involved. Clive, however, seemed to have a cast-iron alibi: he could produce friends to swear he'd been in London on the night of the assault. He might have got away with it, but Sharon was able to undermine his story when she realized he'd given Kylie a birthday card two days late, so had actually been in Ambridge at the time of the attack.

To Eddie's great relief, Clive was arrested and charged with grievous bodily harm. He was then taken to court, found guilty and sentenced to five years' imprisonment. Whether a second lengthy spell in prison has the desired effect of changing his behaviour remains to be seen. Given his track record, the majority of inhabitants in Ambridge, including, sadly, most of his own family, have serious doubts about it.

Ivy **Horrobin**

(Cynthia Cherry)

In one of his unkinder moments, Eddie Grundy commented that Ivy has 'ears like satellite dishes'. One can only hope that they aren't as sensitive in picking up signals, as many disapproving words have been spoken about the Horrobin clan during their years at No. 6, The Green. Ivy has always been proud of what daughter Susan has achieved, and enjoys looking after Susan's children, Christopher and Emma Carter. Her other daughter, Tracy, hasn't been too much of a handful either, but the four sons she's had by husband, Bert, are a real problem. Stewart, Keith and Gary are no angels, but Clive, with his convictions for armed robbery and grievous bodily harm, has brought his mother the most heartache. Even at his worst, she's never disowned him, but kept on visiting him in prison.

She wishes she could see more of Kylie, Clive's daughter by Sharon Richards, although she may never become reconciled to what she considers to be an awful name. She takes on cleaning work when she can, at Blossom Hill Cottage and Arkwright Hall among other places, but scratch cards and bingo remain her main hope of radically improving her standard of living.

Tracy **Horrobin**

Tracy acted as bridesmaid at the wedding of her sister, Susan, to Neil Carter in 1984. It was probably the only occasion in her life when an uninformed onlooker might have been

Birth: 16.7.1975

tempted to murmur, 'What a charming girl!' She lacks the criminal tendencies exhibited by her brothers, but seems allergic to hard work and is unwilling to smile when a surly grimace will do.

Employed at the Bridge Farm dairy from late 1997 to 1999, she became highly skilled in finding new excuses for turning up late, or not at all. To Clarrie Grundy's enormous chagrin, she was made temporary supervisor there, after appearing to be the only person to take Helen Archer's programme of hazard analysis seriously. However, she didn't have the interpersonal skills needed to hold the post, and left after a fierce argument with Colin Kennedy. She went on to work at the Cat and Fiddle before joining the Cat's chef, Owen, when he moved to the Lower Loxley café. She didn't last long there; her interest in Owen was certainly not professional, and her interest in the customers was non-existent. She was asked to leave, and has since been reviewing her career options.

Florrie **Hoskins**

Florrie Hoskins, finding herself pregnant in 1905, disappeared on All Hallows Eve, only to be found later, drowned in the village pond. Martha Woodford wasn't too pleased when Jennifer Aldridge told her that the poor woman had lived in her cottage. Joe Grundy didn't help by pontificating on what souls that haven't properly been put to rest get up to. Once Eddie Grundy and Snatch Foster had mischievously arranged a ghostly apparition, the only way to calm poor Martha's nerves was for Jennifer to fib that the cottage in question was in Lower Loxley.

Cyril **Hubbocks**

Cyril Hubbocks appeared to have found the perfect job when he retired after thirty years on a milk round. As a lifelong angler, he seemed just the man that Brian Aldridge needed to be manager of the new fishing lake at Home Farm in 1992. The project didn't start well: the lake opened a month late, during which time Cyril was on half pay, and later Brian incorrectly suspected him of fiddling the finances. Where Cyril could fairly be faulted was in spending so much time talking with Tom Forrest that he didn't notice Eddie Grundy teaching his son William the delicate art of poaching.

Lady **Hylberow**

(Pauline Seville)

Her encounter with the eccentric Lady Hylberow was surely one of the most extraordinary experiences of the young Christine Archer's life. After Christine rescued her dog, Foxy, from a hit-and-run accident with a car in 1952, Lady Hylberow took a liking to her, though Chris was somewhat mystified when she addressed her as Felicity. It then emerged that Lady Hylberow had lost her own daughter in the Blitz and that Christine bore a strong resemblance to her. A student of ecclesiastical art, Lady Hylberow wanted Christine to accompany her via Italy to Ethiopia to look at pre-Coptic churches, but, when she called at Brookfield to discuss this with Doris, she found that ink had been spilt on some of her valuable books and stalked off, calling the place Bedlam. She tried to patch things up with Christine by booking two theatre seats, but, when Chris turned up at the interval, having been delayed by Dick Raymond, Lady Hylberow pronounced herself totally disillusioned by Christine's apparent obsession with men. She later wrote to Doris withdrawing her offer of the trip and explaining that she didn't want the responsibility of looking after Chris abroad, where she might easily fall prey to the temptations of Latin hotheads.

Mr and Mrs **Ilverton**

(Leslie Parker)

In 1953, Chris and Grace were thrilled with a pony they bought from Mr Ilverton, a smallholder from Netherbourne. They were less pleased, however, when they found out that the sale had broken his daughter Joan's heart. Visiting him to find out the truth, they discovered that the story was to have a happy ending: he and his wife were, in fact, getting Joan another, larger, pony, Trigger.

Mr **Imison**

(Kim Durham)

Mr Imison, the local Trading Standards Officer, had a busy day in July 1984. He first called at Brookfield to watch their sheep dipping in his capacity as 'Diseases of Animals Inspector' before moving on to the Ambridge Farm shop, where he claimed the produce he'd bought was underweight. He also pointed out that, despite a previous warning, there was still no blackboard displaying prices. Betty Tucker rejoindered feebly that it must have been lent to the playgroup.

Bill **Insley**

(Ted Moult)

Newcomers to Ambridge sometimes wonder why Neil Carter owns a patch of land around the Tuckers' house at Willow Farm, not realizing it was a legacy left to him in 1986, on the death of Bill

| Birth: 1.10.1918 |
| Death: 23.9.1986 |

Insley. Derbyshire-born Bill had come to the village three years before, not long after selling his own farm near Ashbourne to the National Coal Board. He had recently lost his wife, so, as a way of making a fresh start, he bought the farmhouse at Willow Farm, and 15 acres on which to breed rare pigs.

He enjoyed socializing with Laura Archer and Colonel Danby, and, in rivalry with Joe Grundy, sought to win the favour of Martha Woodford, attempting to win her over by making her a bird table, among other romantic gestures. He was a good friend to Neil, too. In return for advice about pigs, he let Neil rent the old barn at Willow Farm cheaply, lent him the money to do the repairs necessary to make it fit for a chicken enterprise, and then, disliking battery hen-farming himself, steered him towards the idea of going free-range. His sudden death from a heart attack deprived Ambridge of a most pleasant and generous man.

Karen **Irving**

In 1996, Brenda Tucker was the first to notice when Emma Carter started being verbally picked on by Karen Irving on the school bus. Emma's parents, Neil and Susan, went to see her form teacher about it at once. Neil considered the school's policy of talking to the bully rather than laying blame, too lenient, but Susan thought it was worth trying. In this case, it worked well. Karen, under instruction to do something nice for Emma, lent her a tape, and, within a month, the two girls seemed to be getting on well together.

Mr and Mrs **Jarrett**

'Socially acceptable amateurs' was Mark Hebden's ringing condemnation of the magistrates (Phil Archer among them), who, in 1980, convicted both Mr and Mrs Jarrett of causing a breach of the peace (by disrupting the Hunt) and Mrs Margaret Jarrett of criminal damage (by spray-painting a fence post). The Jarretts had claimed they were innocent and had been ridden at by Hunt members, chiefly Gerald Pargetter, who was in his (stirrup) cups.

Jason

(Brian Miller)

'Orroight, bab?' is Jason's habitual greeting as he arrives with his paint-spattered transistor, apprentice, Clint, and fund of Brummie 'humour', which helps, he thinks, to soften the blow when he has to tell a hapless customer he's discovered woodworm in the beams or deliver one of his so-called 'estimates'. Despite accusations of dubious taste when he and Clint played bullfighters with bones they'd found digging trenches for the church loo (only animal bones, it was revealed), for many years Jason has been Ambridge's builder of choice, though work can take him as far afield as Cradley Heath and Walsall. He's worked at The Lodge, the Dower House, the cricket pavilion and The Bull – but then he does have an ex-wife and three children to support, as well as a live-in girlfriend. In fact, he works so hard that some might have thought he deserved to take off for Torremolinos over the Millennium – unless you were the person (Phil Archer) for whom he was supposed to be working (on the extensive rebuilding of Woodbine Cottage). At least Jason didn't commit the sin there that he did at Honeysuckle Cottage – uprooting most of the perfumed climber that gives it its name.

Jazzer

(Ryan Kelly)

When the Grundys had to move to the Meadow Rise Estate in Borchester in the spring of 2000, the biggest consolation for Ed Grundy was knowing he'd be living near his classmate and good friend Jazzer. Originally christened Jack, Jazzer is one of a large, dysfunctional family. With Ed, Fallon Rogers and his brother on bass, he formed the rock group Dross, for which he provided some sledgehammer drumming. He also taught Ed how to hot-wire stolen cars, thereby confirming Clarrie Grundy's conviction that he was a thoroughly bad influence on her son.

Thorkhil **Jensen**

(Andrew Wincott)

Blond, foreign, good-looking – it's no wonder that Danish student Thorkhil set Sharon Richards' heart beating faster when he arrived to help at Bridge Farm in 1991. When not occupied with Sharon, Thorkhil was a great asset on the farm, keen to muck in and compare the Bridge

Farm experience with Danish methods. It was on Thorkil's initiative that Tony agreed they should do most of the building work on the dairy extension themselves, and his presence even inspired the usually unwilling Sharon to put herself out a bit more on the farm. On his last evening in Ambridge, he took her out for a romantic dinner at Giovanni's, but would not be drawn on the commitment she wanted, still less on her hints that it would be wonderful for Kylie to have a proper father. When they parted at the airport, she told him she'd start saving for her air fare to come and see him, to which he replied, 'Good idea. You do that, Sharon.' But within a month, his letters had started to tail off.

Hilda **Johnson**

(Hilda Birch)

His snobbish mother made Paul's courtship of Christine and their early married life a misery, but Hilda Johnson had nothing to be snooty about: before meeting her wealthy husband, Herbert, she'd been a barmaid at her parents' pub, The Crown, in Borchester. In 1960, she announced that she wanted the share she'd been left by her late husband in the family business so that she could buy into a boarding-house in Bournemouth, where, presumably, she saw out her old age.

Paul **Johnson**

(Leslie Dunn)

When Paul Johnson rode into horse-loving Christine Archer's life in 1954, he must have seemed the fairy-tale knight in shining armour. Fresh from her disappointment over boyfriend Dick Raymond, Christine accepted with alacrity Paul's invitation to ride one of his horses in a two-day show at Belverston. Although Paul notionally worked for his father's firm, horses were his life and he put a lot of business Christine's way. Soon he was boarding out one of his best mares and her two-week-old foal at Chris and Grace's stables. On the night of Grace's death, Paul and Chris were together – they'd been playing

Birth: 10.1.1931
Death: 10.5.1978

badminton in Borchester – and he was a great comfort to her. He encouraged her to keep The Stables going, even suggesting they form a business partnership. In the end, however, she went into partnership with his sister, Sally.

They'd known each other for two years when he proposed in July 1956, though it's tempting to wonder if he might in part have done so in retaliation after a row with his snobbish mother, who never gave Chris her blessing. After wisely holding his bachelor party a full three days beforehand at The Feathers, Paul and Chris were married on 15 December 1956 at St Stephen's.

Paul's father died the following year, leaving him the majority share in the business, and, perhaps resentful of Chris's success while he was having to knuckle down to office work, Paul told her he wanted her to give up showjumping. Chris did so, but she had concerns of her own when Paul's car was spotted outside the home of his secretary, June. He laughed it off, saying they were 'working late'.

When, in 1960, however, Paul's mother wanted to withdraw her capital from the business, Chris was right behind him, offering to sell a horse for seventy guineas and telling him it was the first of many. (She did not, at that time, know just how many she would part with over the years to bale him out.) Refusing her offer, Paul decided instead to sell out to Charles Grenville, but his decision to stay on as general manager led only to resentment and frustration. In Paris for a few days, he ran into a girl named Marianne Peters, who'd supposedly had a crush on him as a teenager. Back in England, he found her a job in Borchester, and who knows where the touching youthful fixation might have led had not Christine found out and made Paul see sense. Barely four years married and already Chris must have been seeing her charming, errant husband in a rather different light.

Over the next decade, though, Paul's waywardness was, thankfully, confined to his working life. Quitting his job with Grenville after trouble over a tractor deal and a discrepancy in the accounts, he whisked Chris off to Newmarket for a year, where he worked in aerial crop-spraying. Back in Ambridge, he bought Wainwright's Garage, and, when this foundered, proposed selling horseboxes in Europe. This plan never got off the ground, but Paul talked himself into a job in the oil industry, working variously in Germany, Wales, and, finally, London.

By this time they had an adopted son, Peter, and Chris was effectively a single parent. She'd refused to move from Ambridge again, but this did at least mean that she had some sort of family life to protect, when, in 1976, Paul confessed to an affair with his boss's PA, Brenda Maynard. Yet again, Chris had to send her rival packing, and, yet again, Paul was out of a job.

He finally accepted work in a local farm machinery business, but was bored and unfulfilled – always, as Chris knew, a dangerous state of affairs. When Paul began to behave secretively, she inevitably suspected another woman, but, when he told her he'd been preoccupied because he was considering setting up a fish farm, her relief was mixed with incredulity. Again, however, swallowing her objections (what he knew about fish farming could have been written on the back of a minnow), she even considered selling the paddock to raise money for the venture. As impulsive as ever, Paul resigned his job and bought 20,000 seven-inch trout before he'd finalized details with Jack Woolley, who was providing the land. Not taking out insurance might have been seen as improvident in anyone but Paul, but all he could see was the 100 per cent return he was expecting on the full-grown fish. Nemesis arrived in October in the shape of an autumn storm. Leaves blocked the pump and all the trout were asphyxiated. Though Jack Woolley waived the rent and Paul asked his creditors for time to pay, he finally had no option but to file for bankruptcy. Debts amounted to £20,000. After twenty years of his charmed, somewhat Walter Mittyish life, Paul's luck had run out. Publicly humiliated and resentful of the Archer family's attempts to help, he spent two months maundering at home before suddenly disappearing, leaving Chris a note saying he could take no more. Their car, which was being bought on hire purchase in Chris's name, was found in London, and Paul himself was eventually traced to Hamburg. When Chris flew out to reason with him, he insisted he was not coming back: he had found a job in Germany and intended making a life there – alone.

In fact, Paul didn't have long to live: he was killed in an accident on the autobahn on 10 May 1978. Given that he'd spectacularly failed to turn up for one bankruptcy hearing, and was under pressure from Chris and Phil to attend the next, it's interesting that the German coroner, in all his rigorousness, recorded a verdict not of accidental death but of death by misadventure. The funeral was held in Hamburg, and Paul was buried in Germany, though it's doubtful whether this impetuous soul, spoilt by his doting mama and indulged by his at first adoring and then long-suffering wife, could rest in peace anywhere.

Peter **Johnson**

(Simon Cornish)

As a child, the adopted son of Paul and Christine had a beautiful singing voice, though his performance at the Christmas carol concert in 1977 was marred by the fact that his father, declared

Birth: 5.9.1965

bankrupt, had disappeared. He got on well with his stepfather, George Barford, who taught him the bugle, and, when Peter left for university in 1983, his ambition was to go into musical administration. When Jill Archer tactfully enquired of Chris in 2000 whether Peter showed any signs of settling down, the response was that he was too busy 'playing the field'.

Elizabeth **Jones** 'Betty' 'Libby'

(Hedli Niklaus)

Libby was the twenty-something milk recorder who caught Tony Archer's eye while Pat was away in Wales nursing her sick mother in 1977. On the pretext of not wanting to waste a double ticket, Tony took her to the Cricket Club dance. But knowing her brother of old, the ever-watchful Jennifer made sure that Libby stayed the night at Home Farm afterwards, just in case.

Percy **Jordan**

(William Eedle)

When Percy Jordan gave up the tenancy of Valley Farm in 1975, he was hopeful that, as he and his wife, Elsie, had no children, his nephew could take it on, but estate manager Andrew

Death: 13.8.1985

Sinclair had to explain that this would not be possible. Everyone was happy, however, when Percy and Elsie were allowed to rent the farmhouse while the land was absorbed into the Berrow Estate. In retirement, Percy helped Tony Archer at Willow Farm and Bridge Farm, and also worked for Paul Johnson in his ill-fated fish-farming venture. He continued as a member of the bell-ringing team, but no longer played cricket, though he'd been a keen village player in his youth. Thus, Percy and Elsie lived fairly uneventful lives in Ambridge, or so it seemed until Percy's death in 1985. It was only then that he bequeathed to Walter Gabriel a photograph album full of photos of Rosie Wynyard taken after her marriage to Piggy Atkins, the Penny Hassett butcher. Had Percy and Rosie had an affair? Sadly, dead men tell no tales, but Ambridge gossips deduced that the rather humourless man they remembered might have had a more dashing side.

Josie

Working mothers all over the country must have sympathized with the plight of Josie, a photographer for the *Borchester Echo*, whose two children, Becky and Henry, were looked after by Hayley Tucker. In late 1999, Josie refused when Hayley asked if she could bring Roy's daughter, Phoebe with her every day, but, when Hayley gave her an ultimatum, Josie caved in, allowing Phoebe to come with Hayley two days a week. Once Henry started school, she had less need for a full-time nanny, so it was a relief when Hayley was offered a job at Lower Loxley in early 2001.

Julie

(Kathryn Hurlbutt)

Jolene Rogers is by no means the first woman working at The Bull to cause a stir with her dress sense. In the early 1980s, Julie made a big impression on the pub's male punters, especially

Birth: 1.4.1964

when she wore the black dress with a split skirt. The pink tracksuit she wore for her daily jog was pretty eye-catching, too. When she first took up the live-in post, replacing recently deceased Polly Perks, she already had a boyfriend, Ahmed, in Birmingham. He wasn't too happy with her working in a pub, and shortly after decided to finish the relationship.

Learning that Julie was footloose and fancy-free was, for the men of Ambridge, like showing the hare to the greyhounds. First out of the traps was Neil Carter, who whisked her off to the Royal Show. Recently wed Eddie Grundy had a liking for her, while David Archer was interested enough to have lunch with her, but it was Neil's flat she moved into after accepting his proposal in February 1983. She wasn't much interested in country life, however, so perhaps it's as well that a trip to the Policeman's Ball with DS Barry induced her to think again. Having already left The Bull for The Feathers, by mutual agreement she left Neil as well.

Keeper's Cottage

Now rented by the Grundys from Jack Woolley, Keeper's Cottage is one of a pair of houses built in 1960 by Charles Grenville to replace some workers' cottages that had been demolished to make way for a new road. The first tenant, Tom Forrest, was given some say in the layout of the house, and was soon renowned for the pride he took in developing the garden, which was to be the source of his, and wife, Pru's, many prize-winning entries in the Flower and Produce Shows.

Colin **Kennedy**

An ex-maths teacher who's swapped protractors for potting up, Colin works in the Bridge Farm dairy. When Helen, in charge during Pat's depression in 1999, promoted Tracy Horrobin to supervisor, Colin resigned in protest and had to be talked round by Pat. His earnestness makes him something of a bore. Simon Gerrard in particular dreads meeting Colin, who likes to expound his theories of what's wrong with the British education system.

Vivian **Kennedy**

(Gordon Walters)

Young, handsome, well-educated, and a district officer who could talk soil samples till the cows came home — what more could any girl want? Well, it clearly wasn't enough for Christine Archer, who was distinctly 'off' with Vivian, when, in 1953, Phil engaged him to analyse the soil on a rough bit of Lakey Hill. First Chris told him crisply that she was too busy to take him on a ride round the countryside, then she refused to accompany him to a dance. When Doris insisted he spend an evening at Brookfield, Vivian was relieved to find Chris wasn't there, and scuttled off before she came home, but Walter hit a cricket ball through his car windscreen and the poor fellow found himself carted back to Brookfield, where Chris did bring herself to tend his injuries. He confessed that he couldn't reconcile her aloofness towards him with gossip he'd heard about her racy encounters with Basil Grove, Dick Raymond and Reggie Trentham, and screwed up his courage to ask her out one last time. She agreed to go punting, but he panicked and fell overboard as a motor-boat approached, dousing for good any flames of passion that might have been ignited.

Kitty and Gary **Kenton**

(Beatrice Kane, Bryan Kendrick)

Kitty had done well enough financially from running a pub with her late husband to be able to buy the tenancy of Hood's Farm for her son, Gary, when it came up for sale in 1959. A cheerful lady, she enjoyed her stay at The Bull while she watched essential work being done on the farm, and took particular pleasure in spending time with Walter Gabriel, who amused her greatly. Less amusing was Gary's lack of success in running a chicken operation. By 1960, it was time to sell up to Charles Grenville.

Kenton's Farm

Kenton's Farm has no connection with Kenton Archer, but was named after Gary Kenton, who briefly held the tenancy at the end of the 1950s. Prior to that, it had been in the hands of the Hood family, who took it over from the Courts, who, in turn, had taken control of the tenancy from Joe Blower in 1955. Squire Lawson-Hope was the landlord in Joe's time, and ownership of the farm passed to George Fairbrother, then Charles Grenville, in whose hands it lost its individual identity, as it was absorbed into the Estate, later owned by Borchester Land.

Satya **Khanna**

(Jamila Massey)

Although Usha Gupta's auntie is in many ways traditional in her attitudes and has often expressed disapproval of Usha's lifestyle, perhaps part of her envies the freedom her niece enjoys. Satya was something of a pioneer herself: while she was part of the Asian community in Uganda, she became the first woman in her family to take a degree. On arriving in England, she had to take in washing for a time to survive financially, but has since become established on a more comfortable footing. She has a strong sense of family duty and regularly visits Ambridge to keep an eye on Usha. This usually entails giving Blossom Hill Cottage a thorough cleaning and the cooking of a wide range of delicious meals and highly fattening sweets. Originally, she wanted her niece to move back to Coventry or Wolverhampton to be near other family members, especially after Usha became the victim of racist attacks in the village in 1995. Gradually, however, she's accepted that there are positive aspects to country living, and now enjoys meeting up with the friends she's made in Ambridge, particularly Marjorie Antrobus, who has an equally experienced and compassionate view of life.

Dawn **Kingsley**

(Patricia Bendall)

In 1962, a year after starting work as John Tregorran's assistant in his antique shop, Dawn Kingsley accepted the offer of a partnership. She had a good eye for a business opportunity, and, after moving to work for Jack Woolley at his New Curiosity Shop, won his confidence sufficiently for him to lend her £7000 for investment purposes. She made him his money back, plus some profit for herself.

A less successful investment was her relationship with artist Robert Heriot. Marriage was presumed to be imminent when she joined him in London, but she returned alone, looking for new work in Borchester.

Bill **Knowles**

Bill became foreman at Home Farm in 1990. A keen astronomer in his spare time, he was considerably less starry-eyed when overseeing Ruth Archer on her year's placement from Harper Adams College. He didn't really believe a woman's place was on the farm, and showed his discontent by constantly finding fault with her. More to his taste was the company of agricultural supply representatives, especially if they were picking up the tab in expensive restaurants. Brian Aldridge, tipped off by Ruth that Bill was spending time with the reps, realized his foreman was fiddling fertilizer costs and sacked him at once.

Conn **Kortchmar**

(Don Fellows)

Conn was the American GI whose wartime romance with Peggy Archer came to light in 1992, when Kate Aldridge and Helen Archer discovered an old letter he'd written, in the attic at Blossom Hill Cottage. Kate couldn't resist writing back to him in the guise of Peggy. Delighted to hear from his old flame, widower Conn soon turned up in Ambridge. When he realized what Kate had done, he gracefully said he'd come to England to see his son and new granddaughter in Bristol anyway. However, he started spending a lot of time in the village.

Recalling one romantic memory after another, Conn, to Jack Woolley's chagrin, was obviously intent on wooing Peggy for a second time. He took her back to some of their wartime trysting places, including the pub in Cambridge where he, like many other GIs, had once scorched his name into the ceiling with a Zippo lighter. Jack grew increasingly jealous, and, mistakenly assuming a bunch of flowers sent to Peggy by Kate had come from Conn, forcefully told the ex-GI it was time he was no longer overpaid, oversexed and over here. Conn dutifully headed back to Boston, leaving Peggy to muse over his parting gift – the Zippo lighter.

Lakey Hill

Although a village landmark and a brilliant spot for scenic views, in the 1950s Lakey Hill was nothing but a problem for Phil. Charged by Fairbrother with reclaiming the land, he had soil samples taken, but, though these revealed enough nitrogenous matter, there was a deficiency of lime and phosphates. Phil nonetheless tried steep ploughing, only to have the tractor stall, with the result that he hit his head and suffered an eye injury. In 1953, a successful pioneer crop of rape, rye grass and turnip was sown on some 30 acres, but when, in 1956, Fairbrother burnt off gorse and heather without a licence, PC Bryden reported him and he was fined £2 for arson. Now absorbed into Brookfield, whose sheep graze the lower slopes, Lakey Hill has become a trysting place for the Archer youth. In 1985, Mark Hebden walked Shula Archer to the top before proposing, and it became their special place. Almost ten years later, Elizabeth and Nigel, whose engagement had been broken off, re-plighted their troth there. What neither couple probably realized was that in 1953 the girls' father had sat there late into the night with Grace Fairbrother, roasting potatoes in the embers of the Coronation Day bonfire.

Martin **Lambert**

(Scott Cherry, David Goodland, Steve Hodson)

After a couple of years working as a vet in Somerset, Martin Lambert joined Bill Robertson's practice in 1984 and set about trying to establish himself locally. First on his 'to do' list was getting a girlfriend. He found Shula Archer highly attractive, and even shoved Eddie Grundy into the Am for being rude to her on Bonfire Night. Shula, whose thoughts were more focused on Mark Hebden, grew tired of Martin's advances, and told him they could only be friends.

Birth: 1955

Finding the right accommodation wasn't easy either. He looked at the possibility of living in Honeysuckle Cottage, until Nelson Gabriel decided to keep it for his own, and daughter Rosemary's, use. Anxious to save money so that he could buy into the practice, Martin was eventually reduced to lodging with the Grundys. It wasn't a successful arrangement: they didn't get the free veterinary services they hoped for, and he didn't get much peace and quiet. By April 1989, when he'd made one last, unsuccessful pass at the now-married Shula, he decided it was time to look for domestic and professional happiness elsewhere.

Lady Isabel **Lander**

(Mary Wimbush)

When, in 1970, Ralph Bellamy asked the recently widowed Lilian Nicholson to hostess a dinner party for him, she realized she was only a substitute for the glamorous Lady Isabel Lander. As the niece of Brigadier Winstanley, Lady Isabel had come to Ambridge to look after him in his declining years, but she was no fortune-hunter from the distaff side of the family. She herself was the daughter of a field marshal, who'd been created an earl for distinguished services to the nation, and owned her own manor house in Sussex and flat in Belgravia. Although local gossips threw her together with 'Squire' Bellamy, their relationship, in fact, had more of a business basis. The Brigadier bequeathed his estate to his niece while he was still alive, and Bellamy advised her about running it.

If she had romantic leanings towards anyone during her time in Ambridge, it was the arty Hugo Barnaby, to whom she sold Nightingale Farm for his arts and crafts centre. But although they spent Christmas 1970 together in Sussex, when her uncle died the following year she sold the estate to Bellamy and moved back to her manor house alone.

Bob **Larkin**

(Lewis Gedge)

Ned Larkin described his brother, Bob, as something of a 'wild 'un' when the latter came to Ambridge in 1957. Everyone else quickly grew to think of him as a complete and utter rogue. As

Death: 21.2.1957

soon as he discovered The Bull, he started to give Pru Harris the benefit of his best chat-up lines. He proposed to her twice, and, even though turned down on both occasions, at least had the satisfaction of getting her to go out with him, much to Tom Forrest's displeasure.

Next he started stealing petrol from private vehicles, with Dan Archer and Joe Blower both suffering the consequences. Because Bob used Ned's gloves while about this nefarious business, suspicion fell on Ned when the gloves were found petrol-soaked. It took a confrontation with Mabel Larkin to get the truth out of Bob.

He went from bad to worse, until finally he was accidentally killed in a struggle over a gun, when Tom Forrest caught him poaching. The Larkins were, of course, upset, but the rest of Ambridge restrained its grief surprisingly well.

Jethro **Larkin**

(George Hart)

In 1985, an article in the *Borchester Echo* began, 'A lucky elephant charm saved an Ambridge man from death this week'. Those who knew farm labourer Jethro Larkin well will not have been surprised that the article referred to him. Half a ton of grass from a silage clamp had fallen on him, and only chance prevented him from being smothered by it. If a man makes his own luck, Jethro should perhaps have put in a little more overtime, as his was a life sometimes blighted by ill-fortune.

Birth: 28.8.1924
Death: 17.6.1987

The eldest son of Ned and Mabel Larkin, he was working in Dorset until 1966, when he returned to Ambridge with wife Lizzie and their two daughters, Clarrie and Rosie. The family moved into a cottage, while he took up a job on the Bellamy Estate. A year later, the Larkins moved into Rickyard Cottage before taking over Woodbine Cottage in 1971.

During this time, Jethro began working for Ambridge Farmers Ltd, at first mainly with the pigs at Hollowtree Farm. 'Slow and steady' seemed to be his motto. He had Van Gogh's ear for instructions he didn't like, and, while he didn't believe in open mutiny, he would conveniently find ways to avoid doing as requested. In 1976, Phil warned him that a loft over a calf-pen needed to be treated with caution, but he went crashing through the floor anyway and broke a leg in the process. It needed considerable persuasion from Mike Tucker to make him put in a claim for compensation.

When Neil Carter came to Brookfield, Jethro took quite a time getting used to him. At first he was worried that the young man was going to replace him, then it was his attitude that was irritating. But eventually he came to accept having Neil around, even finding him something of an ally in the face of Phil's repeated, optimistic attempts to increase efficiency. There were limits to the friendship, however. It was one thing for Jethro and Neil to eat their lunchtime sandwiches together in the Brookfield workshop, quite another to try sharing a car. Part of an inheritance Jethro's Uncle Charlie left him went into buying a Renault hatchback, with Neil making up the difference in cost. Unsurprisingly, it was the cause of considerable argument, until Jethro bought Neil's share outright.

He didn't always get on with David Archer either. He considered him bossy, while David could be disparaging about the older man's age and manner. At one point Jethro even considered leaving Brookfield, but some well-timed compliments about his fence-making healed the rift. At least that was one less thing for him to worry about; bunions and bad gums were frequent causes of discomfort, and he developed a habit of disappearing from the farm at the most inopportune moments to go for treatment.

At home, he relied heavily on Lizzie to keep things running smoothly. When she suffered a stroke and then died of a subarachnoid haemorrhage in 1980, it was a devastating blow for him. His only way of coping was to throw himself into his work. Later, he drew some comfort in training and looking after Gyp, a working Border collie Phil bought for him.

While he accepted elder daughter Rosie's marriage to Dennis Mabbott, he was much less happy when Clarrie started dating Eddie Grundy. He had a series of rows with her, which culminated in him threatening not to give her away at her wedding in 1981. Only when she walked out of Woodbine Cottage and went to stay at Grey Gables for a couple of nights did he relent.

While he was a magnet for ill-luck, he didn't keep it all to himself. In 1983, he accidentally dropped a hay bale on Phil Archer's head, causing some bruising and leaving Phil apparently a little vague. Later, when heavy rain had led to a piano being temporarily left in the Hollowtree pig unit while on its way to The Bull, Jethro found Phil playing it. Not unnaturally, he assumed that anyone serenading porkers had gone soft in the head, and considered himself largely to blame. Over the years, he saw a surprising number of the Archer family in various states of undress.

He witnessed David clambering naked out of a bathroom window, having been locked in by Elizabeth, and, some months later, almost crashed his tractor when Elizabeth's topless sunbathing drew his eye from the rev counter.

His finest moment occurred in 1986, when he played in The Bull's darts team, which beat the Cat and Fiddle. Showing the predatory instincts of a football manager, Dick Pearson then persuaded Jethro to switch allegiance. A successful appearance in the Cat's victory over the Dog and Trumpet was followed by a period of disillusionment with the level of behaviour Dick presided over. Jethro returned to The Bull, not even minding Peggy's refusal to let Gyp sit on the seats.

By 1987, he was increasingly worried about the effects of old age. To convince David that he was still up to the job, he made extra efforts in all his farm work. When, in June, the two of them went to trim some overgrown trees by a farm track, perhaps Jethro was unconsciously trying too hard. Pulling heavily on the rope round a thick branch David was cutting, he was unable to jump clear when it suddenly came away and knocked him flat. As he fell, he struck his head. By the time an ambulance and Dr Thorogood had been alerted, it was too late. David spent a lot of time reliving the accident and wondering how the tragedy might have been avoided, but in the end it was clearly just a question of bad luck.

In his slow, steady way, Jethro had saved a little money and left £10,000 to be shared by Rosie and Clarrie. His was not a spectacular life; although a little unfortunate at times, it is one remembered with considerable affection by those who knew him.

Lizzie **Larkin**

Despite spending much of her married life busily cooking, Lizzie Larkin somehow stayed as thin as a beanpole. The same couldn't be said of her daughters, Rosie and Clarrie, nor of husband, Jethro, with whom Lizzie came to Ambridge in 1966.

Death: 18.9.1981

She ran the Larkin household shrewdly, keeping close note of all expenditures in an account book. One rare extravagance was a second-hand bike bought as a Christmas present for Jethro. The cost of replacing the range at Woodbine Cottage worried her, until Clarrie persuaded Phil

Archer, their landlord, to pay half the cost. Lizzie was so relieved to see the back of the old one that she wasn't angry when Eddie Grundy fitted a second-hand replacement rather than the anticipated brand new one. When she did have time to relax, she liked going to whist drives, and sometimes enjoyed singing. On one memorable occasion she performed a duet with Nora McAuley in the village revue. After a period of feeling unwell and experiencing bad headaches, in September 1980 she suffered a brain haemorrhage and died in hospital. The deep sense of loss Jethro felt was plain to see for a long time afterwards.

Mabel **Larkin** née Bracken

(Kay Hudson)

Mabel and Ned Larkin brought up five children together. Their son Jethro was the only one to settle in Ambridge, after first spending some time in Dorset, but Mabel liked to keep in touch with all of

Death: July 1983

them, especially her daughter Susan, who lived in the North with a husband and two daughters.

Growing restless with life at Glebe Cottage, Mabel was pleased to move into Woodbine Cottage after Ned's retirement from Brookfield in 1967. In the same year, she represented Ambridge at the WI's AGM at the Albert Hall. She got herself into considerable difficulties about what to wear, since her taste in hats left much to be desired.

She sometimes helped Carol Tregorran at the Market Garden, but, after Ned's death late in 1967, began working as a housekeeper for Hugo Barnaby. She moved to Nightingale Farm in 1971, whereupon Jethro and his family moved into Woodbine Cottage. Brian Aldridge hired her as a housekeeper in 1973, a position she maintained for a number of years, before retiring to Manorfield Close. She died within a few years of moving.

Ned **Larkin**

(Bill Payne)

The grandfather of Clarrie Grundy, Ned Larkin started work at Brookfield in 1956, when he was taken on as Simon Cooper's replacement. He and his wife, Mabel, only had themselves to look after, since their five children had already left the nest.

Death: Dec 1967

Strongly protective of his family, he tried to excuse his brother, Bob's, anti-social behaviour as the result of a childhood illness. His initial reaction to Bob's killing by Tom Forrest was to feel angry towards Tom. Only with difficulty did he come to accept that his brother's criminal behaviour had led to his downfall.

He and Walter Gabriel shared a similar sense of fun, and grew to be great friends. Ned helped Walter find his life savings at Arkwright Hall after Gregory Selden had stolen them. On a subsequent trip to the Hall, he crashed through some floorboards, fortuitously uncovering a pile of gold sovereigns. He worried when his daughter Susan had problems with her husband, Charlie, but was pleased when his eldest son, Jethro, came back to Ambridge with his wife and daughters, Clarrie and Rosie, in 1966. Sadly, he wasn't to enjoy their company for long. In December 1967, he passed away, only a few months into his retirement.

Susan **Larkin**

(Patricia Gibson)

Susan Larkin was one of Ned and Mabel Larkin's five children. On marrying her lorry-driving husband, Charlie, she moved to Newcastle, where she had two children by him, Bobbie and Joyce.

In 1959, she came back to stay with her parents, and, although not saying very much, was obviously unhappy with the state of her marriage. While her back was turned, eighteen-month-old Joyce swallowed some paraffin Ned had been using on his car. After an urgent trip to hospital, Susan insisted on taking her children home, a journey made more stylish by dint of being undertaken in Mr Grenville's chauffeur-driven car.

David **Latimer**

(Arnold Peters)

Appointed vicar to the parishes of Ambridge and Penny Hassett in 1968, David Latimer was a mix of the forward-looking and the traditional:

Death: Feb 1973

while he urged parishioners to call him by his Christian name, he had an aversion to marrying couples during Lent or Advent, though he made an exception for Greg Salt and Nora McAuley. He was defeated by ill health and died in 1973 while staying with his mother in Sussex.

Hester **Latimer**

(Penelope Shaw)

A good horsewoman, Hester must have been delighted to move to Ambridge with her husband, David, and their children, Tessa, Kit and Kate in 1968. Sadly, within five years, David had died, and Hester had three months in which to leave the Vicarage. She was touched when nearly £300 was collected for her and presented to her at a sherry party in her honour. She then departed to go and live with her elder daughter, Tessa.

Keith **Latimer**

(Jack May)

George Fairbrother rubbed his hands when mineralogist Keith told him in 1951 that there could be up to three million tons of ironstone beneath his land and the Squire's, and that it would fetch £40 a ton when manufactured. Keith shared Fairbrother's pragmatic attitude to a potential mining scheme and could not understand the concerns of the villagers. Indeed, when Phil Archer approached him wanting a word, Keith assumed it was about the date he'd arranged with Christine, not Phil's fears for his own future at Fairbrother's.

Chris and Keith did go out, but, as they strolled home across the fields, they witnessed the theft of the diamond drilling bit from Keith's equipment. Later, with Phil and Dick Raymond, Keith laid in wait for the vandal's return, but they failed to catch him. Keith was then involved in an argument in the pub between his assistant, Bert Matthews, and Bill Slater, and his guilt at Bill's subsequent death was not assuaged when he discovered that Bill had, in fact, been the saboteur.

Keith gave evidence for a mine at the public inquiry and was disappointed when Mr Crawford, the industrialist to whom the Squire's mineral rights had been sold, was persuaded by the villagers and refused to allow the scheme to go ahead.

Teresa Mary **Latimer** 'Tessa'

(Carol Davies)

Despite – or perhaps because of – being the vicar's daughter, Tessa was an outgoing girl who liked her suede skirts and brightly coloured wet-look boots (well, it was 1970). Although away at university, she enjoyed Hugo Barnaby's company when in Ambridge, and went out regularly with Tony Archer. She also spent one of her vacations hitch-hiking abroad. After her degree, she trained as a probation officer and married a fellow social worker.

Birth: 1949

Bob **Lawrence**

Bob, then in his mid-forties, took over as manager of Carol Tregorran's Market Garden in 1977. A conscientious worker, he had rather a retiring nature, although could be forthright when required. Jack Woolley asked for his advice on running his newly established garden centre, and was taken aback by how drastic some of Bob's suggestions were.

Unlike his namesake, T.E. Lawrence, he was rarely seen in traditional Arab dress.

Elizabeth **Lawson**

(Eileen Barry)

In 1957, before he met Jill, young widower Phil Archer became close enough to Elizabeth to take her to a Valentine's ball, ask her to star in his cine film about the village, and to listen to the dawn chorus in the woods with her. But she had a fiancé, Stephen, in London, and, in May, of that year, she decided to return to him as she and Phil were getting too close. How different things might have been...

Clive **Lawson-Hope**

(Leslie Parker)

Late in 1952, Clive arrived to take over the running of the Estate for his uncle, the Squire. He was the hero of the hour when he took Grace Fairbrother to hospital after she'd been involved in a car crash, and, from that moment, to Phil's discomfiture, Clive seemed to have his sights set on making her his wife. He proposed in February 1953, but Grace avoided giving him an answer until June, when he pompously withdrew the proposal himself.

Phil wasn't the only person to whom Clive didn't endear himself. Tom Forrest chafed at being ordered about by someone with five years' college training as opposed to his thirty-five years' experience, and Walter Gabriel loathed him for trying to evict him from his farm. He fell out with John Tregorran, too, over Christine Archer, and jumped to the conclusion that John had stolen a horse that had gone missing from The Stables, when, in fact, John was trying to reclaim it from some Gypsies. When news came in 1954 that his Uncle Percy had died in Kenya and Clive was to inherit, he asked Christine to accompany him as his wife, but she refused and he left alone for a life under the African sun.

Clive **Lawson-Hope** 'Squire'

(Ronald Baddiley)

Standing by the drawing-room fireplace at the Manor, beneath the carved family coat of arms and drinking his two sherries before dinner, Squire Lawson-Hope epitomized the old order. His connection with the old Ambridge families was impressive: an Archer was in service with the Lawson-Hopes at Waterloo, and a Gabriel was batman to his father at Vimy Ridge. But the Squire's grip on modern life was not so secure, and he was nearly outmanoeuvred by George Fairbrother over the question of ironstone extraction in the village. Like many of the old landed families after the war, the Lawson-Hopes had perpetual money problems, and he hoped that his nephew Clive's arrival to run the Estate in 1952 would put it on a more sound financial footing. By the time Clive left for Kenya, however, the Squire had already tried to sell off Coombe Farm, and, when he announced in May 1954 that he was selling the entire Estate, Dan Archer cannot have been too surprised. Dan bought Brookfield, and the rest of the land was split between Fairbrother and the Bellamy family, while the Manor itself went to Dr Cavendish. The Squire was always disappointed that he had no son to succeed him, although there would clearly not have been much for him to inherit.

Letty **Lawson-Hope**

(Kitty Scoopes, Kay Hudson)

Doris Archer spent her early years in service as lady's maid to Letty Lawson-Hope at the Manor, and was her personal help and confidante in the closing years of her life. In gratitude, Letty left Doris Glebe Cottage for her lifetime (Dan later bought the freehold for her), and, when Letty died, Dan arranged for his old shire-horses, Blossom and Boxer, to be brought out of retirement to draw her coffin on a hay wagon.

Death: 21.4.1958

Barney **Lee**

(Gordon Walters, Michael Ford, Douglas Ditta)

Neither of Barney Lee's forays into Ambridge was a success. Having induced his friend from army days, Jack Archer, to try a combined farming operation in Cornwall in the early 1950s, he fell in love with Peggy Archer. When the farm enterprise fell through, Barney followed the Archers back home, hoping to win Peggy away from Jack. He was soon sent on his way.

He returned in 1976, some six years after the death of his wife, Betty, as the manager of Carol Tregorran's Market Garden. Now that Peggy was a widow, Barney hoped finally to win her hand, but failed again, his cause not being helped by his heavy drinking.

Dr and Mrs **Lenz**

(Harold Kasket)

When Eva Lenz married PC Coverdale in 1980, her parents came over from Germany for the wedding, but the hotel she and her husband were due to stay in didn't suit their requirements, so they stayed at Home Farm. A trip to the theatre in Stratford came to an abrupt end when Mrs Lenz found a lack of English spoiled her enjoyment of the play. When she and her husband returned to the farm unexpectedly early, Brian and Jennifer Aldridge wore themselves out in the attempt to be entertaining.

Lewis

(Robert Lister)

Now semi-retired, Lewis is able to pick and choose which architectural assignments he takes on. Converting a barn at Lower Loxley into an art gallery took his fancy in 1999, and he also masterminded the renovations needed in the main accommodation block. While Nigel and Elizabeth Pargetter were impressed with his professional ability, Julia

Pargetter was attracted by his suave, confident manner, and soon she and Lewis were understood to be close friends. He alone seems able to control the more thoughtless excesses of her behaviour. When she jeopardized the building schedule by providing continual tea-breaks for the builders, a quiet word that she was putting the work, and their friendship, at risk was all Lewis needed to say.

Unable to attend Lily and Freddie Pargetter's christening party in 2000, which was for family only, he showed a facility with handling babies that Julia could only watch and admire. He said that he learnt the knack of pacifying howling infants when his own daughter, Felicity, was young.

Although he was busy when working for the Landmark Trust on the restoration of Arkwright Hall, he is always happy to find time to look after the twins, or to enjoy the company of their grandmother. Unsurprisingly, he is widely seen as an asset at Lower Loxley.

Liam

Liam was a man with a mission and a mobile. Brought in to manage the newly opened shop at Lower Loxley in February 2000, he went everywhere with his ear clamped to a phone, continually ordering and organizing. One of the things he obviously organized was a new job for himself, for within less than a year he was off, leaving Elizabeth and Nigel Pargetter in the lurch. Kathy Perks may have been glad he didn't stick around, however, because within weeks she'd taken over his job.

Lisa and Craig

(Tracey Gardiner, David Phelan)

In October 1992, Bert Fry noticed movement in Rickyard Cottage, and, to Brookfield's amazement, they found they had squatters. The locks had been changed and a young couple, Lisa and Craig, and their baby, Scott, had moved in. Their appearance divided the Archer household. While David and Kenton tried strong-arm tactics, such as letting down the tyres on Craig's car and turning off the water supply, Phil favoured using the law to get the couple out. Jill, meanwhile, felt desperately sorry for them and was concerned about the baby.

Eventually, a solution was arrived at: Jill negotiated for Lisa to get a job at Pat's dairy. Her wages, plus Craig's as a farm labourer would, Jill hoped, with housing benefit, mean that they could afford to rent the cottage. Jill, however, was in for a tough lesson in the vagaries of the benefit system. Lisa's wages led to a reduction in both their level of housing benefit and family credit. Although Jill entertained hopes of their being properly housed in Ambridge, nothing was available, and, when Craig lost his job in May 1993, the trio packed up and left. Jill tried to trace them but to no avail. Only Scott's rattle remained to remind her they had been there at all.

Ewan and Gwynneth **Llewellyn**

(Dillwyn Owen, Margaret John)

Pat's aunt and uncle attended her wedding to Tony in 1974, representing Olwyn, Pat's mother and Gwynneth's sister, who was ill. Lively Gwynneth hit it off at once with Walter Gabriel, but, when she and her husband visited the newlyweds the following year, Tony couldn't wait for them to go home. Pat, however, found her aunt a godsend round the house and she came back to help out after the birth of John.

Alistair **Lloyd**

(Michael Lumsden)

By 1997, Shula Hebden and Caroline Pemberton, who had each lost their husbands, were ironically dubbing themselves the 'merry widows', and, from the moment vet Alistair Lloyd bumped into Caroline

Birth: 1962

and told her his divorce had just been finalized, he was a marked man. It was Caroline who made the first move, asking him to a chamber music concert, but he turned her down, and she feared she was losing her touch. The reality was more believable – he simply fancied Shula. Attending a sick cow at Brookfield, he was delighted to be asked to her and Kenton Archer's joint fortieth birthday, which was being held eight months early on New Year's Eve at Nelson's Wine Bar. There, unable to contain himself till midnight, let alone August, he kissed her in the middle of the party. Caroline was magnanimous in defeat, and Alistair and Shula began going out.

He admitted to her straight away that he had a jaundiced view of marriage – his wife had gone off with his best friend after years of strained silences and blazing rows – but he could sympathise with Shula over the death of Mark, as he had once had a nephew who'd been killed in a car crash. Shula had an early taste of what life with a vet might be like when they had to abandon a meal in a swanky seafood restaurant after Alistair's pager went off. After he'd seen to the emergency, they ended the evening with bacon sandwiches, cocoa and a kiss, and shortly afterwards he sent her a card declaring, 'Vet me be your Valentine'.

In April 1998, Daniel threw a spanner in the works, as children do, when he fell ill with what turned out to be a form of arthritis. Frantic with worry, Shula froze Alistair out and turned for succour to village doctor Richard Locke, with whom she began an affair. She eventually told Alistair that there was someone else, but not who, and he confided in the man he thought was his friend – Richard. It was David Archer who eventually let out the identity of Alistair's rival. Appalled, Alistair confronted Richard and accused him of exploiting his position for sexual advantage.

Richard left the village and Shula clumsily tried to make amends, but Alistair seemed to be having none of it. They were still estranged when Shula was publicly humiliated over the affair at a Cricket Club meeting and abruptly left. Following her outside, Alistair told her that he loved her, and, within a fortnight, had proposed. Shula seemed a little alarmed at the speed with which things were moving, and he took the ring back, only present her soon afterwards with two air tickets to St Kitts, which he thought would be ideal for their honeymoon. Having checked that it really was what he wanted, she agreed to marry him.

Alistair, as is his style, went about things the right way, asking a delighted Phil for Shula's hand, and also making the effort to win round Jill, who feared Shula was rushing into the wedding. They were married in a civil ceremony on Christmas Eve 1999, with Daniel as ring-bearer, and both were touched by the support for their union evidenced by the packed church for the subsequent blessing.

Alistair had always got on well with Shula's young son, but, once the couple were married, Daniel seemed less keen on sharing his mother on a full-time basis. Alistair won him round with patience and a trip to the surgery, during which Daniel fed a rabbit called Mr Lomax.

The corner was turned when Daniel asked Alistair, not Shula, to read his bedtime story.

Daniel and Alistair became inseparable as they sought out all forms of wildlife round the village. The joy of having a daddy on hand for a game of football or cricket (Alistair excels at both) has been enhanced by the move to The Stables, where, for the first time, the family can have plenty of space. Although for the moment Alistair intends to retain his premises at the business units, in time he's expressed an interest in moving his practice to The Stables. Such a move would consolidate his bond with Shula, already made stronger by his adoption of Daniel in late 2000.

His second marriage, after a traumatic divorce, has brought Alistair, as well as Shula and Daniel, the security and support that all of them craved. His was a calming presence during the Brookfield inheritance row, and the entire Archer family have come to rely on his quiet good humour, as well as his veterinary skills. Indeed, the only time he's shown any tetchiness was during a difficult Lent when he and Shula each challenged the other to give up their favourite thing. Alistair gave up alcohol, while Shula denied herself chocolate, and the present from a grateful client of a box of liqueur chocolates was a true test. Alistair's suggestion that Shula should suck out the centres while he ate the chocolate did not meet with a favourable response, and the pair learnt their lesson. These days, they have given up giving up.

Richard **Locke**

(William Gaminara)

Dr Richard Locke responded well in adversity, medical or otherwise. He was a great support to Shula Hebden during her difficulties with IVF treatment and pregnancy, for example, but was equally at home propping up a collapsing innings for the Ambridge Cricket Club. At times, when he was in costume for the Sealed Knot Civil War re-enactments that he revelled in, he even looked a hero. His patients quickly got used to him when he came to Ambridge in 1992. They appreciated his willingness to listen to their problems, instead of reaching automatically for the prescription pad. Even Jennifer Aldridge, who considered his Mancunian accent 'a bit common', found she could open

Birth: 1963

up to him when she came for a repeat prescription for sleeping tablets. He showed as much sensitivity outside the surgery, surprising Elizabeth Archer with his insight into her post-Cameron Fraser mistrust of men.

Nigel Pargetter's worries that Elizabeth might get involved with the new doctor were unfounded. Richard did become interested in Debbie Aldridge, however, after the raid on the village shop, when he thought she wasn't coping properly with the stress it caused. Professional interest became personal for a while, as he convinced her to take part in the Battle of Hassett Bridge re-enactment, and then had to rescue her from the battlefield when she was thrown from her horse. But they argued most of the time they spent together and eventually decided they were better off being just good friends.

It took Richard a while to settle into rural life. Early on he was baffled by Clarrie Grundy's pneumonia-like illness, until Robin Stokes, wearing his vet's hat, put him on the track of Q fever, which is caught from drying prematurely born lambs. Pretty soon, Richard had learnt enough about farming practice to tell an unimpressed Joe Grundy of the need to wear protective clothing while sheep-dipping.

Finding the right place to live proved difficult. He had brief stays at the Brookfield B & B, at a Home Farm holiday cottage, and was a lodger with Marjorie Antrobus for a while. He sold his house in Manchester, and was looking to buy a property in Borsetshire, but it wasn't till Blossom Hill Cottage came up for sale in 1995 that he really saw somewhere he wanted. In the event, Usha Gupta got in first, but, instead of bearing a grudge, Richard was soon inviting her out for a meal. It proved to be an expensive night. Usha heard a rumour that she'd only been asked out as a way for Richard to get at Debbie. Set on revenge, she ordered the most expensive food Nelson's Wine Bar could offer. By the end of the evening, Richard had paid £60 for the privilege of being put down in no uncertain terms. But there was an even more disastrous sequel; as Usha left alone, having turned down the offer of being escorted to the taxi rank, she was attacked by racist thugs. Within seconds, Richard was on the scene, taking care of her.

It was the start of a slowly developing romance. Initially on a purely business footing, he moved into the spare room at Blossom Hill Cottage. As Usha became subject to a series of further attacks, he grew closer to her. By the time she was ready to sell up and move away from Ambridge, he wanted them to put down roots together; he told her he loved her and convinced her to stay.

He continued to be well liked as a doctor, and was flattered when a baby he delivered was given 'Richard' as a second name. The summer and autumn of 1996 were to be trying times, however. Mrs Barraclough, an old lady who was dying of cancer, appreciated the time he spent with her in her final few weeks – so much so that she left him an eighth share of her estate. The woman's son, Ken, made an official complaint against Richard, accusing him of unduly influencing the will and not providing the best possible medical care. An independent review investigated the matter, with the General Medical Council looking at its findings. Although they decided not to refer Richard to the Professional Conduct Committee, he was warned about his record-keeping. When he finally received £10,000 from Mrs Barraclough's will, he gave £5000 to a cancer charity, while the remainder was used as a deposit on the Vicarage, which was to become the new surgery.

As two highly busy professionals, it wasn't easy for Richard and Usha to give their relationship the time it deserved. Cracks were starting to show by the spring of 1998, when fears that Daniel Hebden might have leukaemia brought Shula back into regular contact with Richard. They grew close as a series of tests ruled out the worst of their worries for Daniel; by the summer, they had become lovers. Finding the deceit involved intolerable, Richard moved out of Blossom Hill Cottage and started staying at the surgery, inevitably giving rise to a chorus of village gossip. Usha was devastated to learn that 'the other woman' was one of her friends.

Richard felt the only way forward was to leave Ambridge. He accepted another job in Manchester, assuming Shula would come with him. When she told him their relationship was over, he reacted with disbelief, then anger that he had given up so much in return for nothing. He didn't even have the consolation of leaving on good terms with Usha; she was far too hurt to help him ease his conscience by sharing a civilized farewell.

Richard left quietly in September 1998, and it was no hero's departure. He doesn't seem to have stayed in touch with anyone in Ambridge, though there are some people, especially his practice receptionist, Susan Carter, who remember him with affection. They feel that Shula's actions deprived the village of a good doctor and a good friend.

Sarah **Locke**

Shula was upset when she learnt in October 1983 that her former fiancé, Mark Hebden, was going out with blonde, sporty Sarah, daughter of the senior partner at law firm Locke & Martin. When they became engaged and planned a honeymoon on the Lockes' boat in Devon, Shula's torment increased. Mark and Sarah's wedding, however, was first postponed due to pressure of her father's work, and then cancelled, and Shula could breathe again.

Lawrence **Lovell**   'Larry'

(Stephen Hancock)

Just think, instead of Laurence Oliver and Vivien Leigh, it could have been Lawrence Lovell and Vivien Leigh, because a meeting with the famous beauty is but one of Larry's many claims to fame. Others (all disputed by the sceptical thespians of Ambridge) are that he once appeared in a West End production of *The Desert Song* (though Lynda sniffs that he was only an assistant stage manager) and has been a male model (for knitting patterns, it transpired). Poor Larry. Dismissed by Joe Grundy as being 'all cravats and hair oil', this sad little man, who thinks his left profile looks like Noel Coward, tends to overdo the aftershave in his attempts to woo the ladies. His infatuation with Jill Archer has led to his praising her costumes over the cast performances in many an Ambridge theatrical, and in 1997 he was only persuaded to accept the part of Theseus in *A Midsummer Night's Dream* – he'd originally gone for Lysander – because she was to play Hippolyta. One of the most embarrassing evenings Caroline Pemberton ever endured was when Larry answered her lonely hearts advertisement in *Borsetshire Life* and dropped by to listen to Guy's old 78s. She had to move the furniture to limit his pouncing opportunities.

Lower Loxley Hall

With the addition of a treetop walk, a rare breeds area, a café, shop and art gallery to complement the existing appeal of 7 acres of woodland and 3 acres of formal gardens, Lower Loxley has recently become an even more impressive stately home to visit. The residence of the Pargetter family for centuries, the Hall has Jacobean origins, though has been much added to since, as is reflected in the date of '1702' over the main door.

The current generation of the family, headed by Nigel and Elizabeth, offset the huge cost of maintaining the Grade II listed building not only by opening it to the public but also by promoting it as a conference centre. Many companies find it an attractive venue, in part because of its impressive Great Dining-Room, Jacobean fireplace and neo-classical library. Repairing damage caused by dry rot in the late 1980s, and by an infestation of death-watch beetle a decade later, proved expensive, but the Hall is now in better condition than it has been for years. Set in 70 acres of parkland, which is in turn surrounded by farms belonging to the Lower Loxley Estate, this splendid building is rightly considered one of the jewels of Borsetshire.

Arnold **Lucas**

(George Woolley)

The retired solicitor who rented the Dower House from the Bellamys in 1975 was something of a recluse, who occupied himself tending his conservatory full of cacti, making detailed military models and teaching himself to play the lute. All that close work, however, must have played havoc with his eyes, and it was his housekeeper, Mrs Blossom, who noticed that his sight was failing. She discreetly put his name down for the talking newspaper for the blind, and Jill Archer, then working for the charity, became involved. At first Mr Lucas refused to accept that he needed help, and, by the time Jill had persuaded him to see a specialist in London, his acute glaucoma was inoperable. Still in denial, he was obstructive towards the mobility officer sent from Social Services to assess him, and it fell to Jill to shake him out of his stubbornness by telling him he was a self-pitying snob. This 'cruel to be kind' ruse worked, and he agreed to go on a Social Services rehabilitation course. He could not, however, continue to live alone, so he left the village to live with his married daughter, Phyllida, giving Jill a brooch and a half-moon table in thanks.

Lyttleton Brook

Lyttleton Brook, part of which runs through Home Farm, is a small tributary of the River Am. Brian Aldridge dug out and developed a stretch of it when he decided to diversify his income by creating a fishing lake. It is mentioned in the rhyme: 'Why trouble your head over what to cook, when you can pull trout from Lyttleton Brook', though some authorities question the saying's authenticity.

Humphrey Lyttleton

(Self)

Phil and Christine were intrigued in 1957 when the vicar told them he'd engaged a celebrity in the music sphere to open the village fête. While Phil hoped aloud it wouldn't be some Teddy boy in drainpipe jeans, Chris was closer to the mark when she hazarded that it might be someone from the world of jazz. Sure enough, bandleader Humphrey Lyttleton did the deed.

Rosie Mabbott

Clarrie Grundy's elder sister, Rosie, now lives in Skegness with husband Dennis, after moving there from Great Yarmouth some years ago. Their daughter, Bess, is doing well as an apprentice hairdresser, though son David has yet to settle on a career. Rosie and Clarrie have always had a good relationship, although they don't see each other as often as they would like. When their father, Jethro Larkin, took against Clarrie marrying Eddie Grundy in 1981, Rosie visited Ambridge specifically to support her sister, even though she didn't think much of Eddie herself. In 1984, she had the trauma of almost losing her husband, when Dennis ended up in intensive care after being run over. The following year, Jethro came to visit, but was so put out by Dennis's rudeness that he quickly returned to Ambridge.

The Mabbotts are not well off, but, during the Grundys' recent financial troubles, Rosie offered to pay a phone bill for them and was then willing

Birth: 14.9.1951

to sacrifice her meagre savings if it would help the fight against bankruptcy. Clarrie refused to take the money, which, in truth, would have made little difference, but was greatly touched by the demonstration of sisterly support.

Nellie **Macdonald**

Nellie, who lived about twenty-five miles away from Ambridge in Stourhampton, was a friend of Laura Archer's in the 1950s. When Laura was still not sure where she was going to settle in England, she left Ambridge to stay with Nellie in 1957, but the two strong-minded women soon found they irritated each other. Within three months, Laura was on her way back to Ambridge and Nellie was breathing a sigh of relief.

Clive **Mackenzie**

(Marcus Campbell)

There was an invasion from Down Under in 1976 when Clive and his friends, Bazza from Australia and fellow New Zealander Michele, came sheep shearing at Home Farm and Brookfield. Clive had just finished at Lincoln College, and the trio were travelling round the country in a Land Rover. When it was time for them to move on, Clive persuaded Shula to join him and the others on a trip round Europe.

Adam **Macy**

(Judy Bennett, Jeremy Whitticase)

When he was ten, red-haired Adam Macy had a very nasty accident. Riding with friends on Heydon Berrow, he dismounted hurriedly and came to ground in some scrub, where he startled an adder. He should have said straight away he'd been bitten, but bravely tried to keep quiet about it. By the time Libby Jones took charge of the situation, Adam was becoming seriously ill. He was rushed to hospital,

Birth: 22.6.1967

where a new anti-venom serum, Zagreb, was administered, and, to his family's relief, a swift recovery followed. It was an early sign of just how tough he could be. As Jennifer Archer's illegitimate son by Paddy Redmond, he needed resilience from the start. His birth had caused such a shock wave in Ambridge that his mother, who was refusing to name the father, took Adam to live with her in a dingy flat in Bristol. Within a few months, though, they were back in the village and he was soon getting used to having new faces around. First Jennifer married Roger Travers-Macy, and then, within a couple of years, a baby sister, Debbie, arrived on the scene.

Roger came from a wealthy background and this brought its own disadvantages. In 1970, two incompetent kidnappers, Henry Smith and Chloe Tempest, took Adam from The Bull, hoping to extract a £5000 ransom from Roger's father. Fortunately, a tip-off from Sid Perks, who knew Smith and Tempest of old, helped the police to find Adam before the kidnapping got very far.

Another upheaval came when he was nine. His parents divorced, and Jennifer made a second marriage to Brian Aldridge. Adam was unsettled by this and started to misbehave, until his grandmother, Peggy Archer, got the truth out of him: he was afraid his new stepfather might suddenly go away, just as Roger had. Acting on Doris Archer's advice, Brian talked to Adam about these concerns, and found out that he already knew Roger hadn't been his real father. Tensions eased after this chat. Later, when the question of surnames was raised, Adam was content to remain a Travers-Macy, in line with Roger's wishes. In time, however, this was simplified to just Macy.

When Jennifer went into a maternity home to have Kate, Adam began having bad dreams, and, once again, seemed a little unsettled. Still, he tried to make his mum welcome when she came home by preparing some conker coffee from horse chestnuts for her. It wasn't his fault it tasted disgusting. Despite being academically able when he put his mind to it, he didn't always perform well at school, and needed extra coaching in maths to get into St Peter's Preparatory. From there, he followed in Brian's footsteps and went to Sherborne in 1981. In the same year, he was spotted by Paddy Redmond, on a brief visit to the village, but they didn't meet up and Adam was left none the wiser about who the red-haired stranger was. He was more concerned about his mother's growing friendship with John Tregorran, which he didn't approve of at all.

Being out in the open air was what he liked best. Apart from horse-riding and jumping, he enjoyed rugby, running, swimming and shooting. He did just enough to get himself into the sixth form, where he took English, French and economics A-levels. University was to be the next step, but first he had itchy feet to deal with.

Two years working and travelling in Canada left him in good shape physically. Sixteen-year-old Lucy Perks thought him a looker when he returned to Ambridge, but Elizabeth Archer was more sniffy: he wasn't her type at all. The two years away had helped him decide what he was going to do with his future. At various times, he'd wanted to be a gamekeeper or a showjumper, but now he had his mind set on farming. He went to Newcastle University and graduated with a 2.1 in agricultural economics. Rather than taking the easy option of letting Brian find work for him, he immediately set off for Africa, where he travelled through Kenya, Senegal and Tanzania.

The idea of using his skills in the Third World soon started to appeal. By 1991, he was digging wells for irrigation projects, and, over the next few years, took on a range of new responsibilities. He gained particular satisfaction from increasing milk yields in one small village in Kenya by crossing local and British goats.

He always kept in contact with his family, but was aware that baby sister Alice, growing up without him around, probably regarded him as an exotic stranger who sent fascinating presents once in a while. It was a real pleasure for him to meet up with Jennifer and Brian in South Africa when he became godfather to Kate's daughter Noluthando in 2001. Apart from the opportunity to catch up on a lot of family and Ambridge gossip, it gave Adam the chance to review where he was, and where he wanted to be, in life. He's matured a great deal while abroad. Working in conditions where money is tight, and the outcome invariably important to local communities, he's become adept at making difficult decisions quickly and then putting them straight into practice. His tolerance threshold for bureaucratic niceties and impractical debate is pretty low. He likes the social life he's built up; he finds a week off work passes very pleasantly in Nairobi and never lets a chance go by to get to Lake Victoria. For the moment, he's happy where he is and can't see any reason to leave. But meeting up with his family has at least raised the question: what would life be like for him back in England?

Katherine **Madikane** 'Kate' née Aldridge

(Henrietta Smethust/Susie Riddell, Kellie Bright)

Birth: 30.9.1977

When the going gets tough, Kate literally gets going. From an early upset at Cheltenham Ladies' College, through to having daughters of her own, her response to stress has been to throw a few things in a bag and start moving. It's not that she wants to hurt the people she leaves behind: she just knows she'll make things worse if she stays.

As Brian and Jennifer Aldridge's first child together, she was materially very well cared for. Like Jennifer's other children, Debbie and Adam, she quickly developed a taste for riding, and, by ten years old, was entering gymkhanas on her pony, Velvet. By adolescence, however, she was more interested in getting rides on motorbikes, smoking and helping wreck the Christmas tree on the village green. She justified herself by saying she'd had no love or attention. When Brian and Jennifer weren't able to visit her at boarding school on her thirteenth birthday, she went missing for nine hours. The school felt she was a bad influence and asked her to leave.

She was no better back in Ambridge, running up huge phone bills to a German boyfriend, smoking at rehearsals for the nativity play and sneaking off to the disco in Borchester. Blossom Hill Cottage, vacant since grandmother Peggy Archer married Jack Woolley, quickly became the hub of teenage shenanigans which were to result in the unexpected appearance of Peggy's wartime sweetheart, Conn Kortchmar, in the village.

More dangerously, Kate's new boyfriend, Warren, was a thief. An accident in a car he'd stolen left her with a black eye and a police caution. In desperation, her parents brought in an educational psychologist. Family therapy was arranged, but fizzled out when first Brian, then Kate, found excuses not to go.

She had her good points. She got on well with Lynda Snell and showed courage letting down the tyres on Clive Horrobin's getaway van during the raid on the village shop in 1993. Afterwards, she became withdrawn for a while, and, although she once opened up about her feelings to Jennifer, seemed more comfortable spending time with her New Age friends, such as Spike.

Her growing rejection of conventional values was mirrored in her appearance, with a pierced nose complementing two earlier piercings in each ear. Coming back from Glastonbury in August 1994 to find she'd done badly in her GCSEs, she collected the takings from the riding course and headed off. Her family went through agonies not knowing where she was, until she finally returned the following March to explain that she'd been in Kent, trying to stop a motorway extension. Jennifer was too frightened of driving her away again to be angry, and agreed to her moving into one of the Home Farm cottages. Debbie, by contrast, was furious at her selfish behaviour.

Kate brought two things back with her: memories of a short-lived love affair with another protestor, Luther, and a taste for drugs. Mostly she stuck to cannabis, but seemed willing to experiment, with the result that Richard Locke was called out one night when she seemed hyper. Her parents worried about what she was doing, but weren't in a position to stop it.

Jennifer was more pleased by the reforming influence Kate showed on her new boyfriend, Roy Tucker. Brian thought his daughter better suited to Jolyon Gibson, the well-spoken friend who, to Roy's annoyance, first became Kate's lodger, and then her lover. Unfortunately, he was also a drug dealer, whose idea of a Christmas present was a bottle of temazepam capsules. Feeling depressed on New Year's Eve 1995, Kate took whisky and capsules together, and ended up in hospital.

With Gibson out of her life, she started going round festivals with Roy, selling vegetarian food from a van. But if that brought them closer together, the widening of the Borchester bypass pushed them apart again. Kate gave up her job in the Cat and Fiddle to help organize protests against it. Roy was right to be suspicious when Luther turned up and was invited to stay at Kate's cottage. By the time Kate spent a night in the cells for her part in the protests, it was clear that she and Roy were on two different paths and they split up.

To complicate matters, she was shortly to find out that she was pregnant, and couldn't be sure if Roy or Luther was the father. She didn't want either of them involved, but, after giving birth in a tepee at Glastonbury with Morwenna, a qualified midwife, as her birthing partner, she couldn't stop Roy from establishing his paternity through a DNA test. At first Kate resented his interest in their daughter, Phoebe, but gradually saw the benefits of having another parent to share the responsibility.

She proved to be a capable and loving mother, and seemed to settle into resuming part-time work at the shop as well. But towards the end of 1999, she was feeling stifled in Ambridge. Desperate to get away, she took Phoebe with her to Morocco, only to return within a month, panic-stricken when her daughter contracted gastro-enteritis. She then had to make the hardest decision of her life. Much as she loved Phoebe, she felt she couldn't be a good mother until she had finished her own spiritual quest. Leaving Roy to look after their baby, she set off to travel through Africa.

The journey seems to have been the making of her. In South Africa she met, fell in love with and became pregnant by a young radio journalist, Lucas Madikane. Unhappy at the idea of moving to Johannesburg to further his career, she came back to Ambridge, where she had her second daughter, Noluthando Grace, or Nolly. But when Lucas came over to be with her, Kate finally realized she'd found the love and security she'd always been looking for, and, to her family's surprise, married him on their return to South Africa in spring 2001. Although making the decision to leave Phoebe in Ambridge was an awful choice, she now seems confident that her future lies with Lucas and Nolly in Johannesburg. Perhaps for the first time in her life she has nothing to run away from.

Lucas **Madikane**

(Connie M'gadzan)

Two days after Kate Aldridge prematurely gave birth to her second baby, Noluthando Grace, in January 2001, the father arrived in Ambridge. Lucas Madikane was a young radio journalist who had got

Birth: 1972

together with Kate during her stay in Cape Town. They had split up when she wouldn't agree to relocate to Johannesburg so that Lucas could take up a post with the South African Broadcasting Corporation. In the weeks following the birth, however, he managed to convince Kate that her future lay in going back with him and Noluthando.

Born in Langa, one of Cape Town's oldest townships, in 1972, he was fourteen when his elder brother, Thando, was killed by a stray bullet in an outbreak of township violence during the prevailing state of emergency. His parents, Michael and Delia, encouraged him to study, and three years spent at the Pentech, a technical college on the Cape Flats, paid off when his experience with campus radio led on to a professional job with Radio Good Hope. He is proud of his Xhosa roots and is close to his elder sister, Ntombekhay, and younger brothers Desmond and Anele. He is also professionally ambitious, and committed to helping develop the new South Africa. But undoubtedly the greatest pleasure in his life now, after a hard day's work at the SABC, is coming home to his cherished wife and daughter.

Noluthando Grace **Madikane** 'Nolly'

Few things arrived early on the railways in January 2001, but Kate Aldridge's second baby, Noluthando Grace Madikane, was one of them. Kate was on the Blackberry Line steam railway, seeing if she could settle her differences with Hayley Jordan over the care of Kate's first child, Phoebe, when the contractions started. A hectic dash in Hayley's car ensured the baby was born at Borchester General. Her name, meaning 'one who is loved', is usually shortened to Nolly for everyday use. Together with her father, Lucas, and mother, Kate, Nolly is currently happily living in Johannesburg.

Birth: 19.1.2001

Clare **Madison**

The elegant Clare Madison arrived in Ambridge in 1965 as the girlfriend of Ralph Bellamy. Her estranged husband threatened an alienation of affections charge against Ralph, but he fought back by hiring a private detective, who acquired sufficient evidence against the husband to make him back off. Clare also considered a partnership with Ann Grenville in her gown shop, and was briefly involved with Phil Archer, who was then between wives.

Kenneth **Maitland**

(Lewis Gedge)

In 1953, Grace Fairbrother, believing that Kenneth Maitland knew a lot about horses, let him arrange for her to attend a year-long horse management course in Ireland. Reggie Trentham thought he was a fraud, since he was never actually seen in the saddle. He challenged Kenneth to a point-to-point race, with stakes of £250. Kenneth won, but, in some distress, hurriedly quit his lodgings at The Bull. He left behind papers revealing that he was a genuine horseman, who had been forbidden to ride for two years due to spinal injuries. Also left behind were the torn-up remains of Reggie's cheque.

Adrian **Manderson**

(Howard Ward)

In 1999, Usha Gupta told Tom Archer that the barrister she'd engaged for him in the GM crop trial was one of the best, and he (not unreasonably) thought she was referring to his professional abilities. In court, indeed, he put on a brilliant performance. When, a year later, Adrian asked Usha out, however, it became apparent that she had always admired more than his cross-examination skills.

Manor Court

An eighteenth-century gentleman's house, Manor Court was bought by John Tregorran from Ralph Bellamy in 1968. John's new wife, Carol, brought her market gardening expertise to the land, and, by 1976, Manor Court wine was on sale in The Bull and also featured on the elite Grey Gables wine list. When the Tregorrans left for Bristol in something of a hurry in 1984 (John had been infatuated with Jennifer), the house was sold.

Manor House

Well outside Ambridge, the Manor House was the ancestral home of the Lawson-Hopes. With the sale of the Squire's Estate in 1955, however, it passed out of the family for good. The first owner under the new regime was Dr Cavendish, followed by George Fairbrother, and, subsequently, Charles Grenville. On Grenville's death, the house passed to his wife, Carol. She lived there till her marriage to John Tregorran in 1967.

Manorfield Close

This cul-de-sac of twelve old people's bungalows is conveniently situated opposite the Village Hall. There was drama in 1989 when a tree came down across the road, damaging Mrs Potter's garden. The phlegmatic old lady said her garden was always a mess anyway, and, as Mike Tucker and Eddie Grundy dismembered the tree, Jill gamely passed the residents' meals-on-wheels over the branches. Mrs Perkins and Colonel Danby were both one-time residents of Manorfield Close.

Steve Manson

After many years working at Home Farm, Steve Manson was considered an invaluable and reliable foreman. Happily married, and with a second child due, he would probably have stayed in post if his father-in-law hadn't died, leaving a market garden to run. Steve's decision to leave Home Farm in 1989 to take on this new challenge couldn't have come at a worse time, as Brian Aldridge was in hospital after suffering a head injury at Grange Farm. Jennifer was so annoyed by Steve's action that instead of letting him work out his notice, she intemperately sacked him on the spot.

HRH, The Princess Margaret

(Self)

As chairman of the National Society for the Prevention of Cruelty to Children's centenary appeal, the Duke of Westminster agreed to attend a fashion show at Grey Gables in 1984. To the delight of Jack Woolley and all others present, the society's national president, HRH, The Princess Margaret, put in an unexpected appearance as well. Ambridge's fashion cognoscenti commented very favourably on the yellow outfit she was wearing for the occasion.

Market Garden

A year after arriving in Ambridge, Carol Grey decided to develop a smallholding she'd bought from Dan Archer into a market garden to produce a wide range of fruit and vegetables. With input from George Fairbrother, Carol expanded the business, before selling it in 1959 to Charles Grenville. It passed through the hands of Ralph Bellamy and Jack Woolley during the 1965 buy-out of the Grenville estate, before reverting to Carol's ownership the following year. She sold it again in 1980, when she went to join husband John Tregorran in the USA, and it later closed for good.

Timothy Marne

(Alan Barry)

Timothy Marne, also known as Thomas Macready, aka Trevor Malloy (presumably he kept the initials the same for simplicity), was a barman at The Bull in the late 1970s. Sid and Polly were taken in, but former copper George Barford had Timothy's number, recognizing him from his nefarious past. George tipped off PC Drury, and the silver-tongued, Dublin-born conman fled, claiming a dying mother. That old chestnut.

Johnny **Martin**

(Peter Hempson, Philip Neads, Brian Hewlett)

Johnny Martin was one of the two boys fostered by Tom and Pru Forrest in 1960. After some initial difficulties, he thrived in their care. After passing his eleven-plus examination, he attended Borchester Grammar School, and went on to complete a forestry course in 1967. He started working for Ralph Bellamy before moving to a full-time position on Lord Felpersham's estate in 1971. Although he subsequently lost touch with the Forrests, he returned to Ambridge to pay his respects at their funeral.

Birth: 1951

Maxine the Mohican

With lustrous black hair and a leather-fringed costume, Hull-born circus performer Maxine the Mohican was everything Eddie Grundy thought desirable in a woman. In 1990, with Clarrie on holiday in Jersey, Eddie took to hanging round the circus, giving the big-top belle smouldering looks. Perhaps he lost some romantic credibility when he tripped over a guy rope, and needed first aid from Kathy Perks, but Maxine was still willing to listen to Eddie's offer of sausage and chips at Grange Farm. The affair didn't get any further; disapproving Joe Grundy saw to that.

Jane **Maxwell**

(Mary Wimbush)

Is this the girl Phil Archer should have married? In 1951, Phil employed willowy blonde Jane to work with the poultry at Fairbrother's. A real English rose with her peaches and cream complexion, they soon had more than just a good working relationship. Efficient and industrious, Jane worked so late one night that she fell asleep on a pile of sacks in the office. Phil was crouched, waking her, Prince Charming style, when his girlfriend, Grace Fairbrother, appeared and a chastened Phil had to forbid Jane from working late again.

Jane was also close to journalist Dick Raymond, a liaison promoted, thoughtfully, by Grace, and told him she was a would-be novelist, scribbling in her spare time. But her true feelings were for Phil and she was jealous of Grace. It wasn't that Phil couldn't see Jane's obvious allure: in addition to her good looks, she knew about farming, had a more stable temperament than Grace, and, in short, would make a wonderful farmer's wife....

In early 1952, however, Jane abruptly conceded defeat. She gave Phil a week's notice and left for pastures new. One can only hope she got the makings of a novel from her brief encounter.

Brenda **Maynard**

(Jane Rossington)

When Paul Johnson had an affair in 1976, he avoided the cliché of sleeping with his secretary, alighting instead on his boss's PA, Brenda. He'd already broken things off and confessed to Chris when Brenda turned up in the village, staying at The Bull. It took both husband and wife to convince Brenda that it was all over, and she left to return to her filing duties.

Nora **McAuley**

(Julia Mark, Daphne Neville)

Irish barmaid Nora was not exactly lucky in love. Having come to Ambridge in 1966 to join her fiancé, Paddy Redmond, she broke off the engagement the following year when he determined to move down south. A few weeks later, Nora couldn't fail to spot Paddy's likeness in Jennifer Aldridge's baby – the red hair was a bit of a giveaway – but said nothing. Instead, she consoled herself by looking after Greg Salt, whose parents had recently died. After a rocky courtship, they were married, but, when he left her for another woman, she moved into The Bull to manage the B & B accommodation. She next struck up a friendship with the alcoholic George Barford, and, after his suicide attempt in 1974, she again took pity on a lonely man and moved in with him. His ex-wife and son caused endless problems, but a miscarriage, though traumatic, marked a new start for Nora and George. Ironically, it was so that he wouldn't be alone in the evenings that she gave up the bar job she'd loved. She went to work at the canning factory, where she met someone else – someone who, perhaps, would look after her for a change –and moved to a flat in Borchester.

Harry **McIntyre**

Harry McIntyre was Neil Carter's boss during the time he worked as a sales rep for Borchester Mills, the local animal feed company. When the Grundys ran into trouble paying their feed bill in 1998, Harry was amenable to their plan of paying off the outstanding bill at £50 a week.

Angus **McLaren**

(Ian Sadler, Duncan McIntyre)

Perhaps the chance of fishing on the River Am persuaded keen angler Dr Mclaren to take over Dr Harvey's Ambridge practice in 1959. Over the next fifteen years, he dealt calmly with many of the villagers' medical problems, including the difficulties surrounding Elizabeth Archer's birth and those that arose from Jack Archer's losing battle with alcoholism. By 1974, he was ready to retire, and, accordingly, handed on the practice to his well-liked assistant, Dr Poole.

Frank **Mead**

(Graham Rigby)

Polly Perks's father, Frank Mead, was not entirely stable. Always opposed to alcohol and people enjoying themselves, he was aghast when his daughter found bar work at The Bull. By 1966, his obsessions were even more extreme and he became a compulsive arsonist. He was in and out of the County Mental Hospital for years before dying in 1975 and being buried at Penny Hassett, where he had lived.

Death: 1975

Lizzie **Mead**

(Peggy Anne Wood, Joy Davies)

After a difficult life with her mentally unstable husband, it's perhaps not surprising that Lizzie herself became somewhat truculent in her old age. Sid and Polly had hoped for financial help from Polly's widowed mother to buy a cottage in Penny Hassett in which she could have lived, but she stubbornly refused to leave Ambridge. They bought the cottage anyway, and in 1976 Lizzie eventually went to live with her widowed sister, Joan, at Edgeley.

Miss **Merryman**

What dark passions must have lurked beneath the calm, proficient exterior of Miss Merryman. She acted as Jack Woolley's secretary for years, both in Ambridge, and, prior to that, at the London end of his business empire. But in 1968, as Jack's marriage to Valerie started to wobble, anonymous letters circulated, suggesting that he was having an affair with Carol Tregorran. Miss Merryman was uncovered as the practitioner of the poisoned pen, basing what she wrote on drunken gossip from Fred Barratt. Jack, alas, had no choice but to terminate her employment forthwith.

Meyruelle

The citizens of Meyruelle, a small town in the Languedoc-Rousillon region of southern France, rarely venture further than the Golfe du Lion for their holidays. But in 1993, a delegation headed by the mayor, Monsieur Gustave Touvier, visited Ambridge as part of a town-twinning process initiated by Clarrie Grundy, and further developed by Jack Woolley. Two twinning ceremonies were to follow – one in Ambridge on 15 September 1994, and another in Meyruelle the following year. Those wishing to know more about the charming little French town are referred to a video shot by Mr Philip Archer during the Ambridge contingent's visit.

James **Miller**

(John Goodrum)

James Miller was a land agent who acted as valuer for the Tenant Farmers' Association in 1997. He broke the news to Eddie Grundy that Simon Pemberton had applied to the Agricultural Lands Tribunal for an eviction order, on the grounds that the Grundys were negligent and under-efficient in their use of Grange Farm.

Apart from providing informed support in the preparations for the tribunal's hearing, Mr Miller also brokered a deal with Simon's solicitors after the tribunal had found in Eddie's favour, whereby Simon dropped a damages claim in return for Eddie forgoing compensation and legal costs.

Kirsty **Miller**

(Annabelle Dowler)

Tom Archer met intelligent, dark-haired Kirsty at college. He'd already been charged with trashing a GM rape crop at Home Farm in 1999 when, a few months later, he was accused of involvement in another such incident in Northamptonshire: Kirsty had been arrested at the scene wearing his jacket with his bank statement in the pocket. Now both the young lovers had court cases hanging over them, and bail conditions that precluded their meeting. This was hard for the pair, who were reduced to Romeo and Juliet-type trysts in Borsetshire's woods and Borchester's seedier cafés. After his acquittal, Tom reluctantly told Kirsty that they had to stop seeing each other until her case was heard, but that he did love her.

Kirsty's case was eventually dropped, but, by the time she sought Tom out again, ten months after they'd parted, he was, unbeknown to her, involved with another girl, Lauren Walsh. His attempts to two-time the girls led to major complications when both joined the cast of Lynda Snell's *Mikado*, but they eventually rumbled him and made him grovel. Tom settled for Kirsty, who now works with Helen at Ambridge Organics.

Sandy **Miller**

(Elizabeth Revill)

In a moment of marijuana madness, Sandy Miller concealed some joints in boyfriend Neil Carter's pocket during a police raid on a party in 1974. She denied all knowledge of them being there and made Neil promise not to involve her with the police. He was as good as his word, despite being found guilty of a drugs offence and being put on probation. His reward? Sandy telling him she never wanted to see him again. Pretty typical of Neil's luck with women at that time.

Chris **Mills**

(Tim Treslove)

Due to previous cricketing favours having been refused, considerable bad blood had built up between the Ambridge cricket team and Chris Mills, captain of Darrington, by 1998. In the aftermath of that annus most horribilis for Ambridge, when a merger with Darrington was only narrowly staved off, Chris managed to poach Sean Myerson and Roy Tucker for his own team. The following year, he reported Ambridge for playing two New Zealanders who hadn't been registered with the league, ratcheting up the ill-feeling still further. Consequently, matches between the two villages always have a sharp edge now.

Ann **Moore**

(Self)

Shula Archer too headstrong? Surely not! Yet this was the final verdict of showjumper Ann Moore, who spent a large part of 1974 working with Shula and her horse Mister Jones. Ann had originally thought that Shula had promise and, with tuition, could make the grade as a showjumper. But the teenage Shula was obviously not the stable character she is today.

Bill **Morris**

(Jim Hooper)

When Shula's eyes met Bill's across the canteen trays of Borchester Tech in 1975, she was smitten – captivated by his cheeky grin and trendy polo-necked sweaters. He was studying for a National Certificate in Agriculture, and with his 600-acre family farm on the Welsh Borders, he seemed like a safe bet to invite to supper at Brookfield. But when Bill told Phil outright that Ambridge farmers were out of date, he found he was without a date himself.

Trina **Muir**

(Judith Carey)

Scots-born Trina came to Ambridge in 1973 with a tragic past already behind her: she'd once done competition riding but had been lamed in a bad fall, which had also left her unable to have children. Lilian employed her to run the riding school so that she could spend more time with her young son, and Trina immediately spotted Shula's potential. In 1975 she was instrumental in getting Shula on to a horse management course, and, when Shula's favourite horse, Red Knight, had to be put down after an accident, she helped her to work through her grief by enlisting her help in buying and training his replacement.

Although she settled in well at work, it took Trina some time to find her feet on the Ambridge social scene. Eventually, it was Gordon Armstrong who took a fancy to her, and they began going out, though the relationship did not always run smoothly. When he refused to go to a party at the Tregorrans, she glammed up, went alone and was photographed by the *Borchester Echo*. Gordon was soon round eating humble pie, and their relationship was back on again. In 1977, however, she went home for Hogmanay – and stayed.

Sean **Myerson**

(Gareth Armstrong)

Apart from running the Cat and Fiddle with his business and life partner, Peter, Sean Myerson was also a designer and decorator. He impressed Guy and Caroline Pemberton with his work on the Dower House in 1996, and went on to undertake projects for Phil and Jill Archer and the Aldridges. As an entertaining and genial host behind the bar as well, he was generally well liked. Not everyone was able to come to terms with the fact that Sean was gay, however, most noticeably Sid Perks, landlord of rival pub The Bull and captain of the village cricket team. As a skilled cricketer, Sean should have been an automatic selection, but was consistently overlooked, until the 1997 club AGM almost unanimously elected him to be captain. League success and personal triumph in the Single Wicket Competition followed, but Sean felt obliged to defect to Darrington, after failing to see through a merger of the two neighbouring clubs.

Although he and Peter made quite a success of running the Cat, by July 2000 they were ready for new challenges. But as Sean made clear in his speech at the pub's closing party, the memories they were taking from Ambridge were nearly all happy ones.

Nelson's Wine Bar

A place always in tune with the times, if you wanted a glass of red and a slice of quiche in Borchester in the 1980s, the place to go was Nelson's Wine Bar. Nelson acquired the old warehouse in West St at the beginning of the decade and renovated it as a 1920s speakeasy with Al Capone glowering down from the walls. A couple of years later, on the crest of conspicuous consumerism, it became a cocktail bar, with Nigel Pargetter dispensing the margaritas, before Nelson masterminded yet another makeover. This one was in Palm Court style, and attracted the fabulous Hebe (in the words of the poster) to sing on its opening night. But Nelson had money troubles and it fell to Walter to bale him out and finance another relaunch. One boost to trade was no doubt the appointment of the comely Shane as cook-cum-waiter.

In 1996, the wine bar was transformed again, this time into a café-bar serving speciality teas and coffees. It opened on New Year's Eve, offering free champagne, and, perhaps under its influence, Nelson and Julia kissed on the dance floor. A year later, however, the café-bar was abruptly closed. Shane was seen disappearing with the espresso machine, in lieu of his unpaid salary.

Adrian **Netherbourne**

Caroline Pemberton's Bugatti-owning Uncle Adrian lives at Netherbourne Hall, which, like Lower Loxley, is these days open to the public, the family occupying to the east wing. Lord Netherbourne was a prime mover in arranging for the Borsetshire NSPCC Centenary Appeal Fashion Show to be held at Grey Gables in 1984 and the consequent appearance there of both the Duke of Westminster and Princess Margaret. Jack Woolley can never thank him enough.

Alan **Nicholas**

(Raymond Skipp)

In 1972, Dan Archer and Jack Woolley were travelling back to Ambridge with the locomotive Jack had acquired for the Country Park when they took pity on a young hitch-hiker. Long-haired Alan Nicholas clambered aboard with his guitar, and so it was that this particular rolling stone ended up in Ambridge.

Once there, Alan helped to clean up the engine, regaling Tom Forrest with a spur-of-the-moment song about it. He kipped down at Rickyard Cottage with Tony and they entertained two girls they'd met, though Tony always claimed the night was spent discussing literature – a likely story. Alan certainly fancied his chances with women, although he never got anywhere with Trina Muir, and the mobile librarian he had his eye on turned out to be married. When Alan planned to move on to London, Sid and Tony persuaded him otherwise by offering him the job of chef at the steak bar, despite his lack of experience. But Alan never really settled. Haydn Evans accused him of stirring up Angela Cooper's desire to leave home while himself not having the guts to make his own way in life. With a spring in his step and a song in his heart, Alan strapped on his guitar and left.

Lester **Nicholson** 'Nick'

(Hayward Morse)

Pilot Officer Lester Nicholson ('Nick' as he was known) spent a short but illustrious career in the Canadian Air Force and an even shorter time in Ambridge – just time, in fact, to sweep Lilian Archer off her feet and marry her in May 1969. But within nine months of the wedding he was dead, having fallen in a Canadian hospital while receiving treatment for an ear condition that had seen him invalided out of the services.

Birth: 7.6.1946
Death: 18.3.1970

Nick

When Nelson Gabriel described Usha Gupta's colleague Nick as being one of those young men who talks loudly on his mobile phone and drinks foreign beer from the bottle, it's unlikely that he intended to be complimentary. Nick, a friend of Usha's from university days, came to help her run Hebden & Gupta after Mark Hebden's death. In April 1996, he left to start work for Jefferson Crabtree. His enthusiasm for the new company was one of the factors that helped convince Usha she should enter into a merger with them.

Nightingale Farm

In 2000, Hayley Jordan and Roy Tucker were having trouble finding somewhere affordable for themselves, and Roy's daughter, Phoebe, to live. Then Hayley's existing landlady, Marjorie Antrobus, convinced them that, with the incorporation of another, little-used room, the self-contained flat upstairs at Nightingale Farm could be made quite big enough to meet their needs. Some minor alterations, undertaken by Hayley's dad, followed, and the flat duly became a family home not many months before Roy and Hayley's wedding. Since buying the farmhouse, outbuildings and half acre of land, which were all that remained of the original farm, in 1985, Marjorie had enjoyed the company of several lodgers before Hayley. These included Richard Locke, Ruth Archer and

Nigel Pargetter, although Marjorie's original purpose in purchasing the property had been to accommodate the eight dogs she then possessed. Before her time, the flat had been Neil and Susan Carter's first home, while, during the ownership of Hugo Barnaby, the main part of the building had seen service as a youth club and an arts and crafts centre. Before him, Nightingale Farm belonged to Lady Isabel Lander, who had inherited it as part of the estate of her uncle, Brigadier Winstanley.

Michael **O'Leary**

(Michael Collins)

Big-hearted Doughy Hood must have been sorely tempted to change his will, which was made in favour of his assistant Rita Flynn, when Rita was bowled over by the charms of Mr O'Leary, the foreman of a road-working gang in the village in 1960. But Michael was a good thing, liked by everyone who met him, and there were many well-wishers, when, at Easter 1961, the pair became engaged and moved to Ireland.

Steve **Oakley**

(Matthew Morgan)

After farm worker Steve Oakley's girlfriend walked out, he decided to buy her share of their house near Waterley Cross. Employed at Home Farm for the 1994 harvest, he showed himself to be such a useful worker that he was in demand throughout Ambridge over the next year, supplementing his income by taking on casual work in The Bull when necessary. Then a relationship with Debbie Aldridge went wrong, and after Simon Pemberton wouldn't let him rent 80 acres of pasture to set up his own enterprise, Steve felt it was time to sell up and move to Shropshire.

Alan **Oliver**

Christine and Paul Johnson never had cause to be disappointed in the performance of Red Link, the horse they bought in March 1957 from Tony Stobeman, but probably Red Link's finest hour was when he was partnered by leading rider Alan Oliver at Badminton. The showjumper himself bought the horse from them in December of the same year when Paul, jealous of Chris's time, persuaded her to part with him.

Owen

Borchester-born Owen wielded his spatula in a variety of places, including a bistro in York and a yacht in the south of France, before coming to work at The Bull in 1995. Both his personality and his cooking made such a good impression that The Cat and Fiddle couldn't resist poaching him a couple of years later. Clients at the Cat immediately noticed a marked improvement in the food, which lasted until the pub's impending closure prompted Owen to accept the position of chef at Lower Loxley's new café in May 2000.

Ellen **Padbury**

Chosen to be Miss Ambridge 1977 at the village fête, Ellen Padbury had already made a good impression on Neil Carter when she teamed up with him for a Young Farmers' scavenger hunt. The ease with which she rode pillion was attributable to the many hours she'd spent roaring round Penny Hassett on the back of her brother's motorbike. Michele Brown wasn't so enthusiastic when Ellen left the Nightingale Farm flat in a mess after visiting it with her brother and some friends. Once Neil started investing more time in his hopeless crush on Shula Archer, Ellen was rarely seen again in the village.

Tina **Paget**

(Karen Perkins)

Nineteen-year-old Tina, the daughter of a friend of John Tregorran, visited Ambridge in the spring of 1960. Her formative years, mainly spent in South Africa, had clearly been character building, as she showed when, on Carol Grey's advice, she decided to break a date with Ricky Boyd. When Ricky came to remonstrate with her in John Tregorran's shop, she gave a clear and full account of her feelings by hitting him with a paperweight. It was with some relief that Carol and John saw Tina join up with her parents again soon after.

Elizabeth **Pargetter** née Archer

(Judy Bennett, Nicolette Gorton, Alison Dowling)

Marriage and motherhood seemed to have a calming effect on Elizabeth Pargetter, the youngest child of Phil and Jill Archer. As long as business and domestic matters were running

| Birth: 21.4.1967 |

smoothly at Lower Loxley Hall, she was almost docile. But, as her parents discovered in 2000, when she did everything she could to disrupt what she considered the unfair handing on of the family farm to her brother David, the impulsive, hot-tempered daughter who has caused them so much heartache in the past is never far below the surface. Right from the start, Elizabeth created problems. At birth, her heart had a narrowed valve and a hole between the pumping chambers. Two successful operations by the time she was five enabled her to live a normal life, apart from a delay in attending school full-time. It was laziness, rather than poor attendance, that stopped her passing the exams for Borchester Grammar School, however. Her parents sent her to Cherrington Manor instead, a boarding school, where she succeeded in passing eight O-levels before subsequently being expelled for underage drinking. With a view to going on to study agriculture, she enrolled to do a couple of A-levels at Borchester Technical College in 1984, but had to do a rapid rethink when she failed environmental science.

Rather than farming, she spent a summer selling ice cream, in competition with Nigel Pargetter. Then she took a job touting advertising space for the *Borchester Echo* before developing a taste for journalism. Once she had passed the appropriate exams, the *Birmingham Evening News* took her on in 1990, but she didn't feel comfortable living away from Ambridge. She moved back the following year, in time to start a disastrous affair with Cameron Fraser.

Her previous boyfriends had generally given her parents some cause for concern. Mixed-up Terry Barford hadn't been much of a catch; irrepressibly flirtatious Tim Beecham wasn't much better, while Robin Fairbrother had been a doubly unsuitable boyfriend. Apart from still being married when he got together with Elizabeth in 1987, there was a lot of emotional baggage attached to the fact he was the half-brother of Phil's first wife.

But Cameron was easily the worst of the bunch. When he disappeared from Ambridge in 1992, only just ahead of the Fraud Squad, he left Elizabeth brokenhearted and pregnant. After a great deal of heart-searching, she opted for an abortion, much to her mother's distress. Even more upset was her sister, Shula Hebden. Shula and her husband, Mark, were having difficulty conceiving and would willingly have adopted Elizabeth's child. The rift between the two sisters was not healed until after the christening of David's daughter, Pip, when, for the first time, they were able to discuss the complexity of their feelings about the abortion.

Throughout all Elizabeth's troubles with men, there was always one safe rock for her to cling to, the only person allowed to call her Lizzie. When Shula ditched Nigel Pargetter in 1984, he quickly transferred his affections to Elizabeth. For a number of years they had an on/off relationship, occasionally getting engaged to each other, but neither yet mature enough for marriage. Only in the aftermath of her affair with Cameron did Elizabeth realize how much Nigel really meant to her.

She had started working as marketing manager at Lower Loxley in 1992, a job Nigel had created specially for her. Over the following months, despite some friction with Nigel's mother, Julia Pargetter, they grew increasingly close, and, by January 1994, had become engaged. There was a slight hiccup in the run-up to the wedding, when Elizabeth's naturally jealous temperament led her to resent the amount of time Nigel was spending with recently bereaved Shula. Finally she realized that he was devoted to her alone, and, wearing a cream lace dress with roses in her hair, she married him in September of that year.

Like all newlyweds, they needed time to adjust to marriage. When Elizabeth started going away regularly to do consultancy work for Hugh Stevens, Nigel began to have unfounded suspicions of an affair. Julia was an irritant to both of them, constantly interfering in the business side of Lower Loxley. Elizabeth was pleased to see Nigel becoming much better at standing up to his mother. In April 1999, she watched appreciatively while he told Julia off for disrupting repair work to Lower Loxley. Impressed by his authoritative manner, Elizabeth quickly led him off to the bedroom.

The news that she was expecting twins some months after should not have been a surprise to her. After all, two of her siblings, Kenton and Shula, are twins. But it did create some complications. The pregnancy wasn't easy, with bouts of breathlessness and palpitations indicating that her heart was having trouble coping with the strain. She was admitted to hospital early, and, on 12 December 1999, Baby G and Baby B, later to be named Lily and Freddie, were delivered by caesarean section. Freddie, taking after his mother, caused an immediate panic by having breathing problems. Fortunately, after some days in an incubator, he pulled through. Elizabeth postponed an operation to replace a leaky valve in her heart to throw herself into combining motherhood with the work of running Lower Loxley. Greatly angered and upset when she couldn't persuade her parents to give her and her children a greater share in Brookfield, she drove herself to the point where she had a cardiac arrest in January 2001. As became clear in a reconciliation with her father afterwards, it wasn't so much the financial benefits she'd wanted as the reassurance she was as valued as her brothers and sister.

Now apparently fully recovered, Elizabeth is on better terms with her parents, but can still harbour resentments if she feels others have received preferential treatment in family matters. The suspicion that her own children may be disadvantaged, whether in the division of Brookfield or in any other matter, is quite enough to bring out the tigress in her. When that happens, poor Nigel can only watch and hope that serious damage isn't done.

Gerald **Pargetter**

The portrait of Gerald Pargetter hanging in the drawing-room of Lower Loxley Hall clearly shows his grey eyes and large nose, but can only hint at the unspeakable smell he used to bring in from hunting, according to his wife, Julia. One in a long line of Pargetters, Gerald loved country living, but had no head for figures. In consequence, when he died in 1988, he was leaving Julia, and their children, Nigel and Camilla, an estate that had gone into steep decline.

Death: 28.4.88

Julia **Pargetter**

(Jo Kendall, Mary Wimbush)

Without Bitterness: from Lemons to Lower Loxley was the title of the autobiography Julia Pargetter started to write in 1998. It never got further than the opening pages, thus sparing booksellers the conundrum of whether to file it under fact or fiction. Few people in Borsetshire have ever shown a greater tendency to re-invent their personal history than Julia.

Birth: 17.8.1924

Once ensconced in the centuries-old Pargetter family home, Lower Loxley Hall, she was content to let others believe that she, like her husband, Gerald, came from genteel stock. It was only in 1994, some years after Gerald's death, that the full truth of Julia's past came out, when her sister, Ellen Rogers, came for the wedding of Julia's son, Nigel. Proudly illustrating the social progress Julia had made, Ellen revealed that she had formerly been called Joan and that their father had been a greengrocer, who had wanted both his girls to be secretaries. Showing a lifelong disdain for the mundane, Joan had become Julia, and had set off to find success as an actress and dancer. In the glamour-hungry years of the Second World War, she soon had a phalanx of male admirers convinced that she was the next Marlene Dietrich. One of them, who waited at the stage door for her in Bridlington, was to change her life. First he left her a red rose. The next day she received a fox fur coat and a note reading: 'To warm your heart, as you have warmed mine.' Soon she accepted Gerald Pargetter's offer of marriage, and settled into life on the Lower Loxley Estate.

Two children, Nigel and Camilla, were born. Julia was not instinctively maternal, and left much of their upbringing in the hands of others. She was later to blame Nigel's overly pliable nature on the fact that his nanny was a *Guardian* reader, and therefore not to be trusted. While she greatly enjoyed cooking, Julia was perhaps not completely fulfilled by married life, and was being treated for depression by the last years of Gerald's life. When he died, in 1988, she refused to countenance Nigel's suggestion that she hand on the estate immediately to avoid death duties later. But neither was she prepared to plan a realistic overhaul of Lower Loxley's parlous finances. Instead, she left matters in Nigel's hands, while she took off on a series of extended trips abroad.

She spent time in France and the Caribbean, occasionally returning to Borsetshire for long enough to complain at the way her son was opening up Lower Loxley to the public. Finally, she was persuaded of the business sense in handing Lower Loxley on to Nigel. Nelson Gabriel sometimes invited Julia out during her visits home, partly to give Nigel some respite, and a rollercoaster friendship developed between them, which never quite resolved itself into romance. An interior designer called Asty was another gentleman friend of Julia's. She had plans for him to do some work at Lower Loxley, but he was rather a dubious character, and their friendship faded after they fell out during a holiday together in Barbados.

By the time she had run out of the money to keep travelling, it was clear that Julia had become heavily dependent on alcohol. By 1993, she was ready to admit she was an alcoholic and asked Nigel to help her kick the habit. A Christmas shopping expedition led to a relapse, and there was another false start the following year after she entered a clinic, only to discharge herself and set off on a drinking binge with one of Nigel's credit cards in hand. But she persevered and has now not had a drink for some years. She strongly disapproved of Nigel's involvement with Elizabeth Archer and tried to steer him in the direction of Debbie Aldridge, reasoning that a match with such a wealthy family could go a long way towards solving Lower Loxley's money problems. When that plan fell through, she grudgingly came to accept Nigel and Elizabeth getting engaged. She attempted to take over the wedding arrangements, saying that she wanted to make the ceremony worthy of her son, even if the bride wasn't, but was then furious when she discovered that Brookfield, not Lower Loxley, was to be the centre of operations on the day.

Occasionally, she complains that she receives better treatment from daughter Camilla and son-in-law James, but Julia is actually much happier living at Lower Loxley. She has not been an easy presence for Nigel and Elizabeth to have around while trying to run a conference centre and visitor attraction. If there is a way of disrupting the smooth running of events, Julia will find it. Her commandeering of the main business computer to try her hand at a romantic novel, *Passion's Plaything*, in 1998 was only one example among many. She was also responsible for the appearance of some very sinister debt-collectors, when she reneged on a gambling debt owed to the notorious Ronald Hardwicke. Moreover, her well-meaning efforts at cost cutting are invariably highly expensive. Yet her gift for communication proved invaluable when the art gallery Elizabeth masterminded opened in 1999, and Julia showed herself to be an excellent saleswoman.

She seems much more reconciled to having Elizabeth as her daughter-in-law since the birth of the twins, Lily and Freddie. She's even tried helping to look after them, though her response time to crying in the night is slowed by her need to get hair and make-up just right before leaving her bedroom. Lewis, the architect who oversaw the conversion of a barn into the gallery, has become a close friend, too – so much so that on her seventy-fifth birthday she removed any birthday cards that might have revealed her true age to him. But increasing age and becoming a grandmother haven't changed her too much. She still interferes with the running of Lower Loxley whenever she sees fit, and her flair for self-aggrandisement is still entirely intact. She is only too pleased to confirm that in 1996 she acted in a period drama with 'Marlon'. Only under the most persistent questioning will she acknowledge that the Marlon in question was actually a rather splendid pig.

Lily and Freddie **Pargetter**

You wait five years for Elizabeth and Nigel Pargetter to have children, then all of a sudden, two come at once. Both were born by caesarean section: first of all there was Lily, weighing in at 5lb 11oz, then Freddie, a few ounces lighter. Nigel and Elizabeth didn't have names ready, so Lily became Baby G and Freddie Baby B for a short time.

Birth: 12.12.1999

Baby B had things tough at the start; small and fragile, he spent his first five days in an incubator overcoming breathing problems. The twins developed good, healthy appetites, with Lily seeming marginally greedier. She wore the Archer gown at their christening, while Julia Pargetter, a great believer in the importance of the male hereditary line, insisted that Freddie should have the Pargetter gown.

Elizabeth had some fears that her babies were developing a little slowly, but Jill Archer reassured her there was nothing to worry about. Further support came from the Borchester Twins Club, which Elizabeth started attending. Freddie and Lily were soon thriving; with luck they'll inherit their mother's head for business and their father's good nature. If they're unlucky, it'll be the other way round.

Nigel **Pargetter**

(Graham Seed, Nigel Caliburn, Graham Seed)

As a son of country gentry, Nigel Pargetter may have been born with a silver spoon in his mouth, but, like a great deal else in Lower Loxley Hall, it had probably been bought with borrowed money. Since 1988, when he took on running the hall and accompanying estate on the death of his father, Gerald, Nigel has battled with dry rot, death-watch beetle and a seemingly ever-increasing overdraft to try to make Lower Loxley financially viable. Those people in Ambridge who think of him only as a likeable buffoon who is never happier than when in fancy dress, underestimate his deep commitment to his family's history and traditions. Now he has children of his own to hand an inheritance on to, he is determined to keep Lower Loxley, and as much of its lands as possible, in Pargetter hands.

Birth: 8.6.1959

Earlier days were more carefree. As a child, he had a great fondness for teddy bears, some of whom can still be seen in the Toy Museum at Lower Loxley. Like his father, he was educated at Rugby and then sent out to make his way in the world. He wasn't without talents. Gerald taught him that the secret of making really good cucumber sandwiches lies in blending curry powder with the butter, while Nigel's ability to undo bras through blouses could always revive flagging conversations at parties.

He didn't seem so well suited to work, however. He struggled as a swimming pool salesman, failed to thrive on his Uncle Clarence's beef and maize farm in Zimbabwe, and, although he showed enthusiasm in the great Ambridge ice cream war, when his Mr Snowy van was in fierce competition with Elizabeth Archer's Mrs Snowy outfit, it was never going to be a full-time career. In 1986, he started work at the Stock Exchange, but, by the following year, the Stock Exchange found it could do very well without him.

If Nigel couldn't find his niche as a worker, he was just as unsettled in his personal life. He became very fond of Shula Archer, once he started dating her in 1983, but, much as she enjoyed his company, Shula considered Mark Hebden a much better long-term prospect. After Shula, Nigel turned his attentions to her sister, Elizabeth, or Lizzie as he alone called her. Wearing his trademark gorilla suit to take her back to school was just one of the many flamboyant touches that endeared him to her. They would go out with each other in the gaps between other romances. By 1989, Nigel felt that since Lizzie wasn't looking for the same lifelong commitment he wanted, they should end their relationship. Misunderstanding what he was saying and wanting to prove she could be serious, she proposed to him. For a while they were engaged, until they both realized they hadn't thought it through, and all plans to marry were dropped.

Nigel's new responsibilities after his father's death sometimes made him take a more sober look at life. Contrary to expectation, he quickly established that he was capable of making big decisions in reorganizing Lower Loxley's finances. Despite advice from Rodway & Watson that he should sell Old Court Farm, he opted to re-rent it. He then proved he was his own man by letting it to the Crump family, the existing tenants on an adjoining smallholding, rather than responding to blandishments from various members of the Archer clan, who wanted to take it on instead. He started opening Lower Loxley Hall to the public and held a highly successful medieval banquet there in June 1989, the funds going some way towards paying to repair damage from dry rot.

Nigel's mother, Julia, was horrified at the thought of hoi polloi filing through the family home. Nigel never found contradicting her easy, especially when she had been drinking, but he stuck manfully to the task of expanding Lower Loxley's business base. To this end, he took a major step forward in 1992. On this occasion, however, his motivation was personal as well as practical. He had been looking on miserably while

Elizabeth conducted her unhappy affair with Cameron Fraser and had generously taken her on as marketing manager at Lower Loxley during this time. Together they prepared the launch of Lower Loxley Corporate Entertainments in July. As they worked together over the next months to make the new enterprise a success, their old fondness for each other gradually reasserted itself, and now, shaped by a growing maturity, they realized they were finally ready for marriage.

A bag of nerves on his wedding day in September 1994, Nigel was convinced he would never manage to say coherently '...and thereto I plight my troth'. But the service went well, and since then the marriage has been, for the most part, a good one. A period of coolness in 1997, which almost induced Nigel to start an affair with Caroline Pemberton, was resolved by a bungee jump on the village green, when a worried Elizabeth realized how much she loved her husband and would hate to lose him. Together they have moved Lower Loxley in a new direction as a rural theme park.

More importantly, they have become parents. Nothing has given Nigel as much happiness as fathering the twins, Frederick Hugo and Lilian Rosalind, who appeared on 12 December 1999. Very much a hands-on father, Nigel has even, briefly, tried putting them in cardboard boxes when there was a misplaced concern that they were late in developing sitting skills.

Those who were present at Nigel's fortieth birthday party fondly remember him driving round in an ice cream van and dropping an ice-lolly down Siobhan Hathaway's back. But while he still has the capacity to let rip on occasion, there is another side to him these days. Unintentionally, Elizabeth's fears about Lily and Freddie losing out in the Brookfield inheritance hurt Nigel. He has matured into someone who, having taken on the responsibility of a wife and children, will do everything in his power to provide all they will ever need.

Simon **Parker**

(Alaric Cotter)

On a balmy June night in 1977, the young Shula Archer lay down with Simon Parker on a tartan picnic rug in a Netherbourne cornfield. The earth moved, and so did the moral climate in Ambridge. Phil was always suspicious of Simon, whom he castigated as 'that inky blighter' – a reference to Simon's journalistic career on the *Felpersham Evening Post* and then the *Borchester Echo* – and not without reason. Bursting on to the Ambridge scene with a story about the youth club – or lack of it – entitled 'The Village That Doesn't Want Its Young', Simon later scooped a story about Shula hunting on the dole – and not for jobs. Shula was besotted with him, however, supporting him in his print campaign against the allegedly corrupt councillor Tom Tyrrell, unluckily a friend of *Echo* proprietor Jack Woolley. Simon always thought he was made for higher things, however. After seeing Shula intermittently for a year – he was often late for dates and at one point spurned her for a girl with purple fingernails (varnished, one hopes) – he told her during May Day celebrations in 1978 that he'd been offered work in London. End of story.

Partridge Twins

Far from being the singing teen idols their name suggests, the Partridge Twins are two monosyllabic friends of Eddie Grundy's, whose most notable contribution to local life so far was pulling the traps for a clay pigeon shoot in 1989. Not even Eddie knows their first names, so they are referred to simply as Partridge One and Partridge Two. It is to be hoped that neither has offspring named in the American manner, thus sparing Ambridge the complexities of addressing Partridge Two, the Third.

Lyn **Pasco**

(Jane Galloway)

Almost ten years before Ruth Archer arrived at Brookfield, agricultural student Lyn was blazing a trail as general farm hand at Bridge Farm. Pat was supportive of her agricultural ambitions, but Tony – sceptical from the start – was not impressed when she had trouble rodding a drain, even less so when she told him it was his fault for not having self-locking rods. Lyn also helped with the Home Farm lambing before finding work outside Ambridge, where she might be better appreciated.

Birth: 1978

Fat **Paul**

As the Grundys' money troubles started to get serious in 1999, Eddie looked for help from anyone and everyone. One of his circle, the heavily tattooed Fat Paul, couldn't lend Eddie any money himself, but put him in touch with the loan shark Mike Butcher. It is not known if Eddie calls his friend 'Fat' to his face, or uses 'Corporeally Enhanced' Paul out of politeness.

Peaches

Peaches was a good-looking barmaid who worked at the Cat and Fiddle in the mid-1980s, where she was much admired by Tim Beecham. To be honest, there can't be many attractive young women dispensing alcohol whom he doesn't fancy.

Dick **Pearson**

Landlord of the Cat and Fiddle, Dick Pearson fell ill with liver trouble in 1983 and had to leave his post for a time – an absence much regretted by Joe and Eddie Grundy. While they found Dick convivial company, the relief landlord sent to replace him was anything but. Coming from an army background, and with experience of running a boxing club in Leeds, the new chap didn't seem the sort who'd put up with any nonsense from his customers, so the Grundys wisely decided to decamp to The Bull for the duration of Dick's illness.

Pedro

(Norman Painting)

When eighteen-year-old Shula 'did' Europe with friends in 1976, she fell hard for soulful Spaniard Pedro. When he turned up in England minus sun, sea and sangria, however, the allure had gone, partly perhaps because he spoke no English. Shula took him hunting, but his horse bolted, and, alarmed by country life, he left for London, leaving Shula a red rose in one last lavish Latin gesture.

John **Peel**

(Self)

Blodwyn Pig, Atomic Rooster, the Flock: many of the bands once championed by DJ John Peel had obvious agricultural connections. He had the chance to promote a band with even more distinctive rural roots when Eddie Grundy gave him some demo tapes towards the end of 1991. John was in Ambridge after a chance meeting between Caroline Bone and the controller of Radio 1, Johnny Beerling, when rafting down the Zambezi. This led to the Radio 1 DJs' Christmas lunch being held at Grey Gables. John, impressed by Eddie's celebrity impersonations at the village pantomime, invited him and his family to join the lunch. He was less impressed with the tapes, however, which were returned shortly afterwards.

Caroline **Pemberton** née Bone

(Sara Coward)

Unkindly known by some as 'the village bicycle' – as a result of her somewhat chequered romantic past – Caroline is now a wealthy widow, living in her late husband's home, the Dower House. But her clipped tones and well-groomed presence are more often to be found at Grey Gables, where she has a very full-time job as manager of Jack Woolley's prestigious hotel.

Birth: 3.4.1955

Caroline Bone, as she was born, is of a noble family with a long pedigree. The de Bohuns reputedly came over with William the Conqueror, and fought in the breach at Agincourt and on the beaches of Dunkirk. She is related through marriage to Lord Netherbourne, and her family live at Darrington.

Caroline arrived as hostess/organizer at Grey Gables in 1979 via The Bull, Acapulco and Bristol, where she ran a wine bar. Although she is herself a trained cordon bleu cook, her skills in the Grey Gables kitchen have always lain in the special understanding she has with Jean-Paul, the temperamental French chef. Jack Woolley so valued her handling of him that any threat of Caroline's to leave inevitably met with a promotion: she was made restaurant manager in 1983 and general manager in 1988.

As an attractive single girl in Ambridge – tall and slim with hazel eyes and dark hair – Caroline has always been the focus of a lot of male attention. In the early 1980s, though, while her friend Shula was meeting and marrying Mark Hebden, nothing seemed to go right for Caroline. A boyfriend called Lance chucked her, and Paul Chubb, a pilot in the Fleet Air Arm, went off and married a girl called Philippa. By 1985 she was at a low ebb. Meeting Brian Aldridge at a Hunt Ball, she danced with him all night and they began a torrid affair. Caroline was lucky that it was the dim Tony who saw Brian kissing her passionately in the Country Park: only he would have believed Brian's glib explanation that it was a deferred birthday kiss from weeks ago. After a couple of months, however, Caroline couldn't stand the deception, and told Brian it was all off. When Jennifer later found out and confronted her, a shamed Caroline thought of leaving the district, but her new boyfriend, Matthew Thorogood, was understanding, and she decided to stick it out. In 1987, Caroline moved in with Matthew at Ambridge Farm, but soon felt taken for granted. She moved back into Grey Gables the following year and rapidly put in train plans to build a health club there to enhance its leisure facilities.

In 1990, she met Cameron Fraser, the new owner of the Berrow Estate. Soon he was buying her dinner and parading her at Ascot and his Highland shooting lodge. As he'd done during her relationship with Matthew, Brian tried to needle her with his jealous comments, but Caroline did the sensible thing: had a new hairdo and ignored him. Sadly, Cameron, too, would let her down, not just by dumping her in favour of Elizabeth Archer, but by fraudulently investing £60,000 of her money. It was no wonder that she turned, if not to God, then to his representative on earth in the shape of vicar-cum-vet Robin Stokes. This unlikely liaison flourished, despite Caroline's lack of faith, the visits of his two boisterous sons, and his avowal that he could only countenance sleeping with her within the bounds of marriage. Caroline was thunderstruck. Was this a proposal? Indeed it was, and she and Robin became engaged in 1993.

Caroline was just two days away from her wedding when she was involved in the car accident that killed Mark Hebden and left her badly injured. Recovering slowly, she found she had no common ground with Robin, who – incredibly to her – still believed in a benificent God. She called the whole thing off and the wedding presents were parcelled up and returned.

Apart from men, some of the greatest traumas in Caroline's life have involved animals. Mike Tucker shot her sheepdog pup, Charlie; Jack's bull terrier, Captain, died while in her care; and her horse, Ippy, was stolen. It was horses, however, that brought her together with the man who would, at last, become her husband – Guy Pemberton. She helped him choose a new mount, Moonlight; he bought her another, Maisie, for her birthday, and, within six months, they were married. Another six months on, however, there was heartbreak again when Guy died prematurely of a heart attack. Caroline, beside herself with grief, blamed his son Simon, and also revealed to Shula that Simon, whom Shula had been seeing, had been two-timing her. It was a dreadful time for both women. Their friendship was repaired, but the scars of Guy's death took longer to heal.

Guy left her both the Dower House and his investment in The Bull, and Caroline proved that she'd learnt to be more shrewd financially when she insisted to Sid that if she put in more money to facilitate Kathy's divorce settlement, she'd expect a 51 per cent share of the business. With Jack's total retirement, she became busier than ever at Grey Gables, not least during the filming of a 'docusoap' there in the summer of 2001. As for the men in her life, there have been some developments. A much younger man moved into her home, but, for once, tongues were not set wagging as it was her godson, William Grundy, who became her lodger when his family was evicted from Grange Farm. Her on-off romance with the new owner of the Grundys' erstwhile home, Oliver Sterling, seems to be 'on' again at present, but Guy – the perfect match – is proving a tough act to follow.

Guy **Pemberton**

(Hugh Dickson)

When distinguished-looking widower Guy bought the Estate after the Cameron Fraser débâcle, all of Ambridge, not least the tenants, was relieved to have a landlord who was more of the old school. Rhizomania, coupled with a desire to retire, had, he claimed, brought him to Ambridge, though the real reason was later revealed to be the death of his elder son, Andrew, who had been destined to take over his East Anglian farm.

> **Birth:** 1931
> **Death:** 12.4.1996

Guy quickly established himself as firm but fair, a true countryman, who acted as cricket scorer and stabled his old hunter, Mungo, with Christine Barford. Having had no dairying experience, he consulted Phil about bovine matters and the Brookfield team were delighted when Guy later awarded them the contract to farm his arable acreage. Guy also acted as saviour of The Bull by becoming Sid's partner.

Eminently eligible, he at first seemed perfect for Mrs Antrobus, but, through a shared passion for horseflesh, it was Caroline to whom he eventually proposed. They married on 11 September 1995, but, by the following year, Guy was dead of a heart attack, leaving the Estate to his reprehensible son Simon. Against Caroline's wishes, he was buried next to his first wife in Suffolk.

Simon **Pemberton**

(Peter Wingfield)

Initially, Simon had kept a low profile in Ambridge, and there are many who might wish it had stayed that way. He accounted for his abrasive approach by claiming he'd always felt his father loved him less than his brother, but that doesn't excuse his violence to Shula and Debbie, both of whom were his girlfriends. However, when Debbie brought a case against him in 1997, the court believed his plea of mitigation – he cited the stress of his father's death – and gave him a conditional discharge and £200 fine.

That Simon should get away with it was typical: his arrogance made him think he could get away with anything. Earlier, in 1995, running the Estate after Guy had a riding accident, he argued with Geoff Williams, the farm manager, causing him to resign. He interfered in Guy's recuperation and bitterly opposed his marriage to Caroline. Shula defended him to the village and to her friend, but he betrayed her by having an affair with an old flame, Harriet. Having severed his links with Ambridge, he now spends a lot of time abroad with his irrigation equipment business. One can only feel sorry for those who cross his path, particularly the women.

Penny Hassett

Penny Hassett is little more than two miles away from Ambridge. Its best-known features are, perhaps, the church of St Saviour's, one of the four churches in Janet Fisher's remit, and its pub, the Crown and Cushion, more commonly referred to as the Crown. There is also a small private school for girls, St Margaret's, that Alice Aldridge attends. Shula Archer and Mark Hebden bought a cottage there during their first engagement, but otherwise people from Ambridge don't seem keen on moving to their slightly larger but less attractive neighbour.

Arthur **Perkins**

(Bernard Fishwick)

The Fairbrothers' desire to place a memorial window in the church for Grace in 1959 had ramifications which reached far beyond Phil and Jill's reaction. The stonemason engaged for the job

Death: 4.12.1968

was one Arthur Perkins, a widowed Londoner, who lodged at The Bull, where the landlady's mother, Mrs P, served him his supper. Finding much to impress in his temperate attitudes, the usually unbending Mrs P invited him to her cottage, albeit to dig the garden. Arthur duly proposed, and, though Mrs P was so shocked she had to go and stay with Aunt Laura to recover, she eventually said yes during a drive with Arthur in her pony and trap.

In his retirement, they divided their time between Ambridge and the East End, dogged by Arthur's poor health. He never really recovered from a heart attack in 1965 and died in 1968. He was buried in London within the sound of Bow bells.

Polly **Perkins** 'Mrs P'

(Pauline Seville)

Peggy Archer's mother, Mrs Perkins, always known as Mrs P, bustled into Ambridge in her black duster coat and feathered hat in 1951 and immediately began taking the village to task. Her

| Birth: 6.3.1905 |
| Death: 3.5.1991 |

deceased husband had been a railwayman and she'd been living on her own in the East End, but she'd answered a cry for help from her daughter, who was struggling to cope with three small children and a feckless husband. Mrs P's strict moral code and sharp tongue soon dealt with him.

Although she settled willingly in Ambridge for Peggy's sake, Mrs P was not a natural countrywoman. Offered mushrooms by Tom Forrest, she said she didn't trust those picked from the field – though if she'd thought it through, those in the greengrocer's had surely come the same route. She didn't endear herself to Dan at the start of the hunting season when she told him that anyone who galloped around the countryside 'like they were in a cowboy film' deserved all they got, yet she was frightened of foxes, as well as rats. She couldn't bear the sight of anyone skinning rabbits, and thought it a shame to shoot squirrels as they had such pretty tails. In other aspects of village life, though, she fitted in beautifully. A stalwart of the church cleaning rota, no one could get a shine on the eagle's-head lectern like Mrs P, and she also enjoyed whist drives, the WI and the Over Sixties Club at the Village Hall. Thinly disguised as Gypsy Rose Perkins, she read the tea leaves at several village fêtes, once spookily predicting a mishap for Christine, who promptly tripped over a tent peg and ricked her ankle. In 1986, Mrs P was outraged when Mrs Antrobus, then a newcomer to the village and an innocent in its workings, asked Martha Woodford to tell the fête fortunes. Mrs A was lucky that she didn't suffer the fate of Mabel Bagshawe, whom Mrs P badmouthed over two pots of plum jam Mabel had allegedly 'stolen'. Mrs P then remembered that she had herself given them to Jill.

But beneath her well-corseted breast beat a heart of gold, at least where Walter Gabriel, her long-time friend and confidant, was concerned. Within a year of their meeting, when Walter was under pressure from the Squire's nephew Clive Lawson-Hope to shape up or be thrown off his farm, she offered to lend Walter £400 – a considerable sum in those days – to help him restock. When matters didn't improve, she took things into her own hands, visiting the Squire to intercede on Walter's behalf. This, by the way, was a woman who'd once beaten a stranger over the head with her umbrella for mistreating cattle at Borchester market, but presumably the Squire was more tractable, for he agreed to stop Clive from harassing Walter, and the umbrella stayed safely sheathed.

Mrs P was constantly having her leg pulled about her ongoing friendship with Walter, but she always maintained that he behaved like a perfect gentleman. The closest they came to intimacy, in fact, was when she called round one day to find him washing some underpants. Unable to stop herself from taking over, as was her wont, she insisted she'd rinse them through for him, and, on seeing both the state and the commodious size of his combinations, ripped them up for floor cloths. Only afterwards did she realize that he was actually washing them to wear. As forthright as ever, she offered to buy him some new ones, but a blushing Walter refused, and she made him an egg and bacon pie instead. On another practical note, she gave 'our Peg' some good advice when the latter complained that her husband, Jack, was spending too much on drink. Mrs P. recommended the treatment she'd once meted out to her own first husband, Albert – boiled potatoes and marge for a fortnight, with boiled oxtail on Sundays. This, she said, should convince Jack to be more careful with the housekeeping.

For all her formidable appearance and fierce tongue, Mrs P seemed to spend most of her time in Ambridge fighting off men. Joe Blower, Doughy Hood, and, of course, Walter, fell sway to her charms, but when she did remarry, she contrived to keep her name by settling for Arthur Perkins, a retired stonemason. The marriage was happy but short-lived, and, when Arthur died after eight years, Mrs P returned to the village and pretty much took up where she'd left off. Walter almost ruined the balance of their relationship by his proposal in 1970, and, when he attempted to kiss her in 1976, Mrs P was so scandalized that she refused to accompany him to the Woodfords on New Year's Eve. Instead she went alone. Walter tried to make up by first-footing with a bottle of champagne, but, when he removed the cork it shot out of the bottle, striking Mrs P on the back of the head. Walter had a lot of explaining to do.

Horrified at Jennifer's pregnancy back in 1967, Mrs P and her granddaughter were eventually reconciled, and the new great-grandmother became a favourite babysitter for Jennifer's brood, as well as for Pat and Tony's. Keeping busy, she asserted, kept her young. In 1987, however, she was hurt not to be invited to Christmas drinks at Home Farm and spent most of Christmas Day alone. Pat tried to assure her that no one had been trying to leave her out, but Mrs P got her own back on New Year's Eve by disappearing overnight. On New Year's Day she announced she'd had a lovely evening babysitting for the Tucker children, and was most amused by her family's discomfiture.

From her prime spot in Manorfield Close, Mrs P could keep an eye on 'Mr Gabriel', and, indeed, all the village goings-on. In 1991, however, when Peggy and Jennifer arrived for lunch, the house was still and silent. Mrs P had died peacefully in her chair. At the age of eighty-five, death had come at last. Still, as she was often heard to say, 'There's not much you can do about it, is there?'

Jamie **Perks**

(Benjamin Minchin)

Birth: 20.7.1995

Born just before the stroke of midnight on 20 July 1995, little Jamie's world was turned upside down when his parents' marriage fell apart and his mum, Kathy, took him to live at Bridge Farm. With their move to April Cottage, and better relations between his parents, Jamie looks to be in for happier times, able to concentrate on his Scalextric, bike, remote-controlled car and all the other spoils of the divorced child.

Kathy **Perks**

(Hedli Niklaus)

Birth: 30.1.1953

There's never a good time to be told your husband is having an affair, but, arguably, the middle of your crowded pub on a Friday night is not one of the all-time greats. This, however, was Kathy's experience when Eddie spelt out the reality of Sid's absence from bar duties. Suddenly, with sickening certainty, Kathy knew the truth about all those sweaty sessions at the gym and the fateful night Sid's car was supposed to have broken down. Confronting him in a searing exchange later that same night, she said she needed time to think, but their attempts to patch up their thirteen-year marriage came to a poignant end when she walked off the dance floor at the Tower Ballroom, Blackpool, and they both had to admit it was over.

When Kathy first came to the area in 1984, she already had a broken marrriage behind her. She was a teacher of domestic science (and sex education) at Lucy Perks's school, but her first date with Sid – a meal out – was not a resounding success, and she became involved with local policeman Dave Barry, whom she met when he investigated the theft of the school's video recorder. She helped Dave with the décor of the Police House, but, recognizing his not-so-latent chauvinism just in time, refused to move in with him. In October 1986, she went on a whim to the Mop Fair in Borchester with Sid, and they ended up kissing. Soon Dave had got his marching orders and Sid swiftly proposed, though it took him three attempts before Kathy could be persuaded to accept.

They married on 24 April 1987 at Borchester Register Office, Kathy in a silk dress, and pearls borrowed from Peggy. Lucy went to stay at Bridge Farm while they were on honeymoon, and Kathy probably wished she could have stayed there, for Lucy's diversionary tactics in the early months of their marriage – playing up at school, seeming to get religion, sabotaging BST tests at Brookfield – must have put a strain on the newlyweds. When, in 1989, Kathy's school was amalgamated with another, she was despondent about her career and ripe for an affair. Dave Barry, still on the scene, was only too happy to oblige, chatting her up, to Sid's fury, at a jazz evening in Nelson's Wine Bar. Christmas that year was dull and quiet, Kathy complained, but she made up for it at The Bull's New Year's Eve party, kissing Dave passionately under the mistletoe, and, having sent Sid to bed, making love with her former beau on a pub banquette.

Although she tried to tell herself, and Dave, that it had all been a mistake, she couldn't keep away from him. Matters were made worse by Sid's New Year resolution to be the perfect husband, and, when he arranged a romantic weekend away for the two of them, Kathy had to pretend to be tired to avoid her conjugal duties. Guilt-ridden, she semi-confided in Pat, who advised her see a counsellor. This helped, and, by the summer, Kathy had broken things off with Dave. She threw herself into training for the St John Ambulance Brigade, but, though he'd moved to St Albans, Dave sent her both a birthday card and Valentine gift the following year. Belatedly, Sid realized her deception. He walked out and went missing for six weeks, and, on his return, threw her out. Kathy was fortunate to get a job with accommodation, running the leisure centre at Grey Gables. Sid started divorce proceedings, but it wasn't until Christmas 1991 that both could admit they didn't really want to part. To Lucy's horror, the marriage was repaired, and Kathy was totally supportive of Sid, when, in 1993, Peggy Woolley decided to sell The Bull. After protracted negotiations, Sid bought the pub in partnership with Guy Pemberton, though Kathy initially retained her independence and her job at Grey Gables, covering for Caroline Bone after her accident in February 1994.

In October that year, Kathy and Sid flew to New Zealand for Lucy's wedding, and it was during a moonlit stroll on a beach that their son was conceived. When she discovered she was pregnant, Kathy's first reaction was one of dismay, especially as she and Sid had just embarked on an ambitious plan to open a Civil War-themed restaurant at The Bull. It opened in June 1995 and Jamie was born a month later.

Kathy gave up her job at Grey Gables to run the Hassett Room, but Ambridge had a limited appetite for salmagundi and syllabub, and, a year later, it was replaced by the Family Restaurant, which basically serves chips with everything. Disillusioned, Kathy returned to supply teaching, but the marriage had entered a dangerously stale period. Kathy mocked Sid when he embarked on a health kick, but she should have taken more notice of his newly muscular physique. Jolene Rogers certainly did and they began a highly-charged affair.

When Kathy found out about it, she was devastated. She and Sid tried to work through their problems, but both found it impossible, and, in September 1999, Kathy moved out to live at Bridge Farm, taking Jamie with her. After some trying times, and some aggressive solicitors' letters, there was a Christmas truce when Kathy allowed Sid to watch Jamie open his presents on Christmas morning. Bucked up by her new job running the shop and café at Lower Loxley, Kathy entered 2001 in a more optimistic frame of mind, dropping her claim for alimony and settling for a lump sum of £60,000 and maintenance for Jamie. The move to April Cottage marked a new start for her – again.

Lucy **Perks**

 • SEE: *Lucy Gemmell*

Polly **Perks**   née Mead

(Hilary Newcombe)

Universally loved in Ambridge, Polly was much missed by everyone after her untimely and tragic death in 1982. Driving to the cash and carry warehouse with her friend Pat Archer in the passenger seat, the car skidded on a bend in a muddy lane and hit a milk tanker sideways on. Polly was killed outright and is buried in St Stephen's churchyard. The ones who suffered most, though, were inevitably Polly's husband, Sid, and young daughter, Lucy. In the ensuing years, both made frequent pilgrimages to her grave, often with red roses, Polly's favourite flower.

| Birth: 15.5.1943 |
| Death: 10.2.1982 |

Polly was born and brought up in Penny Hassett and moved to Ambridge when she was twenty to work as barmaid at The Bull. Having turned down a proposal from Greg Salt, she also broke off her subsequent engagement to Sid. The romance was on again, however, when he supported her after it was discovered that her father, who was mentally ill, had been setting fires all round the district and would have to be committed. They were married on 27 September 1966, with Polly's boss's daughters, Lilian and Jennifer Archer, as bridesmaids.

Sid and Polly had plenty to contend with in the early years of their marriage. Jack Woolley had promised them jobs as joint wardens at Arkwright Hall, but, when he decided to close it, they had to think again. With the proceeds from a Premium Bond win, Polly took over the Ambridge Village Shop. As he had a criminal record, Sid couldn't be considered as postmaster, but he gave up his job at Paul Johnson's garage to help out at the shop full-time. There was tragedy in 1969 when Polly miscarried after a raid on the post office, but celebrations in 1971, when, in December, she gave birth to Lucy. Polly's gynaecological problems continued until 1974, when she suffered an ectopic pregnancy, but, though she and Sid briefly considered adoption or fostering, by 1977 they had decided they were content with their lot.

In 1972, Peggy Archer had suggested that the couple take over The Bull, and this they had done, selling the shop to Jack Woolley. Again, Sid's past record meant that Polly had to be the licensee, but they worked well as a team, opening a steak bar, followed by the Ploughman's Bar, and establishing, with Nora McAuley's help, a thriving bed and breakfast trade.

By 1975, the Perkses felt they had so much to be thankful for that they celebrated at upmarket Redgate Manor not once but three times – on her birthday, his birthday and their anniversary. Looking to the future, and, ironically, growing old together, they began to look for a home not tied to the pub. Alighting on Rose Cottage in Penny Hassett, they hoped for monetary help from Polly's widowed mother, but, when she proved intractable, managed to take out a loan secured by Peggy Archer. They took possession of the cottage on 2 January 1976.

A few months later, there was a traumatic incident when Lucy went missing from the pub and was found at her grandmother's bungalow in Manorfield Close. She had swallowed some sleeping pills and lapsed into a coma, but, after an overnight stay in hospital, she was released unharmed. Sid and Polly's fortunes were again on an upswing, when, still in 1976, Polly was nominated as publican of the year. Coming second to Frank Watson of the George Hotel in Borchester, she and Sid spent her £25 winnings on yet another night out at Redgate Manor.

The following year, Sid and Polly had problems with both their staff and their tenants. First, they let Rose Cottage to the feckless Briggs family, who did a moonlight flit owing back rent. Then Nora McAuley quit the pub for the canning factory, and there was a period of uncertainty before Caroline Bone and then Jackie Smith became regular faces behind the bar and at the food servery. But it wasn't until 1979, when Jethro Larkin's daughter, Clarrie, took on the job of barmaid that The Bull had a replacement deserving of the title, and a worthy inheritor of the mantle of Rita Flynn, Pru Forrest and big-hearted Nora. To celebrate, Sid took Polly to – yes, you've guessed it – Redgate Manor for her birthday.

As wife, mother and publican, Polly was fulfilled in all her ambitions, and, in essence, had to look no further than her home, family and friends for satisfaction. She flirted with the idea of a life outside The Bull and thought of gaining a qualification, so enrolled for a hairdressing course one evening a week. But it was found out to be a con and she lost the money she'd paid. Although she declared her intention of joining a properly accredited course at Borchester Tech the following autumn, it came to nothing, as did the proposed canal boat holiday she and Sid thought of taking Lucy on in 1980. When all the places were found to be booked up, the idea was dropped, the truth being that Polly didn't need holidays or hairdressing – she had everything she wanted in life.

That life came to an abrupt end just outside the village one February day – February being a dark and dangerous month for sudden deaths in Ambridge, as the families of Mark Hebden and John Archer would testify. Polly suffered the most tragic of fates for a mother – that of never seeing her child grow up – though she did know that Lucy was considered bright, possibly scholarship material, and she knew, too, that Sid idolized his young daughter. Not as much, though, as he idolized his 'Poll-Doll', from whose death, perhaps, he has never quite recovered throughout all the succeeding years. It is, however, possible – just possible – that in Jolene Rogers he has found another love match, and The Bull another landlady to treasure.

Sid **Perks**

(Alan Devereux)

If it's difficult for some people to imagine the genial publican as Jolene Rogers's red-hot lover, it's harder still to conceive of Sid Perks as a fifteen-year-old tearaway who was sent to an approved

Birth: 9.6.1944

school for breaking and entering. But this was Sid's unenviable record when he came to Ambridge in 1963 and was taken up by fellow Brummie Jack Woolley as someone with whom he could reminisce about Stirchley. Sid prospered under Jack's ample wing, working as his chauffeur-handyman for four years. When, after marriage to Polly, Sid decided to seek other work, Jack still acted as the couple's benefactor, insisting they live at Arkwright Hall. Sid worked briefly at Hollowtree, though, fearing cross-infection, Phil dispensed with his services when he found out that Sid had taken on other work with pigs at Paunton Farm. As luck would have it, the other pig farm was a front for criminal types, who were plotting a mail van robbery, but Sid was instrumental in eventually seeing them brought to justice. He then worked at Paul Johnson's garage, but gave that up to help out in the shop when Polly became postmistress. In December 1969, Sid found Adam Macy's would-be abductors, Chloe Tempest and Henry Smith, lurking near his van. They tried to pump him for information about the child, but Sid refused to give them any, and when, in February 1970, on what can only have been the principle of 'round up the usual suspects', the police arrested Sid himself on suspicion of the kidnapping, he was able to lead them to the real culprits.

In 1971, Polly gave birth to a daughter, and, in June 1972, Sid and Polly got their big break when Peggy Archer suggested they take over The Bull. Jack Woolley quickly stepped in to buy the shop, and, on their first day, the couple happily served free drinks to their customers. Despite his initial disappointment that, owing to his criminal record, he could not be licensee, Sid was soon to be found poring over the farming press so that he could talk about fat lambs with the regulars. Sid and Polly threw themselves wholeheartedly into improving the pub, adding a restaurant and bar, bed and breakfast accommodation and restoring the bowling green. Always an excellent sportsman, Sid also revived the darts team, and, for many years, managed and played for Ambridge Wanderers and captained the cricket team. There was worry in 1974, when Peggy considered selling, but Sid and Polly were reassured when she promised that if ever she did, she'd give them first refusal.

Sid was knocked sideways by Polly's death in 1982, and concerned for his future at the pub. Mark Hebden advised him that he could, in fact, become licensee, and Sid embarked on the difficult role of working single father. Within a couple of years he was grateful for the advice and friendship of Lucy's form teacher, Kathy Holland, though a jealous DS Barry, her former boyfriend, spitefully threatened to report Sid for serving drinks after time. After three proposals, Kathy finally accepted Sid, but only after she'd laid down her conditions: she intended keeping her job, and she didn't want children of her own. On hearing of the engagement, Lucy locked herself in her bedroom and refused to come out, probably the most peaceful few hours they would have for many years.

Strains on both of them at work and the hardships of step-family life led to Kathy resuming her affair with Dave Barry in early 1990 and Sid put two and two together when she received cards and perfume from him in 1991. Furious and humiliated, he went AWOL for six weeks, then walked back into the pub, confronted Kathy and threw her out. They were eventually reconciled, though, at a New Year's Eve dinner dance.

Having pulled together through the sale of The Bull, which finally happened in 1993, Sid and Kathy's relationship was further cemented by the birth of Jamie in 1995. Sid proved to be a doting dad, but, ironically, it was his desire to get fit so that he could play football with his four-year-old son that led to the collapse of the marriage. Sid took to jogging and working out, and in time, at the gym in Borchester, met up with Jolene Rogers, who confessed she'd admired him even before he got into shape. Soon their energetic sexual shenanigans led to lies and guilt, but when Eddie Grundy blew the whistle on the affair, Sid felt he had to try to make a go of things with Kathy: not just his marriage, but his livelihood and his adored son were at stake.

Within three months, however, unable to bear the icy atmosphere, Kathy had quit the pub and her job there, and Jolene, a natural behind the bar, was boosting the takings. With the ugly details of Sid's divorce settled, the pair seem happily secure – without having sacrificed any of their potent sexual chemistry. Maybe, for Sid, it's a case of third time lucky.

Les **Perry**

(John Bull)

Les was a PE teacher at Borchester Technical College, who worked with Neil Carter to set up and run a youth club in Ambridge in the mid-1970s. His enthusiastic and imaginative approach to youth work meant that before John Tregorran offered the use of Nightingale Farm as a venue, he even seriously considered setting the club up in a narrowboat. After his marriage in 1976, he had less free time available, and gradually disengaged from the activities he'd helped initiate.

Peter

Peter was not only Sean Myerson's business partner at the Cat and Fiddle, he was also the significant other in Sean's life. They neither hid nor made an issue of being gay, although the fact that they attended a Gay Pride Rally in June 1997 could still draw disapproving clucking from one or two villagers years after. The only area of Sean's life that Peter didn't share an interest in was cricket, but they were both of the same mind by the summer of 2000: much as they had enjoyed living in Ambridge, it was time to move on.

Marianne **Peters**

(Sheila Grant, Zoe Caldwell)

An adolescent crush had left the naive Marianne still besotted with Paul Johnson at the age of twenty three, and, when they met again by chance in the febrile atmosphere of Paris, in 1960, she was still hoping he'd propose. As he was by now married to Christine, the best he could do was to offer Marianne a job in Borchester, but a watchful Chris was having none of it and issued a firm 'non'.

Sam **Peters**

(Graham Rigby)

Ralph Bellamy's cowman, Sam had to retire on health grounds in 1974 but was reluctant to leave his tied cottage. Jack Woolley thought he'd cracked the problem by offering him the job of car park attendant plus accommodation, but Sam and his wife, Alice, eventually chose to move to Hollowtree Cottage. She took on the job of caretaker at the flats, and Sam found work as a milk tester at Borchester Dairies.

Jane **Petrie**

(Ursula O'Leary)

In 1972, Borchester art teacher Jane Petrie took charge of the arts and crafts summer school at Arkwright Hall. A striking-looking woman, with long dark hair that she usually tied back, she told Walter Gabriel she'd been involved in an unhappy love affair, which ended with citation in a divorce case.

She had a similarly devastating effect in Ambridge: Tony Archer developed such a passion for her that Ralph Bellamy sacked him for neglecting his work. At the end of the summer she left, thereby sparing the swains of the village further heartache.

Angi **Phillips**

(Stella Gonet)

Angi Phillips was one of the first singers to arrive for the production of *Don Giovanni* held at Lower Loxley Hall in December 1994. Overwhelmed by Mrs Antrobus's hospitality, she moved lodgings from Nightingale Farm to a spare room at Grange Farm. While with the Grundys, she gave Edward singing lessons and arranged for Clarrie to see the opera free in return for helping out at Lower Loxley. If she hadn't then gone on a farm walk with Joe, slipped, broken her ankle and consequently been unable to perform, she could have considered it a highly successful visit.

Police House

The new home of George and Christine Barford, the Police House is next door to the shop and close to Woodbine Cottage in the centre of the village. Chris and George have spent time and money on extending the place, but the house was plenty big enough for Dave Barry in 1984. He turned it into a proper bachelor pad, with his Aphrodite lamp and zebra-striped cushions; George and Chris favour a more homely style.

John **Poole**

John Poole came to Ambridge in 1974 as 'young Dr Poole' – old Dr McLaren's assistant – and, having taken over his practice, stayed until 1986 – almost long enough to become 'old Dr Poole' himself. Perennially popular, he pumped Freddie Danby's stomach after he'd eaten three death cap toadstools, and also counselled Jethro Larkin after Lizzie's death. He handed over to Matthew Thorogood in 1986.

Dawn Elizabeth **Porritt**

(Rachel Wright)

Dawn was a well-qualified nanny, who arrived at Home Farm in January 1989 to help Jennifer Aldridge cope with three-month-old Alice. Brian thought she was extremely good-looking, while Jennifer was glad to have someone to take on the work, despite being disconcerted by her broad Midlands accent. In spite of finding Dawn useful, the Aldridges were unwilling to provide her with a proper contract, claiming that they preferred to operate on a basis of trust. Showing a similar approach, Dawn trusted her instincts and soon left to find new employment.

Trudy **Porter**

Starting as a waitress in 1984, faithful Trudy has risen through the ranks at Grey Gables, eventually becoming assistant manager. Although she once flirted with the idea of a job in London and asked Caroline for a reference, she's stayed loyal to Ambridge, where she enjoyed aerobics and disco dancing in her youth, and now has thespian ambitions. Sadly, Lynda Snell found her Titania audition piece more like a middle-aged Moll Flanders. But she did get a non-speaking part.

Mrs **Potter**

And potter she did around Ambridge with the help of her walking frame. A resident of Manorfield Close, she gave Kenton a hard time in 1989 when a similar item to one he'd bought from her for £30 turned up on *The Antiques Roadshow* and was pronounced to be worth thousands. Kenton pointed out that hers had had its handle glued back on, a fact she'd perhaps missed owing to her poor eyesight.

Ken **Pound**

(Michael Collins, Garard Green)

Somewhere in the attic at Willow Farm, a stuffed vampire bat is probably still mouldering in a corner. This unusual item was bequeathed to Mike Tucker by Ken Pound, who, until his death, worked at Ambridge Farm.

Death: 17.11.1983

Farming with his wife, Mary, Ken struggled to make a good living. He had problems getting a decent milk yield from his Friesians and Jerseys, and was no more successful when he moved from running a free-range hen operation to a battery one. The equipment he used was so old that when anything went wrong he could never find spare parts. He was disappointed in 1972, when his son-in-law and daughter, Harry and Marilyn Booker, came to live on the farm, but didn't get fully involved in helping out. Still, he pressed ahead with a range of schemes to make money, including opening a farm shop, initially in partnership with Carol Tregorran, and, later, letting the Bookers run a Sunday market on his land, with the unwished-for consequence that he was fined by the Council for breaking by-laws.

After a rapid deterioration in his health, he passed away in the winter of 1983, leaving his family with memories and Mike with the stuffed bat.

Mary **Pound**

(Ysanne Churchman)

Mary worked with her husband, Ken, to keep Ambridge Farm running for thirty years. More outgoing than he was, she played a fuller part in village life as well. In 1973, she agreed to be the secretary of the local WI, and was elected president in the following year. She took her responsibilities seriously and made accommodation available when a guest speaker, Major Austen Bigsby, had to be booked at short notice and had nowhere else to go. When a ladies' football team was set up locally, she was happy to join in.

Birth: 1918

Walter Gabriel always liked her company, and she got on better with her son-in-law, Harry Booker, than Ken ever did. Harry, who was married to the Pounds' daughter, Marilyn, came to stay at Ambridge Farm for a year in 1972 while he and his wife tried to establish themselves in the district. Mary organized a tremendous New Year's party for the whole family, with the Grundys coming over for the celebrations as well.

She pulled her weight with all the farm work, but, as Ken's health started to fail in 1982, she decided it was time to give notice on the tenancy. After Ken's death the following year, she went to live in Edgeley.

Myra **Prestwick**

(Shirley Stelfox)

Phil was in awe of the fabled Myra Prestwick, fellow JP and scourge of the criminal classes. A widow from the other side of Borchester, she was a friend of Bunty Hebden, who knew her by the unlikely nickname of Mimi. A vigorous committee woman, she served on Borsetshire Conservation Trust and was active in politics, replacing Brian Aldridge when a kick from a Grundy cow ended his hopes of a council career in 1989.

Jim and Mrs **Price**

(Pauline Seville, Kay Hudson)

A visit to the village shop and post office between 1951 and 1968 was usually enlivened by a chat with Mrs Price, who ran the business with husband Jim. He always felt his wife wasn't particular enough about distinguishing between the shop and post office tills, putting it down to her lack of system. What they would have made of the recent computerization and name change the post office has been through is anybody's guess, but it's probably as well they retired long ago to live near their son and daughter-in-law in Cornwall.

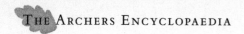

Maggie **Price**

(Rachel Newman)

Shula met Maggie when they were both students at Borchester Tech in 1975, and, as was his wont, Neil Carter developed a crush on her. He sent her a Valentine card, and they went away to a holiday camp on the south coast (strictly separate chalets), but the trip was not a success since she found him boring. Maggie had more luck with the lads on a break with Shula in Devon, but a date with Kenton bore no romantic fruit.

Solly and Heather **Pritchard**

(Richard Griffiths, Joyce Gibbs)

Ruth Archer's parents, Solly and Heather Pritchard, have only one regret about their daughter marrying into the Archer family: they wish Ambridge was a little nearer their home in Prudhoe so that they could see more of Ruth, David and the children. Solly, who manages a factory making bathroom tissue and other paper goods, has trouble taking time off work. Consequently, he and Heather haven't visited Brookfield as often as they would have liked. Guests at David and Ruth's wedding still smile at the memory of Solly's speech, when he wittily extolled the virtues of toilet paper.

Heather is a quietly spoken fund of common sense and support to her family, never more so than during Ruth's ordeal with breast cancer. The first inkling Heather had that something was wrong came when Ruth phoned to ask whether there was any history of it in the family. During the troubled months that followed, Heather spent as much time as she could with her daughter, gently caring for her and helping to coax her into a more positive frame of mind after the operation. She's looking forward to the day when Solly finally retires, and the two of them have a little more time to spend with their loved ones.

Mrs **Pugsley**

According to the date over the main door, Lower Loxley Hall is three hundred years old. Its housekeeper, Mrs Pugsley, is less easy to put an age to. A constant whirr of tea-making and cleaning activity, she is rarely seen at rest while on duty, particularly when Julia Pargetter is in a dictatorial mood. Not given to disclosing personal details, Mrs Pugsley rarely speaks of her husband, though she is known to have one. Presumably he addresses her by her first name, but, perhaps in deference to her quiet air of domestic authority, no one else dares to.

Mr **Pullen**

Mr Pullen's unfortunate bladder complaint has plagued many an Ambridge gathering, but he doesn't let it stop him from participating in village life. Occasionally cantankerous – he cheered the walkout at the 1994 Rural Reminiscences meeting – he narrowly escaped death in 1999, when Eddie, as the mighty Thor, wildly hurled an axe during the fête. Only George Barford's quick thinking saved his life, and the axe crashed through Eddie's van window instead.

Birth: 13.7.1915

Penelope **Radford**

(Angela Rippon)

The lovely Penelope was one of Nelson Gabriel's rather more up-market girlfriends: they'd met in London where her father was a wine merchant. She visited Ambridge in July 1980 and impressed everyone with her cut-glass vowels and clear diction.

George **Randall**

(Raymond Baseley, Chris Gittins, John Hobday, Edward Higgins)

Completely at home on a rural beat, PC Randall kept an eye on Ambridge from 1951 to 1955, was. He made a point of always seeing that sheep-dipping was done correctly and knew the owner of every dog in the district, something Phil Archer hoped would come in useful after Walter Gabriel's sheep were brutally savaged. After four years of coping with mainly minor offences, such as Dan Archer shooting a racing pigeon, he took the chance of promotion and moved on elsewhere.

Peter **Rawlings**

In 1955, Peter Rawlings was a patient of Dr Cavendish, battling against alcoholism. He could have landed in serious trouble with the law when he stole Mrs P's handbag, an action he later claimed to have no memory of. Dr Cavendish was able to get charges dropped by offering to take full responsibility for his future actions. The doctor had a vested interest in helping Peter: he was romantically interested in his sister, Eileen, and had borrowed money from his parents. Peter, motivated by a wish to win over Joyce Richmond, eventually did become teetotal.

Dick **Raymond**

(John Franklyn)

Dick was the first in a long line of the *Borchester Echo*'s cub reporters to have made an impression on the Ambridge scene, and in particular on the Archer womenfolk. Back in 1951, Ambridge was on Dick's patch, and he was happily getting details of births, deaths and marriages from the vicar and other gossip from the landlord at The Bull when a real story – the ironstone scheme – jumped up and bit him on the notebook. He got friendly with Christine, using her as his Ambridge stringer, and it was thanks to a crossed line when phoning his office from Brookfield that he stumbled across plans to sabotage Keith Latimer's drilling equipment. An attempt to catch the saboteur in the act was botched, but Dick's investigative antennae twitched when a button he'd torn off the saboteur's coat matched a missing one from Bill Slater's jacket and the diamond drilling bit was found at Bill's lodgings.

Christine was keen on the dashing reporter, but he went for a job on the *London Evening Gazette*, and was later posted to Malaya as junior South-east Asia correspondent. For a journalist, his letters were disappointingly infrequent and she was hurt when she heard he'd got engaged to a tea-planter's daughter.

Red House Farm

Phil and David Archer were negotiating with Cameron Fraser for a five-year lease on Red House Farm when the slimy Scotsman disappeared in 1992. The farm and its land, some 80 acres to the southwest of the village, were therefore sold along with the rest of Cameron's estate, first to Guy Pemberton, then to Borchester Land. The land is farmed in-hand and the farmhouse is let to commuters.

Paddy Redmond

(John Bott, Cashel Fitzbrien)

He'd originally planned to be a vet, but by the time he started work at Brookfield in March 1965, Ulsterman Paddy Redmond had opted for the farming life. Apart from having agricultural skills, he could play the piano and enjoyed the thrill of motorcycle scrambling. Jennifer Archer found him irresistible, so was understandably put out when Paddy returned from a holiday in Belfast with the news that he was engaged. Soon after, his fiancée, Nora McAuley, came to Ambridge and started work at The Bull. When, in 1967, she and Paddy disagreed about the wisdom of setting up in business on their own, he moved on from Ambridge, leaving not only Nora behind, but a pregnant Jennifer, too.

He might never have known he was the father of Jennifer's son, Adam, if, when he returned for a visit after a fourteen-year absence, Nora hadn't broken the news to him. He was warned off from seeing his son by Brian Aldridge, but accidentally bumped into Adam and Jennifer just before leaving again. Having established a good track record as a farm manager in

Venezuela, among other places, he was heading off to work in Ulster, where it's believed he still is.

Reg

Reg, a tenant farmer of the Pargetters for many years, had mixed feelings about retiring, until Nigel offered him part-time work looking after the rare breeds section at Lower Loxley. Fired with enthusiasm, he put a lot of effort into preparing for the arrival of the Gloucester cattle, Cotswold sheep and other livestock. Since the attraction's opening in spring 2000, he's enjoyed talking to visitors, who are sometimes overwhelmed by the sheer weight of detail Reg passes on about the feeding and breeding habits of his animals.

Frank **Rhodes** 'Dusty'

(Bryan Stanion)

Percy and Betty Hood were taken in by young 'Dusty' Rhodes' well-bred manner, but their daughter Joan knew better. Dusty, having given her a lift home from the Hollerton hop, went on to try and involve her in a series of petty thefts. When he pinched the Youth Club funds in 1958, the police got involved and Dusty did a runner. With Jimmy Grange and Joan hot on his trail, he ended up in a river, and, as a non-swimmer, had to be rescued. A spell in the Cottage Hospital was followed by a stretch on probation.

Anneka **Rice**

(Self)

'Challenge Anneka' was the TV watchword in the early 1990s, as the presenter raced round the country in a catsuit getting things done. When Robert Snell told his wife that Anneka was to be in the Borsetshire area, Lynda was quick to enlist her help in refurbishing the Village Hall, a project for which village enthusiasm was flagging. Anneka rose to the challenge admirably, and made Eddie Grundy's day by donating a signed photograph to his collection.

Kylie **Richards**

(Lucy Jones)

A real child of her time, as evidenced by her name, a tribute to the star of her mother's favourite TV programme, *Neighbours*, Kylie didn't have the best start in life. She was nonetheless a happy soul, winning Bonniest Baby at the fête at the age of eight months. In her time in Ambridge, she was looked after variously by Martha Woodford, Mrs Antrobus, and, once, memorably, Brian Aldridge, after Sharon had secured his babysitting services in a promises auction. Kylie had a great time, but Brian was strangely reluctant to repeat the experience.

Birth: 26.10.1989

Sharon **Richards**

(Celia Nelson)

A bandoned by Clive Horrobin, the father of her baby, when Kylie was just six weeks old, Sharon's life has never really taken the direction she might have wanted – or, indeed, any direction. After homes at the Vicarage and in the Bridge Farm caravan, she acquired a council house on The Green, where for a short time in 1994 she lived with John Archer before leaving for a mother's help position in Leeds. Returning three years later, her hold over John was undiminished. She effectively broke up his relationship with Hayley Jordan, and was hopeful that there might yet be something between them. John, however, sent her packing and she didn't return to Ambridge again until after his death, when Tony eased her anguish by admitting that John had, once, genuinely loved her. It is believed that Sharon has returned to Leeds, where her luxuriant Borsetshire vowels are probably having much the same effect on the male population as they did in Ambridge. Sadly for her, none of her liaisons seems to be lasting – even the dashing Dane, Thorkhil Jensen,

Birth: 7.3.1972

Tony's temporary farm worker, with whom she also went out, returned home without even leaving her a contribution towards her air fare. Such is Sharon's life.

Frank **Richmond**

A rapid turnover of staff gave cause for concern at Grey Gables towards the end of 1976. Michele Brown suggested that manager Frank Richmond might be the cause – she was pretty sure he was on the fiddle. So he was, not only giving short measure at the bar, but also keeping all the tips.

It was only after he'd fled Borsetshire and been apprehended in Liverpool that another theft came to light: Walter Gabriel found sixty-four stolen tins of herring stashed in his timber shed. Faced with the facts, Frank floundered.

Rickyard Cottage

Literally behind the rick yard at Brookfield, the cottage has had many occupiers, starting in the 50s with Simon and Bess Cooper, followed by Ned and Mabel Larkin. Tony stayed there briefly in his 70s bachelor days before it reverted to being the home of Brookfield workers Mike Tucker and then Graham Collard. Despite Graham's assertion that it was too small to swing a cat, it seemed an attractive proposition in 1992 to squatters Lisa and Craig and later to a succession of Jill Archer's holiday guests.

John **Ridley**

(Harry Stubbs)

Only thirty-four when he arrived in 1951, John Ridley was a very hands-on cleric. He once helped Peggy with the pigs at the smallholding, telling her there was little point in preaching 'love thy neighbour' without practising it. Perceptively, he also remarked that he could learn more by listening to Dan Archer, Tom Forrest and Walter

Gabriel chatting about village affairs than by trying to find out for himself. He could also be a very irreverent reverend. Arriving early for his induction service, he interrupted Walter in his hilarious impersonation of the Bishop and enjoyed sharing the joke.

The neighbour he might have loved above all was Christine Archer. He visited her in hospital after a riding accident and tried to enlist her support in getting more young people interested in religion. He then told Dan and Doris they had a charming and beautiful daughter. When, in 1955, he announced he was going to do an exchange with the vicar of a small parish in London, John Tregorran speculated that it was because his affections for Christine weren't returned.

He remained in Ambridge until 1961 and was succeeded by Matthew Wreford.

Harry **Roberts**

Ruddy-cheeked and with a flat cap permanently in place, Harry Roberts looked every inch a pigman. He was taken on to look after the Hollowtree unit at Brookfield in 1996, at a time when no one realized the pigmeat industry was about to go into sharp decline. Within a couple of years he was on short hours. With the help of his wife, he tried to make money from table-top sales, but was still struggling, so, when an offer of work at a garden centre came in November 1998, he parted company with the Archers.

Bill **Robertson**

(Geoffrey Hutchings)

When his father-in-law bought nearby Poston Hall for Bill and his wife, Sally, in 1978, Bill was reluctant to leave Ambridge, but he hadn't always been such a home bird. Son of local vet Ian, Bill spent a summer travelling round the States before college and seriously thought about leaving Ambridge for America. He became a junior partner, though, then took over his father's practice, trying to drum up trade by telling Tony Archer it was a false economy not to have the vet call. Tony still said he couldn't afford it.

Ian **Robertson**

(Lewis Gedge, Robert Sansom)

Dan Archer always put great faith in what he was told by local vet Ian Robertson. Ian had an efficient manner and a good eye for livestock; he diagnosed outbreaks of milk and swine fever at Brookfield, but his most important intervention came in 1956, when he alerted the Ministry of Agriculture to possible foot-and-mouth disease at the farm. It wasn't just his clients who were impressed with his work; by the mid-1970s, his son, Bill, had decided to follow in his father's footsteps and gradually took over the practice.

Sally **Robertson** née Arnold

Attractive Sally married local vet Bill in 1976. She was a keen horsewoman and was fed up when, during a difficult pregnancy, she had to give up riding. In 1979 she ran The Stables for Christine Barford while she and George honeymooned in Tunisia, from where they doubtless brought her an appropriate souvenir – a Berber bridle, perhaps.

Rocco

Julia Pargetter collects interior designers like other people collect fine wines. She acquired the friendship of New York-based Rocco in 1996. Very small and completely bald, he wore a green linen suit and was much given to snapping his fingers. Having failed to impress Nelson Gabriel with his plans for the wine bar, which would have entailed removing a load-bearing wall, he set off in search of places where his talents would be more appreciated.

Mr and Mrs **Rodgers**

(Helena Williams)

A useful pair, the Rodgers lived in Ambridge from 1956 to 1970. He initially worked for George Fairbrother, tending his Hereford herd, while Mrs Rodgers helped Jill Archer with the children both at Hollowtree Farm and at Brookfield. There was drama in 1960, when she rang Phil to say that David had swallowed a safety pin. Hurtling home in a panic, Phil found the crisis averted: the pin had been found stuck in the child's clothes.

Norman **Rodway**

(Michael Bilton)

M r Rodway was senior partner in the family firm of Rodway & Watson when Shula Archer began work there in 1976. Although at first she found him a stickler, she later went on to

Birth: 1917

respect his authority and experience. He was devastated when Cameron Fraser, for whom Rodways acted as land agent, was exposed as a fraudster. Unable to get hold of Shula to break the news, he rang her mother Jill and confided in her instead.

Ellen **Rogers**

(Rosemary Leach)

T wo years younger than her sister, Julia Pargetter, Ellen Rogers has spent most of her recent life running a bar, which she set up with her late husband, Harry, at Denia, on the Spanish coast.

Despite her dread of flying, she came back to England in 1994 for her nephew Nigel's wedding. While in Ambridge she indiscreetly revealed some family secrets, including Julia's hidden past as a greengrocer's daughter and that she had been christened Joan. Like her sister, Ellen enjoyed the company of Nelson Gabriel, and, before returning home, pressed him to come and visit when he could. Together they visited Madrid in 1998, just before Nelson's unexpected disappearance.

Julia also spent time with Ellen in Spain, and managed to run up such horrific gambling debts that she could raise funds only from a moneylender, Ronald Hardwicke, by pretending to co-own the bar in Denia. Although Ellen was furious when she discovered what Julia had done, she retained enough sisterly feeling to give a timely warning about the likely consequences if Hardwicke wasn't repaid. She has had few dealings with her family since, preferring to drink and flirt with the ex-pat community, who keep her profits healthy.

Fallon **Rogers**

(Joanna van Kampen)

Like Kylie Richards, the dangers of being named after a character from your mother's favourite soap are plain to see in Fallon. Good mates with Ed Grundy until an accident while joyriding put her off Ed's dubious charms, she did well in her GCSEs and in 2001 went on to a vocational popular music course at Borchester College. Reluctant resident of The Bull and one-time lead singer in the band Dross, Fallon had an ill-fated crush on Tom Archer. She finds Sid and Jolene's antics 'embarrassing' and Sid's gift of a Boyzone CD did nothing to win her round. As if...

> **Birth:** 19.6.1985

Jolene **Rogers**

(Elizabeth Revill, Buffy Davis)

When Clarrie first saw Jolene (aka Doreen, aka 'The Lily of Layton Cross') singing with Eddie in the Grange Farm cellar, in 1981, her rhinestones glittering and her buckskin fringes swinging, she knew she had a potential love rival. But beyond a close working relationship, nothing ever developed between Eddie and Jolene, who briefly married Wayne Tucson, then lived with a bass player in Huddersfield. Returning to the area in 1996, she formed a new band, the Midnight Walkers, but supplemented her gig income by teaching line dancing at venues including the Cat and Fiddle and The Bull. Having admired Sid's deltoids at the gym in Borchester, by early 2000 they were flexing all kinds of muscles in a number of interesting places, including Jolene's shower. Jolene was quick to tell Sid she loved him, but, when a drunk, embittered Eddie blurted out the truth about the affair to Kathy, she had a nervous few weeks of waiting before Sid and Kathy called it a day. Now installed at the pub, she is proving a real crowd-pleaser and her innovation for the younger crowd, 'The Bull Upstairs', was an instant hit. Having finally got her man, there is no doubt that Jolene and her double-D cups will stand by him.

Rookeries

SEE: *Home Farm Estate*

Dr **Rose**

(Brian Hickey)

Dr Rose was the consultant cardiologist Elizabeth saw when she was pregnant with twins in 1999. Because of her pre-existing heart condition, he made a careful check of her heart and lungs and was able to draw a truthful account from her about the palpitations and tiredness she was feeling. After she started having breathing problems late in the pregnancy, she was again referred to Dr Rose, who expedited her early admisson into hospital.

Rose

Always known as 'Pat's CND friend', spiky-haired, dungaree-clad proto-feminist Rose attended the same women's studies course in 1983. When her 'cruel' boyfriend threatened to leave her, Pat invited her to Bridge Farm, where she spent a lot of time in her room and exhibited such a fascination for fungi that Peggy suspected she was not interested in their culinary properties alone. In 1985, Pat heard that Rose owned two goats and was hoping to start generating her own power.

Rose Cottage

When Polly Perks planted two pink rambling roses round the front door, she had no idea that she and Sid would never see out their retirement in the cottage they'd bought for that purpose. It needed a lot of work when they acquired it in 1975, but busy Sid stripped the walls and retiled the kitchen floor. Kathy met Sid partly through her tenancy of the cottage, but it was sold in 1994 when Sid needed to buy The Bull.

Maureen **Rosewarne** 'Morwenna'

(Wendy Schoemann)

Described by Hayley Jordan as looking like the Wise Woman of Tintagel, Morwenna was the traveller friend Kate Aldridge chose to be her birthing partner in 1998. Jennifer Aldridge's initial concerns about this were somewhat assuaged when she learnt that Morwenna was a properly qualified midwife, who had previously successfully delivered a number of babies without the use of drugs. However, after Phoebe Aldridge's uncomplicated birth in a tepee at Glastonbury, Jennifer grew jealous of the reliance Kate placed on Morwenna, feeling rather pushed out of the picture. The fact that husband Brian's main reaction was to find Morwenna attractive didn't really help either.

Shortly after the birth, Morwenna and some other friends were going to France. Kate wanted to accompany them, taking Phoebe with her, but the father, Roy Tucker, got a court order stopping her. Nevertheless, Kate and Morwenna stayed in touch, so when Kate left Home Farm hurriedly in March 2000, one of Jennifer's first thoughts was to contact Morwenna to see if she had any information. Showing where her loyalties lay, Morwenna said she didn't know where Kate was, but wouldn't have told Jennifer even if she had known.

Graham **Ryder**

(Malcolm McKee)

A sharp-suited smoothie, who lives near the trendy Goat and Nightgown in Borchester, Graham covered Shula Hebden's maternity leave from the Estate office in 1994. He proved himself only too willing to toady to the loathsome Simon Pemberton, whom he greatly admired both for his business acumen and his apparent success with women. Graham, unfortunately, has neither facility, and now in the job full-time, has found another unfortunate role model in Matt Crawford. While he may run with the hare and hunt with the hounds in business, Graham's prowess in the saddle leaves much to be desired. Setting his sights on the widowed Caroline Pemberton in 1998, he rashly asked her to go riding with him, but couldn't control his mount. He took lessons in secret from Shula and sought advice on romantic tactics from Alistair Lloyd, but a break with Caroline in the Lake District, about which she has always maintained a discreet silence, led both of them to conclude that they were better off as friends. Most recently he has valued The Bull as part of the Perks's divorce, and had another disastrous foray in the hunting field. Clearly, Graham is a rider by name and not by nature.

Denise **Ryland**

(Brenda Dunrich)

Like the nice, well-bred girls they were, Christine Barford and Grace Fairbrother visited Denise in early 1952 shortly after she opened her rival stables at Walton Grange, near Hollerton, to ask her to raise her prices so as not to drive them out of business. Denise practically laughed at them, and went on to get Paul Johnson so drunk at a party that she claimed he'd proposed, later admitting she'd invented the whole thing. By the end of the year she'd gone spectacularly bankrupt.

Caroline **Salt**

In the middle of Greg Salt's divorce from Nora, he found out that his girlfriend, Caroline, was pregnant. The divorce was hurried through as a result, and Greg and Caroline married in 1972.

Gregory **Salt**

(Gerald Turner)

For no particular reason that his background reveals, Greg Salt seems to have been the original angry young man. His working life was as choppy as his personal affairs, and he ricocheted between the family farm on Brigadier Winstanley's estate, working for Dan and Phil Archer at Ambridge Farmers Ltd, and running a milk round. He didn't seem to settle to anything, though he was always a conscientious worker, living in at Hollowtree during the 1965 swine fever outbreak and in 1968 refusing to leave Dan in the lurch to take a holiday with his girlfriend, Nora McAuley.

Birth: 1941

Greg and Nora had got together after the death of his father, when she'd kindly gone to the farmhouse and cooked him a meal. He gave up thoughts of emigrating to stay near her in Ambridge, and soon they were engaged, but he was self-conscious and chippy about visiting her in her private sitting-room at Grey Gables, where she worked at the time, and she returned his ring. In his typical style, however, the engagement was soon back on and the pair were married on 23 December 1968. The marriage ended when he met someone else, though he did generously pay Nora an informal maintenance for four years.

Sandy

(Samantha Edmonds)

A fellow student with John Archer in the mid 1990s, Sandy actually had more in common with Tony, and she was soon helping him to restore the old Ferguson tractor he'd bought. She chose to do her college project on organic farming, which gave her every excuse to visit Bridge Farm, much to Pat's chagrin. After an argument with Pat over (false) rumours that he and Sandy were having an affair, Tony stormed off to sleep in the caravan, and Sandy settled for her boyfriend, Trevor.

Sam **Saunders**

(Leslie Bowmar)

Was Sam Saunders the man to blame for Jack Archer's decline into alcoholism? Probably not, but when the genial landlord of The Bull announced his intention to retire in 1952, bibulous Jack was only too keen to learn the trade. Jack's only experience of bars was of propping them up, but Sam allowed him to help out in the evenings and advised him on applying for the licence. Sam then left for Felpersham to live with his daughter Millie.

Bill **Sawyer**

(Kenneth Garratt)

The original Sawyer after whom Sawyer's Farm was named, Bill built it up over twenty years to become a thriving dairy unit. In 1955, he turned from dairying to dog breeding and established a successful kennels, before going into partnership with Walter Gabriel and Agatha Turvey to buy the pet shop in Hollerton. Bill and Mrs Turvey bought out Walter's share of the business in 1963.

Vikki **Schofield**

From good socialist stock, Vikki was the assistant at Nelson's Wine Bar who captured Neil Carter's eye at the opening night party in 1980. They went out for some months, even though Neil was convinced Vikki's widowed mother disliked him. Matters seemed to be improving when he was invited to spend Christmas Day with mother and daughter, but bringing a brace of pheasants proved a faux pas. Vikki definitely didn't approve of game shooting. The relationship folded as she moved on to become a student at Borchester Technical College, as well as an activist in the Borchester Animal Defence Group.

Mrs **Scroby**

(Vera Ashe)

When Mrs Scroby took a break from her cleaning duties and sat down with a steaming mug of tea, you knew you were in for a stomach-churning account of hospital procedures and her internal organs. No wonder that in the mid 50s Doris Archer refused her family's attempts to make her employ the voluble domestic, who once told Mrs P that the best cure for rheumatism was a teaspoon of mustard in a pint of beer, boiled up and drunk hot.

Gregory **Selden**

(Lewis Gedge)

Walter Gabriel and Ned Larkin thought the unusual noises they'd heard at Arkwright Hall in 1959 might have a supernatural cause. They told John Tregorran, who arranged to investigate with Carol Grey, but then didn't appear at the agreed time. Later he was discovered in a secret room, having been hit over the head by Gregory Selden, a Gypsy who'd made the Hall his temporary home. PC Bryden failed in his first attempt to catch Gregory, but he was later caught in possession of Walter's savings. Proudly independent, he refused the services of John's solicitor, Mr Bannister.

Eric **Selwyn**

(John Corvin)

One of a succession of undesirable swains whom Shula Archer paraded before her horrified parents, hi-fi enthusiast Eric (who liked to be known, understandably, as the rather more louche 'Rick') was a jazz-mad thirty-five-year-old whom she met at the Tech in 1974 where he was attending classes to learn how to build his own equipment. No one except Shula was surprised when he arranged to meet her at the Country Park and told her he was married.

Shane

Good-looking, sensitive, caring, intelligent – Shane just had to be gay. As Nelson's customers, male and female, sighed over his cheekbones and his cheesecake (both exquisite), Shane maintained his collection of autographed celebrity photos and pondered on his extravagant Christmas decorations. Having served Nelson faithfully for over ten years from 1985, he struck a stylish and appropriate note at his former employer's funeral in April 2001 by providing some of his signature quiche for the wake.

Lionel Quintus Shaw

(Will Kings)

An early incomer to Ambridge, arriving in 1955, Lionel was a retired company director who settled there with his wife and two children. He was promptly fleeced by Walter Gabriel, who charged Shaw £3 an acre for letting Walter's cattle graze on his pasture. Lionel got his own back by feigning absent-mindedness and leaving the gates open so that the cattle got out. A case of 'the townies fight back', perhaps?

Barry Simmonds

Barry worked part-time at Bridge Farm from 1992 to 1996, and was a useful fill-in when Pat and Tony needed time away. A good bat and medium-paced bowler who used to play for Edgeley, he was immediately enlisted into the cricket team. He continued to lend the team his muscle, even when he got a full-time job in Waterley Cross.

Mr **Simmons**

(Colin Skipp)

Foul play was suspected in 1975 when George Barford and Tom Forrest found a woman's handbag and shoe in the Country Park. They handed them to PC Drury, who kept watch and apprehended Simmons when he returned to look for them. The explanation was disappointingly tawdry: they belonged to sales rep Simmons's lady love, and he was anxious to find and return them to her before her husband found out about their affair.

Andrew **Sinclair**

(James Grant)

On his arrival to manage the Estate in 1962, Carol Grenville was one of the first to note Andrew's rugged good looks, but his relations with her husband, Charles, were nonetheless harmonious. Andrew found his subsequent bosses, the arriviste Jack and the abrasive Ralph, rather less to his taste, and was on the point of resigning in 1974 when Bellamy himself left Ambridge. Andrew was delighted, and remained contentedly in post until his retirement in 1986.

Dorothy **Sinclair** née Arnold

(Joan Ansty)

Dorothy's life was something of a Cinderella story. Slightly crippled, and ashamed of her wastrel brother, Ted, she worked all hours to pay back some money he'd stolen. She toiled in Doughy Hood's bakery, did home hairdressing and took in dressmaking before, to her delight, being offered the job of managing Ann Grenville's gown shop. Prince Charming finally showed up in 1964 in the shape of Andrew Sinclair, the Estate manager. They duly married, had a son and lived happily ever after.

Bill **Slater**

(John Franklyn)

One of the more unsavoury characters to pass through Ambridge over the years, Bill was a nephew of Mrs P's who came to the country to alleviate his asthma. He lodged with her and took

Death: 15.11.1951

on casual farm work; he had no feeling for stock, but was good with machinery. Asked to repair Fairbrother's big tractor in late 1951, he drove it over a hummock and damaged it, to Fairbrother's fury – until, that is, he realized that Bill had unwittingly uncovered some ironstone. The ensuing debate over a potential ironstone mine split the village, but Bill was not alive to hear the outcome. Always an argumentative type, he already had a grudge against mineralogist's assistant Bert Matthews, who was courting a girl Bill had had his eye on. In November, Bill and Bert rowed in the pub over the ironstone scheme and had a fight in the yard. Bill fell, hit his head and complained of feeling dizzy. Mrs P's medicinal cocoa made him sick and he went to bed, but next morning it was impossible to wake him. An inquest proved that he had an unusually thin skull: the slightest knock could have killed him.

Henry **Smith**

(John Baddeley)

Together with his partner-in-crime, Chloe Tempest, Henry Smith was responsible for the kidnapping of Adam Travers-Macy in 1970. Hoping that Roger Travers-Macy's rich father would stump up a £5000 ransom, he sent out threats a month in advance of the actual kidnap, which took place at The Bull. Fortunately, Sid Perks was alert to what was going on, and, thanks to information he gave the police, Adam was returned safely and the kidnappers picked up before any money changed hands. Smith was sentenced to three years' imprisonment for his part in the crime.

Jackie **Smith**

(Maggie McCarthy)

In her year in Ambridge, Jackie turned a lot of heads – Tony Archer, Mike Tucker and Harry Booker all queued up for her to pull their pints. A cockney, and a West Ham supporter, she was an attractive girl who could also be one of the lads. She was lured away from Ambridge by a new boyfriend, who in 1978 got her a job at Borchester Sports Centre.

Bobo **Snell**

The first wife of Robert Snell and mother of their two daughters, Leonie and Coriander, Bobo does not intrude much on the new life Robert has made. In 1994, however, Lynda had the embarrassment of phoning her to find out where Robert was – he'd been visiting his daughters at Christmas and had not come home as expected. No doubt Bobo was delighted to inform her that she had no idea.

Coriander **Snell** 'Caz'

Many find that the results of eating a curry stay with them after leaving the restaurant, but for Robert Snell and his then wife Bobo, these produced their aptly-named daughter. When 'Caz' and her sister, then abbreviated to 'Len', visited for Christmas in 1988, Caz was a keen percussionist – hardly in keeping with the Victorian theme Lynda has planned for 2001.... Merry Christmas everybody!

Birth: 1977

Leonie **Snell** 'Len'

After many years of access visits which mostly took place at the girls' home, Leonie surfaced again to disturb the Snells' life in Ambridge in early 2001, when she requested a £5000 deposit for a flat. Lynda felt it was time the spoilt child stood on her own feet, with the

Birth: 1975

result that Robert, who disagreed, left abruptly for Wales. He returned after a few days having made his point to Lynda – and having given a satisfied Leonie what she wanted. With a Christmas visit planned for 2001, it remains to be seen whether peace and goodwill can possibly reign at Lynda's Victorian extravaganza.

Lynda **Snell**

(Carole Boyd)

Would Ambridge be a better place without Lynda Snell? The answer is almost certainly no. This one-woman whirlwind has rallied the residents behind a number of causes that have

Birth: 29.5.1947

threatened their environment, and has hugely added to the village's quality of life through her single-handed revival of the tradition of the Christmas show. However, there is, as always, a price...

Lynda burst on to the Ambridge scene from Sunningdale in 1986. Keen to throw herself into rural life, she was outraged to find Brian Aldridge's footpaths blocked, and shocked when Eddie Grundy produced Clarrie (the ferret) from inside his coat. Worse was to come when a kindly Tom Forrest brought her two rabbits as a welcome present, telling her she'd only need to skin and gut them.

Having failed in 1987 to be elected to the Parish Council under the banner of 'Snell for a Greener Ambridge', Lynda continued her environmental crusades by herself. Ignorance has never prevented her from interfering, as when she reprimanded Joe Grundy for pulling up wild flowers, when he was in fact destroying ragwort, a noxious weed, but later campaigns were more of a success. In 1998, she prevented a proposed development at Sawyer's Farm when she found the protected species *Gentianella anglica* on the site. She protested first about the building of the Borchester bypass, then its widening, and her traffic calming survey in Ambridge resulted in 'Please Drive Carefully' signs. She also successfully retained the village's picturesque fingerpost.

Although stepmother to Robert's two daughters, Lynda was unable to have children of her own. Instead, her maternal instincts have been diverted into her love of animals, starting with two Anglo-Nubian goats, Demeter and Persephone. When Persephone gave birth, Lynda was as frazzled as any new mother, and Robert eventually disposed of the billy kids. Dining at Grey Gables and seeing goat on the menu, Lynda feared she could be eating her babies, but Robert assured her they were safe in Lower Loxley's Pets' Corner. Lynda's next project was an Afghan pup, Hermes, followed by hedgehogs and even ladybirds. She was also vociferous in her demand that the shop cease to stock tuna that might have been caught at the expense of dolphins.

Lynda first insinuated herself into the village social scene by offering to do fortune-telling at the fête, and, before long, she was running the show, even when, in 1991, she put her back out days before the event and had to be carried around on a litter. In recent years, the committee has wrested back some control, though Lynda still makes her presence felt. The area, however, in which Lynda has most been able to shine is that of amateur dramatics. Who, least of all the long-suffering cast, or Phil Archer at the piano, could forget her *A Midsummer Night's Dream* of 1997, or her triumphant millennium *Mikado*? Somehow, despite setbacks and sniping, Lynda survives, often triumphantly. But she was stung when, in 1999, Larry Lovell's bitchy review of her *Babes in the Millennium Wood* said nothing about the direction, but reserved all its praise for Jill Archer's costumes and the smell of pig when David Archer appeared.

Having suffered the indignity of Robert's bankruptcy, Lynda was sympathetic to Clarrie when the Grundys were evicted, for she does have a softer side. She was hurt when the village sent her to Coventry after her covert filming of their litter-dropping activities in 1991; as far as she's concerned, she only ever does these things for the greater good. Her video camera was put to happier use when she filmed all aspects of Ambridge life for their town-twinning partners in Meyruelle, and was keen to go on the Ambridge trip there in 1993 until she got ringworm and ceded her place to Clarrie. Lynda's French came in handy, however, when the Meyruellois made a return visit, though Mayor Gustave Touvier found her intrusive simultaneous translation of the Rural Reminiscences play confusing. Lynda again tried to thrust herself into the limelight in 1996 when a film company used Lower Loxley as a location, and thought with her artistic leanings she might be in line for an important part. She eventually had to settle for the role of 'Peasant in Crowd'.

For someone who frequently creates such havoc, Lynda has striven to create a relaxing environment at Ambridge Hall. A hay fever sufferer who also has a bad allergic reaction to bee stings, she established a low-allergen garden there, but sadly its water feature, as installed by Eddie Grundy, gushed rather than trickled, and spread unhealthy spores into the air. Her excursion into aromatherapy might have been more successful if she'd resisted talking incessantly throughout each massage. There was retribution when Joe Grundy turned up to claim William's prize massage and she had to see the state of his combinations, but Lynda's humiliation wasn't over. One of her printed cards found its way into the phone box and Lynda received calls from several would-be clients expecting something more than a rub-down with geranium oil. In 2000, Lynda went quiet on the aromatherapy and moved on to another Oriental art, *feng shui*. Her interest in this practice, supposed to promote equanimity, has led to much friction both in her marriage and at Grey Gables, where she's worked as a receptionist since 1995. There, Caroline Pemberton finds her a taxing employee, prone to typing up her panto scripts in work time, but admits that when she concentrates on her job, Lynda can be very efficient.

Some might think that this is yet another example of Caroline's supreme tact: 'efficient' can so often mean 'bossy'. But beneath Lynda's abrasive exterior there's a vulnerable woman who needs the devotion of her patient husband, Robert, and who's always felt threatened by his ex-wife and daughters. Their row in April 2001, when he left her for a week, left her uncharacteristically meek for a while. But don't worry, it didn't last long, and the Victorian Christmas she's planning for Robert and the girls looks set to have all the hallmarks of a vintage Snell production number.

Robert **Snell**

(Graham Blockley)

'How does he put up with her?' the men of Ambridge have often asked themselves, referring to Robert and his wife, Lynda. The answer seems to be twofold. First, Robert has an extremely high tolerance threshold, and, second, incredibly to some, he genuinely loves her, as his understanding foot massages at the end of a long day at Grey Gables or a tiring evening at panto rehearsals prove.

Birth: 5.4.1943

The Snells moved from Sunningdale in 1986, and it seemed at first that self-employed computer software specialist Robert might be as much a thorn in the side of local farmers as his wife. He wrongly accused Phil Archer of cruelty to his cattle by letting his water troughs freeze over, and

Phil was again the target for his wrath over the putative barn conversions. But as the slower pace of rural life took hold, Robert seemed content to fade more into the background, allowing Lynda to act as spokesperson for village campaigns, while he concentrated on what he did best: making the money that supported their affluent lifestyle.

Robert's work seemed to go from strength to strength. In 1992, he went to Switzerland on business, and, in the next couple of years, he spent an increasing amount of time abroad. Lynda wasn't always happy with the arrangement, but usually melted with the promise of a romantic dinner at Grey Gables. By November 1994, however, Robert was, unusually, to be found working from home. He was spotted making phone calls from The Bull, refused Lynda's suggestion of a skiing holiday at Christmas and stood her up for lunch. Her suspicions aroused, Lynda put a private detective on to him, and was devastated when she found a receipt for a £400 ring in the glove box of his car. Although he later gave her the ring, saying he'd been uncommunicative and telling her he was grateful to her for putting up with him over the last few months, her suspicions were not allayed. She was convinced he had another woman. The reality, when Robert revealed it, came almost as a relief: he was in dire financial trouble. A customer had gone bust owing him £13,000, clients in Swindon were refusing to pay up, and, in addition, Robert owed Grey Gables £1000. To cap it all, a last-ditch attempt to save himself by marketing an adapted version of a program he'd written for the canning factory had come to their notice and they were threatening to sue. His bank was prepared to be supportive, but Robert felt he'd let everyone down, and voluntarily wound up his company. At an abusive creditors' meeting, Lynda was fiery in his defence, and her efforts to generate money, with her idea of paying guests at Ambridge Hall, touched him beyond measure. Robert had to take a succession of short-term contracts and agency work, and, though he is now both busy and successful again, their financial circumstances have never quite recovered.

The enforced liquidation has, however, given Robert a less demanding work schedule, and he is more able to indulge in the village pursuits he enjoys. He was glad when local work meant he could participate in The Bull's boules evenings, as he had happy memories from years earlier of winning a conker competition at the pub, beating Joe Grundy with his 'superconk'. But the sport Robert really excels at is cricket. Villagers were excited to find on his arrival that he was a member of the MCC, and quickly snapped him up both as a player and as club treasurer.

Robert has not been able to avoid being sucked into Lynda's passions as well. In the 1999 pantomime, *Babes in the Millennium Wood*, he found himself a last-minute casting choice for the strolling minstrel Allan-a-Dale, despite the slight drawback that he cannot sing a note. With coaching, he managed a passable rendition of 'Greensleeves', but was happy to confine himself to sets and props for *The Mikado*.

Over the years, Robert has tolerated Lynda's goats, her dog, Hermes, and her frequent crusades, but was driven to distraction by her interest in *feng shui*. He had an earful of abuse when he admitted he'd taken three especially lucky dragon pound coins from her 'wealth corner', but it was her attempts to reharmonize their bedroom which really got to him. Returning to bed one night after using the loo, he cracked his shin on a repositioned plant pot, before having to admit to Lynda that her new habit of keeping the seat down had led to a nasty accident in the bathroom. When Lynda protested that she'd only been trying to turn their room into a 'love zone', he remarked that he'd never felt less amorous in his life.

Having endured all that, Robert was aghast to learn in March 2001 that Lynda proposed to *feng shui* the garden, especially as she kept interrupting his work to get him to lug stones about. In parallel, his daughter Leonie was nagging him for the £5000 deposit she needed on a flat, and Robert knew Lynda wouldn't be best pleased. When he told her of Leonie's request, they had a bitter row and he stormed off to Wales to stay with friends, leaving Lynda to face the village gossip. Lynda was lost without him, and relieved when he returned just before Easter, knowing that he'd taught her a lesson. In every aspect of their life, harmony seems to have been restored. It's no doubt down to all that positive *chi*.

Emily **Spenlowe**

(June Spencer)

Emily Spenlowe was one of life's great communicators. The death of her husband, Humphrey, wasn't enough to stop her talking to him: she simply stayed in touch through the use of spirit guides. She also employed her gift for other-worldly matters as a fortune-teller at the 1972 village fête, but mixed up John Tregorran's and Mrs Turvey's readings.

When not exploring the ethereal realm, Emily busied herself on the committee for the Festival of Ambridge and with the WI. Humphrey was probably glad of the peace and quiet when she did so.

Spike

One of Kate Aldridge's longest-standing friends, Spike first got to know her in 1994, when they both went to Glastonbury. When she disappeared from Home Farm shortly after, her mother, Jennifer Aldridge, immediately turned to Spike for help, but all he could tell her was that Kate might have joined a New Age settlement in Somerset. He came to Ambridge again in 1997 to protest against the widening of the Borchester bypass and was back the following year for Phoebe Aldridge's naming celebration. Most recently, he joined Kate and other friends on a trip to Morocco in 1999.

Birth: 1974

Wilfred John Sproggett

(Phil Garston-Jones)

Sadly no longer with us, Wilfred Sproggett was much admired for his birdcraft when he became president of the Borchester Ornithological Society in 1972. An architect by profession, birdwatching was his greatest passion, leaving him little time for affairs of the heart. He resisted Tom Forrest's attempts to partner him off him with Mrs Turvey during the 1950s, when Tom was trying to deflect that good widow's attentions from himself.

Stefan

Stefan soon caused a stir among his co-workers when he started in the Grey Gables' kitchens in 1997. With his brooding eyes and dark, ringleted hair, he could pass for a young god, although unkind whispers suggest he shows less intellectual prowess than one of Jean-Paul's soufflés. Still, you can't have everything.

St Stephen's Church

In the yew-shaded churchyard of St Stephen's lie several generations of Archers and Gabriels, not to mention Mark Hebden and Tom and Pru Forrest. They had all worshipped, and most had been married, at the church, which was consecrated in 1281 and built on the site of an early seventh-century Augustinian church. The building's many architectural features were enhanced in 1959 by a memorial window commemorating Grace Archer. For a place of worship, St Stephen's has been a source of much drama over the years. In 1972, a crossbeam in the bell-tower collapsed and caught Dan Archer's shoulder, while in 1990, the clock weights crashed through the floor, narrowly missing William Grundy. Building work for a ramp and toilet in 1992 revealed ancient timbers, which experts took away for carbon dating. Vicar Robin Stokes, fearing costly excavations, was relieved when they decided to leave things as they were for fear of causing greater damage. The church is a positive haven for wildlife. A colony of flittermice bats took up residence in June 1976, and the following month Dan and Betty Tucker found a swarm of bees making a honeycomb near one of the bells. Mice were the next to move in, chomping through the hassocks and organ stops, taking 'all God's creatures' rather literally.

Oliver **Sterling**

(Michael Cochrane)

After waiting for their children to grow up, Oliver and Jane Sterling divorced amicably and sold up their farm in North Borsetshire. While Jane moved to Sussex, Oliver bought the farmhouse and 50 acres of land at Grange Farm in November 2000. Staying in Penny Hassett while the house was extensively modernized, he built on his contacts with the South Borsetshire Hunt to be taken on as a new Joint Master of Foxhounds.

It was through the Hunt that he became friendly with Caroline Pemberton. By January 2001, he was accepting her help with preparations for his housewarming party, and, by Valentine's Day, he and Caroline were sharing meals and kisses. Ed Grundy and Fallon Rogers played a part in bringing them together by sending out bogus Valentine cards, which were mistaken for the real thing. With Ed and Fallon attending the birth of the romance, it's not surprising that the relationship hasn't always run smoothly since. However, after splitting up for some months, a chance meeting at the kennels on Lord Netherbourne's estate seems to have recently brought them back together again.

Oliver's attempts to hobby-farm haven't been without problems either. The national outbreak of foot-and-mouth disease in 2001 delayed the purchase of a small herd of beef cattle, but, when the movement restrictions were eased, he finally had the satisfaction of bringing livestock back to Grange Farm.

Peter **Stevens**

(Edward Seckerson, Peter Biddle, Anthony Smee, Paul Henry)

In 1960, Tom and Pru Forrest were intending to foster Johnny Martin. But Johnny's best friend, Peter Stevens, did not want to be separated from him. He and Johnny ran away from their children's home and hid in an old windmill near Heydon Berrow. When Tom found them, he promised to try and foster Peter as well.

Birth: 1953

Peter proved, at times, a rude and difficult foster son, but his practical skills were to be his salvation. In 1970, he was taken on at Ralph Bellamy's garage, where he showed himself to be an excellent mechanic. Once Haydn Evans bought the business, Peter found his new employer more difficult to get on with. He was quite happy, in 1977, to leave Ambridge for Borchester, where he could be near his girlfriend. Although he turned up at a surprise birthday party for Pru in 1987, Peter did not stay in close contact with the Forrests, perhaps finding his duties running two garages in Borchester too time-consuming. Nevertheless, he made sure he joined his old companion Johnny in attending Tom and Pru's funeral in 1998, clearly aware of the debt he owed his foster parents.

Sally **Stobeman** née Johnson

(Ann Chatterley)

Paul Johnson's sister, Sally, partnered Christine in The Stables after Grace's death, and, in 1962, against her brother's wishes, married the raffish Tony Stobeman, an old racing crony of Reggie Trentham. Tony's business activities (betting shops and a share in the casino with Nelson Gabriel) kept him in the area until the mid-1960s, but the couple have not been heard of since. They've probably got a stud farm in the Vale of the White Horse or a villa on the Costa del Sol.

Tony **Stobeman**

(Jack Holloway)

His yellow waistcoats – always the sign of a cad and a bounder – should have been a warning to the females of Ambridge, but many still fell under the spell of this old racing chum of Reggie Trentham. Having failed to interest Carol Grey in either his commission agent's business or his own prospects, he romanced Paul Johnson's sister, Sally, and married her in 1962. He was last heard of in 1966, his betting shops and casino having fleeced Borsetshire residents of sufficient money with which to retire.

Oliver **Stokes**

(James Naylor)

Oliver was nine when his father Robin introduced him to Caroline Bone and he always got on well with her. He enjoyed a kite-flying picnic she organized, and when her horse, Ippy, was stolen in 1993, he and brother Sam industriously toured the lanes on their bikes in an attempt to find him. He was pleased that Robin and Caroline were getting married, and was upset when it was called off.

Birth: 1983

Robin **Stokes**

(Tim Meats)

With his Old English sheepdog, Patch, Robin was first spied at the fête in August 1991, and took his first service later the same month. His choice of the contemporary hymn 'Lord of the Dance' set the tone for a thoroughly modern minister who a part-time vicar (an NSM or non-stipendiary minister) whose other job was that of a vet.

Birth: 12.10.1951

Robin's own marriage break-up (his ex-wife and sons lived in Kent) made him sympathetic to those with relationship difficulties. He counselled Shula Hebden after her ectopic pregnancy, and Elizabeth post-Cameron Fraser, but had problems of his own when Saxon remains were discovered in the churchyard and Patch was poisoned in the Country Park. By this time, however, he'd become close to Caroline Bone, though her lack of religious belief would always be a strain for them. They planned to marry nonetheless, but the accident in 1994 that killed Mark Hebden and seriously injured Caroline destroyed her shaky faith.

Caroline eventually told Robin she couldn't marry him, and he was hurt when she later became engaged to Guy Pemberton. He left for a new job in Surrey in 1995, and a loyal Marjorie Antrobus sent him on his way with one of her famous fruit cakes.

Sam **Stokes**

(Monty Allen)

Although Caroline had always got on well with Robin's older son, the minute their engagement was announced in 1993, he started to play up. He went missing from school, then turned up at Hollerton Junction, having travelled there by stealth all the way from Kent. When the happy couple took the boys camping, the brothers bickered all the time. Sam was relieved when the wedding was called off, though perhaps not as relieved as Caroline.

Birth: 1981

Sir Michael **Sturdy**

(William Eedle)

When Gerald Pargetter realized his son, Nigel, was going to court for taking and driving away a car in 1984, he lost little time in engaging the services of the eminent barrister Sir Michael Sturdy to act for the defence.

Much good did it do. Nigel was found guilty as charged and fined.

Bert **Sutton**

(Edward Higgins)

Bert tried everything he could to prevent Walter Gabriel from setting up as a haulier in competition with him, even ringing the Council to complain that Walter was not above faking furniture for sale by John Tregorran as genuine antiques. Bert's efforts were in vain, however, and Walter duly got his haulier's licence in July 1957, having wisely refused the offer of a partnership with the truculent transport king.

Carl **Swift**

Carl, who came to take over as gamekeeper on the Grey Gables shoot in 1999, very quickly managed to anger a wide range of people. George Barford resented being told how to do his job by the man who was going to replace him; Tony Archer was unhappy at being told to shut up at a fox shoot, while Peggy Woolley was outraged when Carl started calling her Peg and putting his arm round her. Before Jack Woolley could have serious words, flirtatious Carl had run off with Natalie, the head barman's wife, thus throwing the future of the shoot into jeopardy.

Emily **Tarbutt**

(Peggy Hughes)

Agatha Turvey's companion preferred gardening to cooking, but the two lived happily enough until 1973 when both were struck down with flu. Mrs Turvey's turned to pleurisy, and Emily had no strength to look after her, with the result that Mrs Turvey died. The house, Lakey View, was left to Emily, but she sold it and went to live with her cousin, Matthew Wreford, former Vicar of Ambridge.

Nancy **Tarrant**

In 1967, Walter Gabriel was distraught to receive a visit from Nancy, pregnant by his son, Nelson. Already fearful that Nelson was the father of Jennifer Aldridge's illegitimate baby, Walter advised Nancy to move away and said he'd send her money. The baby, Rosemary, was subsequently adopted, as was her half-brother, Simon. In 1986, Rosemary arrived in Ambridge and informed the village that Nancy was now married to an engineer whose surname was Wilson, had two sons and lived in Southampton.

Rosemary **Tarrant**

(Nicola Wright)

When Rosemary visited Ambridge in April 2001 for her father's funeral, she told locals that she was engaged on part two of her inspector's exams. Yet, for a policewoman, she's evinced

Birth: 19.8.1967

remarkably little curiosity over the years about Nelson Gabriel's life and criminal past. Unless, of course, she realized that such facts as she might uncover would do her career no good at all. Best, after all, to sum him up, as she did after his death, as an 'international man of mystery'.

Rosemary was put up for adoption by her mother, Nancy, and Nelson didn't even know he had a daughter until she walked into the wine bar in 1986 and revealed to his horror that she was about to start cadet training at Hendon. In 1989, she applied for a posting to the Borchester area, and worked alongside DS Barry.

If Nelson had found it hard to accept that he had a daughter, he found it harder still to accept that she had a sex life. When her boyfriend, Peter, came to stay the weekend at Honeysuckle Cottage, Nelson took sanctuary at Mrs P's rather than confront the issue.

Hebe **Taylor**

(Self)

Steeped in the songs of the 1920s and 1930s, which she'd learnt at her mother's knee when the family were interned in Shanghai after the Japanese invasion, Hebe sang at the opening of Nelson Gabriel's refurbished wine bar in 1984. There was talk of some unspecified relationship between them in the past, but when Nelson, strapped for cash as ever, couldn't pay her fee, Jack Woolley had no trouble in luring her away to Grey Gables.

Chloe **Tempest**

(Eileen Barry)

Chloe was Henry Smith's co-conspirator in the 1970 kidnap and attempted ransom of Adam Travers-Macy. She pretended to be interested in renting a room at The Bull, but was more intent on getting the little boy away to Birmingham. Thanks to a timely intervention from Sid Perks, she and Smith were arrested before too much harm was done. After being committed to the Assizes, the precursor of crown courts, she was found guilty and given a suspended sentence.

Terry

(Theo Bryant)

A product of the splendid YMCA 'British Boys for British Farms' scheme, Terry was employed by George Fairbrother in 1951 to help with the poultry, though his heart really lay with the cows. Phil Archer thought him promising enough to take over from Angus when the latter retired, but nothing came of this, as in 1953 Terry was called up for his National Service, after which, no doubt, his skill at boxing led him in other directions than the bovine.

Len **Thomas**

(Arnold Peters)

In coming to work at Brookfield in 1953, Len Thomas was trying to get away from his problems. He'd married after completing his National Service, only to discover his wife wouldn't be faithful. Leaving her and their young son, David, with his father in Welshpool, Len sent them money from Ambridge and hoped that things would eventually work out. He settled well into his job, but wasn't happy when enquiries were made about his family circumstances. Matters became complicated when he took a liking to Hollerton-based Mary Jones. They'd got off on the wrong foot when Len thought her innocent attempts to draw him into conversation too flirtatious, but soon a mutual love developed. After his wife died in a car crash, Len was disappointed when Mary seemed to avoid him. But she was only waiting for everything to settle down, and, in due course they married and had a son of their own, Owen, as well as bringing David to live with them.

Intending to specialize as a shepherd, Len left Brookfield to work for the Estate, but didn't get on well with Charles Grenville. By 1966, Grenville had suffered enough of Len's sullen manner and sacked him, whereafter the Thomases left Ambridge.

Mary **Thomas** née Jones

(Noreen Baddiley)

Mary had a lively, sociable manner, which was partly a reaction to the tough struggle she faced at home, trying to look after her invalid father on her own, on not very much money.

Although she had plenty of boyfriends, she didn't show any signs of wanting to settle down, until getting to know Len Thomas. It was an attraction of opposites that seemed to be going nowhere because Len's wife, Marion, refused to give him a divorce. Mary decided they would have to stop seeing each other, but then circumstances were radically altered by Marion's death in a car crash. Not wishing to benefit from the tragedy, Mary avoided Len's company for a time, but later agreed to marry him in 1954. They brought his son, David, over from Wales to live with them, and then completed their family by having a child of their own, Owen Leonard.

It wasn't an easy marriage; Len's increasing unhappiness when working for Charles Grenville was reflected in his angry moods at home. When he was sacked in 1966, it was a chance for Mary and Len to move their family away from Ambridge and see if they could start again.

Matthew **Thorogood**

(Crawford Logan)

It's not reported whether Matthew Thorogood brought any shrunken heads with him from his stint in Papua New Guinea, where he'd worked for Save the Children: perhaps he thought Ambridge

Birth: 29.6.1953

would provide him with curiosities enough. Setting up his surgery at Ambridge Farm, which he rented from the Estate, he was soon practising his bedside manner on Caroline Bone, who moved in with him in 1987. A supposedly romantic weekend in Florence was rather spoilt by Matthew's invitation to Mark and Shula Hebden to join the party, and, when Caroline discovered Matthew had offered to put up Nelson Gabriel while Honeysuckle Cottage was repaired, the relationship began to unravel. She moved back to Grey Gables, feeling Matthew wasn't ready to commit to her.

As a doctor, however, no one could doubt his integrity. He was anxious for Walter Gabriel in the final weeks of his life, and in 1989 delivered baby Kylie at the Vicarage. In 1991, however, he received an offer to join his aunt's practice in Somerset. He put his house, Willow Farm, which he'd been renting to the Tuckers, on the market and they eventually bought it for much less than Matthew had paid four years previously.

Titcombe

In theory, a head gardener's duties at Lower Loxley should be confined to overseeing the gardens and the staff who manage them, but Titcombe has always taken responsibility for looking after the Pargetters' peacocks as well. Relishing a challenge, he threw himself into recent developments in the grounds, including the provision of a nature trail and a treetop walk. He briefly showed a theatrical side to his nature when he took part in the 1998 production of *Jack and the Beanstalk*, but is more usually found, workboots on, taking care of his precious lawns, shrubs and flowerbeds.

Richard **Todd**

(Self)

Film star Richard Todd opened the village fête in 1962. His fame and good looks naturally drew a bumper crowd, and an autographed programme from the occasion doubtless reposes in many an Ambridge attic to this day.

Gustave **Touvier**

(Claude le Sache)

In 1993, genealogists in Ambridge started to wonder whether the Grundys had Gaulish ancestry; certainly Mayor Gustave Touvier, who headed the town-twinning delegation from Meyruelle, seemed to have a lot in common with Joe Grundy – even his compatriots agreed he didn't have a shred of tact.

Unable to speak any English, he communicated principally in body language. He pinched Lynda Snell's backside while staying at Ambridge Hall, but spent more time eyeing up the earthy charms of Clarrie Grundy, so it's as well that Robert Snell thought to take him shooting before diplomatic relations soured completely.

Arthur **Tovey**

(Harry Stubbs)

Arthur, who managed Carol Tregorran's Market Garden and orchard, kept himself to himself. He never married, and lost his only living relative, a cousin, in 1973. Contenting himself with Walter

Death: 1976

Gabriel's friendship and an interest in stock-car racing, he went his own quiet way through life until 1976, when he hit an overhead power cable with a ladder he was carrying. He died as a result of the injuries he sustained, with the subsequent inquest recording a verdict of death by misadventure. John Tregorran was left £9000 to distribute, as he saw fit, to charities.

Mr and Mrs **Travers-Macy**

(Fred Yule, Beatrice Kane)

Roger Travers-Macy rarely felt close to his wealthy but relatively elderly parents. Matters came to a head in 1968, when Mr Travers-Macy threatened to cut off all financial support after Roger became engaged to unmarried mother Jennifer Archer. However, Laura Archer persuaded him to change his mind, and, in time, Mr Travers-Macy grew fond of his new step-grandson, Adam. He received a ransom note demanding £5000 at the time of Adam's kidnapping, but, due to the kidnappers' incompetence, had no need to act on it. Mrs Travers-Macy enjoyed visiting Jennifer and Roger, during their relatively short marriage, to such an extent that she became something of a nuisance in Jennifer's eyes. John Tregorran had reason to be grateful to her, however: in 1972, she gave him the last existing copy of the Ambridge Mummers Play.

Roger **Travers-Macy**

(Jeremy Mason, Peter Harlow)

In 1965, Laura Archer was rescued from a car accident outside The Bull by the timely intervention of a young man calling himself Roger Patillo. In gratitude, she offered him a job as her

Birth: 9.3.1944

chauffeur, which he was happy to accept. Soon he struck up a friendship with Lilian Archer and confided in her that he was really Roger Travers-Macy, but had changed his name in response to the indifference his wealthy family showed him. The whole sad story came out: ignored by his older brother and sister, he chose 'Patillo' as a pseudonym because it was the name of a villa in the south of France where he used to spend school holidays.

Where, in more robust times, he would have been driven from the village at the end of a pitchfork for fibbing about his identity, Ambridge in the 1960s made him welcome. Laura even rewarded him for passing on a good Stock Exchange tip by buying him a guitar. He didn't stay with her for long. The opportunity to become a partner with John Tregorran and Henry Featherstone in Featherstone's bookshop in Borchester came his way, and Roger made up his differences with his father in time to raise the necessary capital.

Before long, he'd moved into Blossom Hill Cottage, and, shortly after, with Featherstone, bought out John Tregorran's share of the business.

Having acquired a car, he started giving Lilian driving lessons. She was unhappy about the amount of attention he was showing Valerie Woolley, but his true interest lay elsewhere. He started visiting Jennifer Archer, and young baby Adam, in Bristol. Liking soon turned to love, and, although Jennifer tried to cool their relationship because she felt guilty about taking away her sister's boyfriend, Roger was too hip and sophisticated for her to resist.

They married in the autumn of 1968. Mr Travers-Macy, who disapproved of Jennifer, withdrew his threat to cut Roger off without a penny after Laura had appealed to his better nature. Once their honeymoon in Ibiza was over, the newlyweds moved into a flat over the bookshop, with Blossom Hill Cottage being kept for weekends. Together they faced the trauma of Adam being kidnapped in 1970, and then, later in the same year, had a child of their own, when Debbie was born.

Although he loved the children, Roger wasn't happy with the marriage. He started travelling a lot, as he made more connections in the book trade. When he was taken on as a buyer for a firm of antiquarian booksellers in 1974, the travelling increased to such an extent that, feeling almost deserted, Jennifer left Borchester, and went with the children to live with Christine and Paul Johnson in Ambridge.

A final break-up was inevitable. By 1975, Roger was living in North Acton with the woman he wanted to become the second Mrs Travers-Macy. He asked Jennifer for a divorce, which duly came through in February of the following year. Although he sent his good wishes when Jennifer married Brian Aldridge, Roger insisted that Debbie and Adam should retain his surname. Over the next few years, his contact with the children was a little perfunctory, not going beyond the odd card or present. Then, at the start of the 1990s, he was on his own again, the woman he left Jennifer for having walked out on him. His thoughts turned back to his first marriage, and he made the effort to visit Ambridge for Debbie's twenty-first birthday party in 1991. He arranged to meet her a second time in Nelson's Wine Bar, and was delighted when Jennifer, who thought Debbie was surreptitiously seeing Simon Gerrard again, also turned up. Events spiralled from this point on.

Roger gave Debbie a brand new car and thereby made it obvious to Brian that he was back on the scene. A meal at Home Farm, designed to show how civilized they could all be, quickly became a disaster, as Jennifer and Roger reminisced about the old days, and Brian, feeling threatened, retreated to the lambing shed. Debbie warned her father about the bad effect he was having. Roger responded by congratulating Brian on his parenting skills and apologizing for any disruption he'd caused. Far from going away, however, he started meeting Jennifer secretly. The pretext for seeing her was that he needed help to stay in touch with Debbie, but soon their old love was re-ignited. They became more reckless about being seen together: after spotting them shopping for a picnic in Underwoods, Jill Archer was moved to warn Jennifer she was playing with fire. In the end, Debbie was probably the biggest influence in ending the affair. When Roger met her for lunch, the coldness in her manner, as she told him to steer clear of her mum, seemed to bring home how much damage he'd done. He said he was planning on leaving, and proved as good as his word.

From that point on, Roger got in touch with his daughter only intermittently. Naturally, he came to Ambridge when he heard about her involvement in Mark Hebden's accident. He also tried to help when

Debbie was considering buying a share of Nelson Gabriel's antiques business. He offered her an advance of £10,000 on her inheritance, only to let her down by being unwilling to stand as a guarantor for the rest of the loan she needed. To Jennifer's surprise, he's always stayed in touch with Adam, regularly sending letters to Kenya. He was pleased when Debbie brought Simon Gerrard to meet him before their wedding in May 2000, and, though perhaps a little hurt, understood why he couldn't really be asked to attend the ceremony. The sad fact is, as Brian Aldridge would be the first to tell you, Roger is very often at his best when he's at a distance.

Maureen **Travis 'Mo'**

(Roberta Kerr)

'All my friends call me Mo,' the farmer's wife at Hill Farm assured Neil Carter. He'd gone there on feed business and soon found himself being made welcome to call again. Mo Travis was quickly on good terms with Neil's wife, Susan, as well. They talked about two of their respective children, Becky and Emma, who were in the same class at school. A friendship rapidly sprang up between the two women, but Mo was really focusing elsewhere.

Unhappy in her marriage to Geoff, she played upon Neil's sympathies to get some emotional comfort. He was disconcerted when matters got as far as kissing, but felt drawn to her for company in 1994, while Susan was serving her sentence in jail.

Once, while Geoff was away, Neil even brought the children over to stay at Hill Farm, but resisted Mo's offer to sleep with him. Gossip started to spread, and, after her release, Susan heard it, with the result that she and Mo almost came to blows. Eventually Susan came to believe Neil's promise there hadn't been an affair and wasn't surprised to hear from Geoff that Mo had acted in the same way with other men before.

Dolly **Treadgold**

Divorcée Dolly Treadgold was five or six years older than Eddie Grundy when they got engaged in 1979, but it wasn't the age difference, nor the fact that Dolly's real name was Lesley, that caused the relationship to founder. It was Dolly's wandering eye that Eddie found unsettling, so, not wanting to spend his entire married life in competition with other men, he called the whole thing off. Nevertheless, they stayed on good enough terms after Eddie's marriage to Clarrie Larkin for Dolly to come round and cook when Clarrie was away for a while.

Anna-Louise **Tregorran**   'Ann'

Ann, as she was generally known, was the daughter of Carol and John Tregorran, born in September 1969. She learnt to enjoy travelling at an early age, spending a month in Turkey with her

Birth: 23.9.1969

parents when she was six years old. Later she often accompanied her father on his trips abroad.

Jill Archer, who together with Lady Isabel Lander and Hugo Barnaby, was one of Ann's godparents, still likes to hear how she's getting on, although it's now a long time since she was last in Borsetshire.

Carol **Tregorran**   née Grey (formerly Grenville)

(Anne Cullen)

Carol Grey came to Ambridge in 1954 to buy Dan Archer's smallholding. Once in possession of it, she set about turning it into a market garden, but soon found the strain of running it single-handed overwhelming, so, over the next few years, employed a succession of people, including Jack Archer, to share the work.

She formed a close friendship with John Tregorran, who was instrumental in helping her find out about her parents – unmarried artists – who had given her up for adoption when she was only two. John had hoped to marry her, but she chose Charles Grenville instead, marrying him in the autumn of 1961, and having a son, Richard, by him in December 1962. She and Charles remained good friends with John and his new wife, Janet. She was with John when they received news that Janet had been killed and Charles injured in a dreadful road accident.

Early in 1965, Charles died in America. The romance with John revived and they married in 1967, with their daughter, Anna-Louise, being born two years later. John's frequent absences on lecture tours seemed to put a strain on the marriage, and Carol went through a difficult stage, culminating with an appearance in court on a charge of shoplifting, which she was cleared of. By the end of the 1970s, the couple seemed more committed to making their marriage work, and by 1990 had decided to leave Borsetshire for Bristol to start a new life.

Gwen **Tregorran**

(Ann Kindred)

Gwen was married to John Tregorran's brother, Bernard, until he was killed in a car crash in 1951. John provided her, and her son, Bobbie, with some financial support until, in 1957, she came to Ambridge to announce she was to be married for a second time, to a man called Duncan Livsey. Thereafter, her contact with her former in-laws was extremely sporadic.

Janet **Tregorran** née Sheldon

(Judy Parfitt)

Perhaps on the rebound after the love of his life, Carol Grey, had married Charles Grenville, John Tregorran fell in love with and proposed to the attractive-looking Ambridge district nurse, Janet

Death: 31.10.1963

Sheldon. They were married from the Grenvilles' house on 29 June 1963, but were only to enjoy a few months together. At the end of October that year, Janet was being given a lift by Charles Grenville when they were involved in a crash in which she was killed instantly.

John **Tregorran**

(Basil Jones, Philip Morant, Simon Lack, Basil Jones, John Bott, Roger Hume)

A former university lecturer who had been freed from the normal constraints of work by a large win on the football pools, John Tregorran originally came to Ambridge in a caravan in 1954, apparently not intending to stay for long. He attracted a number of girlfriends, but found Carol Grey the most appealing woman in the village. They met when he accidentally ran his motorcycle into her car on the road by Coombe Farm. He soon proposed to her, and, although Carol dismissed this as a joke, over the next few years they conducted an intermittent courtship. When Carol decided to marry Charles Grenville instead, in September 1961, John sought consolation elsewhere, and, within two years, had married Janet Sheldon.

Fate clearly intended John and Carol to be together, though: their respective spouses died prematurely, and, by February 1967, they were doing what Ambridge had always expected them to do, finally marrying each other. The course of the marriage wasn't entirely smooth; John's long absences on lecture tours and a reported affair with Jennifer Aldridge when they worked together on a history of Ambridge indicated that something wasn't quite right at home. Nevertheless, in 1990, the Tregorrans were still together, when, with daughter Anna-Louise, they left Ambridge for Bristol, where they are living to this day.

Ann **Trentham**

(Margaret Joynson)

Despite already having a fiancé in the United States, Ann Trentham was happy to flirt with Phil Archer during her Christmas 1953 visit to Ambridge, when, thanks to cousin Reggie, she was staying at the Country Club. Although Phil was later to rescue her when she fell in the Squire's lake, she had by then taken a liking to her former tutor, John Tregorran. John, however, resisted her attractions and started going out with Carol Grey instead.

Reggie **Trentham**

(Peter Wilde)

Considered one of the best amateur riders in the county, Reggie Trentham was anything but sporting in his approach to life. Running the Grey Gables Country Club during the 1950s seemed to

Death: 1964

leave him plenty of time for other interests. He won the Hollerton Point-to-Point, only to be stripped of his prize for using aggressive tactics. He was equally competitive when playing cricket for Waterley Cross, and, on at least one occasion, fractured a batsman's ribs with his short-pitched bowling.

Mike Daly, who had reported his behaviour during the point-to-point, became a particular focus for hostility. Reggie spread untrue rumours about Mike's war record, and even brought a wartime colleague of Mike's, Valerie Grayson, to the village, in the hope of digging up embarrassing details of the past. He quickly became interested in Valerie for her own sake, however, and, after a protracted courtship, eventually married her. They had a daughter, Hazel Anne, in 1956, and two years later sold Grey Gables and left Ambridge. When Valerie returned with Hazel in 1964, it was with the news that Reggie had died in the Bahamas. Although he wasn't greatly lamented, both Phil and Dan Archer could remember times when Reggie had shown them kindness.

Sheila **Trevelyan**

(Ann Kindred)

A former acquaintance of John Tregorran, Sheila's interest in him was re-awakened when speaking to Walter Gabriel and Mrs P at the Hollerton Easter Carnival in 1958. Two days later, she turned up for an extended stay at The Bull.

Taken on as an assistant at John's bookshop, she used Carol Grey's absence on holiday to engineer an engagement with him. It lasted a month, until she decided that Tony Stobeman was a more interesting proposition.

Subsequently, she wrote *Glasshouse Village*, a somewhat scathing account of her stay in Ambridge, to which she also sold the film rights. Cineastes worldwide have been holding their breath for over forty years now.

Zebedee Tring

(Graham Rigby)

Zebedee was generally happier in the company of his pets – Gyp, the dog, and Queenie, the cat – than he was with other people. Having been made redundant from his road-making job in 1970, he accepted Jack Woolley's offer of work at Arkwright Hall, where he stayed for three years, until resigning in protest at being expected to do cleaning duties. For a short while he then worked for Hadyn Evans, but, on 28 December 1973, was found dead in his cottage by Tom Forrest and George Barford.

Death: 28.12.1973

Matthew Trugg

(Lewis Gedge)

Doughy Hood couldn't imagine the chaos he'd unleash when he kindly agreed to put up his old shipmate from the *Jovaritch* for a few days in 1958. When Hood's assistant Rita Flynn didn't take to him, Trugg tried to blackmail Doughy to get rid of her, saying he'd reveal Doughy's whereabouts to Clarice Conway, whose attentions he was avoiding. Then, having tried to sell Jill Archer's stolen handbag to Ned Larkin in The Bull, he saw sense and scarpered before PC Bryden could catch up with him – and before he could do any more harm.

Ben Truscott

(Philip Morant)

Tony's fiancée, Mary Weston, kindly gave up an evening in April 1974 to talk to the WI about her work as a farm secretary, but she little knew where it would lead. Believing she'd cited him unfavourably, curmudgeonly Penny Hassett farmer Truscott threatened to sue for slander and it was only when Mary cleverly collected written statements from all at the meeting, proving she'd never spoken his name, that he dropped his case against her.

Betty **Tucker**

(Pamela Craig)

If Betty Tucker has a fault, it's probably that she's too accommodating – who else would have put up with Mike over the years? Having said that, when she sets her mind to something, Betty can be very determined, as proved by her resolve in January 2001 to spend her 'nest egg' on some hens which would provide just that. Although the start of her joint enterprise with Neil Carter was delayed by the foot-and-mouth outbreak, Betty refused to waver.

Birth: 4.8.1950

Farming is in Betty's blood: she was brought up on a smallholding, so it was no surprise when, even within the small confines of Rickyard Cottage, she set about breeding pedigree sheepdogs. The first two litters were disappointing, however, and Betty turned to bees, before alighting on goats as a good prospect. Husband Mike was sceptical, but Betty found an outlet for the milk at the healthfood shop in Borchester and made a go of it.

These schemes were a sort of displacement activity, however, for Betty was desperate to start a family. Mike thought they should wait till they had a place of their own, but Betty came off the pill without telling him, and Roy was born in February 1978, by which time Mike was happy to play the proud father.

The only downside of the move to Willow Farm, also in 1978, was the enforced sale of Betty's goats and bees, but she filled her time by offering bed and breakfast, which went well until she fell pregnant again and couldn't face cooking the guests their bacon and eggs. Brenda was almost born in The Bull, where Mike and Betty had gone for a meal with Pat and Tony Archer, but luckily Betty was rushed to hospital in time.

Haydn Evans's retirement in 1982 meant that the Tuckers had to look for another home. Ambridge Farm, vacated by Mary Pound, wasn't exactly welcoming. The house needed rewiring and replastering, and the children found it spooky, but it was the best they could do and Betty supported Mike as he worked hard to modernize the place. Her farm shop, Betty's Barn, however, quickly went out of business.

Having already seen Mike nearly broken by a TB outbreak at Willow Farm, Betty must have noticed the approaching signs of strain in her husband throughout 1985. Mike was overstretched and undercapitalized, the interest on the overdraft was frightening and he owed money left, right and centre. Early in the New Year, a cheque he'd written to Borchester Mills bounced, the phone was cut off and the cows were repossessed. Mike had no option but to declare himself bankrupt. The bank accounts were transferred into Betty's name and Mike's bank accounts were frozen.

It would have been a terrible blow for anyone, but it was worse for someone as proud as Mike. The Tuckers were allowed to stay at Ambridge Farm through the summer at a nominal rent, but they had to be out by Michaelmas. Betty and the children moved briefly to The Bull, while Mike took a live-in herdsman job in the south of the county. It's a measure of how bad things were that Betty was thrilled to get a job cleaning for Jennifer Aldridge simply because the family could have a cottage thrown in. The job, however, caused more problems than it solved when Brian took a fancy to her, offering her mid-morning drinks and suggesting she frolic in the swimming pool with him. Betty fled and told Mike, who threatened to punch Brian's lights out. Sadly, he was restrained, but it made the Tuckers determined to escape from beneath the Aldridge yoke.

In 1988, Mike agreed to them renting Willow Farm from Matthew Thorogood, albeit on a somewhat insecure basis, and Betty continued her cleaning jobs until Jack offered her a position at the shop. Mike whinged, feeling emasculated, but Betty knew they needed the full-time wage.

Mike's accident at the Estate in May 1991 came at a bad time: he'd already argued with Betty over her application for one of the village's low-cost houses. Betty did her best to support her husband, as, having lost the sight of one eye, he became both a depressive and a fantasist. One day he'd be talking up his compensation claim and imagining time shares in Spain, the next he'd be drinking heavily and feeling useless. Sid Perks gave her a consoling cuddle, and, when she moved the children into The Bull at Christmas, something might have developed, as he was living apart from Kathy, but Betty knew Mike needed her.

Mike agreed to treatment for his depression, but when his eventual compensation payout was only a quarter of what he'd been expecting, Betty feared he'd plummet down again. Mike's big plans for buying a logger or a new van were troubling for her: she felt their only hope was to get a foot on the property ladder. This was made possible when Matthew Thorogood, who was leaving the village, had to drop the price of Willow Farm and finally accepted their low offer out of both sentimentality and desperation.

Betty should have been able to breathe a sigh of relief, but, in April 1993, Clive Horrobin and an accomplice held her hostage in the village shop. It took Betty a long time to get over the ordeal, and to this day she is terrified that Clive might again return to the village, as he did in 1997.

A doting Nana to her granddaughter, Phoebe, Betty has never liked Kate, and was uncomfortable at being made to feel the poor relation in comparison to the Aldridges. She was therefore delighted when Roy and Hayley were married in May 2001. But even being the mother of the bridegroom couldn't eclipse her finest hour. On her fiftieth birthday, a date she shares with the Queen Mother, Mike and the family treated her royally so that she too could be 'Queen for a Day'.

Brenda **Tucker**

(Helen Cutler, Amy Shindler)

At the age of eight, Brenda Tucker was miming into a hairbrush and trying to be Kylie Minogue. Her ambitions are somewhat more realistic these days, as, with the help of her mentor, Wayne Foley, she becomes more proficient at radio techniques, working as a trainee journalist on Radio Borsetshire. She's already a thorn in the side of agribusiness with her investigative pieces on the GM crop trashing and Borchester Land's development plans.

Birth: 21.1.1981

Considered from childhood to be mature, sensible and responsible, Brenda's only babyhood aberration was when she fell in with Kate's Blossom Hill Cottage gang at the age of eleven. A year later she was back in her dressing-up/drama phase when she took part in the re-enactment of the Battle of Hassett Bridge in a costume made out of Lynda Snell's old curtains. Good A-level grades in theatre studies, English and media studies would have taken her to university, but, like her practical and hardworking mother, Brenda preferred to get on with things – and to be earning money rather than spending it. Brenda's radio role helped make Betty's fiftieth extra special when she was Wayne's birthday guest on his show. Lucas Madikane's name has no doubt also gone down in Brenda's bulging contacts book.

Brenda's appetite for life was temporarily diminished in the summer of 2001 when she was deceived by Scott, Lilian Bellamy's toyboy, who fed her the usual lines that any 'other woman' is doomed to hear. After Lilian threw Scott out, Brenda had hopes that they might set up house together, but Scott quickly left in search of richer pickings, leaving her sadder and wiser.

Hayley **Tucker** née Jordan

(Lucy Davis)

Now married to Roy, when Hayley first came to the village in 1995 it was as the girlfriend of Roy's best friend, John Archer. Hayley and John had met at the Ice House, a club in Birmingham.

Birth: May 1977

Inviting her to the Lower Loxley Point-to-Point, where he had a stall selling hot pork rolls, John was counting on Hayley's help, but she retorted that she hadn't come all that way to skivvy. Her first encounter with the countryside was not altogether a happy one: she got her boots covered in cow dung and was chased by the Lower Loxley heifer, Elly May. It would take more than that to put the determined Brummie off, though, and, by the summer, she was an item with John, and well enough entrenched to do face-painting at the fête. Now a qualified nursery nurse, she also started her first job for Josie at Waterley Cross, looking after little Becky.

As 1996 was a leap year, Hayley hatched a plan. On 29 February she proposed to John, assuming he'd refuse, but hoping to get a present out of him to make up. To her amazement, the worse for drink, he accepted, and she had to string him along. Admitting her ruse later, the sobered-up John was so relieved that he did indeed buy her the silk dress she'd had her eye on.

They continued happy until the summer, when they went on holiday to Corfu. The holiday snaps showed John with his arm round a variety of girls (never Hayley), and, on their return, he seemed to expect her to help with his pigs without a word of thanks. Hayley told him they were finished, but their separation was brief. Hayley was peeved when she thought John had no special plans for Valentine's night in 1997, but he surprised her by whisking her off to a posh restaurant in Birmingham and asking her to live with him. Interestingly, they looked at and rejected the flat at Nightingale Farm (John didn't fancy living in close proximity to Mrs A), before settling on April Cottage. By this time everyone in the family liked Hayley so much that even Peggy Woolley didn't disapprove of her grandson 'living in sin'.

They might be living there still had not Sharon Richards, John's first love, come back on the scene in 1997 to revive their pheromone-fuelled affair. One ghastly night in November, Hayley returned from a cancelled babysitting engagement to find John and Sharon in a state of undress on the sofa. She packed her things and returned to Birmingham. John realized straight away how stupid he'd been, but, though still in love with him, Hayley was resolute. By the New Year, Hayley was sharing her woes with Roy Tucker, then estranged from the pregnant Kate Aldridge, and they spent a miserable Valentine's night commiserating about their former partners. When John heard from Roy that Hayley was still interested, he made plans to surprise her. On Shrove Tuesday, he took her to the classy Mont Blanc restaurant for their Mardi Gras night, and asked her to marry him. But it was all too soon for Hayley and she refused.

Hayley was away at a holiday village with Becky and Josie when John was killed, and, on her return, fell sobbing into Pat's arms, blaming herself for his state of mind on the day he died. At his funeral, she spoke movingly and played a record that she said reminded her of him: 'Wonderwall' by Oasis.

It was Hayley who inspired John's brother, Tom, to take on his pigs, and it was Hayley's idea to go into sausage production. When Tony had to tell her that she couldn't be a partner in the pigs, only an employee, she was deeply hurt, and withdrew her labour and goodwill. She nonetheless supported Tom in 1999 throughout his GM crop trial, and, though she knew it was a risk, acted as messenger between him and his girlfriend, Kirsty Miller.

By November 1999, she was comforting Roy Tucker again when Kate departed with their daughter, Phoebe, for Morocco, and, in December, she was able to be a practical help when Kate returned, left Phoebe with him, and took off again. Roy was touched when Hayley effectively blackmailed Josie, her employer, into letting her take Phoebe to work with her, and, on Millennium Eve, Hayley and Roy kissed passionately on the village green.

But it's not always easy to go from being friends to being lovers, and Hayley confided in Marjorie Antrobus about her feelings before she and Roy finally got together. In July 2000, Roy suggested they live together at Nightingale Farm, and Marjorie adapted the accommodation with help from Hayley's father and brother. Unbeknown to Hayley, Roy had planned a romantic proposal on New Year's Eve, but Kate turned up and turned everything upside-down. Hayley feared both for her own security and for Phoebe's, and, though Roy did propose, was too shell-shocked to give him an answer. The next day, though, when he repeated the question, emphasizing that his relationship with Kate was well and truly over and that he needed Hayley to fight for Phoebe with him, she happily agreed.

It was ironic that after Kate had gone into labour on the Blackberry Line steam railway, it should be Hayley who was with her for the birth of Nolly, but really, who better? Hayley's caring instincts have led to her being something of a Pied Piper for the children of Ambridge, while she's supported her adored Mrs A through two cataract operations. Tom Forrest also took to her, telling her she reminded him of his Pru. Hayley's abundance of love doubtless comes from her close-knit family. Her dad is a lorry driver and her brother, Gary, a keen Villa supporter. But Hayley's guiding influence has probably been her Nan, with her fund of Brummie sayings and a touching courtship story of her own: she met her husband while strawberry picking in the Vale of Evesham. It seems only right that Hayley's own happy ending should have occurred not so very far away.

Mike **Tucker**

(Gareth Armstrong, Alexander Wilson, Terry Molloy)

It's tempting to think that reaching the age of fifty marked a new maturity, an acceptance almost, in Mike Tucker. When Pat Archer was in the depths of her depression, he proved an understanding listener,

| Birth: 1.12.1949 |

and he showed up at the Grange Farm dispersal sale in a display of solidarity, for Mike had been there himself – declared bankrupt and also depressed.

Everything had looked so promising when he came to Ambridge in 1973. He was newly married to Betty and they settled into Rickyard Cottage while he assumed the job of Ambridge Farmers' Ltd's dairy unit manager. A union man of strong convictions, he set about reviving the local branch of the NUAAW and became the local branch secretary. When Jethro Larkin fell through the loft over the Brookfield calf-pens, he persuaded him to claim compensation and presented him with the resultant cheque at a meeting at The Bull. Although he flatly refused to join the bell-ringers or the Ambridge Chorale, he enjoyed a pint and a game of darts, and helped run the Youth Club on a regular basis. Mike felt mithered when Betty talked about having a family, but, when she became pregnant in May 1977, he accepted the situation with good grace – eventually. In November the same year, he approached Haydn Evans about becoming his partner when Tony Archer moved on to Bridge Farm. He had £2000 of the necessary £6000 saved, and would raise the rest, he declared, with a loan. Haydn agreed, and the Tuckers and the Archers ended up living together while renovations at Bridge Farm were completed. Tony was pleased to have a drinking buddy, but was less sure about Mike's fondness for country and western music.

Roy's birth brought out something of the old Neanderthal in Mike: although he chose the baby's name, he wanted nothing to do with changing nappies. Instead he got on with farming, taking on contract milking, which incensed Haydn, chopping down the Willow Farm willows, which incensed him even more, and, more successfully, taking over Des Drayton's Ayrshires and also his milk round. The herd and a bottling plant were soon installed at the farm, and everything seemed to be going well, especially when Brenda was born in January 1981.

In August 1982, however, the three-yearly test for bovine TB revealed a reactor in Mike's herd. Movement restrictions were imposed, and it took the rest of the year before the herd were declared disease-free. In the meantime, Mike had given up on-farm bottling and was buying in pasteurized milk from Borchester Dairies.

The next blow was Haydn's decision to retire. This meant that by 1983, the Tuckers were on the move again, this time to Ambridge Farm as tenants of the Estate. There Mike worked day and night to build up a busy mixed farm: sixty-five Ayrshire milkers, thirty-five followers, 105 acres of grassland and 60 acres of cereals. And all the time he was still doing a daily milk round.

Mike's hard work couldn't help him, though, when the bank refused to increase the overdraft on which he was already paying some £700 a quarter in interest. He already owed Borchester Mills, the contractor and the vet: he had assets, but no liquidity. The inevitable happened in early 1986, when the cows were repossessed, the bank called in its loan and Mike declared himself bankrupt. Rags to rags in just ten years.

The next few years were dismal for the Tuckers. They returned to Willow Farm as Matthew Thorogood's tenants, with Mike picking up farm work where he could and bitterly unhappy that Betty, with her job in the shop, was now the main breadwinner. No sooner had he got what seemed like more regular work on the Estate than he was involved in an accident when a hydraulic pipe hit him in the eye. An operation for a detached retina was not a success, and Mike became withdrawn and bitter when Betty had to take on the milk round, too. Over the course of 1991, Mike's mental health deteriorated as he refused to be helped, so much so that he picked a fight with his old friend Tony in The Bull and defiantly planted alder instead of ash at Home Farm. He finally cracked when Jim Ascott, on whose land Mike had hoped to raise sheep, decided to let it go into set-aside, as he'd make more out of it. Hardly knowing what he was doing, Mike set out with a petrol can to torch Ascott's barn, but was stopped in time by Eddie Grundy. When Mike left ten-year-old Brenda alone to cook chips, Betty had finally had enough and took the children to stay at The Bull. They were reconciled only after Mike was found sobbing on Christmas Day and agreed to treatment.

In 1992, Betty persuaded Mike to put down the £33,000 compensation for his eye accident as a deposit on Willow Farm, which was up for sale, and, by early 1993, the Tuckers were back there again, this time as owner-occupiers. There Mike started a market garden, supplying Pat and Tony's farm shop, and took on half of Neil Carter's hens. Neil had just given the go-ahead for a joint pick-your-own strawberry venture when Mike's market garden was trashed by racist thugs who had a bone to pick with Roy. The strawberries escaped, however, and ran successfully until 1999, though Mike gave up the market garden in 1997.

Now working increasingly in forestry and landscaping, most of Mike's problems lately have been to do with Brenda's infatuation with Scott and Roy's altercations with Kate over their daughter, Phoebe. He was a distinctly unmerry man in Lynda's *Babes in the Millennium Wood* in 1999, as Kate had taken off for Morocco with the child. Mike was cheered, though, by Roy's wedding to Hayley. He jokingly dubbed the couple the 'Posh and Becks of Borsetshire' for their grand plans, but he swelled with pride just the same.

Roy **Tucker**

(Ian Pepperell)

Roy Tucker was leading a fairly blameless life in Ambridge when he first met Kate Aldridge in 1995. A timid child, who then went through a craze for pop music and Aston Villa, he got two A grades and six Bs at GCSE, and progressed smoothly to A-levels in maths, economics and business studies. He played cricket for the village, and, by the age of seventeen, was regarded by the likes of Martha Woodford as a nice, clean young man: even the long hair and adolescent spots had gone.

Birth: 2.2.1978

He was puttering past on his bike when he came across Kate smoking in the bus shelter. After receiving a lecture on how bad it was for her (Roy has never smoked or done drugs), Kate demanded to know what he did for kicks: sang in the church choir, perhaps? It seemed like an attraction of opposites, but Roy and Kate, to Betty's horror, began going out.

Roy got an even worse reception when he introduced Kate to his mates from Borchester: they laughed at her hippy attire, while she found them boorish and strangely threatening. When they got rough with Roy, who'd missed a 'planning meeting' for a so-called 'hit', he told her it was a bit of housebreaking. But in fact the seemingly angelic Roy was mixed up with a racist gang who were targeting Usha Gupta. After his father's market garden was trashed, Kate put Roy on the spot and he gave names to the police. He was beaten up for his pains, but at least was let off with a caution while the gang proper stood trial.

In September 1995, Roy and Kate traded in their moped and motorbike respectively and bought a 250cc motorbike. But Kate felt Roy was reverting to being boring when he refused to let her ride it till she'd passed her test, and then tried to put her off her friendship with public schoolboy Gibson, whose interests, naturally, her mother was promoting. In December, at a disastrous party at Kate's cottage, Gibson taunted Roy about his fascist friends, and Roy accused Kate of sleeping with him. Their relationship was off, but Roy was anguished when he heard in January 1996 that Kate had apparently attempted suicide on New Year's Eve. It turned out to be an accident: Gibson had let her down, and she'd mixed whisky and pills. A protective Roy fought Gibson when he found him using Kate's cottage to deal drugs, and, by the time of his eighteenth birthday, he and Kate were back together. In June, they went together to the Fleadh Festival, and, seeing the number of food vans doing a good trade, decided this would be something they could do together in Roy's gap year before he started his accountancy and finance course at the University of Felpersham. So 'Pulsations' was born, but their van broke down, and, by October, Roy had found a more reliable source of income as a waiter at Grey Gables, something that he'd continue throughout his university years.

A year later, having just started at college, Roy admitted to his father that things were rocky with Kate. They parted again, and Roy was dumbfounded to learn in a chance remark from Hayley Jordan in January 1998 that Kate was pregnant. He demanded his rights, but Kate told him he had none: the baby wasn't his. Roy determined to have blood tests to prove that it was. Roy and Kate came together briefly through the death of their friend and Kate's cousin John Archer, but, when Kate gave birth to her baby girl in a tepee in Glastonbury, she didn't even tell Roy she'd been born.

Having avoided his calls, Kate tried to take the baby to France, but Roy obtained a last-minute court order to forbid this, and, furthermore, ordered blood tests. These proved that the baby (still known only as 'Baby') was indeed Roy's, and, in a last-minute capitulation, Kate agreed that Roy could have contact without going through the courts. The child was eventually named Phoebe at a naming ceremony on Lakey Hill.

Roy and Kate had finally reached some sort of accommodation, but, in November 1999, Kate told him that Ambridge was 'doing her head in' and she intended taking Phoebe to Morocco. This was bad enough, but when gastro-enteritis meant she had to rush the child home, Roy was beside himself. After a few days back in the village, Kate was off again, this time leaving Phoebe in Roy's care and admitting that, at that point, he was a better father than she was able to be a mother.

During her absence, Roy and Hayley became close and they set up home with Phoebe at Nightingale Farm. In December 2000, he confided to his sister that he wanted to propose to Hayley, and selected an emerald and diamond ring with which to surprise her. But with her usual immaculate timing, Kate returned on New Year's Eve, somewhat spoiling the moment. Hayley nonetheless accepted Roy's heartfelt proposal, but there was more heart-searching to come. Kate was pregnant by a man she'd met on her travels, and, soon delivered another daughter, followed by a bombshell: she wanted Phoebe to return to South Africa with her and her partner, Lucas Madikane. Although ostensibly for a visit, Roy was more than suspicious. Luckily, Lucas's sensible counsel dissuaded Kate, and Roy was free to look forward to his wedding day, 7 May 2001. His surprise to Hayley this time was a three-day honeymoon in London.

As the newlyweds settle down at Nightingale Farm, and, with Kate safely in South Africa with her new family, Roy's life looks more secure than for some time. His prospects as assistant manager at Grey Gables are assured, he has a wife and daughter whom he adores... All he needs now is for the next cricket season to be a good one and his cup will surely overflow.

Wayne **Tucson**

The so-called 'Singing Oilman', Wayne's association with Jolene Rogers, whom he married just before Fallon was born in 1985, was short-lived, both professionally and personally. He remains in contact with his daughter, taking her shopping and bowling on access visits, but that's as far as it goes. When asked in the summer of 2000, he made it plain that he and his current girlfriend would not want Fallon to live with them full-time.

Greg **Turner**

(Marc Finn)

When Brian Aldridge needed a new head gamekeeper for the Home Farm/Estate shoot in 1998, he invited the man then running the Blackwater shoot, Greg Turner, to interview. Greg clearly made a good impression, because, once the requisite references had been received, he was offered the job. While Brian manoeuvred to make Sammy Whipple's cottage available for him, Greg moved into one of the holiday cottages. It was soon evident that he was more interested in getting on top of his new job than in making a good impression socially. He was quick to tell Mrs Antrobus she needed to keep her dogs on a lead when taking them across Estate land, and was on the point of shooting Lynda Snell's dog, Hermes, when it got too close to some newly arrived pheasant poults. Only Lynda putting herself between dog and gun averted a canine catastrophe.

George Barford considered the new keeper virtually unapproachable, while Jennifer Aldridge was unimpressed when Greg cancelled a Home Farm lunch engagement at short notice. Another Aldridge, Debbie, considered Greg harsh in his attitude towards William Grundy, who, eager to gain more gamekeeping experience, had offered his assistance on the shoot, only to be told it wasn't required. Seemingly determined to have a good first season's shooting, at whatever cost in goodwill, Greg refused to cooperate with George about sharing beaters with the Grey Gables shoot. He offered higher wages than his rival, but a lack of local knowledge led to a disappointing first day's shooting, when he misjudged the effect of a wind change on his birds, and directed the guns to the wrong drive. For the first time he showed he wasn't invulnerable to other people's opinions when he later admitted to Debbie over a drink that he felt quite deflated about his misjudgement.

By the following year, and now settled in his own cottage, he was asked to take over the Grey Gables shoot temporarily, in addition to his own duties, while Jack Woolley found a replacement for the retiring George Barford. During a handover period, when the two keepers worked side by side, there was a degree of friction between them over the question of egg collection and other matters, before George grew to accept that the younger man really knew his job. When a satisfactory replacement couldn't be found, Jack Woolley reluctantly agreed for his shoot to be merged with the larger enterprise, and Greg became responsible for running the permanently enlarged operation. He was initially unsure about the one condition Jack attached to the deal – namely that William Grundy should be taken on as an underkeeper – but soon seemed comfortable with the idea.

Although his work kept him exceptionally busy, he did make time to become involved in some aspects of village life. He took part in the 1999 Single Wicket Competition, and was later to be cajoled into entering a quiz team at The Bull. He didn't seem to need close companionship, but got on well with David Archer. It was while on a visit to Brookfield that he revealed he was highly competent at first aid. When Pip scalded herself trying to help make coffee, it was Greg, rather than David, who was first to react, swiftly running cold water over the scald. He later explained that, prior to becoming a gamekeeper, he had worked with young people on outdoor pursuits courses and was consequently used to dealing with emergencies.

It was unusual for him to talk about his past, other than occasionally to discuss some of his earlier gamekeeping experiences with William. He admitted that he came to the work later than most, starting as an underkeeper for a man called Henry Lightfoot, whom he described as being very fond of pubs and reliant on his working dog, Sammy, to get him home after turning out time. For much of the time, Greg seemed content with his own company. William earned his respect for his hard-working attitude, and, on one occasion at least, his gratitude, when Greg accidentally let the heaters go out in the incubators. Brian Aldridge almost stumbled on this costly error, but William managed to cover for his immediate superior. Nevertheless, Greg still didn't grant William the time off he needed to be able to attend the Game Fair, although he later made a point of exonerating his apprentice of any involvement when Eddie Grundy brought a caravan close to the rearing pens to use as temporary accommodation.

Recent times have put extra pressure on Greg. The outbreak of foot-and-mouth disease in 2001 meant he had to be increasingly vigilant about walkers straying on to farm and shooting land. At the same time, he faced the dilemma of being against the proposed housing development, but being unable to speak out freely because ultimately his employers were Borchester Land, who stood to make the most gain if it were permitted. It wasn't until August 2001 that Greg really unburdened himself about his past personal life; and indeed what a burden it was. Following the ugly break-up of a previous marriage, his ex-wife had taken his two children to France and prevented Greg from having any contact with them. The recipient of this news, which explained much of Greg's social reticence, was Helen Archer. To the surprise of them both, they had become involved, and Greg eventually agreed that their relationship could become public. But very few knew about Greg's failed marriage, and even fewer about his estranged children.

Agatha **Turvey**

(Courtney Hope)

Wealthy widow Agatha took a shine to Tom Forrest after he helped her with some odd jobs, and he spent much of the 1950s trying to

Death: March 1976

dodge her advances. She once lured him round to her house by claiming she'd heard a funny noise, which turned out to be a snail on the window pane. He also had a lucky escape one Christmas, when, having told the village that they were spending the day together, she decided instead to visit her sister, Marian. After Tom's marriage to Pru, she turned her attention to Walter Gabriel, but he deflected her by filling the field next to her garden with pigs, and they embarked on something of a love-hate relationship. Despite this, they collaborated for two years on the Hollerton pet shop venture, and, in 1965, he was the only one who remembered her birthday.

Mrs Turvey came to a sad end in 1976, when she went out too soon after a dose of the flu and contracted pleurisy. Her live-in companion, Emily Tarbutt, was also struck down with flu, so was unable to nurse her, and it was days before anyone else called to see how they were. Simon Parker wrote her obituary for the *Felpersham Evening Post*.

Tom Tyrell

Building magnate Tom Tyrell was a highly respected member of Borsetshire society, who acted not only as a councillor with a place on the Housing Committee, but also as a Justice of the Peace. He was clearly unhappy when, in 1977, *Borchester Echo* journalist Simon Parker started to pursue a story about alleged improprieties in council contracts. Tyrell's good friend Jack Woolley used his position as proprietor of the *Echo* to pressure Simon into resigning, only to reinstate him after it transpired that Tyrell had indeed been accepting gifts to help certain firms get subcontracting work.

Underwoods

Underwoods department store in Borchester is Jennifer Aldridge's second home. She shopped in their food hall for gourmet treats for her lunchtime liaisons with her ex-husband, Roger Travers-Macy, she's exchanged many a confidence in their coffee shop, and, in times of trouble, Brian knows she can always be bought off with the promise of a new designer outfit to be charged to her store card.

Vicarage

This four-bedroomed bungalow with garage was built in 1974 next to the church in the grounds of the Old Vicarage. There used to be an Aga in the reasonably-sized kitchen, and a log fire in the living-room, but no cleric has lived in it since the departure of Robin Stokes in 1995. In 1997, it was bought by Dr Richard Locke and converted into the doctor's surgery.

Dave Walker

(Graham Padden)

When Lynda Snell thought her husband, Robert, was having an affair in 1995, she engaged private eye Dave to confirm her suspicions. He shadowed Robert for weeks, but told Lynda his movements were more indicative of someone with money troubles than another woman. Lynda was scornful and dismissed him, but not before she'd been spotted with Dave in two seedy cafés, giving rise to gossip that she herself was seeing another man.

Mrs Walker

(Gillian Goodman)

For a time in the late 1980s and early '90s, Eunice Walker would leap on her moped in Penny Hassett and set off on her part-time cleaning duties. She had started working for the Aldridges when Jennifer's pregnancy in 1988 meant she needed extra help around the house. Since Mr Walker already worked as a gardener at Home Farm, it was easy enough to arrange for his wife also to be taken on. Soon after, Eunice put herself forward to clean at Lower Loxley as well. (As an ex-employee of Lady Lockheart at Hassett Hill Manor, this was much more the class of property she was used to looking after.) She was very clear about what she was and wasn't prepared to do: there was to be no bed-making, heavy lifting was out of the question and the very thought of having to do Ruth Archer's laundry, while the latter was on placement at Home Farm, was enough to make her hand in her notice. She continued at Lower Loxley for a while longer, until Julia Pargetter decided she was surplus to requirements, and sent Eunice, dusters and all, off on her bike.

Lauren **Walsh**

(Cathy Sara)

Tall, attractive and blonde, Lauren Walsh demonstrated a marvellous singing voice when she took on the role of Yum-Yum in Lynda Snell's millennium year production of *The Mikado*. When she learned her supposed boyfriend, Tom Archer, was in fact two-timing her with his regular girlfriend, Kirsty Miller, who was also in the cast, Lauren walked out of rehearsals. Behind the scene machinations from Hayley Jordan led to Lauren and Kirsty calling a truce and mutually making Tom suffer for his duplicity. Lauren returned to sing triumphantly in performance, and was happy to forget all about Tom, as she started going out with a new beau, Martin, instead.

Samantha **Walton**

(Dionne Inman)

A classical guitar aficionado in her spare time, nursery nurse Samantha Walton proved to be a quiet, helpful presence while staying at Grange Farm to gain work experience in 1985. She had all the qualities needed to make her attractive to Eddie Grundy, in that she was female and not in possession of a bus pass. Not only did she have to fend off his advances, she also had to employ her first aid skills when called upon to save young William Grundy from choking. Eddie's thank-you gift, a brooch in the shape of a piglet, somehow seems inadequate recompense for all she had to endure.

Benjamin **Warner**   'Ben'

(Don Henderson)

This rather alternative character from Walthamstow bought the cottage backing on to Mark Hebden's Penny Hassett garden in 1982. His presence proved troubling for Shula Archer, who became fascinated with him, even when he shaved his head and began sporting a kaftan. By 1983, Ben was on the move again, but not before being apprehended by the police, having stolen £400-worth of goods in different local burglaries. He was sentenced to twelve months in prison, half of it suspended.

Warren

When Kate Aldridge wanted a boyfriend in 1992, rather than checking out the gang at Sunday School or looking through the local Boy Scout troop, she opted instead to go out with car-stealing, joy-riding Warren. After a crash in a stolen Alfa Romeo left Kate shaken up and Warren with a fine and twelve months' probation, Brian and Jennifer Aldridge forbade their daughter to have any further dealings with the ne'er-do-well. For once, Kate had the sense to do as she was told.

Bobby **Waters**

(Alaric Cotter)

Formerly the tenant at Heydon Farm on the Brigadier's estate, hard-working Bobby moved on via a job at Brookfield to manage Ralph Bellamy's 120-strong dairy herd at the same time that Tony Archer had been taken on as a trainee. In August 1975, Bobby had an accident in the milking parlour, but a suspected hairline fracture of one of the bones in his spine happily proved to be nothing more than muscle strain. He was back at work by October, where he carried on contentedly, and presumably without incident, until his retirement.

Fiona **Watson**

(Carole Boyd)

In 1967, feisty Fiona refused to accept her job description when she saw that Ralph Bellamy had given her the title 'shepherdess': she was, she maintained, as much a shepherd as any man. Indeed, her pedigree was good: she'd attended Studley College and had worked with sheep on the Welsh borders. She became friendly with Tony and they tried to form an Ambridge branch of the YFC, but, in 1970, she married a farm manager and moved away.

Mr **Watson**

(Patrick Connor)

If Shula found Norman Rodway a hard taskmaster, the other partner in Rodway & Watson's estate agents was equally pernickety. In 1978, he reprimanded Shula for colouring in the wrong house of a pair on sale particulars, though she'd been given the wrong information, but, when he subsequently implied she'd accepted an offer on a cottage too quickly, she stood her ground. This seemed to give him new respect for her, and he bought her a horse brooch for her birthday.

Nick **Wearing**

(Gareth Johnson)

A paler version of Nigel Pargetter, public school-educated Nick was the son of an old friend of Phil Archer, who asked if Phil could find work Nick for a year between school and agricultural college, after which he would take over the running of the family estate. A live-in placement was arranged at Bridge Farm, but before long Nick was working at Brookfield, lodging with Neil Carter at Nightingale Farm and taking out Jennifer Aldridge's au pair, Eva Lenz. Italian opera and modern jazz were just a couple of his passions, but he was a tad too over-enthusiastic when he promised to take Eva badger-watching at dawn and broke her bedroom window lobbing stones at it to wake her up. A trip with her to the Royal Show was more successful from his point of view, though not from Jennifer's. She was incensed when Eva wasn't back till the next day: the pair blithely explained that they'd driven on to London.

By the autumn of 1978, Nick's attentions had switched to Shula Archer, and he accompanied her on her round-the-world trip the following year. The Archers, however, were cross with him, too, when he abandoned her in Bangkok and trekked on to Australia by himself.

Godfrey **Wendover**

In 1988, Peggy Archer was much taken with the cut of retired naval officer Godfrey Wendover's jib when she had to sort out a problem in the barn conversion he had rented from Rodway & Watson. Despite her children mistakenly fearing that Godfrey was a pirate, only anxious to get his hands on Peggy's treasure chest, the two of them got on well together and all was plain sailing for a while. They went to the Three Counties Show, and, falling under the old sea-dog's spell, Peggy started bringing maritime knick-knacks into The Bull as decoration, a ship's bell proving particularly irritating when the punters couldn't resist repeatedly ringing it.

> **Birth:** 1923

Trying to inject the 'naughty' into nautical, Godfrey then invited Peggy to spend a month on holiday with him in Spain. She turned him down, but, undeterred, he continued to attempt close manoeuvres, much to the chagrin of the onlooking landlubber Jack Woolley. However, a misjudged laugh as Peggy outlined plans for entering her cat Sammy into a pet show in 1989 sank Godfrey's chances for good. A man who didn't love animals could never sail in convoy with her, she decided, so Godfrey was left to paddle his own canoe elsewhere.

Mary **Weston**

(Catherine Crutchley)

Tony Archer met Mary at a Young Farmers' dance, and, though there was an instant attraction, the dozy Don Juan didn't think to ask her name. It was a happy coincidence, then, when Mary turned up at Willow Farm as the travelling farm secretary Tony had engaged to help with his paperwork. Soon they were engaged in another sense, with the wedding date set for 27 July 1974. In April, Mary gave a talk to the WI about her work, as a result of which a farmer named Ben Truscott claimed she'd slandered him. Although Mary apologized by letter, Truscott took this as an admission of guilt. He told her he intended to take her to court, while Mary's boss helpfully informed her that if she lost the case, she'd be out of a job. Luckily, she had the idea of gathering written statements from those at the WI meeting. These proved that she'd never mentioned Truscott by name, and he dropped his case against her, but Mary's relationship with Tony seems to have suffered from the stress. Their wedding was first postponed, then cancelled. In October of the same year, Tony heard that she was to marry her boss, Mr Seymour, who'd obviously decided that she was an asset to more than just his secretarial agency.

Charles **Wharburton**

(Harry Stubbs)

This aerodynamic airman was in charge of salvage operations when a jet plane crashed into Brookfield's wheat in 1952. Having discussed compensation with Dan, Wharburton spent the rest of his time in Ambridge with Mrs P, whose cottage was just the place, he hinted, a chap might like to retire to. His son, Jimmy, who lived with relatives, turned up looking for his father, and Mrs P generously allowed the boy to stay until his father's leave was fixed. Then it was 'chocks away' for them both.

Sammy and Joan **Whipple**

Sammy had something of a chequered career as Home Farm's shepherd from 1976 to 1998. He missed the start of lambing in 1978 in order to be with his dying father, Frank, but was later to miss a great deal of time from work through a series of illnesses, not all of which were considered genuine by his employer, Brian Aldridge.

He tended to be set in his ways, and, although competent in his work, seemed uncomfortable taking orders from Debbie Aldridge, on the grounds of her age and sex. By 1998, Brian was keen to move Sammy and his wife, Joan, out of their tied cottage on the farm in order to have it available for the new gamekeeper, Greg Turner. With Usha Gupta acting as his legal representative, Sammy fought Brian's attempts to make him redundant. Usha won the case, but her pleasure in doing so was quickly undermined when Sammy accepted £15,000 from Brian to move anyway. He and his wife left Ambridge for Felpersham, where they moved into Sammy's sister's home, opposite the football ground.

Ben **White**

(Will Kings)

If only Ben White had put as much time into looking after his bakery as he did into minding other people's business, he might well have been more popular in the Ambridge of the early 1950s. He complained that Squire Lawson-Hope's elm trees were a menace to the public, mistakenly claimed Jack Archer had been drunk at the time of a traffic accident and then, as vice-president of the Hollerton Homing Club, was responsible for George Fairbrother and Dan Archer being taken to court for the shooting of racing pigeons. He wasn't much missed when he sold the bakery to his former apprentice, Doughy Hood, in 1956.

Harry **White**

(Gordon Walters)

Harry was the son of Jim White, one of the workers on the Lawson-Hope Estate. By the time he was eighteen, he was in trouble with his father for being involved with poaching. Worse was to come: in 1962, together with an accomplice, Chuck Ballard, Harry tried to blackmail Carol Grenville. He had stolen a set of love letters sent to her some years previously by John Tregorran. He wanted £200 for their safe return, but, instead, found himself being arrested by PC Bryden when he and Chuck went to collect the money.

Geoff **Williams**

Mild-mannered Geoff was for many years the farm manager on the Berrow Estate but fell out famously with Simon Pemberton. In 1995 after several confrontations, Geoff felt he was being set up to fail, so handed in his resignation. He tried to get his revenge in 1997 by turning up glowering at the dispersal sale, but his presence in fact put prices up as everyone knew he was bidding for the cattle.

Harriet **Williams**

Flame-haired Harriet was an ex-girlfriend of Simon Pemberton's who appeared again when he was going out with Shula Hebden in 1996. Simon's claims that Harriet kept phoning him because her marriage was in trouble and she needed a shoulder to cry on were transparent to everyone but Shula, but when Harriet turned up at Guy's memorial service and Caroline recognized her from a photograph, Shula could suddenly see the full picture and Simon was forced to admit they'd been having an affair.

Willow Farm

Now home to Mike and Betty Tucker, Willow Farm was a full working farm in 1972, the year that Haydn Evans bought it for his son, Gwyn. After Gwyn left for Canada, Tony Archer entered into partnership with Haydn until 1978, when he moved on to Bridge Farm. Mike Tucker took over Tony's role as partner until 1983, when Haydn decided to sell up and move back to Wales. While the Tuckers went to Ambridge Farm, the land at Willow Farm was largely bought up by Phil Archer and Brian Aldridge. A newcomer to the area, Bill Insley, then bought the farmhouse and 15 acres from Phil, and let Neil Carter rent the old barn to keep chickens. On Bill's death in 1986, Neil inherited the barn and 8 acres, where he still has his pigs, while Matthew Thorogood bought the farmhouse. The Tuckers rented it from 1988 onwards, glad to have a home after the heartbreak of becoming bankrupt at Ambridge Farm. They eventually bought the house in 1993. Since then, Mike has tried running a market garden there for a while; he and Neil ran a pick-your-own strawberry enterprise on Neil's share of the land for five years. Currently, it's the site for Neil and Betty's free range hens.

Bruno **Wills**

(Matthew Morgan)

Bruno helped Clive Horrobin conduct an armed raid on the village shop in 1993. As Debbie Aldridge pleaded for Jack Woolley's life, Bruno got cold feet and argued with Clive about what they should do next. After they had escaped by car, Bruno stayed at large longer than Clive, leading to fears that he might reappear in the village to threaten witnesses. Eventually he was caught, and, despite denying all the charges against him, was convicted after being positively identified as one of the culprits.

Judy **Wilson**

When Laura Archer's will, in which she intended to leave Ambridge Hall to Freddie Danby, was found to be unsigned, adverts had to be placed in New Zealand newspapers asking for Laura's next of kin. Great-niece Judy Wilson came forward. Not wishing to live in England, she sold the Hall, and hasn't stayed in close contact with Ambridge since, but did invite Phil and Jill Archer to her wedding in 1993 when she married her boyfriend, Keith, in Sydney, Australia.

Brigadier **Winstanley**

(Godfrey Baseley)

It's probably a good job that the Brigadier wasn't around to witness the proposed anti-hunting legislation: a countryman through and through, he lived (and died) for country sports. For many years joint master of the Hunt, he broke three ribs and wrenched his knee when his horse threw him after an anti-hunt protester waved a placard as long ago as

1969. He had already bequeathed his estate to his niece, Lady Isabel Lander, before his death on the hunting field in 1971.

Terry **Wogan**

(Self)

Who better to welcome the mellifluent Irishman to Ambridge than the usually tongue-tied Pru Forrest? This she did in 1989, when the celebrity arrived to take part in a golf match at Grey Gables and booked into the Royal Garden Suite. But even he was lost for words when she presented him with a jar of her mouth-watering damson jam.

Woodbine Cottage

Woodbine Cottage, a tied property owned by Brookfield Farm, stands opposite the village green and next to The Bull. When a lorry skidded off the road and demolished a good chunk of it in September 1999, tenants Bert and Freda Fry had to relocate to the Brookfield bungalow for several months while extensive repairs were carried out. By virtue of Bert's employment at Brookfield, they had been living in Woodbine Cottage since 1988. For a time, the convenience of life in the well-appointed bungalow undermined the Frys' wish to go home, but once they realized that central heating had finally been installed and the kitchen had been thoroughly modernized, they were only too pleased to go back. Before them, the cottage had been home to Jethro and Lizzie Larkin and their daughters for seventeen years. Clarrie Grundy has fond memories of her time living there with her parents and sister, Rosie, and can still remember her grandmother, Mabel, living there prior to that. Sadly, Mabel was on her own for most of her time in the cottage, as husband Ned died in 1967 within a short time of their moving in. They were the first tenants while the cottage was under the management of the Archer family, Ambridge Farmers Ltd having just bought the property from Ralph Bellamy beforehand.

Joby **Woodford**

(George Woolley)

F ive years after coming to Ambridge to work in forestry for the Bellamy Estate, Joby Woodford fell in love with and married Martha Lily in 1972.

Death: 7.1.1983

He wasn't happy with her working at the garage, but agreed she should take a part-time post at the shop. A true craftsman in wood, Joby made some excellent furniture for the garden centre, and was always willing to undertake carpentry chores in the village. By common consent, he excelled himself with the bus stop shelter and bench he made for the Queen's Jubilee in 1977.

A man of practical rather than academic talents, his inability to read became common knowledge only when Doris Archer, having forgotten her spectacles, asked him to read out the poem in a birthday card she was going to buy for Tom Forrest. Quick-thinking Joby invented a verse on the spot. Unfortunately, the real verse was comically insulting, but Tom didn't see the joke. Joby eventually tackled the problem by enrolling on an adult literacy course, and, with the support of his tutor, Miss Minshull, he developed a passion for crosswords.

He died suddenly in 1983, much to the regret of not only Martha, but all his many friends in the village.

Martha **Woodford**

(Mollie Harris)

W ell before the widespread use of e-mail and the Internet, Ambridge had its own way of spreading information rapidly. From the 1970s to the '90s, Martha Woodford rarely let customers

Birth: 31.7.1922
Death: 17.1.1996

leave the village shop without a juicy piece of gossip to accompany their groceries or stamps; the latest news about John Archer's unsuitable friendship with Sharon Richards, for example.

Martha was from Penny Hassett originally, where she had been married to a postman, Herbert Lily, until his death in 1961. So it was as Martha Lily that she came to Ambridge to work part-time at the Ambridge Hall field studies centre in 1970. After soon falling out with Zebedee Tring, she was forced to find other work and took up cleaning for, among others, The Bull and Doris Archer. It wasn't the most satisfying way to make a living, so, in 1972, she approached Jack Woolley about the possibility of working at the village shop. Initially, he turned her down, and Martha settled for serving petrol at Ralph Bellamy's garage instead. But, by January of the following year, she had been taken on part-time at the shop, and when the manager, Angela Cooper, did a sudden flit to be with her boyfriend, Martha was willing to step into her shoes, despite some concerns about the post office side of the business.

By now, Martha was no longer a Lily, having married forestry expert Joby Woodford on Christmas Day 1972. They set up home in Bluebell Cottage, before moving on to April Cottage. Although they got on well together, perhaps they sensed that something was still missing in their marriage. The greatest regret of Martha's time with Herbert had been the stillbirth of a son. She and Joby were now too old to have a family of their own, but they were happy to offer accommodation to Neil Carter, a young apprentice who had come to work for Ambridge Farmers. In some ways they regarded him as a son, standing staunchly by him when he was taken to court for the possession of drugs planted on him by a girlfriend in 1974.

Martha continued to work hard at the shop. She successfully introduced an off-licence section, and, in response to competition from Harry Booker, a home delivery service, too. Overcoming some reservations from Joby, she even coped with longer opening hours being introduced, so it came as a shock when Jack Woolley put the shop up for sale in 1979. Together with Carol Tregorran and Peggy Archer, Martha considered trying to buy it, but the asking price was too great. She was relieved when Jack eventually took it off the market, and her job remained secure.

Joby occasionally helped out at the shop, most memorably selling Doris Archer an inappropriate birthday card for Tom Forrest, so there was nothing unusual in his assisting Martha with stocktaking in January 1983. But the stomach-ache that was keeping him from his own work was more serious than either of them suspected. He suddenly collapsed and died. Martha coped with the trauma of his death by combining an early return to work with an unsuccessful attempt to reach Joby through the services of Ivy, a spiritualist medium, who sported bright green eye make-up.

There were other brushes with the apparently supernatural. Martha served a turn as fortune-teller Madame Arcati at the 1994 village fête.

Earlier, Jennifer Aldridge's researches into village life revealed the possibility that the ghost of Florrie Hoskins might be haunting Martha's house. Snatch Foster and Eddie Grundy couldn't resist the temptation of organizing a ghostly appearance at Martha's window. She was to have the last laugh, though, by pretending she could communicate with spirits, much to the consternation of mischief-making Kate Aldridge and William Grundy when they tried their hand at haunting her.

Less ethereal visitations came in the form of Joe Grundy and Bill Insley, who both fancied their chances with Martha once she had been widowed. She allowed the rivalry between them to get her garden gate mended and a pile of logs chopped. She even ended up with two bird tables, one made by each of her lovesick suitors. Joe dropped out of the contest when he grew tired of running errands for her, while Martha let Bill fade gently out of the picture.

She took something of a shine to Freddie Danby, who proved a lively dancing partner when they got out a pile of old records. She found herself knitting a scarf for the Colonel in competition with Marjorie Antrobus, who was also growing fond of him. In time, Martha became good friends with Marjorie. In 1989, misunderstanding a casual invitation to remain as long as she liked sitting in the window at Nightingale Farm, Martha invited herself to stay for an extended holiday, until Marjorie's patience ran out and she asked her unexpected guest to leave.

The shop, with its bubbling mix of work and gossip, remained at the centre of Martha's life for many years, but gradually it started to become too much for her. VAT was difficult to understand, but not as bad as the rearrangements Mr Woolley made when a slipped disc forced Martha to take time off work. In 1989, she told Jack she was ready to retire. She carried on working part-time for years after, however, while Betty Tucker took over management duties. After the armed raid on the shop in 1993, it was Martha who helped Betty regain her confidence on her first day back at work.

When Bert Fry called to take her to a village meeting in January 1996, he found her lying dead in the garden, with a bunch of snowdrops in her hand. Janet Fisher led the funeral service, while Marjorie addressed the congregation about her friend. It was decided that the Susan Grundy memorial garden should henceforward commemorate Martha as well, in recognition of all she had done for Ambridge. Jack Woolley closed the shop for a day as a mark of respect. For once, the gossiping had stopped.

Jackie **Woodstock**

(Anne Louise Wakefield)

Euphemistically dubbed 'bubbly' by the bachelors of Borchester, in 1980 Jackie was David Archer's girlfriend. She then dallied with Mark Hebden after he and Shula Archer split up, introducing him to, amongst other things, the Borchester Buzzards Hanggliding Club. They lived together at his cottage, and she proposed, but they parted company in 1983 after he accused her of, surprise, surprise, flirting with other men on a skiing holiday.

Hazel **Woolley**

(Hilary Armstrong, Jan Cox, Hilary Newcombe)

At his eightieth birthday party in 1999, Jack Woolley was keen to show guests the card sent to him by his stepdaughter, Hazel. He was pleased to have proof of her continued affection for him,

Birth: 15.2.1956

not realizing that it was only due to his wife, Peggy's, efforts that Hazel had been persuaded to make even this token gesture; the idea of actually attending the party was far too much effort to expect from such a wayward character. In her defence, she had quite an unsettled upbringing. She was born in Ambridge in 1956, the daughter of Reggie and Valerie Trentham. When her parents moved to the Bahamas, she went with them, only to return with her mother to the village after Reggie's death. She didn't immediately approve of Jack Woolley's courtship of her mum, but was gradually won over by his considerate manner, which led him, among other things, to give her a beloved puppy called Honey. Although Jack and Valerie's marriage wasn't to succeed, Hazel was delighted to be adopted as Jack's daughter in 1968. Sadly, the warmth between them didn't survive her growing up and moving away to an insecure life on the fringes of the media world. Since then, they've had only the most occasional contact, usually prompted by Hazel's need for money, but Jack still thinks of her as a good-hearted girl and is always hopeful of seeing more of her.

Jack **Woolley**

(Philip Garston-Jones, Arnold Peters)

In 1974, Jack Woolley asked Peggy Archer to marry him. Not only did she turn him down, but she also resigned from her job at Grey Gables to ensure there could be no mistaking her intentions.

Birth: 19.7.1919

Sixteen years later, he asked the same woman the same question and this time she said yes. Lesser men might have relinquished their dream in the intervening period, but not Jack. Above all else, he has the gift of never giving up.

A native of Stirchley, Birmingham, he wasn't born into money, but, by a mix of entrepreneurial flair and sheer sticking-power, had successfully established himself as a businessman by the time he came to Ambridge in 1962. Over the following years, he was to develop a wide range of commercial interests in the village and its wider environs. His most visible achievement was buying, then upgrading, the Grey Gables Country Club into one of Borsetshire's most luxurious and respected hotels. He oversaw the addition of a golf course, swimming pool and health club to the existing facilities, as well as, for many years, maintaining a shoot in the adjoining Country Park. A reputation for fine cuisine was ensured by hiring Jean-Paul Aubert as head chef, while Jack's decision to employ Caroline Bone to help him run the business was inspired. When the time finally came for him to retire, she was the ideal woman to leave in charge.

He also invested in the *Borchester Echo*, and dabbled in several other enterprises, as well: the New Curiosity Shop was a short-lived outlet for unusual gifts, while Arkwright Hall operated as a recreation centre and then as a field studies centre, before gradually falling into disrepair. He also ran a racehorse, Grey Silk, although this was more for fun than for profit.

The most important of his acquisitions, as far as many Ambridge residents were concerned, was the village post office and shop, which he bought from Sid and Polly Perks in 1972. Angela Cooper, Martha Woodford and Betty Tucker, its current manager, all managed it for him in turn and found him a supportive proprietor, if rather inclined to interfere unnecessarily.

A man of his means was an obvious target for the avaricious. In 1973, he was injured during a robbery at Grey Gables, and, two decades later, was caught up in Clive Horrobin's raid on the shop. Either incident could have proved fatal, for Jack had a history of heart problems, including a heart attack, and eventually had to be fitted with a pacemaker to correct an irregular heartbeat.

It was his personal rather than his business life that caused him most stress, however. When he came to Ambridge, he had already been a widower for some time. Within a couple of years, recently widowed Valerie Trentham caught his eye and he set about wooing her. Part of his campaign was getting to know Valerie's daughter, Hazel, better; to the extent that he even arranged for her to move from her existing boarding school to one nearer Borchester.

Jack and Valerie married on 2 February 1966, but were soon drifting apart. Valerie bored by life back in Ambridge, and trying to inject some excitement into it, began seeing Roger Travers-Macy. Shortly after legally adopting Hazel, Jack was faced with his wife walking out on him. They divorced in 1974. When he learned of Valerie's death nine years later, he unjustly blamed himself for turning her into an alcoholic. He never stopped looking on Hazel as a daughter, and seemed oblivious to her callous manner towards him. When did Hazel come to Ambridge? Only when she needed a handout.

A Staffordshire bull terrier was to be a more loyal companion. Jack got Captain as a three-month-old in May 1978, and, over the next thirteen years, they were virtually inseparable. Never the best behaved of dogs, Captain once disgraced himself by being much too amorous with one of Mrs Antrobus's Afghan hounds. On another occasion, he mauled a wig Jack had bought. At least it wasn't the other way round. He was also, when stuck on the roof at Grey Gables, the cause of his master taking a very nasty tumble. Captain may have been a washout in the best trick competition at the village fête, but there was some consolation in 1989, when he won the dog-most-like-its-master prize.

The pain of Captain's death in 1991 was partially eased for Jack by, at long last, having Peggy at his side. They had remained friends since his first proposal, and, once she had established boundaries, often worked happily alongside each other when she returned to Grey Gables. At different times they had other romantic interests, but, by the start of the 1990s, were realizing that they were better suited to each other than to anyone else. They danced well together at a Valentines' Ball, and then enjoyed a visit to the Chelsea Flower Show. Like the Ambridge Rose Jack had specially commissioned, love bloomed. Shortly after they had been married by the Bishop of Felpersham, Jack romantically insisted on carrying Peggy over the threshold of The Lodge, which they were going to make their home.

Marriage called for re-adjustment. New routines had to be established and occasional hitches, such as the unexpected appearance of Peggy's wartime sweetheart, Conn Kortchmar, had to be dealt with. Peggy sold The Bull, but had a hard struggle persuading her new husband that he needed to retire as well. She didn't really succeed until after his eightieth birthday. With his various enterprises running smoothly without him, he then took an interest in restoring Arkwright Hall. When he hurt himself falling through a jammed door, Peggy put her foot down and insisted that professional help was needed to do it up.

Despite suffering from angina, Jack's only happy when he's busy. In the past he's served as a parish councillor, been involved in organizing village sports and judged the Flower and Produce Show. He has a passion for amateur theatricals and his dance of the seven veils as Widow Twankey in a recent pantomime is already the stuff of local legend. He may no longer be working, but, as Peggy has found out to her cost, he's a hard man to slow down.

Margaret **Woolley**   'Peggy', née Perkins (formerly Archer)

(June Spencer, Thelma Rogers, June Spencer)

When enjoying a soak in the bath, Peggy Woolley sometimes hums a war-time tune: 'Love Is the Sweetest Thing'. It's a sentiment she agrees with, but had to wait a long time to really experience for herself.

Birth: 13.11.1924

Marriage to her first husband, Jack Archer, was often anything but sweet. They fell in love during the Second World War, when she was an ATS stores orderly, whose cheery London manner proved irresistible to the young private from Borsetshire. By the early 1950s, though, the gloss had started to wear off, as Peggy struggled to look after three children, Jennifer, Lilian and Tony, on the meagre returns Jack made on their Ambridge smallholding. She couldn't have wished for better in-laws than Dan and Doris Archer, and having her own mother, Mrs Perkins, move into the village also helped, but it wasn't easy to cope with her husband's mercurial changes of mood and plan. As Phil Archer noted, they always seemed at loggerheads.

Jack becoming landlord of The Bull should have been a step in the right direction, but he was more adept at drinking than managing, so, in November 1953, Borchester Brewery insisted that Peggy should take over the licence. A few years later, with Laura Archer's help, she and Jack bought the pub for £5300. From then on, until she let the pub to Sid and Polly Perks almost twenty years later, she juggled the demands of owning and running it with bringing up her children and keeping an eye on a husband becoming increasingly fond of alcohol and gambling. Although she would never have wished it on him, Jack's death from liver failure in 1972 was in some ways a merciful release for Peggy.

Her children also lived life as though competing to put grey in her hair. Jennifer provided an unplanned pregnancy, the kidnapping of her son, Adam Travers–Macy, and plenty of tempestuous moments in two marriages for Peggy to worry about. Lilian set off major alarm bells with her depressive, alcoholic habits before and after the end of her marriage to Ralph Bellamy. While Tony was never quite as difficult, his financial and domestic problems usually ended up being poured into his mum's ear. In recent years, granddaughter Kate Aldridge has been a frequent source of worry, but the most harrowing time for Peggy came in 1998, when her grandson John Archer was killed in a tractor accident. She showed all her strength of character in supporting Pat and Tony's family during the aftermath.

For a long time through all this, she had her own career to think of. First of all there was running the pub, but, after Jack Archer's death, she was ready for a change of direction. Although she remained The Bull's owner, in 1973 she also became Jack Woolley's personal assistant at the Grey Gables Country Club. She worked there on and off over the next few years, as well as having a phase in the office of Rodway & Watson, and providing emergency cover for Martha Woodford at the village shop in 1979, an exercise she repeated many years later by covering for unreliable Kate.

Men always found her attractive. Even while she was still married, an old wartime friend of Jack Archer's, Barney Lee, took a shine to her, so much so that four years after Jack's death he came to Ambridge and tried to court her. They became friends, but nothing more. At different times, Clive Turner and Robin Freeman showed romantic interest, while Jack Woolley was a constant admirer, whose proposal Peggy turned down in

1974. It wasn't until the end of the 1980s that she really seemed keen on a new relationship, when, to Jack Woolley's chagrin, she started to get close to ex-naval man Godfrey Wendover. Matters were obviously hotting up between them when they wore matching pirate outfits to run a stall at the village fête, but then Godfrey completely blew his chances: he failed to show proper respect when Peggy's cat, Sammy, was entered for the Midland Counties Cat show.

Only one man in her life really understood how important a pet could be. Seizing his chance, Jack Woolley accompanied Peggy to the show. Evenings spent ballroom dancing were to follow, and soon, in the not entirely romantic surroundings of the Grey Gables kitchens, Jack was proposing for a second time. Recognizing how much mellower and better suited to her he had become over the years, Peggy finally said yes.

Before the wedding she had nightmares about turning up in a purple turban, but on the appointed day, 1 January 1991, Peggy looked stunning in a cream dress and apricot hat. She and Jack drove off in an open-topped vintage Bentley, prior to spending a fabulous honeymoon in St Lucia. On their return, they had The Lodge renovated to become their new home. The only check to their happiness was Mrs P's death in the same year.

Realizing they needed to shed business commitments if they were to have time to make the marriage work, Peggy sold The Bull to Sid Perks and Guy Pemberton in 1993, and began to wage a long campaign to convince Jack to retire. She finally persuaded him, after his eightieth birthday in the summer of 1999. Since then they have been able to enjoy a few extra holidays and trips out; a handful of rose petals are an especially treasured souvenir of the Queen Mother's Centenary Pageant that they attended in July 2000. Peggy is a traditionalist, and, although she had the grace to compliment Janet Fisher on her sensitivity at John Archer's funeral, prefers to worship at All Saints, Borchester, as long as St Stephen's has a female vicar. She also strongly disapproves of law-breaking, as was clear when Tommy Archer helped wreck the Home Farm GM trial. However, her efforts to close the ensuing rift between Jennifer and Tony's families gave a good indication of what her main priorities have always been. Whether as a struggling young mum, or in her more comfortable retirement, she has never stopped trying to protect her loved ones. So now, as she sinks back in the bath, perhaps fondly remembering gliding with Jack over the Tower Ballroom dance floor on the Ambridge millennium trip to Blackpool, few would begrudge her the right to sing a quietly contented song.

Valerie **Woolley** née Grayson (formerly Trentham)

(Ann Johnson, Jenny Lee, Heather Canning)

Perhaps Valerie Grayson's wartime experiences working in intelligence left her unable ever to feel completely settled afterwards. When she came to Ambridge in 1952, she was renewing an

> **Death:** 1.8.1983

acquaintanceship with her wartime colleague Mike Daly. However, she soon grew closer to Reggie Trentham, who agreed to employ her as a hostess at the Country Club. They married in 1953 and had a daughter, Hazel, three years later. In 1958, the Trenthams left Ambridge to live abroad, but were only to have limited time together, as Reggie died in the Bahamas in 1964.

Valerie came back to Ambridge and started to work at Grey Gables once more. Jack Woolley persuaded her to marry him in 1966, having already arranged for Hazel to move boarding schools in order to be closer to them. It wasn't a happy marriage, and Valerie was soon seeking consolation in the arms of Ralph Bellamy, as well as trying to draw Roger Travers-Macy into an affair.

She and Jack separated in 1968, although they didn't divorce until 1974. Increasingly dependent on alcohol, her health suffered over the next few years, resulting in her death in 1983. Jack considered himself responsible for her alcoholic behaviour, but the truth is that Valerie had seemed destined to lead a troubled life.

Matthew **Wreford**

(John Carlin)

Matthew was Vicar of Ambridge for seven years from 1961–68, and his stay coincided with one of the most controversial episodes in village history: Jennifer Archer's illegitimate baby. Fearful of telling her parents she was pregnant, Jennifer wanted Matthew to do it for her, but he wisely counselled her that, though he'd always be available to her for support, this was something that she had to find the courage to do. It was good advice.

Norman **Wynford**

(Robert Chetwyn)

Having studied at the Farm Institute and done a couple of years' practical in Lincolnshire, Norman Wynford started farming in Ambridge in 1957 full of plans for a small dairy herd and rearing pigs and chickens. He was delighted to clinch a deal with Hollerton Council, who paid him handsomely for 5 acres of turf from his best pasture, but then it all started to go wrong, and, as ever, over a woman.

Norman had fallen in love with Julie from Hollerton. He needed £200 to lend to his intended's parents as a deposit on their house, and, in 1959, in desperation, tried to sell Phil Archer some cattle for a ridiculously low sum. Phil, ever the gentleman, refused to take advantage of him. Instead, he lent Norman the money, saying he'd have it back when Norman sold the stock at a better time. But there was more to it than that: Norman confessed that his father, Thorpe, who'd bought him the farm, was putting the financial screws on as he didn't approve of Julie.

When Norman dug in his heels over his choice of fiancée, Thorpe announced he was selling up, and Phil's generosity more than paid off. Not only did Norman return his money, but in 1960 Phil stepped in smartly and bought the farm as an investment.

Thorpe **Wynford**

(John Sharp, Tom Harrison)

Striking a cunning deal in 1956, Thorpe lent Walter Gabriel the money to buy his farm as a sitting tenant, then bought it from him at a keen price for his son, Norman. Although eager for Norman to get married, Thorpe didn't approve of his son's choice, and, when he couldn't talk him out of it, washed his hands of the affair. He bumped into Phil Archer in Felpersham, told him he was going to sell and Phil swiftly stepped in with an offer.

Wynford's Farm

Prior to its purchase by Thorpe Wynford for his son, Norman, in 1957, this had been Walter Gabriel's farm. It subsequently passed via Phil Archer to Charles Grenville, who in 1963 rented it to Paul and Christine Johnson. They managed to buy it, and the adjoining paddock, but sold the paddock to raise money for Paul's ill-fated fish farm. After Paul's bankruptcy in 1978, the house was repossessed and Chris moved to The Stables.

Mrs **Yelland**

(Margaret Parker)

Centenarian Mrs Yelland had lived in Ambridge all her life, and the teenage Lilian Archer was intrigued by her reminiscences, when, in 1963, she paid a visit to the house she lived in with her daughter. Lilian was particularly interested to find out if the old lady could remember anything about the Gabriel family and was delighted to be shown a letter written by Walter's granny, Meg.

Marvin **Young**

There was so much concern about Marvin Young's behaviour when he sprayed the Pounds' farm shop with paint in 1975 that he was remanded for medical reports. He didn't turn out to be such a bad lad, however. By the following year he was delivering the *Felpersham Evening Post* after Martha Woodford had decided to stop selling it in the village shop. He's probably a dot.com millionaire by now.

Zoe

(Sunny Ormonde)

Frantic with worry when their daughter Kate disappeared in 1994, Brian and Jennifer Aldridge went in search of her at Glastonbury.

There they encountered a New Age traveller, Zoe, who shortly afterwards turned up again at Home Farm, claiming to have news of the missing girl.

Over the next few weeks, Zoe pretended she was in touch with Kate in order to con money and other benefits from the Aldridges. Finally, she was sent on her way when Brian found her stealing from Jennifer's handbag. When Kate finally returned, it transpired she had never met Zoe in her life.